T0210531

Lecture Notes in Computer Science   8628

Commenced Publication in 1973
Founding and Former Series Editors:
Gerhard Goos, Juris Hartmanis, and Jan van Leeuwen

More information about this series at http://www.springer.com/series/7409

Bertram Ludäscher · Beth Plale (Eds.)

Provenance
and Annotation of Data
and Processes

5th International Provenance
and Annotation Workshop, IPAW 2014
Cologne, Germany, June 9–13, 2014
Revised Selected Papers

 Springer

Editors
Bertram Ludäscher
University of Illinois
Urbana-Champaign, IL
USA

Beth Plale
Indiana University
Bloomington, IN
USA

ISSN 0302-9743   ISSN 1611-3349 (electronic)
Lecture Notes in Computer Science
ISBN 978-3-319-16461-8   ISBN 978-3-319-16462-5 (eBook)
DOI 10.1007/978-3-319-16462-5

Library of Congress Control Number: 2015933500

LNCS Sublibrary: SL 3 – Information Systems and Applications, incl. Internet/Web and HCI

Springer Cham Heidelberg New York Dordrecht London

Printed on acid-free paper

Springer International Publishing AG Switzerland is part of Springer Science+Business Media
(www.springer.com)

Preface

This volume contains the proceedings of the 5th International Provenance and Annotation Workshop (IPAW), held during June 10–11, 2014 at the German Aerospace Center (DLR) in Cologne, Germany. For the first time, IPAW colocated with the Workshop on the Theory and Practice of Provenance (TaPP). Together the two leading provenance workshops anchored ProvenanceWeek 2014, a full week of provenance-related activities that included a shared poster session, a panel on reproducibility in science, and tutorials on the W3C PROV standard, on provenance analytics, and the uses of provenance in cell biology. The week was rounded out with afternoon-long birds-of-a-feather activities around constructing a provenance record from data when provenance was not collected in the first place, and benchmarking of provenance systems. This collection constitutes the peer-reviewed papers of IPAW 2014. These include 14 long papers which report in-depth the results of research around provenance and four extended abstracts that discuss tools and services that were presented in the form of a system demonstration. Finally, we have included 20 short abstracts of the joint IPAW/TaPP poster session. The final papers, demos, and poster abstracts were selected from a total of 53 submissions. All full-length research papers and demo papers received a minimum of three reviews.

The papers of IPAW 2014 provided a glimpse into state-of-the-art research and practice around the capture, representation, and use of provenance. Since provenance often results in graphs, and large ones at that, several of the papers in this collection proposed abstract graph models and methods with well-defined properties, properties that can hold even when sanitized for potentially sensitive information. Tools are the focus of a number of papers in this collection; these are innovative software applications that solve a particular problem and are evaluated experimentally. They are often converging on the W3C PROV model for provenance interchange. Some papers discussed tools that enable provenance capture from software compilers, from web publications, and from scripts, using existing audit logs, and employing both static and dynamic instrumentation. New methodologies for provenance aggregation and use appeared in the collection as well. We see the evaluation of a linked data approach to provenance publishing, the generation of documentation from provenance, and application of provenance to protect attribution in scientific discovery.

In closing, we would like to thank the members of the Program Committee for their thoughtful reviews, Dr. Andreas Schreiber (Local Chair) and Carina Haupt for their excellent organization of IPAW and ProvenanceWeek 2014 at DLR, and—last but not least—the authors and participants for making IPAW the stimulating and successful event that it was.

December 2014

Bertram Ludäscher
Beth Plale

Organization

Program Committee

Ilkay Altintas	University of California, San Diego, USA
Khalid Belhajjame	PSL, Université Paris-Dauphine, LAMSADE, France
Shawn Bowers	Gonzaga University, USA
Adriane Chapman	The MITRE Corporation, USA
James Cheney	University of Edinburgh, UK
Susan Davidson	University of Pennsylvania, USA
Tom De Nies	Ghent University - iMinds - Multimedia Lab, Belgium
Kai Eckert	University of Mannheim, Germany
Juliana Freire	NYU Polytechnic School of Engineering, USA
James Frew	Bren School / UCSB, USA
Daniel Garijo	Universidad Politécnica de Madrid, Spain
Yolanda Gil	USC/ISI, USA
Paul Groth	VU University Amsterdam, The Netherlands
Trung Dong	Huynh University of Southampton, UK
H. V. Jagadish	University of Michigan, USA
David Koop	NYU Polytechnic School of Engineering, USA
Carl Lagoze	University of Michigan School of Information, USA
Timothy Lebo	Rensselaer Polytechnic Institute, USA
Qing Liu	CSIRO, Australia
Shiyong Lu	Wayne State University, USA
Bertram Ludäscher	University of California, Davis, USA
Tanu Malik	University of Chicago, USA
Marta Mattoso	COPPE- Federal Univ. Rio de Janeiro, Brazil
Deborah McGuinness	Rensselaer Polytechnic Institute, USA
Simon Miles	King's College London, UK
Paolo Missier	Newcastle University, UK
Luc Moreau	University of Southampton, UK
Beth Plale	Indiana University, USA
Yogesh Simmhan	Indian Institute of Science, India
Curt Tilmes	NASA GSFC, USA
Jan Van Den Bussche	Hasselt University and University of Limburg

Contents

Provenance Discovery and Data Reproducibility

System Demonstrations

Joint IPAW/TaPP Poster Session

Standardization of Provenance Models, Services, Representations

ProvAbs: Model, Policy, and Tooling for Abstracting PROV Graphs

Paolo Missier[1](✉), Jeremy Bryans[1], Carl Gamble[1],
Vasa Curcin[2], and Roxana Danger[2]

[1] School of Computing Science, Newcastle University,
Newcastle upon Tyne, UK
pmissier@acm.org
[2] Imperial College, London, UK

Abstract. Provenance metadata can be valuable in data sharing settings, where it can be used to help data consumers form judgements regarding the reliability of the data produced by third parties. However, some parts of provenance may be sensitive, requiring access control, or they may need to be simplified for the intended audience. Both these issues can be addressed by a single mechanism for creating abstractions over provenance, coupled with a policy model to drive the abstraction. Such mechanism, which we refer to as *abstraction by grouping*, simultaneously achieves partial disclosure of provenance, and facilitates its consumption. In this paper we introduce a formal foundation for this type of abstraction, grounded in the W3C PROV model; describe the associated policy model; and briefly present its implementation, the `ProvAbs` tool for interactive experimentation with policies and abstractions.

1 Introduction

Provenance, a formal representation of the production process of data, may facilitate the assessment and improvement of the quality of data products, as well as the validation and reproducibility of scientific experimental datasets. This expectation predicates on an assumption of interoperability between mutually independent producers and consumers of provenance. The W3C PROV generic provenance model [1] is intended to facilitate such interoperability, by providing a common syntax and semantics for provenance models, and thus enable provenance-aware data sharing at Web scale.

1.1 Abstracting Provenance

For provenance to be useful, it must be represented at a level of abstraction that is appropriate to the consumer. For example, system-level provenance which includes individual system calls and I/O operations may be appropriate for

This work was funded in part by EPSRC UK and DSTL under grant EP/J020494/1.

B. Ludäscher and B. Plale (Eds.): IPAW 2014, LNCS 8628, pp. 3–15, 2015.
DOI: 10.1007/978-3-319-16462-5_1

system auditing purposes, while a higher level description may be more appropriate to determine how a document evolved to its final version, e.g. through a series of edits involving multiple authors. In some cases, the higher abstraction can be computed from the detailed representation. One such case occurs when provenance describes the execution of a workflow or dataflow, which can itself be described at multiple levels of abstraction. Early work on *provenance views* (*Zoom*) [2] is an example. Here users specify the abstraction they require on the workflow, and that is used to compute a corresponding abstract view of the workflow's trace. More generally, however, a trace may represent arbitrary process executions and data derivations, and one cannot rely on a formal description of the process to specify a suitable abstraction.

The problem of abstracting over provenance in such a more general setting has been addressed in later work, notably the ProPub system [3]. Here the main goal is to ensure that sensitive elements of the trace are abstracted out, by means of a redaction process. In ProPub, users specify edit operations on a provenance graph, such as anonymizing, abstracting, and hiding certain parts of it. ProPub operates on a simplified provenance model (which pre-dates PROV) which only includes use/generation relations, and adopts an "apply-detect–repair" approach. First, user-defined abstraction rules are applied to the graph, then consistency violations that may occur in the resulting new graph are detected, and finally a set of edits are applied to repair such violations. In some cases, this causes nodes that the user wanted removed to be reintroduced, and it is not always possible to satisfy all user rules.

1.2   Contributions

Our work is motivated by the need to control the complexity of a provenance graph by increasing its level of abstraction, as well as to protect the confidentiality of parts of the graph. Our specific contributions in this paper are threefold. Firstly, we define a *Provenance Abstraction Model* (**PAM**) centred on the *Group* abstraction operator. *Group* replaces a set of nodes $V_{gr} \subset V$ in a valid PROV graph PG with a new abstract node, resulting in the modified graph PG'. The rewriting preserves the validity of the graph, in the sense made precise below, and it does not introduce any new relations into PG', which are not justified by existing PG relations. A formal account of this operator is given in Sect. 3. A preliminary but more extended account of this work appears in our technical report [1].

Secondly, we present a simple policy model and language for controlling abstraction, based on the assumption that provenance *owners* want to control the disclosure of their provenance graphs to one or more *receivers*, with varying levels of trust (Sect. 4). The model lets the owners associate a policy, *pol*, to a graph. Policy evaluation results in a *sensitivity* value $s(v, pol)$ being associated to each node v. Assuming, as in the Bell-Lapadula model [4], that a *clearance level cl* can be associated to each receiver, the nodes V_{gr} to be abstracted in PG according to *pol* are those for which $s(v, pol) > cl$.

Finally, we present the `ProvAbs` tool, which implements both *Group* and the policy language. `ProvAbs` has been demonstrated on our confidentiality preservation use case, in the context of intelligence information exchange [5].

1.3 Related Work

In addition to the Zoom and ProPub prototypes cited above, strands of research that are relevant to this work include (i) provenance-specific graph redaction, (ii) graph anonymization, and (ii) Provenance Access Control (PAC). Provenance redaction [6] employs a graph grammar technique to edit provenance that is expressed using the Open Provenance Model [7] (a precursor to PROV), as well as a redaction policy language. The critical issue of ensuring that specific relationships are preserved, however, is addressed only informally in the paper, i.e., with no reference to OPM semantics.

Extensions to the relational data anonymization framework to graph data structures, specifically for social network data, have been developed [8–10]. The approach, involving randomly removing and adding arcs, will not work for PROV, however, as it would result in new, false dependencies. More relevantly, PAC is concerned with enforcing access control on parts of a provenance graph, in the context of secure provenance exchange. An analysis of the associated challenges [11] notes that provenance of data can be more sensitive than the data itself. In a similar setting, [12] accounts for the possibility of forgery of provenance by malicious users, and of collusion amongst users to reveal sensitive provenance to others. However, the paper stops short of providing any hints at technical solutions, and indeed it is not clear how these problems are specific to provenance, as opposed to data sharing in general. Finally, our policy language is loosely related to an XACML-based policy language [13] the access control system for provenance, where path queries are used to specify target elements of the graph.

2 Essential PROV

We now introduce the PROV concepts that are required for the rest of the paper. The PROV data model [1] defines three types of sets: (i) Entities (*En*), i.e., data, documents; (ii) Activities (*Act*), which represent the execution of some process over a period of time, and (iii) Agents (*Ag*), i.e., humans, computing systems, software. The following set of core relations is also defined amongst these sets:

$$\text{usage:} used \subseteq Act \times En \qquad \text{generation:} genBy \subseteq En \times Act$$
$$\text{derivation:} wasDerivedFrom \subseteq En \times En \qquad \text{association:} waw \subseteq Act \times Ag$$
$$\text{delegation:} abo \subseteq Ag \times Ag \qquad \text{attribution:} wat \subseteq En \times Ag$$

For simplicity and due to space constraints, in this paper we restrict our scope to just *En*, *Act*, and relations *used* and *genBy*. The extension of this work to Agents and their relations (*abo*, *wat*), is available from our extended tech report [5]. The extension to other core relations such as *wasDerivedFrom* is straightforward and will not be discussed here.

We denote instances of these relations as $genBy(e, a)$, $used(a, e)$, etc., where $e \in En, a \in Act$. Following common practice, we view a set I of such binary relation instances as a digraph $G = (V, E)$, where $V = En \cup Act$ and E is a set of labelled edges, and where $x \overset{r}{\leftarrow} y \in E$ iff $r(x, y) \in I$.[1] Finally, we denote the set of all such provenance graphs as $PG_{gu/ea}$, to indicate that they only contain $genBy$ and $used$ relations amongst En and Act nodes.

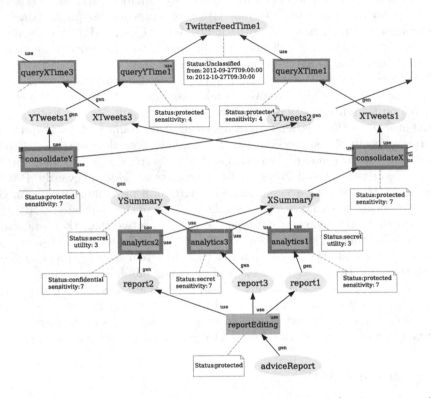

Fig. 1. Example provenance graph of a complex document production process. The `ProvAbs` model is designed to abstract some of the elements in the graph, for instance to avoid their disclosure. Coloured boxes denote `ProvAbs` sensitivity annotations, explained in Sect. 4 (Color figure online).

Figure 1 shows an example of a $PG_{gu/ea}$ graph, where ovals and rectangles represent Entities, Activities, and Agents, respectively. The graph describes a document, `advice-report`, which was ultimately derived from twitter feeds captured at different times, through a series of query, consolidation, and analysis activities. The agents to whom the documents and activities are ascribed are omitted for simplicity. Note also that the nodes are decorated with user-defined properties, such as `Status`.

---

[1] Conventionally, we orient these edges from right to left, to denote that the relation "points back to the past".

A set of formal constraints are defined on the PROV data model. These are described in the PROV-CONSTRAINTS document [14]. Two groups of constraints are relevant here. The first (Constraint 50 — typing[2]) formalises the set-theoretical definitions of the relations given above. Additionally, Constraint 55[3] stipulates that entities and activities are disjoint: $En \cap Act = \emptyset$.

The second group concerns temporal ordering amongst events. PROV defines a set of instantaneous events which mark the lifetime boundaries of Entities (generation, invalidation), Activities (start, end), and Agents (start, end), as well as some of the interactions amongst those elements, such as generation and usage of an entity by an activity, attribution of an entity to an agent, and more. Optionally, events may be explicitly associated to PROV elements. In the following, we denote the start and end of an activity a by $startEv(a)$, $endEv(a)$, respectively, and the generation and usage events for an entity e and activity a with $genEv(genBy(e, a))$, $useEv(used(a, e))$, respectively (as mentioned, Agents are beyond the scope of this paper). PROV events form a preorder, which we denote $\preceq$. The relevant temporal constraints are expressed as follows.

- **C1: generation-generation-ordering (Constraint 39):** If an entity is generated by more than one activity, then the generation events must all be simultaneous. Let $e \in En, a_1, a_2 \in Act$, and let $genBy(e, a_1)$ and $genBy(e, a_2)$ hold. Then the following must hold:

$$genEv(genBy(e, a_1)) \preceq genEv(genBy(e, a_2)) \text{ and}$$
$$genEv(genBy(e, a_2)) \preceq genEv(genBy(e, a_1))$$

- **C2: generation-precedes-usage (Constraint 37):** A generation event for an entity must precede any usage event for that entity. Let $a \in Act, e \in En$, and let $used(a, e))$, $genBy(e, a)$ hold. Then:

$$genEv(genBy(e, a)) \preceq useEv(used(a, e))$$

- **C3: usage-within-activity (Constraint 33):** Any usage of $e \in En$ by some $a \in Act$ cannot precede the start of a and must precede the end of a. Let $used(a, e)$ hold. Then:

$$startEv(a) \preceq useEv(used(a, e)) \preceq endEv(a)$$

- **C4: generation-within-activity (Constraint 34):** The generation of e by a cannot precede the start of a and must precede the end of a. If $genBy(e, a)$, then:

$$startEv(a) \preceq genEv(genBy(e, a)) \preceq endEv(a)$$

A *valid* PROV graph is one that satisfies all the constraints defined in the PROV-CONSTR document [14]. Within our scope, a valid $PG_{gu/ea}$ graph is one that satisfies the constraints defined here.

---

[2] http://www.w3.org/TR/prov-constraints/#typing.
[3] http://www.w3.org/TR/prov-constraints/#entity-activity-disjoint.

3 Abstraction by Grouping

Simple edits that can be applied to a graph to protect confidentiality of its content include removing individual nodes or edges. Alternatively, the node's identity can be changed, or the values associated to any of its properties can be removed. These straightforward edits are legal in PROV and they will not be discussed further.[4] We are instead concerned with edits that replace a group of nodes with a new abstract node.

3.1 Core Concepts

To model this type of abstraction, we are going to define a *Group* operator which takes a graph $G = (V, E) \in PG_{gu/ea}$ and a subset $V_{gr} \subset V$ of its nodes, and produces a modified graph $G' = (V', E') \in PG_{gu/ea}$, where V_{gr} is replaced with a new single node. *Group* is closed under composition, thus allowing for further abstraction by repeated grouping (abstraction of abstraction). Let $v_{abs} \in V'$ be an abstract node in G'. We denote the set V_{gr} of nodes in G that it replaces by $source(v_{abs})$.

In order to understand the requirements for defining *Group*, consider the replacements in Fig. 2. On the left, nodes $V_{gr} = \{a_1, e_4, e_5\}$ are replaced with a new node e'. Simply using the original edges to connect the remaining nodes to e' leads to type constraint violations, namely for the new edges $e_1 \leftarrow e'$, $e_2 \leftarrow e'$, and thus to an invalid graph.

Now consider Fig. 2(b), where $V_{gr} = \{e_1, e_3, e_4, e_5\}$. In this case, the simple strategy or replacing V_{gr} with e' and reconnecting the remaining nodes leads to the two cycles: $\{genBy(e', a_1), used(a_1, e')\}$ and $\{genBy(e', a_3), used(a_3, e')\}$. Such cycles are legal, and in particular they are consistent with temporal constraints C1-C4 above. Indeed, it is easy to imagine a situation where an activity a first generates an entity e, and then makes use of e. For instance, a could be a programming artifact, i.e., an object that first instantiates a new object e, and then makes use of e. In this case, the event ordering is

$$startEv(a) \preceq genEv(e, a) \preceq useEv(a, e) \preceq endEv(a) \tag{1}$$

Yet, we argue that *introducing* new cycles during abstraction is undesirable. Intuitively, this is because cycles make stronger assumptions on the possible temporal ordering of events than those in the original graph, and thus are only representative of a restrictive class of graphs. To elaborate more precisely on this point, we first introduce new definitions of generation and usage events for an abstract node v_{abs}, from the corresponding events associated to $source(v_{abs})$. For this, consider the definition of generation and usage in [1]:

---

[4] Note that removing an arbitrary node may result in disconnected fragments of the graph, as in general one cannot simply add edges to reconnect the remaining nodes, unless those can be inferred from standard PROV constraints. For instance, if activity a is removed from the graph: $\{used(a, e_1), genBy(e_2, a)\}$, this results in two disconnected nodes e_1, e_2, because no relationship can be inferred between them from the original graph.

Generation is the *completion of production* of a new entity (Sect. 5.1.3).
Usage is the *beginning of utilizing* an entity (Sect. 5.1.4).

An abstract node v_{abs} can be thought of as representing the collection $source(v_{abs})$ in the new graph. Thus, its "generation" is logically defined as the completion of production of its source nodes, that is, its associated generation event should be the *latest* generation event from within its source. Note that associating a generation event to an abstract node requires the existence of a generating activity. Although this is not always provided as a result of abstraction by grouping, *Inference 7* in [1] ensures that such generating activity exists. Thus we can formally define generation for abstract nodes, as follows.

Definition 1 (Abstract node generation event). *Let* $V_{gr} \in V$ *and* v_{abs} *be a new abstract node, with* $source(v_{abs}) = V_{gr}$ *and generating activity* a. *Define:*

$$genEv(genBy(v_{abs}, a)) = \max_{e_i \in source(v_{abs})} genEv(genBy(e_i, a_i))$$

where a_i *is the generating activity of* e_i.

Symmetrically, we associate a usage event to v_{abs}, which is the *earliest* usage event for the nodes in $e_i \in source(v_{abs})$.

Definition 2 (Abstract node usage events). *Let* $V_{gr} \in V$, $G' = (V', E')$ *be the new abstract graph, and let* $v_{abs} \in V'$ *be a new abstract node. If there exists an activity* $a \in V'$ *such that* $used(a, v_{abs})$ *holds, then*

$$useEv(used(a, v_{abs})) = \min_{e_i \in source(v_{abs})} useEv(used(a_i, e_i))$$

where a_i *is an activity that used* e_i.

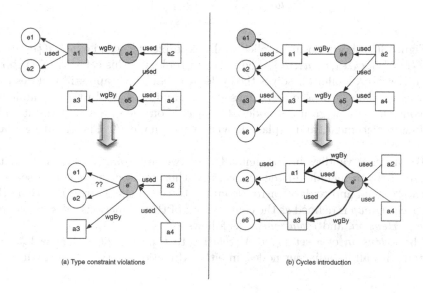

(a) Type constraint violations　　　　(b) Cycles introduction

Fig. 2. Issues with naive replacement of groups of nodes.

With these definitions in place, temporal constraint (1), which applies to simple usage-generation cycles in the graph, translates into the requirement that *every* entity $e_i \in source(v_{abs})$ be generated before *any* use of e_i. This constraint ties to each other the generation and usage time of the nodes that are abstracted. In the original graph, however, there is no such requirement: the generation of any entity is, in general, independent of that of others. This suggests that a new generation-usage cycle in the abstract graph adds constraints that are not present in the original graph, and should therefore be avoided. Note that ProPub [3] also insists on avoiding cycles, but the formal argument in support of this requirement does not appear to be clearly grounded in semantics.

To summarize, the requirements for *Group* when G is rewritten into G' are: (i) no type constraint violations must occur in G', (ii) no new relationships that are not also present in G are introduced in G', and (iii) no new usage-generation cycles are introduced in G'.

3.2   Convexity, Closure, Extensions, and Replacement

Intuitively, the reason for cycles such as the one in Fig. 2(b) is that set V_{gr} is not "convex", that is, there are paths in G that lead out of V_{gr} and then back in again. This observation suggests the introduction of a preliminary *closure* operation, aimed at ensuring "convexity" and therefore acyclicity. This is defined as follows.

Definition 3 (Path Closure). *Let* $G = (V, E) \in PG_{gu/ea}$ *be a provenance graph, and let* $V_{gr} \subset V$. *For each pair* $v_i, v_j \in V_{gr}$ *such that there is a directed path* $v_i \rightsquigarrow v_j$ *in* G, *let* $V_{ij} \subset V$ *be the set of all nodes in the path. The Path Closure of* V_{gr} *in* G *is*

$$pclos(V_{gr}, V) = \bigcup_{v_i, v_j \in V_{gr}} V_{ij}$$

Figure 3(b) shows closure applied to the example of Fig. 2, i.e. $pclos(\{e_1, e_3, e_4, e_5\}, G) = \{e_1, e_3, e_4, e_5, a_1, a_3\}$. The result of replacing this set with e' is shown in (c). However, while this solves the cycle problem, the graph still violates type constraints, namely on the new edges $e_2 \leftarrow e'$ and $e_6 \leftarrow e'$. In this example, we can construct a new group of nodes, $\{e', e_2, e_6\}$, on the graph that results from the first replacement, and replace it with a new node e''. The resulting graph (d) is valid.

To preserve validity in the general case, we are going to first extend the closure in (b) to include e-nodes e_2, e_6, and then replace the resulting set with e'' (the "extend and replace" arrow from (b) to (d) in the figure). Following this approach, *Group* is defined as the composition of three functions: *closure*, defined above, *extension*, and *replacement*, as follows.

The *extension* of a set $V_{gr} \subset V$ relative to type $t \in \{En, Act\}$ is V_{gr} augmented with all its adjacent nodes, in either direction, of type t. Formally:

Definition 4 (*extend*). *Let* $G = (V, E) \in PG_{gu/ea}$, $t \in \{En, Act\}$.

$$extend(V_{gr}, G, t) = \{v' | (v, v') \in E \wedge v \in V_{gr} \wedge type(v') = t)\} \cup$$
$$\{v | (v', v) \in E \wedge v \in V_{gr} \wedge type(v') = t)\} \cup V_{gr}$$

In our example:

$$extend(\{e_1, e_3, e_4, e_5, a_1, a_3\}, G, En) = \{e_1, e_3, e_4, e_5, a_1, a_3, e_2, e_6\}$$

Note that all sink nodes in $extend(V_{gr}, G, t)$ are of type t by construction.

Replacement. Let $G = (V, E)$, $V'_{gr} \subset V$ be obtained using *extend*, and let v_{new} be a new node symbol that does not appear in V. Function *replace* replaces V' with v_{new} in V, and connects v_{new} to the rest of the graph, as follows. Let $\vartheta_{out}(V'_{gr})$, $\vartheta_{in}(V'_{gr})$, and $\vartheta_{int}(V'_{gr})$ denote the set of arcs of G leading out of V'_{gr}, leading into V'_{gr}, Each arc $(v', v) \in \vartheta_{out}(V'_{gr})$ is replaced with a new arc (v_{new}, v), and each arc $(v, v') \in \vartheta_{in}(V'_{gr})$ is replaced with a new arc (v, v_{new}), both of the same relation type. Arcs in $\vartheta_{int}(V'_{gr})$ are removed along with the nodes in V'_{gr}. Indeed, all sink nodes in V'_{gr} are of type t as noted above, and so is v_{new} by construction. Thus, sink nodes are replaced by a node v_{new} of the same type. Since the arcs have the same type as those they replace, it follows that *replace* preserves type correctness. It is also easy to verify that each new edge in G' can be mapped to an existing edge in G (proof omitted).

Definition 5 (Replace). $replace(V_{gr}, v_{new}, G) = (V', E')$, *where:*

$$V' = V \setminus V_{gr} \cup \{v_{new}\}$$
$$E' = E \setminus (\vartheta_{out}(V_{gr}) \cup \vartheta_{in}(V_{gr}) \cup \vartheta_{int}(V_{gr})) \cup \vartheta'_{out}(V_{gr}) \cup \vartheta'_{in}(V_{gr})$$

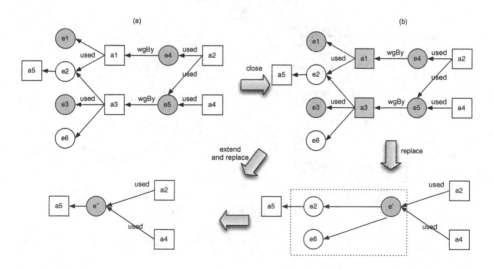

Fig. 3. Grouping by closure and extension.

3.3   T-Grouping

We can now define *Group* as a composition of closure, extensions, and replacement. In general, nodes in V_{gr} can be either *En* or *Act*. It is necessary to specify the type of the replacement node, as this may lead to different results. To make this explicit, we denote the operator by **t-grouping** (i.e., **e-grouping** or **a-grouping**, respectively). In the next section, we clarify how user-defined policies are used to control the application of **t-grouping** to a provenance graph.

Definition 6 (t-Grouping). *Let $G = (V, E) \in PG_{gu/ea}$, $V_{gr} \in V$, $t \in \{En,$ Act$\}$, and let v_{new} be a new node with $type(v_{new}) = t$. Then:*

$$Group(G, V_{gr}, v_{new}, t) = replace(extend(pclos(V_{gr}, V), V, t), v_{new}, G)$$

Note sink nodes in the closure are homogeneous and are replaced by a node of the same type t. This satisfies the necessary condition for *replace* to perform correctly. Figure 4(a-1, a-2) illustrates $Group(G, \{e_4, a_2\}, v_{new}, Act)$, while Fig. 4(e-1, e-2, e-3) shows $Group(G, \{e_4, a_2\}, v_{new}, En)$. Note that a new pattern arises in the case of *e-grouping* as shown in Fig. 4(e-1, e-2). Now the extension leads to $V_{cl} = V_{gr} \cup \{e_5\}$, which in turn leads to the pattern shown in Fig. 4(e-3), involving two generation events for the new entity e_N. Although this is a valid pattern, the two generation events must be simultaneous by C1 above. The intuitive interpretation for this pattern is that each of the two activities generated

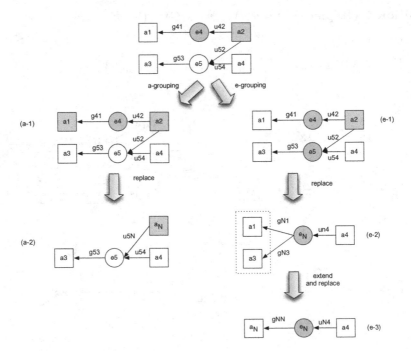

Fig. 4. e-grouping and a-grouping

one entity in $source(e_N)$, and that the abstraction makes these two events indistinguishable. Formally, nothing further needs to be done to the graph. However one can restore the more natural pattern whereby one single generation event is recorded for e_N, by propagating the grouping to the set of generating activities. In the example, this leads to the graph in Fig. 4(e-3).

4 Policy Model

Having outlined the grouping operator, we now present a simple policy language to let users specify one or more grouping sets V_{gr} for abstraction. We refer to these users as Policy Setters (PS). Our approach consists of two phases. The first phase involves annotating each node n with a *sensitivity* value $s(n)$ and/or a *utility* value $u(n)$. These annotations are independent of any intended receiver of the abstracted graph. In the second phase, a grouping set V_{gr} is generated for a specific receiver r, denoted $V_{gr}(r)$ for clarity. We assume, as in Bell-Lapadula [4], that a pre-defined clearance level $cl(r)$ is associated with r. The nodes to be abstracted are simply those with sensitivity higher than $cl(r)$: $V_{gr}(r) = \{v \in V | s(n) \geq cl(r)\}$.

A policy is a sequence of rules. Each rule (i) identifies a set of nodes, and (ii) assigns a sensitivity to each of those nodes. Node selection is achieved using a simple form of path expressions on the graph, combined with filter conditions. Keeping simplicity of use by non-expert PS in mind, we have chosen a simplified fragment of regular path expressions on graphs [15]. The example rules in Fig. 5 apply to the graph in Fig. 1:

```
list classifications   [Unclassified, Classified, Protected, Secret];
for all (act used data)
    where (data.Status >= Secret in classifications (def true)) setSensitivity(act, 7);
for all (process used data)
    where (data descendantOf d14)) setSensitivity(data, 10);
```

Fig. 5. Example Policy rules

The rules are executed in sequence. **List** declares a domain-specific *ordered* enumeration of constants, called **Classifications**. The path expression in the first command is a simple pattern where **act** and **data** are variables, and **used** is the *used* relation. The pattern is then matched against the graph and the variables are bound to nodes. The filter condition predicates on the values of properties associated to the nodes. Here the value of **data.Status** is expected to be one of the constants in the **classification** list. This predicate selects all nodes with value *at least* **Secret** in the ordered list. The activity nodes that satisfy the conditions have their sensitivity set to 7.[5] Rather than allowing arbitrary regular path expressions in the language, we expose specific traversal operators. One example is *descendantOf*, which returns all nodes reachable from

---

[5] A default value can be specified, i.e. for the cases where a **data** node has no **Status** property, or the property has no value.

a given start node. An example of its use is the second rule above. Rule evaluation binds variables `process` and `data` to activity and entity nodes a, e, respectively, such that $used(a, e)$ holds and e is any node that is reachable from node with id `d14` (a constant value).

Utility is the counterpart to sensitivity. It denotes the interest of the provenance owner in ensuring that a node be *retained* as part of the graph, as it represents important evidence which is not sensitive. Recall from our earlier example that grouping may remove non-selected nodes in order to preserve validity, a possibly undesirable side-effect. The utility values associated to different nodes are used to quantify such loss of utility. Let $V_{ret} = V \setminus V_{gr}$ be the set of nodes not intended for grouping, and $V'_{ret} \subset V_{ret}$ the nodes which were in fact retained after grouping. The residual utility is simply

$$RU_V = \frac{\sum_{n \in V'_{ret}} u(n)}{\sum_{n \in V_{ret}} u(n)} \tag{2}$$

which is maximized for $V'_{ret} = V_{ret}$. Policy setters who experiment with different policy rules, i.e., using a test set of provenance graphs, may use RU_V as a quantitative indicator of utility loss associated with a given policy and receiver.

4.1 ProvAbs Tool

The Provenance Abstraction Model is implemented as part of a project involving confidentiality protection for provenance. The main purpose of the `ProvAbs` tool is to let a PS explore partial disclosure options, by experimenting with various policy settings and clearance level thresholds. Users may load a graph in PROV-N format [16] and either specify a policy interactively, or load a predefined policy file. The output consists of a graphical depiction of the graph, annotated with its sensitivity values (these are the coloured boxes in Fig. 1), as well as the final abstract version of the graph. The residual utility value (2) is also returned. Provenance graphs are stored in the Neo4J graph database (neo4j.org). Policy expressions are evaluated using a combination of the Neo4J Traverse API and Cypher queries. `ProvAbs` and its documentation are publicly available.[6]

5   Summary

In this paper we have presented a Provenance Abstraction Model (PAM) and its implementation, `ProvAbs`. PAM is based on a *Group* operator, which replaces a set of nodes in a PROV graph with a new abstract node while preserving the validity of the graph. A simple notion of convexity of the set of nodes to be replaced ensures that the rewriting does not introduce new cycles. Due to space limitations, the scope of this paper is limited to $PG_{gu/ea}$ graphs, which only include generation, usage relations on Activity and Entity nodes. A more comprehensive model, including its extension to Agents, can be found in our

---

[6] http://bit.ly/1dxg9X1.

report [5]. Encouraged by this initial study, we are now developing a more comprehensive model of abstraction that accounts for larger fragments of PROV — a complex specification in its own right.

References

1. Moreau, L., Missier, P., Belhajjame, K., B'Far, R., Cheney, J., Coppens, S., Cresswell, S., Gil, Y., Groth, P., Klyne, G., Lebo, T., McCusker, J., Miles, S., Myers, J., Sahoo, S., Tilmes, C.: PROV-DM: The PROV Data Model. Technical report, World Wide Web Consortium (2012)
2. Biton, O., Boulakia, S.C., Davidson, S.B., Hara, C.S.: Querying and managing provenance through user views in scientific workflows. In: ICDE, pp. 1072–1081 (2008)
3. Dey, S.C., Zinn, D., Ludäscher, B.: PROPUB: towards a declarative approach for publishing customized, policy-aware provenance. In: Bayard Cushing, J., French, J., Bowers, S. (eds.) SSDBM 2011. LNCS, vol. 6809, pp. 225–243. Springer, Heidelberg (2011)
4. Bell, D.: The Bell-LaPadula model. J. Comput. Secur. **4**(2), 3 (1996)
5. Missier, P., Gamble, C., Bryans, J.: Provenance graph abstraction by node grouping. Technical report, Newcastle University (2013)
6. Cadenhead, T., Khadilkar, V., Kantarcioglu, M., Thuraisingham, B.: Transforming provenance using redaction. In: Proceedings of the 16th ACM Symposium on Access Control Models and Technologies, SACMAT 2011, pp. 93–102. ACM, New York (2011)
7. Moreau, L., Clifford, B., Freire, J., Futrelle, J., Gil, Y., Groth, P., et al.: The Open Provenance Model — core specification (v1.1). Future Gener. Comput. Syst. **7**(21), 743–756 (2011)
8. Zheleva, E., Getoor, L.: Preserving the privacy of sensitive relationships in graph data. In: Bonchi, F., Malin, B., Saygın, Y. (eds.) PInKDD 2007. LNCS, vol. 4890, pp. 153–171. Springer, Heidelberg (2008)
9. Bhagat, S., Cormode, G., Krishnamurthy, B., Srivastava, D.: Class-based graph anonymization for social network data. Proc. VLDB Endow. **2**(1), 766–777 (2009)
10. Liu, K., Terzi, E.: Towards identity anonymization on graphs. In: Proceedings of SIGMOD, pp. 93–106. ACM, New York (2008)
11. Braun, U., Shinnar, A., Seltzer, M.: Securing provenance. In: Proceedings of the 3rd Conference on Hot Topics in Security, pp. 4:1–4:5. USENIX Association, Berkeley (2008)
12. Hasan, R., Sion, R., Winslett, M.: Introducing secure provenance: problems and challenges. In: Proceedings of the 2007 ACM Workshop on Storage Security and Survivability, StorageSS 2007, pp. 13–18. ACM, New York (2007)
13. Cadenhead, T., Khadilkar, V., Kantarcioglu, M., Thuraisingham, B.: A language for provenance access control. In: Proceedings of ACM Conference on Data and Application Security and Privacy, CODASPY 2011, pp. 133–144, ACM, New York (2011)
14. Cheney, J., Missier, P., Moreau, L.: Constraints of the provenance data model. Technical report (2012)
15. Mendelzon, A.O., Wood, P.T.: Finding regular simple paths in graph databases. SIAM J. Comput. **24**(6), 1235–1258 (1995)
16. Moreau, L., Missier, P., Cheney, J., Soiland-Reyes, S.: PROV-N: the provenance notation. Technical report (2012)

ProvGen: Generating Synthetic PROV Graphs with Predictable Structure

Hugo Firth[✉] and Paolo Missier

School of Computing Science, Newcastle University, Newcastle upon Tyne, UK
{h.firth,paolo.missier}@ncl.ac.uk

Abstract. This paper introduces *provGen*, a generator aimed at producing large synthetic provenance graphs with predictable properties and of arbitrary size. Synthetic provenance graphs serve two main purposes. Firstly, they provide a variety of controlled workloads that can be used to test storage and query capabilities of provenance management systems at scale. Secondly, they provide challenging testbeds for experimenting with graph algorithms for provenance analytics, an area of increasing research interest. *provGen* produces PROV graphs and stores them in a graph DBMS (Neo4J). A key feature is to let users control the relationship makeup and topological features of the graph, by providing a seed provenance pattern along with a set of constraints, expressed using a custom Domain Specific Language. We also propose a simple method for evaluating the quality of the generated graphs, by measuring how realistically they simulate the structure of real-world patterns.

1 Introduction

Every piece of data ever produced, either manually or automatically, has a provenance. This is metadata that provides an account of how the data was created. Examples include a blog's author, the history of a piece of software along with its contributors, the instruments used to take a measurement, and their settings; or a description of an experimental process used to produce a scientific result. The PROV data model for provenance [MMB+12], endorsed in 2013 by the W3C, provides a formal and domain-agnostic grounding for provenance, in the form of UML and OWL models, and RDF, XML, and relational (PROV-N [MMCSR12]) serializations. We refer to PROV instances as digraphs, where nodes are of three possible types: *Entities* (for data, documents, anything that has provenance), *Activities*, which model the execution of a data consumption and production process; and *Agents*, to whom Entities can be attributed, and who hold responsibility for carrying out Activities. The edges represent instances of relationships amongst the nodes, which are documented in the PROV-DM specification [MMB+12].

The provenance traces associated with a homogeneous data collection (a scientific data repository, all the blogs hosted on a particular site, all the artifacts associated with a complex software project) also naturally form a collection. Such collections grow in size both with the number of underlying data products, and

B. Ludäscher and B. Plale (Eds.): IPAW 2014, LNCS 8628, pp. 16–27, 2015.
DOI: 10.1007/978-3-319-16462-5_2

with the complexity of their production process. Figure 1 suggests how different collections can be placed into a space defined by volume, i.e., the number of traces in a collection, and by the typical size of a trace within a collection. For instance, many small traces (upper left) may be associated with a large repository of scientific data, while complex software with a long history may be represented by many large traces (upper right), as exemplified by the Git2Prov [DMV+13] tool.

Arguably, the value of provenance comes not only from querying the content of individual traces, but also from analytics, which can only be computed on whole collections. It is therefore important for practical applications to demonstrate the effectiveness of a data and service architecture to manage large bodies of provenance, with special focus on the upper quadrant of our size/volume space. Thus, we expect that the design of scalable repositories for provenance traces should be a natural concern in provenance management. A number of recent efforts have been documented on nascent provenance management infrastructure [CAB+13, CLFF10, LLCF11, MMW+12], and there is evidence of the emergence of applications that require provenance querying in a variety of settings (e.g. [MOnH+13, ddOOn+12]). However, unlike other "big data" domains such as Linked Data and more generally RDF triple stores, where performance benchmarking is established practice, to the best of our knowledge no community-made benchmarking and commonly accepted datasets that are specific to provenance are available.[1] This makes it difficult to benchmark and compare different implementations with regards to storage techniques, query models, and analysis algorithms.

This is somewhat counter-intuitive, given the amount of provenance that is generated, in domains such as those alluded to above. In fact, only a handful of real datasets are currently available through a community process, i.e., the first ProvBench initiative in 2013 (http://bit.ly/1fBOswR)[2], and even fewer conform to the recent PROV standard and are therefore interoperable. Existing benchmarking datasets which apply to RDF triple stores[3] are not adequate, because they fail to account for the specific data model and semantics of PROV, as well as for the specific requirements of provenance query and analysis.

1.1 Contributions

Our assumption is that synthetic PROV graphs can be a valuable complement to emerging natural provenance collections, provided that their structural properties reflect specific provenance patterns, with control over their repetition and variability, and at varying scales. Such graphs can be used both for benchmarking

---

[1] The use of community datasets for comparing the performance of predictive models has also long been commonplace within the data mining and KDD community, where challenge datasets are regularly used.

[2] Further contributions are expected from the second ProvBench in 2014 (http://bit.ly/1c0q5rS).

[3] The W3C maintains a list of those http://bit.ly/1lhjvvn.

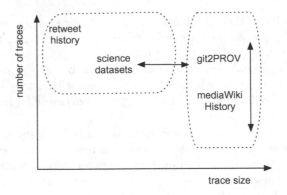

Fig. 1. A simple space for homogeneous provenance collections

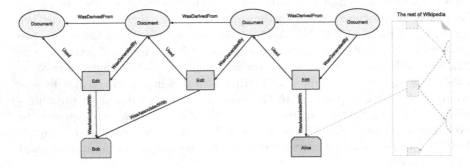

Fig. 2. The *document revision* provenance pattern in Wikipedia includes multiple derivation and editing activities by multiple user or bot agents.

emerging provenance management systems, as well as to test analytics algorithms that operate naturally on large provenance collections.

Our main contribution (Sect. 2) is the design and implementation of *prov-Gen*, a PROV generator that is designed to help populate the space described in Fig. 1. *provGen* "grows" collections of synthetic PROV graphs in a way that conforms to real-life provenance patterns. These are currently user-defined and modelled after patterns found in specific domains, and which reflect the nature of the data generation process described by the provenance. For instance, the prevalent provenance pattern for a Media Wiki website, which we refer to as the "document revision" model, involves multiple revisions of articles, by multiple editors (Fig. 2). Git repositories exhibit similar patterns, which reflect the revision history of the code. These patterns are different, for instance, from those for the provenance of data generated using a workflow, which reflect the consumer-producer graph structure of the dataflow specification.

Users control the "shape" of the graph being generated by *provGen* by providing two main elements. The first is a *seed graph*, which determines the specific types of nodes and the relationships amongst them to be considered, in an otherwise random generation process. The second element is a set of constraints, expressed using a dedicated Domain Specific Language (DSL), which limit the possible ways in which nodes and relationships are added. These two elements ensure a predictable general shape for the generated graph, as well as its compliance to PROV.

As discussed later, *provGen* relies on a graph DBMS backend (Neo4J). In particular, the generation algorithm is based on graph rewrite rules that are implemented using a combination of Cypher queries and Create statements.

1.2   Related Work

A growing body of research is devoted to generating large bodies of synthetic graph data, either using purely random models [KN09, ER60], or by generating graphs that exhibit specific statistical properties [BA99, BB05, LCKF05]. One example is the *preferential attachment* model. Popularised by Barabasi and Albert [BA99], this model states that as new vertices are added to a graph, the probability of creating a relationship with node n is inversely proportional to the degree of n. This model generates a graph with a degree distribution which follows a power law.

An issue common to these models, emphasised for instance in a comprehensive survey on graph generators [CF06], is their focus on enforcing global properties of the generated graph, such as degree distribution, clustering coefficient, etc. A potential reason for this focus is that these generators aimed at simulating social networks [PBE13, BB05], the statistical properties of which are based on large sets of examples, and thus are fairly well understood [MMG+07]. In contrast, our generation strategy relies on user-specified patterns, rather than a large set of pre-existing examples (in the future, we hope to be able to use patterns that have been automatically discovered from existing graphs, by means of standard graph mining techniques [KK04]). This has the advantage that the overall topology of the graph can be made to reflect desired semantic properties of the data, such as the average number of usages for a certain type of entity, the average number of association of an agent with activities, and so forth. Pham *et al.* [PBE13] are amongst the few to have addressed this problem. However, they focus on a loosely related issue, namely the correlation between node and relationship properties, such as an increased likelihood to be called "Joachim" if you live in Germany, and on generating realistic synthetic value dictionaries accordingly.

2   Graph Generation Model

Graph generation in *provGen* is an iterative process which starts from a single node. At each iteration, a collection of predefined *atomic rewrite* rules is used to add a set of new nodes or relationships to the current graph. These rules account for all possible relation types that are defined in the PROV-DM specification. As an example, consider the definition of the $used(a, e)$ relation between an activity a and e an entity e. Three atomic graph rewrite rules are defined for this relation, namely (i) given an entity node e, add a new activity node a and an edge $used(a, e)$; (ii) given an activity node a, add a new entity node e and an edge $used(a, e)$; and (iii) given a pair of unrelated nodes (a, e), add edge $used(a, e)$. Since each single PROV relation type induces three atomic rewrites, and we consider 13 types of relations from PROV, at each iteration *provGen* can potentially fire any of 39 different rules.

Users can control the execution of these rules and the overall effect of the generation process in three complementary ways, namely (i) by specifying a *seed graph*, (ii) by adding a set of constraints, and (iii) by specifying additional execution parameters. We now describe these in some detail.

1. Seed graphs. A seed graph specification restricts the set of rules to choose from, to only those corresponding to the relations that appear in the graph. As an example, the document revision pattern depicted in Fig. 2 may be expressed as follows, using PROV-N syntax:[4]

```
entity(e1, [ prov:type="Document" ])
entity(e2, [ prov:type="Document" ])
activity(a, 2013-11-16T16:00:00, 2013-11-16T16:05:00, [prov:type="edit"])
agent(ag, [ prov:type='prov:Person' ])
used(a, e1, 2013-11-16T16:00:00)
wasGeneratedBy(e2, a, -, [ ex:fct="save" ])
wasAssociatedWith(a, ag, -, [ prov:role="contributor" ])
wasDerivedFrom(e2, e1, a)
```

Using this graph, *provGen* determines that only *wasGeneratedBy*, *used*, *was DerivedFrom* and *wasAssociatedWith* rules are to be used. Furthermore, it will associate the properties and values found in the seed graph, for instance `prov:type="edit"`, to the new nodes and relations.

2. Constraints. Even with this restriction, unconstrained generation would lead to a graph with arbitrarily high node degree and branching factor, which would bear little resemblance to the seed trace provided, except in its relationship makeup. To further control the generation process, the second user input consists of an additional set of constraints, specified using a natural and intuitive syntax. Constraints are syntactically similar to workflow *control-flow* patterns [VTKB03], expressing the required states of data being created.

Constraints consist of three structural components, as shown in the examples of Table 1, namely a *determiner*, an *imperative*, and a *condition*. The determiner is either variable (`an Agent`) or invariable (`the Agent, a1`) and determines the elements to which a constraint applies. Requirements on these elements are specified by means of the Imperative clause. For instance `has in degree` (the requirement) `at most 1` (a qualifier) allows a new incoming edge to be added to any Entity that has none. The qualifier may optionally include a probability distribution, as in the second example. This determines the likelihood that

---

[4] Domain-specific properties have been added to nodes and relations to denote the role of entities, activities, and agents in the pattern.

Table 1. Examples of user-defined constraints for graph generation.

Determiner	Imperative		Condition
	Requirement	Req. qualifier	
an Entity	has in degree	at most 1;	
an Agent	has relationship "WasAssociatedWith"	between 1, 1000 times, with distribution gamma(..., ...),	unless it has relationship "ActedOnBehalfOf";
an Activity	has relationship "Used"	exactly 1 times,	unless it has property {"prov:type"="create"};
an Entity	has relationship "WasDerivedFrom",	at least 1 times,	unless it has relationship "WasGeneratedBy" with the Activity, a1, AND a1 has property {"prov:type"="create"};

an action be taken in order to satisfy the requirement, namely the generation of a new *WasAssociatedWith* relation. Furthermore, a condition specifies the applicability of an imperative to a determined element, i.e. **when** (selective condition) or **unless** (greedy condition). Thus, the second constraint inhibits the creation of a new *WasAssociatedWith* relation for any Agent that already has a *ActedOnBehalfOf* relation associated to it. Conditions admit the use of logical connectives, as in the third and last constraint examples, and may predicate on properties that are mentioned in the seed graph, such as **prov:type** (pre-defined) or **ex:name** (user-defined). Finally, the last constraint shows an example of variable usage (**a1**).

Note that these constraints are in addition to those defined in the PROV-CONSTR document [CMM12]. For instance, *provGen* will not create a graph where entities are generated by multiple activities. The sketch in Fig. 3 shows the different patterns obtained when generating the graph with and without enforcing the constraints.

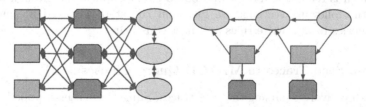

Fig. 3. Sketch of PROV graphs generated with and without enforcing user constraints

A more complete account of the constraint DSL can be found as part of the *provGen* documentation[5].

---

[5] The provGen website: http://bit.ly/1w5Aj22.

3. Execution Parameters. Finally, users may specify additional execution parameters to control the number of distinct (unconnected) graphs to be generated,
as well as the average number of nodes and edges per graph. More advanced
parameters can be used to control the average height (maximum depth) and
width (maximum breadth) for each graph generated.

The combination of seed graph, constraints, and execution parameters leads
to collections of PROV graphs that approximate real traces from different
domains, and which can be used to populate selected areas of our provenance
state (Fig. 1). In Sect. 4 we briefly sketch the evaluation method we are using to
test the quality of generated graphs, with respect to a large testbed of provenance
graphs with known topological properties.

Overall, *provGen*'s generation process consists of a nested iteration loop. In
the inner loop, *provGen* iterates over the set of active atomic rewrite rules. When
a rule fires, any constraint that applies to the elements that it is operating upon
is checked, and if any of those constraints is violated, the rule has no effect. This
process is repeated in the outer loop, until a halting condition is satisfied, i.e.,
the desired size is reached, and the DSL constraints are satisfied.

3   Mapping the Model to Graph DBMS Queries

provGen is implemented using the Neo4J graph DBMS[6] as a back end. In particular, both atomic rewrite rules and user constraints are transparently compiled
into CREATE and MATCH statements expressed in Cypher, Neo's declarative graph
pattern language[7]. Queries (in addition to CREATE statements) are required at
each iteration to test the requirements and conditions associated with user constraints (Table 1). This compilation step provides isolation from the data layer,
delegating graph traversal to the underlying DBMS, and also provides flexibility for retargeting the graph generator to a different back end. A native graph
DBMS also offers a more natural data model for PROV than a more traditional
RDBMS solution.

The *provGen* architecture is shown in Fig. 4. Components are deployed on a
server, which is reachable from a web based client application through a REST
API. In the following sections, we focus on the steps involved in generating
Cypher queries from rewrite rules and user constraints.

3.1   From Seed Traces to MATCH Query Clauses

The first step involves parsing the seed traces. Since these user-supplied samples
of PROV data may be serialized into multiple formats, parsing relies upon several third party libraries, including the OWLAPI[8] and ProvToolbox.[9] This step

---

[6] The Neo4j project: http://bit.ly/Pwux7U.
[7] Cypher documentation: http://bit.ly/1klIlMK.
[8] The OWLAPI project: http://bit.ly/N9hsPM.
[9] The ProvToolbox project: http://bit.ly/1fV95nN.

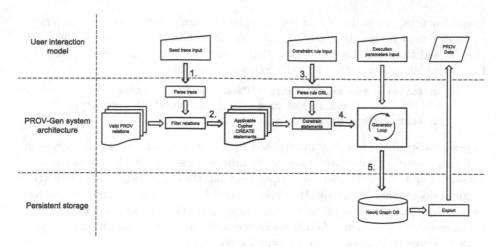

Fig. 4. *provGen* system architecture.

results in a subset of the 39 pre-defined atomic graph rewrite rules, mentioned in Sect. 2, to be selected for the generation step.

Rewrite rules are statically mapped to Cypher queries. As an example, below we show the queries responsible for creating the PROV *used* relationship. Note that multiple queries are required in order to account for the directed nature of PROV relationships and the ability to create a edge between two pre-existing nodes.

```
(1) MATCH (a:Activity {})  CREATE (a)-[:USED {}]->(:Entity {})
(2) MATCH (a:Entity {})  CREATE (a)<-[:USED {}]-(:Activity {})
(3) MATCH (a:Activity {}), (b:Entity {})  CREATE (a)-[:USED {}]->(b)
```

Query fragment (1) matches any node a of type Activity, it creates a new Entity node, and it connects it to a using a *used* relationship. Symmetrically, (2) adds a new Activity node to any existing Entity node. Finally, (3) takes a pair of *existing* nodes a (Activity), b (Entity) and again creates a *used* relationship between them.

The examples above show empty brackets, to indicate that no properties are associated to the nodes and relationships. However, all properties associated to the elements of the seed trace are also associated to corresponding elements of the new graph. Thus, for example activities would have a property prov:type, inherited from the activity node in the seed graph above.

3.2   Constraints as WHERE Clauses

The DSL parser[10] separates the component elements of each constraint, namely *determiner*, *imperative* and *condition*. Requirements may be expressed on various

---

[10] The parser is implemented using Scala parser combinators: http://bit.ly/1cURrAo.

graph features, i.e., nodes in/out degree, relationship, property, etc.... Each type of requirement is compiled into a Cypher query `WHERE` clause. These clauses are then added to the `MATCH` statements that represent the atomic rewrite rules, to form complete queries. Consider the following example:

```
an Activity has relationship ''Used'' exactly 1 times,
            unless it has property {''ex:name'':''create''};
an Activity has degree at most 5;
```

These constraints are easily interpreted in the context of a document revision pattern, where activities are edits of document versions, which produce a new version. For these activities, we stipulate that they use only one entity (the original document). Activities that create new documents are exceptions, noted by the `ex:name=create` property, and these activities are allowed to use zero or more input documents. Additionally, we add an upper bound to an Activity node's degree to illustrate a more complex constraint.

The constraint is compiled into query fragments (4) and (5) in the Cypher query below, where they are merged with the `MATCH` and `CREATE` clauses of atomic query (1) from the example above:

(1) **MATCH** (a:Activity {})
(4) **MATCH** (a)-[r]-()
(5) **WHERE NOT** a.ex_name = "create" **AND NOT** count(r) >= 5
(1) **CREATE** (a)-[:USED {}]->(:Entity {})

The query specifies at the same time the node and relationship generation, and the constraint. The `MATCH` clauses bind variables a and r to an Activity and to the set of its edges, respectively (either incoming or outgoing, as no direction is specified). The `WHERE` clause ensures that the `CREATE` statement (which creates a new *used* relationship) is only executed on a if the `''ex:name''` property is not "create", and the number of edges in set r is at most 4.

3.3   Generator Loop

The generator loop (Fig. 4) accepts a collection of atomic create operations, selected and constrained as described above, and repeatedly iterates over it, executing each associated Cypher query against the underlying graph database.

The generator loop has several halting conditions: both explicit, where execution parameters, detailed in Sect. 2, halt generation as the order $|V|$ and size $|E|$ of the graph reach their specified maxima; and implicit, where constraint rules may prevent the execution of individual operations in order to avoid violating specified range requirements. Note that limits in cardinality imposed by execution parameters may be met before the minimum requirements of a constraint rule are satisfied. When this is the case, *provGen* gives priority to the user constraints, to ensure that those are not violated.

4   Evaluation Methodology

The main purpose of *provGen* is to fulfill the need to generate a possibly large number of provenance graphs for data domains where provenance is not yet routinely collected, or is not abundant. Yet, our evaluation of the system's effectiveness relies on precisely those domains where large provenance collections are available. Specifically, we evaluate *provGen* by comparing selected properties of existing "real-world" provenance graphs, which we call *control* set, to those of generated graphs (the *test* set) intended to emulate them. Using this approach, we aim to empirically demonstrate that *provGen* may be configured to generate datasets that are "similar" to those produced by multiple different sources of provenance.

Our evaluation is ongoing. Here we illustrate the approach using one single control set, namely a set of Wikipedia provenance traces, representative of the *document revision* pattern, taken from the ProvBench repository and compliant with PROV.[11] The control graphs include about 4,000 nodes and 6,000 relationships. Our test set consists of two synthetic datasets of roughly the same size as the control, produced using *provGen* with a user-created seed trace for the document revision pattern, along with constraints and parameters.

In this initial evaluation we have considered three simple criteria. Firstly, we note that in the control set, which follows the linear Wikpedia pattern (Fig. 2), each Entity is used exactly once. Thanks to our user constraints, this is easily replicated exactly in the test set. Secondly, as example criteria we additionally consider the *number of associations per Agent*, and the *average number of entities with distinct titles contributed to, per Agent*. In the control, each Agent has 2.4 associations on average (std dev. 6.2), while in our test set it has 2.9. The average number of contributions per Agent is 1.1 in the control (std dev 0.8), while in the test is 1.8. Encouraged by these preliminary results, we are now in the process of more extensively testing *provGen* using a variety of criteria that can be easily measured both on control and on test graph.

5   Conclusion

In this paper we have presented *provGen*, a PROV-specific graph generator driven by user-defined seed graphs, which represent provenance patterns, and additional user-defined constraints designed to enforce semantics properties of the generated graph. Constraints are expressed in a dedicated "plain english" constraints language.

One feature that sets *provGen* apart from existing approaches to graph generation is that it provides users with local control over topological features and statistical characteristics of the graph. Constraints are evaluated locally for each node created, thus avoiding the complexity of verifying them globally. *provGen* is implemented using a Neo4J graph database back end. Graph rewrite rules and user constraints are both mapped to Cypher queries. Rewrite rules are mapped

---

[11] ProvBench'2013 CFP: http://bit.ly/1fBOswR.

to CREATE clauses, while constraints are compiled into WHERE clauses. The two are blended together into complete Cypher queries, so that graph generation relies entirely on Neo4J's native query engine.

We have also briefly discussed our approach to evaluating the effectiveness of *provGen* in generating "real-world" provenance, i.e., by comparing some of its key statistical properties with those of real graphs within the same class. We are currently experimenting with a variety of seed graph patterns, and more extensively evaluating *provGen*'s capability to mimick real provenance. Currently seed patterns must be manually designed or discerned. In future, an attempt to collate a collection of patterns common to provenance data, as has been done with workflow specifications [VTKB03], could prove useful.

Graph generation performance is another concern we are currently addressing. Generating large scale graphs requires efficient execution of the MATCH–CREATE-WHERE queries shown above, on graphs of increasing size. We are finding that Neo4J may not be an optimal choice, as it is geared for OLTP workloads with consequent transaction management overhead. However, our architecture is flexible and allows for experimentation, as changing the back end simply requires retargeting the mapping of rules and constraints to a different query language.

References

[BA99]   Barabási, A.L., Albert, R.: Emergence of scaling in random networks. Science 1–11 (1999)

[BB05]   Batagelj, V., Brandes, U.: Efficient generation of large random networks. Phys. Rev. E Stat. Nonl. Soft Matter Phys. **71**(3 Pt 2A), 036113 (2005)

[CAB+13] Chebotko, A., Abraham, J., Brazier, P., Piazza, A., Kashlev, A., Lu, S.: Storing, indexing and querying large provenance data sets as RDF graphs in apache HBase. In: 2013 IEEE Ninth World Congress on Services, pp. 1–8. IEEE, June 2013

[CF06]   Chakrabarti, D., Faloutsos, C.: Graph mining. ACM Comput. Surv. **38**(1), 2–es (2006)

[CLFF10] Chebotko, A., Shiyong, L., Fei, X., Fotouhi, F.: RDFProv: a relational RDF store for querying and managing scientific workflow provenance. Data Knowl. Eng. **69**(8), 836–865 (2010)

[CMM12]   Cheney, J., Missier, P., Moreau, L.: Constraints of the Provenance Data Model. Technical report (2012)

[ddOOn+12] de A.R. Gonçalves, J.C., de Oliveira, D., Ocaña, K.A.C.S., Ogasawara, E., Mattoso, M.: Using domain-specific data to enhance scientific workflow steering queries. In: Groth, P., Frew, J. (eds.) IPAW 2012. LNCS, vol. 7525, pp. 152–167. Springer, Heidelberg (2012)

[DMV+13] De Nies, T., Magliacane, S., Verborgh, R., Coppens, S., Groth, P.T., Mannens, E., Van de Walle, R.: Git2PROV: exposing version control system content as W3C PROV. In: Poster and Demo Proceedings of the 12th International Semantic Web Conference, pp. 125–128 (2013)

[ER60]   Erdös, P., Rényi, A.: On the evolution of random graphs. In: Publication of the Mathematical Institute of the Hungarian Academy of Sciences, pp. 17–61 (1960)

[KK04]   Kuramochi, M., Karypis, G.: An efficient algorithm for discovering frequent subgraphs. IEEE Trans. Knowl. Data Eng. **16**(9), 1038–1051 (2004)

[KN09]   Karrer, B., Newman, M.E.J.: Random graph models for directed acyclic networks. Phys. Rev. E **80**(4), 046110 (2009)

[LCKF05] Leskovec, J., Chakrabarti, D., Kleinberg, J.M., Faloutsos, C.: Realistic, mathematically tractable graph generation and evolution, using kronecker multiplication. In: Jorge, A.M., Torgo, L., Brazdil, P.B., Camacho, R., Gama, J. (eds.) PKDD 2005. LNCS (LNAI), vol. 3721, pp. 133–145. Springer, Heidelberg (2005)

[LLCF11] Lim, C., Lu, S., Chebotko, A., Fotouhi, F.: OPQL: a first OPM-level query language for scientific workflow provenance. In: 2011 IEEE International Conference on Services Computing, pp. 136–143. IEEE, July 2011

[MMB+12] Moreau, L., Missier, P., Belhajjame, K., B'Far, R., Cheney, J., Coppens, S., Cresswell, S., Gil, Y., Groth, P., Klyne, G., Lebo, T., McCusker, J., Miles, S., Myers, J., Sahoo, S., Tilmes, C.: PROV-DM: The PROV Data Model. Technical report, World Wide Web Consortium (2012)

[MMCSR12] Moreau, L., Missier, P., Cheney, J., Soiland-Reyes, S.: PROV-N: The Provenance Notation. Technical report (2012)

[MMG+07] Mislove, A., Marcon, M., Gummadi, K.P., Druschel, P., Bhattacharjee, B.: Measurement and analysis of online social networks. In: Proceedings of the 7th ACM SIGCOMM Conference on Internet Measurement - IMC 2007, p. 29. ACM Press, New York (2007)

[MMW+12] Marinho, A., Murta, L., Werner, C., Braganholo, V., da Cruz, S.M.S., Ogasawara, E., Mattoso, M.: ProvManager: a provenance management system for scientific workflows. Concurrency Comput. Pract. Experience **24**(13), 1513–1530 (2012)

[MOnH+13] Mattoso, M., Ocaña, K., Horta, F., Dias, J., Ogasawara, E., Silva, V., de Oliveira, D., Costa, F., Araújo, I.: User-steering of HPC workflows: state-of-the-art and future directions. In: Proceedings of the 2nd ACM SIGMOD Workshop on Scalable Workflow Execution Engines and Technologies, SWEET 2013, pp. 4:1–4:6. ACM, New York (2013)

[PBE13]   Pham, M.-D., Boncz, P., Erling, O.: S3G2: a scalable structure-correlated social graph generator. In: Nambiar, R., Poess, M. (eds.) TPCTC 2012. LNCS, vol. 7755, pp. 156–172. Springer, Heidelberg (2013)

[VTKB03] Van der Aalst, W.M.P., Ter Hofstede, A.H.M., Kiepuszewski, B., Barros, A.P.: Workflow patterns. Distrib. Parallel Databases **14**(1), 5–51 (2003)

Applications of Provenance

Walking into the Future with PROV Pingback: An Application to OPeNDAP Using Prizms

Timothy Lebo[✉], Patrick West, and Deborah L. McGuinness

Tetherless World Constellation,
Rensselaer Polytechnic Institute, Troy, NY, USA
lebot@rpi.edu
http://tw.rpi.edu

Abstract. Adding provenance to existing systems can benefit users, but comes at an expense that may be difficult for some to justify. This trade-off can be overcome by *increasing* the value of provenance, by *decreasing* the cost to add it – or by doing both. This paper offers a contribution for each. First, we develop further the W3C PROV pingback technique so that it may reach its potential to interconnect provenance records that would traditionally sit in isolation, thus *increasing* their value. Second, we *reduce* the expense to publish the provenance of existing host systems by using minimal coupling to the Prizms Linked Data platform. Using an Earth Sciences scenario and the OPeNDAP data transport architecture as an example host system, we investigate how PROV pingback could work in practice, demonstrate its potential, and identify outstanding issues that must be addressed before it can be widely adopted.

Keywords: PROV · Provenance · Pingback · Linked Data · Discovery

1 Introduction

The provenance community reached a significant milestone in 2013 when the World Wide Web Consortium (W3C) published its PROVenance documents. With a core model for provenance standardized, the community is now better prepared to turn their attention to subsequent challenges in research and application. In application, work may now focus on the relatively easier task of creating extensions that suit specific uses, which benefit from a common abstract structure and a growing set of interoperable tools. PROV was designed to suit Linked Data design principles [12], and publishing PROV as Linked Data offers great potential for distributed and uncoordinated discovery, access, and use of others' information. Conversely, PROV can benefit Linked Data by offering its consumers insight into how their distributedly-collected data came to be.

Unfortunately, the potential advantages of pairing PROV with Linked Data have yet to be seen at a scale as grand as the Web it uses. Now that PROV is a prominent fixture in the toolbox, a broader development community needs compelling reasons to adopt the W3C Recommendation and they need practical

© Springer International Publishing Switzerland 2015
B. Ludäscher and B. Plale (Eds.): IPAW 2014, LNCS 8628, pp. 31–43, 2015.
DOI: 10.1007/978-3-319-16462-5_3

answers for how to do it. Because existing host systems are often large and heavily invested in technologies not well suited to adopting Linked Data design to publish provenance records, solutions are needed to bridge the gap between existing systems and an interconnected Web of provenance with other systems. Our work aims to provide a technical foundation for such solutions, by developing PROV Pingback and applying designs from the Prizms platform.

PROV Pingback [9] has the potential to drastically interconnect provenance records that would traditionally sit in isolation. In contrast to the rest of PROV, which describes *how to describe* provenance so that anyone with the record may read about an object's history, PROV Pingback enables parties to discover what happened to objects they created *after they have left their purview*. It addresses the practical need for upstream parties to obtain provenance recorded downstream, and does so with a simple technique based on the HTTP Link header.

The Prizms system emerged from the need to create high quality Linked Data [11] and has evolved into a Linked Data platform geared towards replicability, reproducibility, and transparency of the data that it publishes. Prizms supports the many Extract-Transform-Load processes that may be required to integrate a variety of others' data about a topic of interest, and it provides for consistent provenance capture, metadata descriptions, and hosting using best practices.

The contribution of this paper is two-fold. First, it presents an approach to publish provenance of existing systems with very little effort; it allows them to expose provenance records without the overhead of publishing the records themselves and while benefiting from Linked Data principles. Second, this paper investigates the use of the PROV Pingback technique by applying it to a realistic scenario, demonstrating its potential, and identifying outstanding issues that need to be addressed before it can be mature enough for mainstream adoption. The work presented here can be used to both *increase* the value of provenance while *reducing* the effort required to add provenance to existing systems.

2   The State of the Linked PROV Cloud

Almost a year after standardization, PROV has not yet flourished within Linked Open Data (LOD). We present here two lightweight measures of PROV's LOD presence using two resources popular within the Linked Data community: Open-Link Software's LOD Cache and datahub.io's dataset catalog. Attempts to provide a "State of the Linked PROV Cloud" suggest two challenges that the approach in this paper aims to address. First, it is possible that it is still too difficult for many to publish provenance in a manner that benefits a wider audience. Second, it is too difficult to discover existing provenance, even with Linked Data principles in place. Although widespread publication and discovery may not be a problem within individual applications (since first parties *receive* portions of provenance from which they can work), it remains an issue for those who wish to repurpose others' existing data as an independent third party.

Table 1. Occurrences of PROV terms appearing in LOD Cache (20 Feb 2014).

Entity	33
wasDerivedFrom	24,975,410
hadPrimarySource	7,874
generatedAtTime	3,376
wasGeneratedBy	33
wasAttributedTo	33
Activity	214
used	214
startedAtTime	214
wasAssociatedWith	214
generated	214
wasInformedBy	106
endedAtTime	108
Agent	1

2.1 PROV Occurrences in OpenLink Software's LOD Cache

OpenLink Software's LOD Cache is a collection of 51 billion[1] RDF triples assembled over a period of years, and continues to grow as datasets come to the attention of its maintainers. We submitted SPARQL queries to find occurrences of the 50 classes and 68 properties in PROV. Table 1 shows the occurrences of the only fourteen PROV terms that occurred in the dataset. Most term's occurrences are inconsequential, except perhaps prov:wasDerivedFrom's 24 million (~12M from DBPedia pointing to Wikipedia pages and ~12M from wikidata.org). Unfortunately, these results do not portray a thriving PROV LOD ecosystem.

2.2 PROV Occurrences in datahub.io's Dataset Catalog

The datahub.io site should provide a more comprehensive and unbiased view of Linked Data, since anyone may contribute dataset listings. In addition to gathering entries for many other contemporary datasets, the site was used to organize the famous "LOD cloud diagram" between 2007 and 2011[2], which established conventions for describing Linked Datasets within the CKAN data portal platform. According to the metadata at datahub.io[3], fifteen datasets use the PROV vocabulary. Nine were created by the authors, so we set those aside. DBPedia is one, but we already saw it through the LOD Cache (above). That leaves five independent PROV adoptions (imf-linked-data, bfs-linked-data, fao-linked-data, oecd-linked-data, ecb-linked-data), but imf-linked-data can also be seen through

---

[1] http://lists.w3.org/Archives/Public/public-lod/2013May/0154.html.
[2] http://lod-cloud.net.
[3] http://datahub.io/dataset?tags=format-prov.

the LOD Cache and all five were created by the same author and thus share similar structure. So, a community-based perspective on the use of PROV in LOD does not portray a thriving PROV LOD ecosystem, either.

3   Approach

In this section, we describe our approach to easily create provenance leveraging the Prizms Linked Data platform, since it appears still too difficult to publish provenance according to Linked Data principles and it is still too difficult to discover provenance in LOD. First, we introduce the Prizms platform by creating datasets about the *structural* provenance of our example host system, OPeN-DAP. OPeNDAP is a data transport architecture and protocol widely used by earth scientists to access remote data, such as satellite weather observations. We chose to use the OPeNDAP system to highlight how a system that *does not* use Linked Data principles can benefit from publishing its provenance records as Linked Data. Next, we describe how a minimal coupling to Prizms can publish a host system's *behavioral* provenance, and discuss the distinction between *structural* and *behavioral* provenance. Then, we describe the addition of PROV Pingback to accept reports of downstream derivations of our host system's data products. Finally, we demonstrate how the host can use its accumulation of clients' provenance to easily lead others to those downstream derivations.

3.1   Prizms' "SDV" Dataset Organization: Source, Dataset, Version

We apply Prizms' SDV organization principle throughout our approach. Prizms is a Linked Data platform designed to sustainably gather, integrate, and publish third party data to produce an integrated corpus about topics of interest. Prizms combines a few organizational principles, several existing toolsets, and commodity version control (Git) to facilitate coordination and collaboration among distributed team members. As a consequence, Prizms' design facilitates within-team replicability and, by extension, reproducibility by external parties.

The SDV organization principle [11] organizes the many individual Extract-Transform-Load (ETL) processes that a data corpus or application may require according to three fundamental provenance aspects:

- *Source*, the agent (person, organization) providing the dataset.
- *Dataset*, a logical, abstract portion of the agent's data.
- *Version*, a concrete portion of an agent's abstract dataset.

Each of these three provenance aspects is identified using a concise identifier that follows a few conventions[4] (e.g. `usda-gov`, `national-nutrient-database`, and `release-26`) with the objective that a consumer could identify the original source agent, and the source agent could identify the dataset and version in their original holdings. The three aspects form a hierarchy for the datasets and serve as a naming scope for the entities mentioned within the datasets.

---

[4] https://github.com/timrdf/csv2rdf4lod-automation/wiki/SDV-organization.

In the following example that we use to illustrate our approach, we establish six *abstract datasets* from three different *sources*. Because the datasets overlap in content but are created by drastically different means, it is important to organize them so that they can be properly managed. By following the SDV principle to organize provenance datasets, we are able to achieve provenance of provenance using the same mechanisms that are in place to express provenance of datasets.

3.2 A Concrete Basis: Modeling the Structure of the Host System

When a client requests a data product, its provenance often describes *behavioral* influences, such as the kinds of operations applied (e.g. filtering and aggregation), the mechanisms performing the operations, and their input data sources. It can be helpful, both from a designer's perspective and from a user's perspective, to supplement *behavioral* provenance with *structural* provenance. Structural provenance includes descriptions of the mechanisms performing the operations and how those mechanisms came to be. For example, software modules' code repository changes are a rich source of their structural provenance. Provenance of an unfamiliar host system's structure can help when designing the provenance of its behavior, since its components can be described *a priori* (e.g. modules' versions, lifespans, and contributing developers) and can be directly referenced.

We described the structural provenance of OPeNDAP with three datasets. The first is a PROV-O representation of its Subversion (SVN) history[5]. The second is a curated list of software components along with their home in the code repository. The third connects the first two datasets by elaborating the SVN file path hierarchy. The following table shows the SDV aspects assigned to the structural provenance datasets, referred to in this paper as S1, S2, and S3.

	Source	Dataset	Version	Size
S1	opendap-org	opendap	svn	1.9MT
S2	us	opendap-components	2014-Jan-07	1.4KT
S3	us	opendap-svn-file-hierarchy	2014-Jan-20	1.0MT

S1's source agent is the OPeNDAP community; the dataset is the software itself, and its version is the latest SVN state. The repository's XML log was transformed with XSLT to produce PROV-O[6]. S2 and S3 originated from the authors. S2 started as a spreadsheet and was transformed into Description of a Project[7] RDF using Prizms' tabular converter. S3 was constructed by SPARQL querying for SVN file paths within S1/S2 and elaborating their hierarchy. These three datasets together describe the host system's *structural* provenance and provided a basis for its *behavioral* provenance when handling data requests.

---

[5] The OPeNDAP source code is maintained at https://scm.opendap.org/svn/.

[6] Details at https://github.com/timrdf/prizms/wiki/Publication:-IPAW-2014.

[7] https://github.com/edumbill/doap/wiki.

3.3   Minimal Modifications to the Host System (e.g. OPeNDAP)

While it remains the host system's responsibility to record its own behavioral provenance (including references to its structural provenance), Prizms is used to reduce the effort required to publish those records as Linked Data. Figure 1 illustrates the coupling between Prizms and the host system, in relation to the downstream client that reports its derivations via PROV Pingback. In the upper left of the sequence diagram, a USGS LiDAR file CA_OrangeCo_2011_000402.nc is used by the host system to respond to the client's HTTP request for chunk-7. While the host system processes the request as normal, it does only two additional things (Sect. 3.3, Fig. 1). First, it logs the provenance of its handling to a new file s/d/v/record.ttl. Second, it adds HTTP Link response headers pointing to A and P for the response's provenance and pingback, respectively. The host system required only five new parameters to coordinate with Prizms: Prizms' base URI (http://opendap.tw.rpi.edu), data directory root, and Pingback service URI (/prov-pingback), along with the SDV source and dataset identifiers for the dataset of provenance records (us and opendap-prov, respectively).

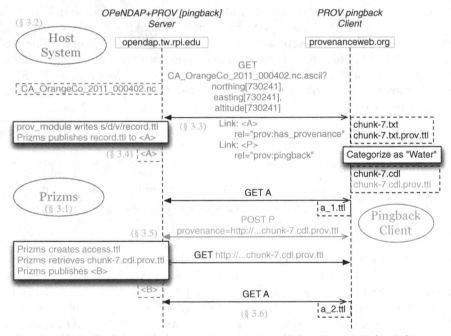

The minimal coupling between the host system (upper left) and Prizms (lower left), in relation to a pingback client (right). Section numbers indicate where each interaction is described in this paper.

Fig. 1. Sequence diagram among host system, Prizms, and pingback client.

3.4   Prizms Publishes Host System's prov:has_provenance Target

Prizms' automation monitors for unpublished datasets to publish. The log file that the host system writes (e.g. s/d/v/record.ttl, above) triggers Prizms to publish it as Linked Data. The dataset URI A that results from writing the record in directory s/d/v/ is the same URI that the host system returns in its prov:has_provenance Link header – this coordination is the extent of the coupling required for our approach. Although a custom publishing trigger was required to determine which records to publish in the dataset us/opendap-prov, it is available to be reused for other applications of our approach and employs the Vocabulary of Interlinked Data (VoID)[8] and PROV-O metadata that Prizms provides by default. A VoID Dataset A is named using its SDV aspects, its data dump is described and made available on the Web, and the provenance of loading its dump file into a new SPARQL endpoint named graph is described. These best practices for publishing Linked Data facilitate its discovery and access.

3.5   Prizms Accepts Pingback Pointers

As shown to the right of Fig. 1, the client captures its own account of its request for a portion of the LiDAR file (e.g. in chunk-7.txt.prov.ttl). When making the HTTP request to the host system, the client must remember the pingback URI provided in the response header (P, Fig. 1) so that it knows where the host will accept reports of its derivations (see [9]). Once the client derives a product chunk-7.cdl from the host's response, records provenance of its derivation in chunk-7.cdl.prov.ttl, and hosts it on the Web, the client can then report its results back to the host by accessing the pingback URI P. If the client manually loads the pingback URI using a Web browser, the service provides a description about the original request and accepts the client's URL for provenance about chunk-7.txt. The service also describes to the user how the pingback may be performed automatically via HTTP POST using the *curl* command.

Prizms' automation, which is centered around the SDV principle, allowed for a minimal pingback service implementation; it required less than 200 lines of code and can serve as a basis for other applications. When any Data Catalog Vocabulary (DCAT)[9] access metadata is situated within Prizms' data root, Prizms acts on it to retrieve, integrate, and publish it. So, the pingback service's only responsibility is to accept the pingback pointer and write it as access metadata into the same data root that the host system used for dataset A, using different SDV aspects similar to those shown in the table below. Doing so creates a new dataset B which is a local copy of the provenance hosted by the client.

Unfortunately, because pingback pointers could be provided and hosted by anyone on the Web, we cannot blindly trust that their contents are not malicious (e.g. executable code). To ameliorate this problem, we use Prizms' trigger and secondary dataset frameworks to delete any pingbacks whose contents are not

---

[8] http://www.w3.org/TR/void/.
[9] http://www.w3.org/TR/vocab-dcat/.

RDF containing PROV assertions. A dataset C is created for each batch of filtering. The following table shows the SDV organization for the three datasets created by the server after a single "request, pingback" cycle. Dataset A (Fig. 1) contains the provenance recorded by the host system during the client's original request. Dataset B (Fig. 1) contains the host's copy of the provenance reported by the client via pingback. Dataset C is the host's aggregate of all its copies of provenance reported by clients within a recent duration (e.g. daily).

	Source	Dataset	Version
A	us	opendap-prov	20140206-1391
B	provenanceweb-org	prov-pingback	20140206-1391-1e2
C	us	pr-aggregate-pingbacks	2014-Mar-03

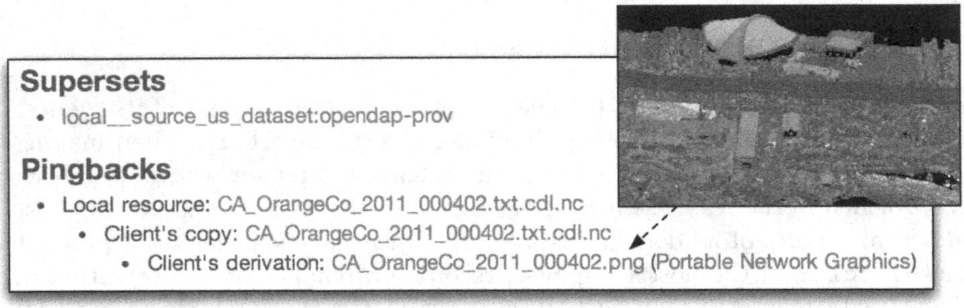

Supersets
- local__source_us_dataset:opendap-prov

Pingbacks
- Local resource: CA_OrangeCo_2011_000402.txt.cdl.nc
  - Client's copy: CA_OrangeCo_2011_000402.txt.cdl.nc
    - Client's derivation: CA_OrangeCo_2011_000402.png (Portable Network Graphics)

(a) A portion of the HTML view of the prov:has_provenance dataset A, after a client has posted a PROV Pingback and Prizms has rehosted it as dataset B. The inset image shows a portion of the LiDAR rendering that the client derived.

```
select distinct ?host_input ?client_copy ?client_derivation ?format ?F
where {
  ?host_response
    foaf:isPrimaryTopicOf <A>;
    prov:wasDerivedFrom [ prov:specializationOf ?host_input ].

  ?host_input
    ^(prov:wasDerivedFrom | prov:wasQuotedFrom) ?client_copy.
  ?client_copy
    ^(prov:wasDerivedFrom | prov:wasQuotedFrom)+ ?client_derivation.
  optional {  ?format ^dcterms:format ?client_derivation
    optional {?format  dcterms:title  ?F} }
}
```

(b) SPARQL query used by host to find downstream derivations of its data responses.

Fig. 2. Query and view of downstream derivations.

3.6 Walking into the Future

Figure 2a shows part of the HTML view when navigating to dataset A, the host's original record of the client's request for `chunk-7`. Even though the client's categorization and rendering (`chunk-7.cdl`, `CA_OrangeCo_2011_000402.png`) were created *after* this request, the host is still able to find and link to these derivations when describing the original request. Because Prizms accumulates the provenance pointed to by clients' pingbacks, it is able to use the single SPARQL query in Fig. 2b against only its own endpoint to find and offer links to client's subsequent derivations. The top portion of the query matches within the host system's account (dataset A, Fig. 1), and the bottom portion matches within the clients' (dataset B). The URL that the client requests (and that the host handles) is the natural link between accounts. With all of the relevant provenance in a single store and partitioned according to its source, the host is able to provide a variety of other Linked Data views to its clients. For example, the host can list all served requests with the files that they used, or the host can show the popularity of the files it serves based on the number of requests that used them or the number of downstream derivations that they contributed to.

4 Discussion

Related Work. Many methodologies exist for making systems provenance-aware. Of the dozen desiderata that Chapman and Jagadish [3] outline, our approach contributes to four: (1) building toward interoperability of provenance systems, (2) providing support for querying data and provenance together, (3) making provenance available to the user, and (4) capturing provenance of non-automated processes. PrIMe [13] provides a step-by-step guide that we used in part to address the question *"What derivations have others made of this given data entity?"*. Because our approach does not address *what* a host system should record of its behavior, a methodology such as PrIMe can be used to address such challenges. Groth et al. [4] present a technology-independent architecture of provenance systems, and discuss many valuable design considerations. Our low coupling approach follows their *SeparateStore* and *ContextPassing* patterns, yet after aggregating pingbacks it behaves similar to their *SharedStore* pattern.

Previous work has investigated Linked Data and provenance. Carroll et al. [2] established the central concept of a named graph. The concept has since been used by others [14], if only to capture provenance implicitly. The provenance recorded by our Prizms system employs the VoID and SPARQL Service Description vocabularies to describe named graphs as first class PROV entities. Hartig [6] distinguishes between *recordable* vs. *reliant* provenance on the Web. While the former is recorded by systems that can directly monitor their executions, the latter is accessed from third parties and requires evaluation to be trusted. PROV Pingback depends on (and benefits from) the combination of these two kinds of provenance and adds another means by which to obtain provenance from the Web (Hartig suggests DNS WHOIS, semantic sitemaps,

POWDER, and Web service descriptions). Similar to our findings, he also concludes that *"there is only very little provenance-related, RDF-based metadata available on the Web"* and points to lack of vocabularies, tools, and community sensitization/motivation as possible reasons. In follow on work, Hartig and Zhao [7] attempt to overcome the problem of missing provenance about Linked Data by offering a provenance vocabulary and extending several Linked Data publishing tools to automatically provide provenance. Instead of focusing on Linked Data provenance of Linked Data, we broadened the applicability of our Prizms provenance-aware Linked Data production platform by repurposing it to publish and interconnect provenance about non-Linked Data systems.

Advantages and Limitations of Our Approach. A key characteristic of our approach is the ability to frame PROV Pingback as a more fundamental dataset accumulation problem, thus reusing existing toolset's automation, metadata, and provenance to achieve a qualitatively different kind of interconnectivity. SDV organization is a centerpiece of Prizms' dataset accumulation, and stands as a design principle for systems that depend on many data sources. It can be seen as an answer to the request from Harth *et al.* [5] for a "social dimension" of Web provenance, so that data consumers can discuss sources at a higher level of abstraction. They call for a formalism that could describe data placement policies for URI spaces. While SDV organization satisfied the need to identify socially-contextual sources and embeds source attribution within the design of entities' URIs (e.g., 300k, 1.1M, and 50 resources within /source/opendap-org, /source/us, and /source/provenanceweb-org, respectively), it similarly suffers from the DNS ambiguity that Harth *et al.* describe and would thus also benefit from a formalism for URI space ownership. Such a formalism could serve as a foundation for trusting those URI spaces and would have impact both when surveying Linked Data and when deciding if a pingback pointer is acceptable. The VoID vocabulary, with its uriSpace property[10], might be a starting point for such a solution.

Our approach requires Linked Data design. While it may be considered a limitation by the host system, it allowed easy interconnection of distributed provenance systems with a simple RDF union. The dependency on HTTP Link also requires the host system to serve its data over HTTP. On the other hand, our approach allowed us to reuse existing vocabularies such as Friend of a Friend (FOAF) and existing instances such as DCTerms' file formats[11]. SPARQL 1.1 property paths also made it easy to traverse the many steps in a provenance graph to find all derivations. In our effort to gauge PROV's adoption in LOD, we considered several other sources that did not prove to be fruitful. Our objective was to find occurrences *in the wild*, *after* standardization, and discoverable using [semi-]automated means. Crawling all of Linked Data is the most comprehensive approach, but doing so is nontrivial [8]. A middle ground is for some to index Linked Data so that many others may perform centralized searches. The LOD

---

[10] http://www.w3.org/TR/void/#pattern.
[11] http://provenanceweb.org/instances/dcterms:FileFormat.

Cache that we used is one example, but its manual, single-owner growth makes it a biased sample. Swoogle is a well-known index, but did not return any PROV terms. Sindice is a newer index that continues to accept pointers via a different pingback mechanism [10], but its accessibility has recently faded. Ping the Semantic Web, used in previous surveys [6], simply no longer exists. An alternative is to use a Linked Dataset catalog that anyone can contribute to. This has existed at http://datahub.io/tag/lod for seven years and is what we used as our second measure. In our view, this seems to be the best approach to discovering Linked Data sources. The Prizms system automatically provides the appropriate VoID descriptions and submits them to datahub.io on a weekly basis. Such a lightweight collection of pointers can facilitate more automated means to monitor and cache Linked Data sources. For example, Buil-Aranda et al. [1] currently monitor all SPARQL endpoints listed.

Future Work. Despite its powerful ability to interconnect provenance records, PROV Pingback has a high potential for abuse (this is why our example service is not regularly available). Similar to many internet technologies, potential abuses need to be managed and can be mitigated through supporting infrastructure and tooling. Different applications should be able to control policies to adjust the tradeoff between discoverability and abuses. Hosts can reduce their risk by being selective about which clients it offers pingback services to, based on information about the client or its request. A cautious pingback service should verify that every pingback submission is worthwhile, either by its URL (literally), URL contents, or by authenticating the client as a member of a trusted group. URL blocklists and whitelists can be helpful, but can become tedious to manage. URL contents should be handled with caution, perhaps to the point of performing it within a protected space and aborting it if it does not appear to be in an expected format. Any retrieved provenance should describe at least one derivation of a data product that the host served, otherwise it is not relevant. Authenticating the submitting client as a member of a trusted group could be achieved in a variety of ways, but one that does not require a priori coordination would allow for increased contributions and discoverability. Manual curation steps could also be used to validate any aspect used to determine worthwhile submissions.

A more complete and up-to-date State of the Linked PROV Cloud would serve as a design guide for provenance practitioners interested in adopting Linked Data principles, since it could verify that their published provenance is discoverable using traditional Linked Data means. Searches for terminology occurrences could be broadened by looking for non-PROV provenance terms or PROV extensions, accounting for reasoning, and by monitoring any dataset listed at datahub.io. Developers could use such a corpus to choose terms most appropriate for their application, based on quantitative measures of any term's adoption.

We anticipate compounded advantages of a "Prizms network" when both clients and servers use the Prizms platform to propagate pingbacks. Techniques to combine PROV pingback with existing mechanisms such as Twitter's "retweet" feature could accelerate community discovery of downstream derivations.

Scalability of PROV Pingback should also be investigated, and simplifications of PROV Pingback could allow more direct usage by accepting the URI of the derivation itself and reusing the prov:has_provenance mechanism to find its provenance. Finally, the approach we presented should next be applied to *real* applications, not just *realistic*. In the case of LiDAR, we expect to apply it to a project with bathymetric and territorial data of New York State's Lake George.

5   Conclusion

The symbiotic combination of PROV and Linked Data – both PROV *as* Linked Data and PROV *of* Linked Data – offers significant potential for distributed and uncoordinated discovery, access, and use of information. Unfortunately, these advantages have yet to be seen at a scale as grand as the Web it uses. Based on two lightweight measures that we present, it appears still too difficult or too uncompelling to publish provenance in a manner that benefits a wider audience.

We presented an approach to publish the *structural* and *behavioral* provenance of existing host systems by using minimal coupling to the Prizms platform, so that the host system's provenance records may benefit as Linked Data even if its data cannot. We further described an implementation of the PROV Pingback technique, demonstrated its potential to interconnect provenance records that would traditionally sit in isolation, and explored outstanding issues that need to be addressed before pingback can be widely adopted. By *decreasing* the cost to add provenance, and by *increasing* the value of provenance by forming an interconnected Web of provenance with other systems, the approach we describe can facilitate the adoption of provenance within a wider variety of applications.

References

1. Buil-Aranda, C., Hogan, A., Umbrich, J., Vandenbussche, P.-Y.: SPARQL Web-querying infrastructure: ready for action? In: Alani, H., et al. (eds.) ISWC 2013, Part II. LNCS, vol. 8219, pp. 277–293. Springer, Heidelberg (2013)
2. Carroll, J.J., Bizer, C., Hayes, P., Stickler, P.: Named graphs, provenance and trust. In: Proceedings of the 14th International Conference on World Wide Web, WWW 2005, pp. 613–622. ACM, New York (2005)
3. Chapman, A., Jagadish, H.V.: Issues in building practical provenance systems. IEEE Data. Eng. Bull. **30**(4), 38–43 (2007)
4. Groth, P., Jiang, S., Miles, S., Munroe, S., Tan, V., Tsasakou, S., Moreau, L.: An architecture for provenance systems. Technical report, University of Southampton (2006)
5. Harth, A., Polleres, A., Decker, S.: Towards a social provenance model for the web (2007)
6. Hartig, O.: Provenance information in the web of data. In: LDOW (2009)
7. Hartig, O., Zhao, J.: Publishing and consuming provenance metadata on the Web of Linked Data. In: McGuinness, D.L., Michaelis, J.R., Moreau, L. (eds.) IPAW 2010. LNCS, vol. 6378, pp. 78–90. Springer, Heidelberg (2010)

8. Hogan, A., Umbrich, J., Harth, A., Cyganiak, R., Polleres, A., Decker, S.: An empirical survey of linked data conformance. Web Semant. Sci. Serv. Agents World Wide Web 14, 14–44 (2012). Special Issue on Dealing with the Messiness of the Web of Data
9. Klyne, G., Groth, P. (eds.), Moreau, L., Hartig, O., Simmhan, Y., Myers, J., Lebo, T., Belhajjame, K., Miles, S.: PROV-AQ: provenance access and query. W3C Working Group Note NOTE-prov-aq-20130430, World Wide Web Consortium, April 2013
10. Stuart Langridge and Ian Hickson. Pingback 1.0. Technical report (2002)
11. Lebo, T., Erickson, J.S., Ding, L., Graves, A., Williams, G.T., DiFranzo, D., Li, X., Michaelis, J., Zheng, J.G., Flores, J., Shangguan, Z., McGuinness, D.L., Hendler, J.: Producing and Using Linked Open Government Data in the TWC LOGD Portal. In: Wood, D. (ed.) Linking Government Data, pp. 51–72. Springer, New York (2011)
12. Lebo, T., Sahoo, S., McGuinness, D. (eds.), Behajjame, K., Cheney, J., Corsar, D., Garijo, D., Soiland-Reyes, S., Zednik, S., Zhao, J.: PROV-O: the PROV ontology. W3C Recommendation REC-prov-o-20130430, World Wide Web Consortium, October 2013
13. Miles, S., Groth, P., Munroe, S., Moreau, L.: Prime: a methodology for developing provenance-aware applications. ACM Trans. Softw. Eng. Methodol. 20(3), 8:1–8:42 (2011)
14. Sheridan, J., Tennison, J.: Linking UK government data. In: LDOW (2010)

Provenance for Online Decision Making

Amir Sezavar Keshavarz[✉], Trung Dong Huynh, and Luc Moreau

Electronics and Computer Science (ECS),
University of Southampton, Southampton, UK
{ask2g10,tdh,l.moreau}@ecs.soton.ac.uk

Abstract. It is commonly believed that provenance can be utilised to form assessments about the quality, reliability or trustworthiness of data. Once presented with contradictory or questionable information, users can seek further validation by referring to its provenance. While there has been some effort to design principled methods to analyse provenance, the focus has mostly been on offline use of provenance. How to use provenance at runtime, i.e., as the application runs, to help users make decisions, has been barely investigated. In this paper, we propose a generic and application-independent approach to interpret provenance of data to make online decisions. We evaluate the system in CollabMap, an online crowd-sourcing mapping application, to make decisions about the quality of its data and to determine when the crowd's contributions to a task are deemed to be complete.

Keywords: Provenance · Online decision making · Validity measure · Reliability measure

1 Introduction

It is commonly believed that provenance can be utilised to form assessments about the quality, reliability or trustworthiness of data [6]. Provenance is defined as a "record that describes the people, institutions, entities, and activities involved in producing, influencing, or delivering a piece of data or a thing" [7]. It is a crucial piece of information that can help a consumer make a judgement as to whether something can be trusted [8].

A provenance-aware system can generate the provenance of its data and make it accessible to other systems that may use it for other purposes. However, the provenance that is recorded can be application-specific. In order to use it, other systems may require it to be recorded differently and the original application to rerun as a result. This may not be possible nor efficient. As such, we need a principled mechanism for application-specific interpretation of provenance. For example, consider a provenance-aware system that requires users to interact with the system and generate some data. Another application might need to make decisions based on the ratings of the data and users that can be computed from the provenance recorded by the first application. Such a system will need to be able to: (1) Interpret application-specific provenance, (2) Compute ratings for

© Springer International Publishing Switzerland 2015
B. Ludäscher and B. Plale (Eds.): IPAW 2014, LNCS 8628, pp. 44–55, 2015.
DOI: 10.1007/978-3-319-16462-5_4

the entities generated, and (3) Use provenance-based ratings to make decisions in a timely manner.

In order to address these requirements, we introduce an online provenance analysis system that is composed of the following. First, we propose a generic Annotation Computation Framework (ACF) that enables applications to attach application-specific annotations to elements of a provenance graph and to compute new annotations from these.

Second, we put forth a statistical Quality Model (QM) that computes three ratings for data entities and users from their provenance: (1) a *validity measure* for data entities with different validity labels ("valid", "invalid", or "uncertain"), (2) a *reliability measure* for each user reflecting how consistently good their performance is, and (3) a *finish measure* with different finish labels ("finished", "unfinished") that expresses if further user contributions are required.

Finally, we devise an Online Annotation Computation System (OACS) that enables a provenance-aware system to make decisions in a timely manner from its provenance. OACS defines a contract according to which a provenance-aware system should model its provenance, submit it to the OACS, and retrieve ratings (in the form of an annotated provenance graph).

We evaluate the ACF, OACS, and QM in a crowd-sourcing application. To support online quality-based decision making, QM rates each task in the crowd-sourcing application as either finished or unfinished by using validity and reliability measures. The OACS, alongside with QM, helps increase the confidence on validity measure by analysing the performance of users (reliability measure) *during* the execution of the crowd-sourcing application.

To the best of our knowledge, online use of provenance for quality-based decision making has not been previously investigated. Our framework with the online mechanism provides a foundation that enables a provenance-aware system to make online decisions based on provenance of data.

Our contributions are fourfold:

1. A generic Annotation Computation Framework to allow application-specific interpretation of provenance;
2. An Online Annotation Computation System to assist a provenance-aware system to make online decisions during execution time;
3. A statistical quality model that uses provenance to compute (1) validity measure for data entities, (2) reliability measure for users, and (3) finish measure for data entities. It also increases the confidence on validity measure by using reliability measure in an online environment;
4. An evaluation of ACF, OACS, and QM in a crowd-sourcing application called CollabMap.

The remainder of this paper is structured as follows. In Sect. 2, a crowd-sourcing application in which provenance is recorded is introduced. Section 3 and 4 present ACF and OACS, respectively. We specialize online decision making to online quality-based decision making by implementing a statistical Quality Model and show how CollabMap utilises computed ratings to make online quality-based decisions (Sects. 5 and 6). Section 7 presents and discusses the evaluation of ACF, OACS, and the QM. Section 8 provides the related work and Sect. 9 outlines the future work.

2   Scenario: A Crowd-Sourcing Application

CollabMap is a crowd-sourcing application that recruits people to augment existing maps by identifying buildings outline and drawing their evacuation routes from buildings to nearby roads. Participants are required to verify tasks by others by providing positive or negative votes on buildings and evacuation routes, helping CollabMap to determine their validity. The quality of data generated by a crowd with different backgrounds and expertise is inevitably varied. Therefore, two mechanisms to ensure data quality were suggested for CollabMap.

1. Online Majority Voting: The first version of CollabMap (CollabMap-V1) [9] employed a customized adaptation of majority vote. If total sum of positive and negative votes is above +3, then the building is marked as valid. If the score reaches −2, the building is marked as invalid. Provenance was recorded in CollabMap-V1 but was not used to assess the validity of data.
2. Offline Provenance Network Analysis: In the second version of CollabMap (CollabMap-V2), Huynh et al. [5] extracted a set of provenance network metrics from provenance of data to learn about patterns that correlate with quality of data. This approach was not used online either.

User's reliability was not considered for decision making in either of the above versions. Therefore, to improve the quality assessment done by CollabMap in an online environment, we set the following requirements for our system.

Requirement 1. *To compute a validity label ("valid", "invalid", or "uncertain") for each data entity (buildings and evacuation routes). "valid" data entities are to be included in the final result, while "invalid" data entities are to be discarded. In cases where the validity label is "uncertain", further users would be employed to verify the "uncertain" data.*

Requirement 2. *To compute a reliability measure for each user, so that we can use these measures to increase confidence on validity label by analysing users' reliability.*

Requirement 3. *To compute a finish measure for each data entity to decide to continue or terminate a task.*

Provenance would be used to capture all these measures while CollabMap is executing. In this context, use of provenance offers the following benefits: (1) a generic foundation that provenance recorded in CollabMap can be used in a provenance-aware rating application to compute such measures and (2) a data model that captures all the changes and decisions that are made in CollabMap by using above measures in an online environment.

3   Annotation Computation Framework (ACF)

Provenance-based rating can be decomposed in a generic part involving a provenance graph traversal and annotation manipulation, and an application-specific part computing actual ratings for a given purpose in an application. ACF implements the generic part and allows for instantiations to add the application-specific part.

Annotations are utilized as a generic mechanism to enable any information to be attached to elements of a provenance graph. Following provenance record presents the use of an application-specific annotation for a building. The annotation, `validity`, represents validity label of the building.

```
entity(ex:building1,[ex:validity="valid"])
```

New annotations can be computed for a node from existing annotations for the same graph. In order to compute new annotations, both forward and backward computations are supported. Forward computation is the computation of annotations by following relations between nodes along the direction of time; and vice-versa for backward computation.

Three fixed rules are considered to support computation of annotations. Forward computation rule is defined by (1). In this rule, given there is a directed relation from an influencee ($n2$) to an influencer ($n1$), and influencer ($n1$) has an annotation ($ann1$), a new annotation for the influencee is computed based on $ann1$ and defined by $F_{forward}$. To allow application-specific interpretation, a function F is required to compute the new annotation. Backward computation rule has a similar definition except an influencee node has an annotation and a new annotation for the influencer is computed.

The third computation rule, aggregation rule (See 2), is applied when a node ($n1$) has more than one annotation (e.g. $ann1$, $ann2$, $ann3$, ...). In this case, a new annotation, ($aggAnn$), is computed based on all its existing annotations (defined by F_{Agg}).

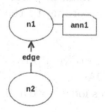

IF G $\vdash$
    $node(n1, ann1)$
    $node(n2)$
    $edge(e; n2, n1)$ (1)
    THEN there exists $ann2$ such that
      $ann2 = F_{forward}(G, e, n1, n2, ann1)$
      $update(G, n2, ann2)$

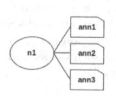

IF G $\vdash$
    $node(n1, ann1)$
    $node(n1, ann2)$
    $node(n1, ann3)$ (2)
    . . .
Then there exists $aggAnn$ such that
    $aggAnn = F_{Agg}(G, n1, [ann1, ann2, ann3, ...])$
    $update(G, n1, aggAnn)$

To ensure termination, we introduce a global counter that acts as a bound for termination. After each computation step, the counter is deduced by one. By limiting the number of computations, we guarantee that computation rules will eventually terminate.

4   Online Annotation Computation System (OACS)

OACS introduces a contract according to which a provenance-aware system should model its provenance. This contract makes two assumptions on the provenance with respect to: (1) the structure of provenance data, and (2) the annotations to be incrementally computable.

An important capability of provenance is to express revisions of the same resource. "Plan for revisions" recipe [8, Section 4.1.4] is used for this purpose. Each version of a resource is connected to a single general resource using the prov:specializationOf relation. Each version is related to its previous one using prov:wasRevisionOf relation. Assumptions 1 and 2 are as follow.

Assumption 1. *Provenance is expected to be structured according to the "Plan for revisions" recipe, so data entities are continuously rated by OACS.*

Assumption 2. *OACS expects annotations of any version of a resource to be computable by using the annotations of its previous version without the need for the full provenance of its previous versions.*

The following describes the steps through which a provenance-aware system should submit its provenance data and retrieve newly computed annotations.

Step 1 Whenever there is new provenance data that needs to be annotated, the provenance-aware system is required to bundle up all new assertions (A bundle is a named set of provenance descriptions [7]);

Step 2 In this bundle, the system is required to identify each element of provenance graph to be "annotated" as a distinct element according to the two contractual Assumptions 1 and 2;

Step 3 Submit this bundle to the OACS;

Step 4 When a response from OACS is ready, the system can retrieve a provenance bundle that contains the new annotations from OACS;

Step 5 New annotations can then be used to update the system's local state and to make application-specific decisions;

Step 6 Return to Step 1.

In a decision making situation, as an application is executing and more knowledge is generating, the application is presented with updated information which decisions are based on. In order to validate the updated information and new decisions, the decision makers can consider their provenance. As such we decided to use bundle to allow provenance of provenance to be expressed.

5 Quality Model (QM)

5.1 Validity Measure (VM)

Requirement 1 requires data entities to be annotated with a validity label ("valid", "invalid", or "uncertain"). Table 1 summarises the annotations processed by VM.

Table 1. Annotation Assertion (AA) and Annotation Computation (AC) in Validity Measure for a data entity D (building or evacuation route)

Annotation	Description	Value	Level
Vote	Value of user (U) vote for D	$Vote(D,U)$	AA
Coordinates	Coordinates of a building	$Coord(D)$	AA
Edges	Total number of edges	$Edge(D)$	AA
Positive votes	Number of positive votes for D	$P(D)$	AC
Negative votes	Number of negative votes for D	$N(D)$	AC
Validity label	Validity label of D	$V(D)$	AC

The beta family of probability density functions model the distribution of a random variable representing the unknown probability of a binary event where $T(D)$ is an example of such a variable to model [11]. In (3), $Beta(\alpha, \beta)$ returns the probability of D being valid provided α and β, where α and β are hyper-parameters to define the shape of the density function.

$$Beta(\alpha, \beta) = \frac{\alpha}{\alpha + \beta} \tag{3}$$

Hence, validity measure $(T(D))$ is given by:

$$T(D) = Beta\Big((P(D)+1), (N(D)+1)\Big) \tag{4}$$

Now, validity label $(V(D))$ can be defined by two thresholds $t1$ and $t2$:

$$V(D) = \begin{cases} valid & \text{if } T(D) \geq t2 \\ invalid & \text{if } T(D) \leq t1 \text{ or } Edge(D) < 4 \text{ for building} \\ & \text{or } Coord(D) \text{ has self-intersecting lines for building} \\ uncertain & \text{if } t1 < T(D) < t2 \end{cases} \tag{5}$$

By analysing CollabMap-V1, 0.7 and 0.3 are the threshold we chose for $t1$ and $t2$ respectively, to select valid and invalid data entities.

5.2   Reliability Measure (RM)

Requirement 2 requires each user to be annotated with a reliability measure. A user can have two roles in CollabMap: identifiers (those who generate data) and verifiers (those who verify generated data). For identifiers, we are interested in computing their total number of "valid" and "invalid" identifications. For verifiers, we are interested in computing the total number of "aligned" (positive vote on a valid data or negative vote on an invalid data) and "non-aligned" (positive vote on an invalid data and negative vote on valid data) verifications. Table 2 summarises the annotations processed by RM.

Table 2. Annotation Assertion (AA) and Annotation Computation (AC) in Reliability Measure for a user U - D can be a building or an evacuation route

Annotation	Description	Value	Level
Good identification	Total number of good D identification for U	$M(I,G,D,U)$	AC
Bad identification	Total number of bad D identification for U	$M(I,B,D,U)$	AC
Aligned	Total number of aligned votes for U	$M(V,A,D,U)$	AC
Non-aligned	Total number of non-aligned votes for U	$M(V,N,D,U)$	AC
Identification reliability	Reliability of U in D identification	$R(I,D,U)$	AC
Verification reliability	Reliability of U in D verification	$R(V,D,U)$	AC

User reliability, $R(I,D,U)$ and $R(V,D,U)$, is computed by applying (3):

$$R(I,D,U) = Beta\Big(\big(M(I,G,D,U)+1\big), \big(M(I,B,D,U)+1\big)\Big)$$
$$R(V,D,U) = Beta\Big(\big(M(V,A,D,U)+1\big), \big(M(V,N,D,U)+1\big)\Big)$$

$$(6)$$

5.3   Finish Measure (FM)

Requirement 3 requires each data entity to be annotated with a finish measure, which is computed from reliability measure. Table 3 summarises the annotations processed by FM.

Table 3. Annotation Assertion (AA) and Annotation Computation (AC) in Finish Measure for data entity D (building or evacuation route)

Annotation	Description	Value	Level
Cumulative users' reliability	Total cumulative users' reliability	$C(D)$	AC
Finish label	Label showing if a task is terminated	$F(D)$	AC

Finish measure, $C(D)$, is computed by applying (7):

$$C(D) = \sum_{U \in VD} R(V, D, U) \quad \text{where VD is the set of all verifiers of D} \quad (7)$$

Now, the finish label $(F(D))$ can be assigned based on the finish measure:

$$F(D) = \begin{cases} Yes & \text{if } C(D) \geq t2 \\ & \text{or } C(D) \leq t1 \\ & \text{or Edge}(D) \leq 4 \text{ for building} \\ & \text{or Coord}(D) \text{ has self-intersecting lines for building} \\ No & \text{if } t1 < C(D) < t2 \end{cases} \quad (8)$$

By analysing CollabMap-V1, $+1.5$ and -1.5 are the threshold we chose for $t1$ and $t2$ respectively, to annotate a data entity as finish assuring the crowd's contributions to the data entity is deemed to be complete with high confidence.

6 Decision Making in CollabMap

CollabMap-V3 uses the measures computed in Sect. 5 to make a decision on next course of action:

$$\text{Decision} = \begin{cases} \text{Continue} & \text{if } F(D) = No \\ \text{Terminate} \begin{cases} \text{Not-Accept} & \text{if } \Big(F(D) = Yes \text{ and } V(D) = Invalid \Big) \\ & \text{or } \Big(F(D) = Yes \text{ and} \\ & \qquad V(D) = Uncertain \text{ and} \\ & \qquad C(D) \leq -1.5 \Big) \\ \text{Accept} & \text{if } \Big(F(D) = Yes \text{ and } V(D) = Valid \Big) \\ & \text{or } \Big(F(D) = Yes \text{ and} \\ & \qquad V(D) = Uncertain \text{ and} \\ & \qquad C(D) \geq 1.5 \Big) \end{cases} \end{cases} \quad (9)$$

7 Experiments and Results

For a preliminary evaluation, we develop several hypotheses that we validate by applying online quality-based decision making to CollabMap-V3 and examining the results. We designed an experiment where 22 users were recruited to work with CollabMap-V3 which ran over 60 h.

Hypothesis 1. *The validity label reflects the actual validity of data as verified by an expert.*

Method 1. We asked an expert to verify all the identified data entities. Then we compared the expert's opinion with the dataset of data entities that were accepted or not-accepted by CollabMap-V3.

Analysis 1. In total, 237 buildings were identified (235 annotated as finished and 2 as unfinished; CollabMap accepted 75 % of all finished buildings and discarded the rest as they were annotated as invalid). 183 evacuation routes were identified (around 80 % annotated as finished and 20 % as unfinished; CollabMap accepted above 98 % of all finished ones). The dataset of data entities in CollabMap-V3 matched the verified data by expert; thus verifying Hypothesis 1.

Hypothesis 2. *User's reliability measure reflects the actual performance and reliability of a user.*

Method 2. We formed a control group where we asked two users to consistently draw valid buildings, two users to consistently draw invalid buildings, and two users to consistently provide verification votes opposed to what they reckon to be true (to provide negative verification votes for valid data entities and vice versa for invalid data entities).

Analysis 2. Figure 1a represents the reliability measures for two users. The reliability measure for all users are similar at the beginning. As they continue engaging with the system, RM updates users' reliability measure based on their performance. The reliability measure for User 433, who consistently draw invalid buildings, decreased from 50 % to less than 2 % (blue dashed line). Whereas the reliability measure for User 427, who consistently draw valid buildings, increased from 50 % to 98 % (red line). At this point, we can validate Hypothesis 2 as users' reliability measure truly reflects their performance.

Hypothesis 3. *If reliable users verify a data entity, the task can be terminated faster than when unreliable users verify a data entity.*

Method 3. We evaluate if (1) QM can incrementally learn the reliability of users and (2) the reliability measure of users was used to terminate the task.

Analysis 3. Figure 1b represents the proportion of finished and unfinished data entities over time. As expected, at the beginning, the growth ratio of unfinished data entities (white boxes on top) is higher than finished data entities (red pattern filled boxes). However, as RM is gaining knowledge about users, the growth ratio of finished data entities are higher.

Figure 1c represents the total number of data entities that are being annotated by their validity and finish labels over the time. At the beginning, as RM does not have enough knowledge about the users, most data entities are annotated as Unfinished-Uncertain (blue triangle-dotted line). As time progresses,

RM gains enough knowledge over users to annotate data entities as Finished-Valid/Invalid (the rapid jump in green diamond-dashed line). We can observe another growing trend and it is those data entities that are annotated as Finished-Uncertain (red square-solid line). This shows that QM reduces the number of votes required when it has gained enough knowledge about the participants. We expect more growth in this line had we let our trial continued. The reason is at the beginning, all users have the similar reliability measure and it takes time to annotate a data entity as finished. As time progresses, reliable users are identified and they will have a higher reliability measure (reliability of some users were measured as above 90 %) which means the data entity is annotated as finished earlier.

Figure 1d represents an average number of votes required to annotate a data entity as finished. The total number of requested votes depends on the finish measures. After one day of execution, there is a decreasing trend that QM requires less votes to annotate a data entity as finished. CollabMap-V1 requires at least 3 votes to terminate a task. As can be seen from Fig. 1d, the average total number of votes requested for a finished building over times, was reduced to 2.5. At this point, it is possible to verify Hypothesis 3. Although at the beginning, QM may require more verification votes, there is a decreasing trend in requesting verification votes toward the end.

8   Related Work

Provenance can be used to estimate quality of data and data reliability based on the source data [10]. Golbeck reviews trust issues on the World Wide Web [3] and identifies provenance as a key element necessary to derive trust. One trustworthiness [2]. Dai et al. [2] propose a method to compute trust scores for data, depending on the trust of the information used to generate it. In order to assess quality of data and reliability of users, Allen et al. [1] describe a provenance system, PLUS, that uses provenance of data to detect potential malicious behaviour and help users assess trust in information. On the same venue of work, Hartig et al. [4] propose a model for Web data provenance and an assessment method that can be adapted for specific quality criteria. None of these works used provenance to infer trustworthiness of data nor performance of users in an online environment. Our approach motivates the use of provenance in an online environment where quality-based decisions can be made in a timely manner.

The issue of data quality and user reliability can be observed in crowd-sourcing applications. In a crowd-sourcing application, tasks are broken down into smaller activities and are allocated to the crowd; upon completion, some rewards are issued. There are mainly two issues associated with some crowd-sourcing applications: (1) quality of generated data, and (2) evaluation of user performance. To assure quality, the crowd-sourcing application assigns the same labelling task to multiple users. When multiple labels are provided for the same task, the crowd-sourcing application fuses all labels to estimate the actual label. Whitehill et al. [12] present a probabilistic model to compute the expertise of

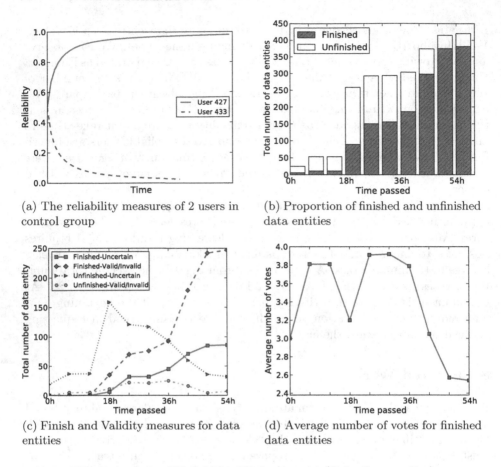

(a) The reliability measures of 2 users in control group

(b) Proportion of finished and unfinished data entities

(c) Finish and Validity measures for data entities

(d) Average number of votes for finished data entities

Fig. 1. Analysis of CollabMap-V3 deployment (Color figure online)

each user, difficulty of each task, and the label of each task. Our proposed QM is similar to this approach in computing a validity and reliability measures, however in contrast, we use reliability measures to decide to continue or terminate a task while the application is executing.

9   Conclusion

In this paper, we have presented a principled approach for online application-specific interpretation of provenance that consists of: (1) a generic part involving a provenance graph traversal and annotation manipulation, (2) an application-specific part computing the annotations for data quality assessment and task termination.

We carried out a preliminary analysis of the approach on CollabMap, a crowd-sourcing application for designing evacuation maps. We showed that it is able to classify data with high accuracy by analysing the reliability of contributors while the application is executing. We also demonstrated that with our framework, CollabMap was able to make online decisions whether to terminate or continue a task.

Going forward, we plan to deploy CollabMap and ACF in a wider community, employing more users for a complete empirical evaluation of our framework. It would allow us to evaluate how accurately ACF can help CollabMap to terminate tasks. Furthermore, we plan to use user's reliability measure to decide whether to accept or reject a user's contribution and to explore dynamic task allocation to users based on their reliability.

Acknowledgements. This work is funded by the EPSRC ORCHID Project (EP/-I011587/1).

References

1. Allen, M.D., et al.: Provenance for collaboration: detecting suspicious behaviors and assessing trust in information. In: 2011 7th International Conference on Collaborative Computing, pp. 342–351. IEEE (2011)
2. Dai, C., Lin, D., Bertino, E., Kantarcioglu, M.: An approach to evaluate data trustworthiness based on data provenance. In: Jonker, W., Petković, M. (eds.) SDM 2008. LNCS, vol. 5159, pp. 82–98. Springer, Heidelberg (2008)
3. Golbeck, J.: Trust on the world wide web: a survey. Found. Trends Web Sci. 1(2), 131–197 (2006)
4. Hartig, O., Zhao, J.: Using web data provenance for quality assessment. In: SWPM, vol. 526 (2009)
5. Huynh, T.D., Ebden, M., Venanzi, M., Ramchurn, S.D., Roberts, S., Moreau, L.: Interpretation of crowdsourced activities using provenance network analysis. In: First AAAI Conference on Human Computation and Crowdsourcing (2013)
6. Moreau, L.: The foundations for provenance on the web. Found. Trends Web Sci. 2(2–3), 99–241 (2010)
7. Moreau, L., Groth, P.: Prov-dm: The prov data model. Technical report (2013). http://www.w3.org/TR/prov-dm/
8. Moreau, L., Groth, P.: Provenance: an introduction to prov. Synth. Lect. Semant. Web: Theory Technol. 3(4), 1–129 (2013)
9. Ramchurn, S.D., Huynh, T.D., Venanzi, M., Shi, B.: Collabmap: crowdsourcing maps for emergency planning. In: Proceedings of the 5th Annual ACM Web Science Conference, pp. 326–335. ACM (2013)
10. Simmhan, Y.L., Plale, B., Gannon, D.: A survey of data provenance in e-science. ACM SIGMOD Rec. 34(3), 31–36 (2005)
11. Teacy, W.L., Patel, J., Jennings, N.R., Luck, M.: Travos: trust and reputation in the context of inaccurate information sources. Auton. Agent. Multi-Agent Syst. 12(2), 183–198 (2006)
12. Whitehill, J., Ruvolo, P., Wu, T., Bergsma, J., Movellan, J.R.: Whose vote should count more: optimal integration of labels from labelers of unknown expertise. In: NIPS, vol. 22, pp. 2035–2043 (2009)

Regenerating and Quantifying Quality of Benchmarking Data Using Static and Dynamic Provenance

Devarshi Ghoshal[1]([⊠]), Arun Chauhan[1,2], and Beth Plale[1]

[1] School of Informatics and Computing, Indiana University, Bloomington, IN, USA
{dghoshal,achauhan,plale}@cs.indiana.edu
[2] Google Inc., Mountain View, CA, USA

Abstract. Application benchmarks are critical to establishing the performance of a new system or library. But benchmarking a system can be tricky and reproducing a benchmark result even trickier. Provenance can help. Referencing benchmarks and their results on similar platforms for collective comparison and evaluation requires capturing provenance related to the process of benchmark execution, programs involved and results generated. In this paper we define a formal model of benchmark applications and required provenance, describe an implementation of the model that employs compile time (static) and runtime provenance capture, and quantify data quality in the context of benchmarks. Our results show that through a mix of compile time and runtime provenance capture, we can enable higher quality benchmark regeneration.

1 Introduction

Application benchmarks are an important way to establish the speed of a new system or library. But benchmarking a system can be tricky and reproducing a benchmark even trickier; a single compile time parameter can give vastly different results depending on whether it is set or not. Analyzing and recording benchmark results is a manual task that depends on the knowledge of the evaluator. The manual nature increases the possibility of missing information, incorrectly logged results and skipped parameters and configurations that affect the program behavior. All these factors affect the quality of the results generated by the benchmark process.

The metadata required to assess the quality of benchmark results to reproduce program behavior and quality of the evaluation process can be complex and expensive. Provenance is a type of metadata used to capture the lineage of data. Provenance from benchmark executions can be used to describe the lineage of benchmark results and the evaluation process involved. It helps in understanding the quality and enables regeneration and referencing of benchmarks. Essentially provenance traces for benchmark results account for the following – (a) ensuring benchmarks were executed correctly, (b) understanding the set of parameters and configurations used for generating the results and (c) keeping track of the benchmarks and their results for evaluation.

B. Ludäscher and B. Plale (Eds.): IPAW 2014, LNCS 8628, pp. 56–67, 2015.
DOI: 10.1007/978-3-319-16462-5_5

For standard application benchmarks, guaranteeing the correct execution of benchmarks and keeping track of the results require intelligent provenance capturing techniques. Log based provenance capture mechanisms [GP13] can be used for collecting provenance from benchmarking. But it is important to guarantee that neither the results are tampered with nor important factors affecting the results ignored. Existing provenance management frameworks [CCPR13, GT12] manage provenance at the application granularity. For benchmarking data, provenance needs to be managed for both the application (benchmark) and the target system (hardware or software or both) for the benchmark. Additionally, existing provenance capturing techniques often require modifications to the filesystem [GT12, MRHBS06], application specific program instrumentations [CCPR13, ABGK13] and/or trapping system calls [GT12] which are not viable due to varied nature of benchmarks and high-degree of system perturbations.

In this paper we identify essential characteristics of provenance in benchmarking and propose a formal model of provenance from application benchmarks. We describe a framework based on the provenance model that captures provenance from application benchmarks both statically at compile time and at runtime in order to validate, regenerate and reference results for future research. This paper makes the following contributions:

- a formal model of benchmark applications and required provenance
- an implementation of the model that employs compile time (static) and runtime (dynamic) provenance capture
- quantification of data quality in the context of benchmarks
- a PROV representation of the data model for provenance of benchmarking applications.

The remainder of the paper is organized as follows. In Sect. 2 we discuss related work. Section 3 proposes a formal model of provenance capture from application benchmarks. Section 4 describes our methodology and the implementation for identifying and capturing provenance using the provenance capture model. We evaluate our model and framework in Sect. 5. Finally, we present our conclusions in Sect. 6.

2   Related Work

Use-cases of provenance. Provenance capture, representation and use has been studied for e-science workflows [Mea05], file systems [MRHBS06], semantic web [CBHS05] and databases [CCT09]. The use of provenance in determining the quality of scientific data and data provenance has also been shown [SP11]. Provenance from scientific executable document systems [Yea12] are also implemeted. But using provenance for quantitative and qualitative analysis of benchmarking results has not been studied earlier.

Models of provenance capture. Several models have been proposed to identify and capture provenance [CAA07]. Bower et al. [BML12] proposes a dependency rule language for capturing fine-grained provenance from workflow traces but requires user-defined rules and runtime traces. We mostly rely on static analysis of source code for fine-grained provenance.

Provenance identification and capturing mechanisms. Provenance-aware solutions [MRHBS06], and language extensions [CAA07] for provenance identification have been proposed. Provenance capture by analyzing audit logs and semi-automated code instrumentation [GT12,CCPR13] have also been developed. We developed output-monitoring and compiler-driven provenance identification mechanisms for collecting provenance from application benchmarks.

Quality assessment. Quality of provenance data and using provenance for understanding the quality of data [CP12,HZ09] are important aspects of quality measurement in provenance. But very little or no work has been done to quantify data and provenance quality at the system level. In our work we quantify the quality of benchmark result, which is a provenance artifact, based on the level of intrusion through external factors.

3   Formalization of Benchmark Provenance

In this section we provide a formal representation of a benchmarking application and use that to define provenance capture.

3.1   Model of Benchmarking

A benchmark application has specific properties where a property is a pair $(n : v)$ where n is the name of the property and v is the corresponding value. A property can either be a static characteristic of the program (or set of programs that build the application) or a dynamic value only known at runtime. If we consider M execution instances of an application with N distinct properties, we can define two categories of properties as follows:

Variants: A set of properties that changes or may change for an execution instance, $i \in M$, of the application. Hence for a particular variant property, its value varies with i. The *variant* set is then defined as,

$$\forall i \in M, Variant(i) = \{(n : v_i) \mid \exists\, n \in N,\ s.t.\ v_i = f(i,n)\} \qquad (1)$$

Since benchmarks are executed multiple times, results are concluded by aggregating individual output from each instance of the benchmark execution. Hence, it is important to unify the variants from all benchmark execution instances in order to preserve the provenance of the final output. Unifying variants over all execution instances $i = (1, \dots, M)$ gives the total set of variants as,

$$\mathbb{V} = \bigcup_{i=1}^{M} Variant(i)$$

$$= \bigcup_{i=1}^{M} \{(n : v_i) \mid \exists\, n \in N,\ s.t.\ v_i = f(i,n)\} \qquad (2)$$

Practically, variants for application benchmarks consist of resource usage like CPU load at the time of benchmark execution and available memory, configuration parameters etc.

Invariants: A set of properties that remains constant over multiple execution instances of an application. The value of an invariant is only dependent on the name of the property. Invariants are, therefore, defined as,

$$\forall i \in M, \; Invariant(i) = \{(n : v)| \; \exists \, n \in N, \; s.t. \; v = g(n)\} \qquad (3)$$

Since invariants are independent of the execution instance i, unification results in distinct (n:v) pairs of an application benchmark as,

$$\mathbb{I} = \bigcup_{i=1}^{M} Invariant(i)$$

$$= \bigcup_{i=1}^{M} \{(n : v)| \; \exists \, n \in N, \; s.t. \; v = g(n)\} \qquad (4)$$

Examples include names of the programs, associated libraries, create-date of the benchmark binary, hostname(s) etc.

Since a benchmark is used for evaluating a system, where we define a system S as a software or hardware entity that has certain properties, we can define benchmark as a partial function,

$$\beta : (\mathcal{I}_\beta, \mathbb{V}, \mathbb{I}, S) \mapsto \mathcal{R}_\beta \qquad (5)$$

where $\mathcal{I}_\beta$ is the set of input-data, $\mathbb{V}$ is the set of variants, $\mathbb{I}$ is the set of invariants, S is the evaluated system and $\mathcal{R}_\beta$ is the set of output results.

To summarize, a benchmark with a set of properties $\mathbb{V}$ and $\mathbb{I}$, evaluates a system S generating the result-set $\mathcal{R}_\beta$ for an input-set $\mathcal{I}_\beta$. It is a partial function because invariants do not map to the result-set but are properties that are unique to the benchmark.

3.2   Model of Provenance Capture

We base our model for provenance on the model of benchmarking defined above. We make no assumptions about the equivalence of inputs and outputs of a benchmark and that collected by our model of provenance capture. So, we denote the output result-set collected by our model of provenance as $\mathcal{R}_\mathcal{P}$. Similarly, we also consider the input data-set collected by the model of provenance as $\mathcal{I}_\mathcal{P}$.

Static Provenance. We define static provenance capture as a function that maps a benchmark to its invariants.

$$\delta : \beta \mapsto \mathbb{I} \qquad (6)$$

Any property that does not vary with different execution instances of a benchmark program but identifies it uniquely is considered during static provenance capture. Hence, artifacts for static provenance capture can be determined statically without executing the benchmark.

Runtime Provenance. Runtime provenance capture, on the other hand, captures provenance information for every execution instance of a benchmark. It depends on the runtime characteristics and parameters of benchmark execution. We define runtime provenance capture as a function that maps a set of results to a set of inputs, corresponding benchmark and variants.

$$\gamma : \mathcal{R}_{\mathcal{P}} \mapsto (\beta, \mathcal{I}_{\mathcal{P}}, \mathbb{V}) \qquad (7)$$

All data-items that affect the benchmark results but can only be determined during benchmark execution are captured during runtime provenance capture.

3.3   Quantification of Data Quality

Since no assumptions are made about the equivalence of inputs and outputs of a benchmark and the captured provenance, there may be discrepancies between the published inputs and outputs of a benchmark and that collected through provenance capture. In the ideal situation, $\mathcal{R}_{\mathcal{P}} \equiv \mathcal{R}_{\beta}$ and $\mathcal{I}_{\mathcal{P}} \equiv \mathcal{I}_{\beta}$.

Trust. We define $\| \mathcal{R}_{\mathcal{P}} - \mathcal{R}_{\beta} \|$ to denote the quantitative difference between the results, i.e., the number of results that differ in the two sets. Similarly, $\| \mathcal{I}_{\mathcal{P}} - \mathcal{I}_{\beta} \|$ denotes the quantitative difference between the inputs. For a set of invariants, $\mathbb{I}$ and variants, $\mathbb{V}$ of a benchmark, β the trust, $\mathbb{T}$ of the result data-set is then measured by the following equation:

$$\mathbb{T} = \left(1 - \frac{\| \mathcal{R}_{\mathcal{P}} - \mathcal{R}_{\beta} \|}{max(| \mathcal{R}_{\mathcal{P}} |, | \mathcal{R}_{\beta} |)} \right) \left(1 - \frac{\| \mathcal{I}_{\mathcal{P}} - \mathcal{I}_{\beta} \|}{max(| \mathcal{I}_{\mathcal{P}} |, | \mathcal{I}_{\beta} |)} \right) \qquad (8)$$

where,
$\| X - Y \|$ returns the count of mutually exclusive elements of X and Y,
$| X |$ is the cardinality of a set X.

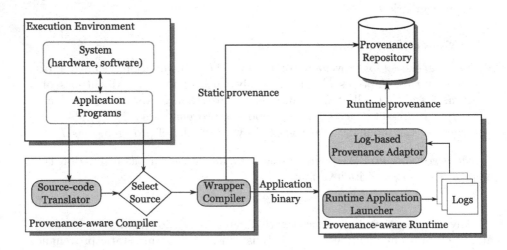

Fig. 1. Framework for capturing provenance for benchmarking data.

In other words, if the input and result generated by a benchmark differs from what its provenance says, then the data is not trustworthy. For simplicity, we consider each input and result to be of equal importance. We also assume that the values of invariants and variants are always within the range of the values captured through provenance. A direct result that follows through the above quantification is the measure of *reproducibility* which is a property of the benchmark result and is a boolean value that determines if a benchmark result is reproducible or not. It is defined in terms of 'trust'.

Definition: Given a set of invariants $\mathbb{I}$ and variants $\mathbb{V}$, a result-set $\mathcal{R}_\beta$ is reproducible for a benchmark β iff $\mathbb{T} = 1$.

4   Provenance-Aware Benchmarking Framework

The formal model is the foundation upon which is built the framework for capturing provenance from application benchmarks as shown in Fig. 1. The framework has two pieces: a static capture component that is built into compile time activity. Run-time is also made provenance-aware through runtime capture.

4.1   Static Provenance Capture

We propose a provenance-aware compiler for static capture of provenance. The compiler is implemented as a wrapper over standard gcc or icc compilers. To enable provenance-aware compilation, a user replaces all calls to the corresponding compiler by call to the wrapper compiler provcc which captures 'invariants' as provenance elements during program compilation. Essentially,

$$\mathsf{provcc} : \beta \mapsto \mathbb{I}$$

where, β is a benchmark and $\mathbb{I}$ is a set of invariants.

4.2   Runtime Provenance Capture

The runtime provenance capture is divided into two modules – (a) provenance-aware runtime and (b) provenance adaptor.

Provenance-Aware Runtime. The second piece of the solution, a provenance-aware runtime, executes and captures provenance information including the variants, inputs and results for a benchmark. All benchmarks are executed via the runtime application launcher provrun which can capture the results from both stdout and files. From our provenance model, provrun is the mapping function δ.

$$\mathsf{provrun} : \beta \mapsto (\mathcal{I}_\mathcal{P}, \mathbb{V}, \mathcal{R}_\mathcal{P})$$

where, β is a benchmark, $\mathcal{I}_\mathcal{P}$ is the set of inputs captured by provrun, $\mathbb{V}$ is a set of variants, $\mathcal{R}_\mathcal{P}$ is the set of output results captured by provrun.

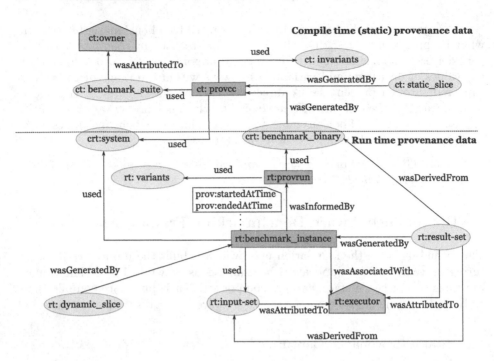

Fig. 2. PROV model for capturing provenance from application benchmarks.

Provenance Adaptor. The second phase of the runtime provenance capture collects, combines and translates provenance information captured in log files into a single provenance graph. It shows the lineage of benchmark results for all execution instances of a benchmark on a system. The complete provenance graph is generated by combining the provenance information collected statically during compilation and dynamically by the runtime system.

4.3 Fine-Grained Provenance Capture

The compiler wrapper is augmented with an additional source-to-source translator module that allows for source-code instrumentation for fine-grained provenance capture. This module allows users to automatically identify and mark regions in the code to generate provenance information. We developed the module using the ROSE compiler framework. It builds a system dependency graph for the benchmark programs and marks regions of the code based on the granularity of provenance information. This module is responsible for generating two slices of the benchmark program: a static slice created during compilation and a dynamic slice generated during benchmark execution. Static slice is used for deriving the mapping between inputs and outputs and preserving the interprocedural dependencies. Whereas the dynamic slice is used to capture the actual parameters passed across the functions for generating the output.

4.4 PROV Model for Benchmark Provenance

Figure 2 shows the PROV data model for application benchmarks. Based on the formal model of provenance capture, the PROV model shows compile-time and run-time provenance capture from application benchmarks. The owner is a PROV agent who is responsible for creating a benchmarking suite. The executor, on the other hand, is a PROV agent who executes a benchmark or evaluates a system using a benchmark. Each benchmark execution has an associated time attribute that captures the start and end time of execution. Invariants and variants are captured as part of the provenance by the provenance-aware compiler and the runtime respectively. Fine-grained provenance is captured by generating the static and dynamic slices of a benchmark program. Finally, the output result is derivation from the benchmark binary and the input data-set which are used to evaluate a system.

5 Evaluation

We experimentally evaluate our methodology using six benchmarks from the NU-MineBench [NOZ+06] benchmarking suite and analyze both overheads and significance of provenance capture from benchmarks. NU-MineBench contains a mix of several representative data mining applications from different application domains. It is used for computer architecture research, systems research, performance evaluation, and high-performance computing. The applications used are: **HOP** – a density-based data clustering. **Apriori** – association rule mining. **ScalParC** – decision-tree based data classification. **K-means** – (and Fuzzy K-means) for data clustering. **ECLAT** – association rule mining. **Semphy** – structure learning algorithm that is based on phylogenetic trees.

Tests were run on a quad-socket, 8-core (32 total cores) AMD Opteron system with 512 GB of memory running 64-bit Red Hat Enterprise Linux. For evaluating the runtime overhead, benchmarks are executed 10 times. As a micro-benchmark, we measure runtime overhead and for higher quality benchmark regeneration, we evaluate the model and the framework along three dimensions – (a) computing if the result is reproducible (quality quantification), b) what is required to regenerate the result (reproducibility data) and (c) how can the result be regenerated (reproducibility steps).

Runtime Overhead. Executing the benchmarks through the provenance-aware framework shows no or very little overheads as shown in Fig. 3a. This is because the benchmark execution is completely uninterrupted and provenance information is logged only in two stages – (a) prior to the execution and (b) when the execution completes. However, we also capture fine-grained provenance by running an instrumented version of the benchmark. In order to enrich provenance information, benchmark programs are marked at specific regions during compilation by the provenance-aware compiler. For this evaluation we only mark function calls which tracks inter-procedural data flow in order to derive the exact mapping between inputs and outputs. This instrumentation results in relatively high overheads as shown in Fig. 3b.

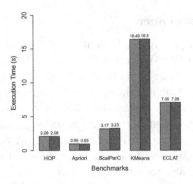
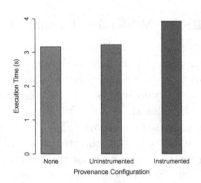

(a) Benchmark execution through provenance-aware runtime

(b) Benchmark execution with different granularity of provenance capture for ScalParC

Fig. 3. Performance overhead in benchmark execution through provenance-aware framework. There are very little or no overheads for provenance capture without instrumenting the benchmark. However, fine-grained provenance capture through source-code instrumentation starts incurring higher overheads.

Table 1. Quality assessment derived from provenance

	HOP	Apriori	ScalParC	K-Means	ECLAT
Num results	1	3	5	45	12
$\| \mathcal{R}_\mathcal{P} - \mathcal{R}_\beta \|$	0	1	2	0	1
Trust value	1.00	0.67	0.60	1.00	0.92

Table 2. Elements of compile time (static) provenance as captured by provcc

Benchmark	Srcs	Objs	Compilation-flags	Opt-flags	Linker-library
HOP	6	6	-fopenmp -Wno-write-strings	-O	libm
Apriori	5	5	-fopenmp -DBALT	-O2	libm
ScalParC	4	4	-fopenmp	-O2	libm
K-Means	4	4	-fopenmp	-O2	libm
ECLAT	14	11	-Wno-non-template-friend	-O3	libm, libc
SEMPHY	23	15	-Wall -Wno-sign-compare -DLOG	-O3	../../lib
			-ftemplate-depth-32		libSEMPHY.a
					libEvolTree.a

Quality Quantification. We calculate trust values for different benchmarks by introducing discrepancies in the result data-set by introducing errors as shown in Table 1. These errors are either system or human errors of reporting results, missing information, inconsistent values of variants etc. For example, for the

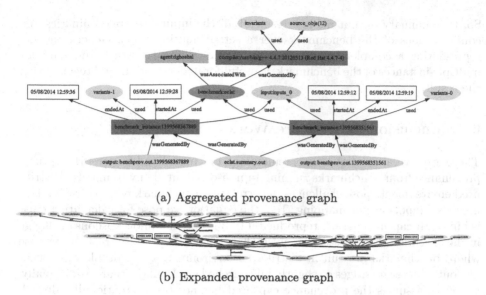

(a) Aggregated provenance graph

(b) Expanded provenance graph

Fig. 4. Provenance graphs for ECLAT - (a) shows the aggregated view of the original provenance graph as shown in (b) for 2 runs of the ECLAT benchmark.

ECLAT benchmark run, if we change the value of the `support` parameter from 0.0075 that is captured through provenance to 0.0080, we are unable to reproduce the output result as predicted through our reproducibility metric. This is because the trust value, $\mathbb{T}$ is less than 1. For benchmark results, **trust value** $= 1$ iff $\parallel \mathcal{R}_\mathcal{P} - \mathcal{R}_\beta \parallel = 0$. In other words, a result can only be trusted and hence reproduced, when the benchmark and its provenance points to the same result-set.

Regeneration Using Provenance. Provenance for regenerating benchmarking data can be categorized into two phases based on our capture model – (a) information useful for regenerating the application benchmark and (b) information for regenerating the benchmark results. For regenerating the benchmark application, we capture its provenance that includes the compilation flags, platforms, source programs (invariants) etc. Table 2 shows a list of provenance elements that are captured using the provenance-aware compiler. For regenerating the benchmark results, associated runtime characteristics (variants) and the input data along with the provenance of the application benchmark are captured. In case of fine-grained provenance, the detailed mapping between inputs and outputs and interprocedural dataflow are also captured.

Since benchmark results are most often an aggregation of individual runs of a benchmark, the correlation between individual results and configurations are important to record as part of the provenance. A connected provenance graph shows the importance of recording, correlating and linking individual provenance traces of a benchmark. As shown in Fig. 4 the aggregated results for ECLAT are written to a single output file through different runs of the benchmark.

So, the summary output file is a result of all the inputs, compiled binaries and configurations of the benchmark over a set of multiple runs. Generating and representing a complete provenance graph describing the steps and data for multiple instances of the benchmark, is useful for understanding and regenerating the result.

6 Conclusion and Future Work

There are several open questions remaining. The model and framework captures provenance from benchmarks running in non-distributed environments. Distributed environments pose challenges in correlating benchmark results, tracing failures, and input-output mapping. Too, the equation we pose for calculating trust is binary. It captures perfect reproducibility but does not allow epsilons of change in the execution trace or static analysis that do not compromise trust. In the case where benchmarks are run in distributed environments, acceptable differences like out of order messages or slightly mismatched clocks may occur. Additionally, the work assumes the provenance captured has not been intentionally altered. Our approach assumes availability of benchmark source-code. In the absence of source-code or provenance-aware compilers, special techniques should be developed for identifying and correlating provenance from benchmarking applications transparently without user intervention. The amount and granularity of fine-grained provenance sufficient for validating benchmark execution also needs further research. Finally, post-processing can be done by mining the result-set and associated provenance in order to automatically derive conclusions about the evaluation process and system's performance.

Acknowledgements. This work is funded in part by the National Science Foundation OCI 1148359.

References

[ABGK13] Alper, P., Belhajjame, K., Goble, C.A., Karagoz, P.: Enhancing and abstracting scientific workflow provenance for data publishing. In: The Joint EDBT/ICDT 2013 Workshops, New York, NY, USA, pp. 313–318 (2013)

[BML12] Bowers, S., McPhillips, T., Ludäscher, B.: Declarative rules for Inferring fine-grained data provenance from scientific workflow execution traces. In: Groth, P., Frew, J. (eds.) IPAW 2012. LNCS, vol. 7525, pp. 82–96. Springer, Heidelberg (2012)

[CAA07] Cheney, J., Ahmed, A., Acar, U.A.: Provenance as dependency analysis. In: Arenas, M. (ed.) DBPL 2007. LNCS, vol. 4797, pp. 138–152. Springer, Heidelberg (2007)

[CBHS05] Carroll, J.J., Bizer, C., Hayes, P., Stickler, P.: Named graphs, provenance and trust. In: The 14th International Conference on World Wide Web, New York, NY, USA, pp. 613–622 (2005)

[CCPR13] Cheah, Y.-W., Canon, R., Plale, B., Ramakrishnan, L.: Milieu: lightweight and configurable big data provenance for science. In: 2013 IEEE International Congress on Big Data (BigData Congress), pp. 46–53, June 2013

[CCT09] Cheney, J., Chiticariu, L., Tan, W.-C.: Provenance in databases: why, how, and where. Found. Trends Databases 1, 379–474 (2009)

[CP12] Cheah, Y.W., Plale, B.: Provenance analysis: towards quality provenance. In: 8th IEEE International Conference on eScience, October 2012

[GP13] Ghoshal, D., Plale, B.: Provenance from log files: a bigdata problem. In: Proceedings of the Joint EDBT/ICDT 2013 Workshops, New York, NY, USA, pp. 290–297 (2013)

[GT12] Gehani, A., Tariq, D.: SPADE: support for provenance auditing in distributed environments. In: Narasimhan, P., Triantafillou, P. (eds.) Middleware 2012. LNCS, vol. 7662, pp. 101–120. Springer, Heidelberg (2012)

[HZ09] Hartig, O., Zhao, J.: Using web data provenance for quality assessment. In: The Workshop on Semantic Web and Provenance Management at ISWC (2009)

[Mea05] Wong, S.C., Miles, S., Fang, W., Groth, P.T., Moreau, L.: Provenance-based validation of e-science experiments. In: Gil, Y., Motta, E., Benjamins, V.R., Musen, M.A. (eds.) ISWC 2005. LNCS, vol. 3729, pp. 801–815. Springer, Heidelberg (2005)

[MRHBS06] Muniswamy-Reddy, K.-K., Holland, D.A., Braun, U., Seltzer, M.: Provenance-aware storage systems. In: The Annual Conference on USENIX 2006 Annual Technical Conference, Berkeley, CA, USA (2006)

[NOZ+06] Narayanan, R., Ozisikyilmaz, B., Zambreno, J., Memik, G., Choudhary, A.: Minebench: a benchmark suite for data mining workloads. In: 2006 IEEE International Symposium on Workload Characterization, pp. 182–188, October 2006

[SP11] Simmhan, Y., Plale, B.: Using provenance for personalized quality ranking of scientific datasets. Int. J. Comput. Appl. (IJCA) 18(3), 180–195 (2011)

[Yea12] Yang, H., Michaelides, D.T., Charlton, C., Browne, W.J., Moreau, L.: DEEP: a provenance-aware executable document system. In: Groth, P., Frew, J. (eds.) IPAW 2012. LNCS, vol. 7525, pp. 24–38. Springer, Heidelberg (2012)

Provenance Management Architectures and Techniques

noWorkflow: Capturing and Analyzing Provenance of Scripts

Leonardo Murta[1], Vanessa Braganholo[1]([✉]),
Fernando Chirigati[2], David Koop[2], and Juliana Freire[2]

[1] Universidade Federal Fluminense, Niterói, Brazil
{leomurta,vanessa}@ic.uff.br
[2] New York University, New York, USA
{fchirigati,dakoop,juliana.freire}@nyu.edu

Abstract. We propose noWorkflow, a tool that transparently captures provenance of scripts and enables reproducibility. Unlike existing approaches, noWorkflow is non-intrusive and does not require users to change the way they work – users need not wrap their experiments in scientific workflow systems, install version control systems, or instrument their scripts. The tool leverages Software Engineering techniques, such as abstract syntax tree analysis, reflection, and profiling, to collect different types of provenance, including detailed information about the underlying libraries. We describe how noWorkflow captures multiple kinds of provenance and the different classes of analyses it supports: graph-based visualization; differencing over provenance trails; and inference queries.

1 Introduction

While scripts are widely used for data analysis and exploration in the scientific community, there has been little effort to provide *systematic* and *transparent* provenance management support for them. Scientists often fall back on Workflow Management Systems (WfMSs), which provide infrastructure to automatically capture the input, intermediate, and output data involved in computations, allowing experiments to be managed, assessed, and reproduced [12,16,18]. Although WfMSs play an important role in bridging the gap between experimentation and provenance management, they have limitations that have hampered a broader adoption, notably: moving to a new environment can be difficult and requires a steep learning curve, and wrapping external scripts and libraries for use in a WfMS is time-consuming. In addition, data analysis tasks that use multiple tools require each to be integrated with the WfMS. When this is not possible (or desirable), scientists often run scripts to orchestrate analyses and connect results obtained from multiple tools.

Collecting provenance of scripts when not using a WfMS is challenging. First, unlike most pipelines supported by dataflow-based systems, *scripts can encode a control flow and include cycles*, which makes it more difficult to identify which functions contributed to the generation of a given data product. Second, *determining the correct level of granularity to capture is hard*: very fine-grained provenance may overwhelm scientists with a large volume of data to analyze, while a

© Springer International Publishing Switzerland 2015
B. Ludäscher and B. Plale (Eds.): IPAW 2014, LNCS 8628, pp. 71–83, 2015.
DOI: 10.1007/978-3-319-16462-5_6

coarser granularity may omit important information. In contrast, workflows in a WfMS have well-defined boundaries for such capture, which are determined by how the underlying computational modules are wrapped. Finally, since *scripts run outside of a controlled environment* such as a WfMS, one cannot make many assumptions (e.g., the presence of a version control system) beyond the involvement of source code and an interpreter/compiler, which makes it difficult to track library dependencies and changes in files.

Some of the existing approaches that do not require a WfMS rely on scientists to modify the experiment scripts to include annotations or calls to provenance capture functions [1,3,7]. Such approaches are intrusive, time-consuming, and error-prone. Others require scientists to use a version control system to track changes to the source code, or are not entirely automatic, requiring input from scientists [3,10]. There are also approaches that capture provenance at the operating system level [6,8,17], which monitor system calls and track processes and data dependencies between these processes. These systems, however, do not have visibility into what happens inside the scripts underlying the processes.

In this paper, we propose a new approach to capture provenance of scripts that addresses the aforementioned challenges. We review the existing types of provenance representation and argue that, in the absence of a controlled environment, a new kind of provenance – *deployment provenance* – is necessary to capture detailed data about the underlying libraries. We then present no-Workflow (**not** only **Workflow**), a tool that implements the proposed approach, and describe how it *transparently* captures provenance of scripts, including control flow information and library dependencies. noWorkflow is *non-intrusive* and relies on techniques from Software Engineering, including abstract syntax tree analysis, reflection, and profiling, to collect different types of provenance without requiring a version control system or an instrumented environment. The tool supports three different types of analyses, including visualization and query mechanisms, to help scientists explore the captured provenance and debug the execution, as well as to enable reproducibility. Although noWorkflow was developed for Python, a language with significant adoption by the scientific community, the ideas presented here are language-independent and can be applied to other scripting languages.

2   Provenance of Scripts

WfMSs provide a controlled environment in which workflows are executed—the workflow engine orchestrates the invocation of the computational modules of a workflow. Since provenance is captured for these invocations, the provenance granularity is determined by how computations are modeled inside the workflow system, i.e., how libraries are wrapped. Scripts, in contrast, lack this well-defined structure and the isolation provided by the workflow engine. Thus, to capture the provenance of scripts, we have to address two important challenges: how to represent information about the environment and how to determine the level of provenance granularity.

2.1   Provenance Representation

There are two types of provenance for scientific workflows: prospective and retrospective [5]. Prospective provenance describes the structure of the experiment and corresponds to the workflow definition, the graph of the activities, and their associated parameters. Retrospective provenance captures the steps taken during the workflow execution, and while it has similar (graph) structure, it is constructed using information collected at runtime, including activities invoked and parameter values used, intermediate data produced, the execution start and end times, etc. The wrapping required by a WfMS to orchestrate the execution of modules from a tool or library naturally creates a level of abstraction for the execution: the module is a black box and its details are hidden. Because the wrapped libraries are integrated with the WfMS, it is possible for the system to track and control them, e.g., to detect that a wrapped library has changed and to upgrade the workflows accordingly [13].

For scripts, this abstraction is absent. Therefore, it is important to capture detailed information about the computational environment (e.g., library dependencies and environment variables) where the script runs. Consider, for example, the Python script in Fig. 1, which runs a simulation to predict weather using historical data about temperature and precipitation. For simplicity of exposition, the real (and expensive) simulation performed by *simulate* is defined in a separate module (*simulator*) not shown in the example. This script depends on 703 distinct modules, although only four are explicitly declared (lines 1–4). Suppose we run the experiment script once and obtain a result. If later, software is installed (or upgraded) that silently updates one of the modules on which the experiment script depends, the next execution may produce a different result, even though its source code remains unchanged. If these dependencies are not systematically captured, it may be difficult to understand why results are different between executions that are apparently identical.

The provenance needed here is neither prospective nor retrospective, and it needs to be captured right before execution. Borrowing terms from software engineering, where software goes through three phases, i.e., *definition, deployment,* and *execution* [9], we define three types of provenance needed for scripts:

- *Definition Provenance* captures the structure of the script, including function definitions, their arguments, and function calls; it corresponds to prospective provenance.
- *Deployment Provenance* captures the execution environment, including information about the operating system, environment variables, and libraries on which the script depends. As discussed before, this may change from one execution to another, even if the source code remains the same. In addition, it extends beyond dependencies a programmer explicitly defines, and the concrete library versions that are loaded depend on the deployment environment.
- *Execution Provenance* captures the execution log for the script (e.g., function activations, argument values, and return values); it corresponds to retrospective provenance.

```
01. import csv
02. import sys
03. import matplotlib.pyplot as plt
04. from simulator import simulate
05.
06. def run_simulation(data_a, data_b):
07.     a = csv_read(data_a)
08.     b = csv_read(data_b)
09.     data = simulate(a, b)
10.     return data
11.
12. def csv_read(f):
13.     reader = csv.reader(open(f, 'rU'), delimiter=':')
14.     data = []
15.     for row in reader:
16.         data.append(row)
17.     return data
18.
19. def extract_column(data, column):
20.     col_data = []
21.     for row in data:
22.         col_data.append(float(row[column]))
23.     return col_data
24.
25. def plot(data):
26.     # getting temperature
27.     t = extract_column(data, 0)
28.     # getting precipitation
29.     p = extract_column(data, 1)
30.     plt.scatter(t, p, marker='o')
31.     plt.xlabel('Temperature')
32.     plt.ylabel('Precipitation')
33.     plt.savefig('output.png')
34.
35. # main program
36. data_a = sys.argv[1]
37. data_b = sys.argv[2]
38. data = run_simulation(data_a, data_b)
39. plot(data)
```

Fig. 1. Example of a Python script (*simulation.py*) that predicts temperature and precipitation in the near future.

2.2   Provenance Granularity

As discussed above, in WfMSs, provenance is captured at the level of an activity, and what happens inside an activity is not taken into account by the provenance infrastructure. In contrast, such boundaries are not well-defined in the context of scripts. Thus, an important question is how to determine the level of granularity at which to capture provenance for scripts. One alternative would be to use approaches that capture provenance at the operating system level [6,17]. Since these systems intercept system calls (e.g., file reads and writes, execution of binaries), they produce a high volume of very fine-grained information that represent data dependencies between processes. It can be difficult to explore this information and connect it to the underlying experiment specification. Consequently, identifying which experiment activity influenced the generation of a given data product can be challenging. On the other hand, if we consider the entire script as a black-box, and capture provenance at a coarse granularity, it would be impossible to know which functions contributed to the generation of a given data product.

We posit that functions in a script are a suitable choice for provenance capture—this is most likely to be meaningful to users since it is closer to the experiment specification. We note, however, that even this level may be overwhelming. For instance, profiling the (very small and simple) script of Fig. 1, we observed 156,086 function activations. This includes functions called by functions that are used in the main experiment script, such as `plt.scatter` (line 30). Clearly, analyzing this volume of information is hard and time-consuming; an alternative is to capture only the activations related to functions that are defined by the programmer (i.e., that have user-defined functions as source or target). In the example, this entails all activations related to the main program along with functions `run_simulation`, `csv_read`, `extract_column`, and `plot`. This approach significantly reduces the amount of captured information, and makes it easier for users to keep track of what is happening throughout the execution.

3   noWorkflow

As a proof of concept, we built noWorkflow, a command line tool written in Python that transparently captures provenance of Python scripts. Running noWorkflow is as simple as running a Python script: `now run <script>`. In noWorkflow, the execution of a given experiment script is called a *trial*. Each trial is assigned a sequential identification number that is automatically generated. Provenance for each trial is captured and stored for future analysis. The system distinguishes a *function call* from a *function activation*: the former is related to definition provenance and can be captured by statically analyzing the source code while the latter is related to execution provenance. For example, in Fig. 1, `data.append` is a single function call (line 16), but it may have many activations at runtime, with different arguments and return values, because it is inside a `for` loop. In what follows, we describe how noWorkflow, in the absence of a controlled execution environment, captures and stores the different types of provenance (see Fig. 2). We also discuss useful analyses that can be performed over script provenance.

3.1   Provenance Capture

Definition Provenance. To capture definition provenance, noWorkflow uses the *abstract syntax tree* (AST) of the script to identify all user function definitions, function calls, arguments, and global variables referenced in the script. We chose user-defined functions as the granularity for provenance capture (Sect. 2.2), and the AST is used to capture the source code of each function definition. In the example (Fig. 1), the source code of `run_simulation` (lines 6–10) is entirely stored, which allows the tool to monitor the evolution of each function definition independently. In addition, noWorkflow stores the source code of the

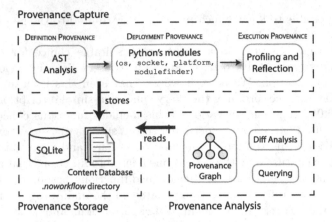

Fig. 2. Architecture of noWorkflow.

entire script. All this information is associated with an experiment trial, thus making it possible to know which function definitions belong to a specific trial.

Each function is then analyzed to capture the objects referenced inside it, including arguments, function calls, and global variables. These objects are associated with the corresponding function definition. Consider for example the function `run_simulation` in Fig. 1: noWorkflow captures two arguments (`data_a` and `data_b`, on line 6), and two function calls (`csv_read` on lines 7 and 8, and `simulate` on line 9). Despite the fact that `csv_read` is called twice in `run_simulation`, we register this information only once as a dependency from `run_simulation` to `csv_read`. At runtime, noWorkflow is able to distinguish between different function activations of the same function call as well as different activations of different calls from the same function definition.

Deployment Provenance. noWorkflow captures two different types of deployment provenance: environment and module (i.e., library) dependencies. This provenance is captured right before the execution of the experiment script begins, and is associated with an experiment trial. noWorkflow uses libraries provided by Python to capture environment information, including `os` to capture operating system information, `socket` to capture the host name, and `platform` to capture information about the machine architecture and Python environment. noWorkflow also uses Python's `modulefinder` library to find the transitive closure of all module dependencies. For each module that this library finds, our tool stores the library name, version, file name (including its full path), and source code (if available).

It is possible that environment and module dependencies change during the script execution. In this case, to precisely capture this information, deployment provenance would need to be gathered dynamically, right before each function activation. However, since this situation is very rare (and advised against), and to avoid introducing a large overhead, we have opted for capturing deployment provenance right before executing the script.

Execution Provenance. Execution provenance includes function activations, argument values, return values, global values, start and finish times for each function activation, as well as their context, and the content of all files manipulated by the experiment script during execution. noWorkflow captures this information through *profiling* and *reflection*.

noWorkflow implements specific methods of the Python profiling API and registers itself as a listener. During an execution, the profiler notifies the tool of all function activations in the source code. Notice that this goes very deep into the execution flow—recall that our simple simulation script has 156,086 function activations. As discussed before, to avoid overloading users with large volumes of information, thus overcoming the granularity challenge, noWorkflow only registers function activations related to user-defined functions. For the script in Fig. 1, noWorkflow registers that `csv_read` calls `data.append` (line 16), but it does not register functions that `data.append` calls. At this moment, we also capture the start time of the function activation, together with the values of every argument, return, and globals that may be involved in the function activation.

While monitoring only user-defined functions reduces the volume of information to be captured, it may miss an important aspect of the experiment: file access. Explicit *open* system calls in the script will be captured, but if *open* is called from a function not defined by the scientist (e.g., `plt.savefig` on line 33 of Fig. 1), this information would be missed by noWorkflow. noWorkflow addresses this issue by using reflection to alter the behavior of a system call. We implement a new function that overwrites the system's *open* function and alters its behavior so that every time *open* is called, we capture the content of the file, store it, call the original *open* system call, and then capture and store the file's content *again*. Thus, noWorkflow preserves the content before and after a file is accessed, allowing us to detect, for instance, if a file has been modified.

Notice that reflection is not enough to identify which function called *open*. To make this association, noWorkflow uses an *activation stack*: every time there is an activation of a user-defined function, it is pushed onto the stack, and when the activation finishes, it is popped from the stack. When *open* is called, the function on top of the stack is tagged as being responsible for opening the file. Figure 3 shows an example: when `plt.savefig` is called from the user-defined function `plot` (line 33), its activation is pushed to the stack; when *open* is called to save *output.png*, `plt.savefig` will be on top of the stack, thus allowing noWorkflow to link it to the modified file. Right before popping an activation from the stack, its end time and return value are registered. If a function is activated several times, noWorkflow registers all activations and links them with the activation on top of the stack that triggered them. This allows noWorkflow to keep track of function activation dependencies, together with the source code line that corresponds to this call and all information previously discussed in this section.

3.2   Provenance Storage

Because transparency is one of our goals, noWorkflow includes an embedded
storage mechanism that does not require any installation or configuration. All
provenance is automatically stored to disk in a directory named *.noworkflow* in
the script directory. This directory holds both a relational database for structured data and a database for file contents. These databases are linked together
by means of SHA1 hash codes.

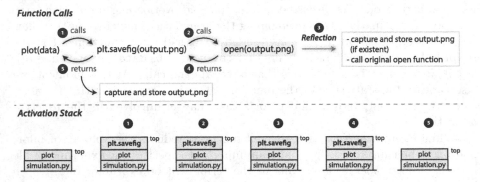

Fig. 3. Example of how reflection and activation stack work on noWorkflow. When
open is called (2), the file is captured before executing the original system call function
(3), and since `plt.savefig` is on top of the stack, noWorkflow knows that this function is the one responsible for opening the file.

noWorkflow uses SQLite to store structured data which includes definition
provenance (e.g., function definitions and objects they reference, including function calls), deployment provenance (e.g., environment variables and module
dependencies), and execution provenance (e.g., runtime information about trials,
file accesses, function activations, and object values). Hash codes are also stored
whenever possible, e.g., SHA1 hashes of the source code of a function and of files
before and after access. In contrast, file contents are stored directly to disk in
what we call the *content database*. To avoid OS limitations regarding the number
of files that can be stored in a directory, we use the same strategy Git uses to
store files: file content is stored in a directory that corresponds to the first two
characters of its SHA1 hash in a file named by the remaining characters of the
SHA1 hash. noWorkflow maintains all files involved with the experiment, and
all SHA1 hashes stored in the relational database have a counterpart file stored
in the content database. Data in the SQLite database is always associated with
a given execution of the experiment script (i.e., a trial). This allows noWorkflow
to save disk space: whenever the hash code of a given file is the same, the hash
is stored in the database, but not the file itself again. In addition, the provenance storage in noWorkflow eases *reproducibility*: scientists can simply share
the *.noworkflow* directory with their collaborators to exchange provenance data.

3.3   Provenance Analysis

While captured provenance aids reproducibility, another important goal is facilitating the *analysis* of provenance to locate, understand, and compare techniques. The current version of noWorkflow supports three different analysis techniques: *graph-based, diff-based,* and *query-based.*

Graph-Based Analysis. Graph-based analysis is facilitated by *visualizing* the provenance of a trial in a graph which provides an overview of the script execution and supports comprehension of both functional and non-functional attributes. However, the provenance of even simple scripts may consist of a large number of function activations, particularly in the presence of loop structures, which may lead to visualization overload problems. For this reason, noWorkflow first *summarizes* the provenance before producing its activation graph. Our overall approach is based on a three-step strategy: summarization, construction, and drawing.

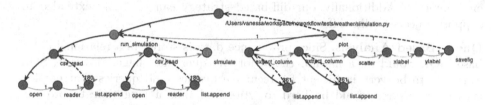

Fig. 4. Graph-based visualization generated from the example in Fig. 1.

The summarization step aggregates different activations of a function call if they belong to the same context (i.e., same loop). The idea is to aggregate the provenance by activation stack, function call line number, and function name. Therefore, each function call may have multiple activations together with their activation arguments, return values, and timestamps. The second step consists of building a graph from the vertices generated by the summarization step and edges extracted from the function activation sequence. There are three types of edges: *call,* when a function calls another function; *sequence,* when two functions are called in sequence within the same activation stack; and *return,* when a function finishes its execution and the control flow returns to the function in the top of the stack. Finally, the third step is rendering the graph. Each vertex is labeled with the function name and is colored according to the traffic light scale (shades from green to yellow to red) [4]: function calls with faster activations are colored in shades of green, while the ones with slower activations are colored in shades of red. Each edge displays the number of times the control flow passed through it, and each edge type has a different shape to ease the visual distinction: *call* edges are thicker and darker, *sequence* edges are thinner and lighter, and *return* edges are dashed, thicker, and darker. There is also a tooltip window that provides detailed information about each node (activation).

Figure 4 shows the graph-based visualization generated from the example of Fig. 1. From the graph, we can observe that the script called both `run_simulation` and `plot` in sequence. It is also possible to see that `run_simulation` is much slower than `plot`, and that there are four loop structures in the script, summarized by noWorkflow: two loops occurring inside `csv_read` and two loops occurring inside `extract_column`.

Diff-Based Analysis. In some provenance analysis scenarios, it is crucial to contrast two trials to understand why results differ. There are many aspects that influence the generation of an output, including script modifications, environment variable changes, and module updates. noWorkflow provides a mechanism to contrast two trials and identify changes that may influence the results. This mechanism allows comparison of the basic attributes of trials (e.g., date, script, and arguments), environment variables, and module dependencies, showing which attributes have changed, and which variables and modules have been added, removed, or replaced. This is especially useful for reproducibility, since it becomes easy to compare two executions of the same experiment in different environments. Additionally, our diff-based strategy can be easily extended to support object-specific diffs.

Query-Based Analysis. Since provenance data is stored in a relational database, SQL would be a natural choice for the query language. However, SQL is known to be very inefficient for recursive queries, and queries that employ transitive closures would be hard to write and take a long time to process. To overcome this limitation, we provide an inference-based query mechanism based on Prolog. noWorkflow is able to export Prolog facts and rules of a given trial which can then be used to query the collected provenance data. The facts follow the same structure of the relational tables that we use to store provenance data. To make queries easier, noWorkflow also provides a set of Prolog inference rules. As an example, the rule `access_influence` can be used to find out which files may have influenced the generation of a given file. Running the query `access_influence(File, 'output.png')` returns a list of files that may influenced the generation of *output.png*, which, in the case of our example, are *data1.dat* and *data2.dat*. Note that, since we export the Prolog facts, any Prolog system can be used. New rules can also be added by users.

4   Related Work

Different mechanisms for provenance capture have been proposed, and some can be applied to scripts. Tools that capture provenance at the operating system level [6,8,17] monitor system calls and track processes and data dependencies between these processes. Because the dependencies are recorded at the process level, it can be difficult to reconcile the provenance with the script definition as these systems cannot see what happens inside the processes. The provenance captured by noWorkflow is of a different nature—it represents dependencies within processes at the function level. In this sense, our approach is closer to the work by Cheney et al. [2]. They proposed a formalism that uses techniques based on program analysis slicing to represent the provenance of database queries so that it is possible to show how (part of) the output of a query depends on (parts of) its input. In contrast, we focus on provenance of (general) scripts, not just database queries. Another important distinction is that noWorkflow captures additional dependencies: it captures deployment provenance and, in addition to function and variable dependencies, it also captures general data dependencies from file reads and writes.

Several tools capture provenance from scripts and connect it to the experiment data. Bochner et al. [1] proposed an API and a client library to capture provenance for Python scripts. Gavish and Donoho [7] introduce the notion of a Verifiable Computational Result (VCR), where every result is assigned a unique identifier and results produced under the exact same conditions have the same identifier to support reproducibility. Unlike noWorkflow, these tools are intrusive and require users to change their scripts and include specific API method calls. Sumatra [3] collects provenance information from Python scripts. It is able to capture input and output data produced by each run (as long as they are explicitly specified by the user), parameters, module dependencies, and platform information. It is also able to detect when a module the script depends on has changed. The source code, however, needs to live in a version control system so that changes from one version to another can be detected. ProvenanceCurious [10] is another tool that can infer data provenance from Python scripts. It also uses AST analysis to capture every node of the syntax tree, and it uses a graph to provide query capabilities. However, for every operation, it requires input from the users regarding whether or not the operation reads or writes persistent data—this information is transparently captured by noWorkflow.

The approach taken by Tariq et al. [19] makes use of the LLVM compiler framework to automatically insert provenance capture at each function entry and exit. Thus, similar to noWorkflow, their approach is transparent—users do not need to manually annotate their code. However, there are important differences between the two approaches. Since Tariq et al. rely on a compiler, they are restricted to capturing static information. noWorkflow, on the other hand, captures both static and dynamic information. The latter is crucial for interpreted languages such as Python, since the underlying program (and objects) can change during runtime. In addition, noWorkflow captures dependencies that involve global variables within a function; these are ignored by Tariq et al., since they do not capture what happens inside functions. While our current implementation selects user-defined functions to track, we would like to explore mechanisms such as the one used by Tariq et al. to allow users to have more control over the captured provenance.

5   Conclusions and Future Work

We have presented noWorkflow, an approach to capture provenance of experiment scripts. Compared to previous approaches, the main benefits of noWorkflow are: (i) it is completely transparent—users do not need to instrument their code; (ii) it systematically captures three types of provenance—definition, deployment, and execution provenance—using non-intrusive mechanisms; (iii) it does not require users to change their modus operandi: scripts can be *outside* of a controlled environment and neither changes to the source code nor a version control system are required; (iv) it provides support for different kinds of analyses over the captured provenance data (graph-based, diff-based, and query-based); and (v) it simplifies reproducibility, allowing scientists to exchange provenance by sharing the *.noworkflow* directory with their peers. noWorkflow is available as open source software at https://github.com/gems-uff/noworkflow. Preliminary experiments show that its overhead is not burdensome.

One direction we plan to explore in future work is how to integrate provenance at different levels (e.g., operating system level with function level). We also plan to further investigate techniques for summarizing and visualizing provenance graphs [11,14], including all three types of provenance, as well as for contrasting different trials [15]. Last, but not least, we note that graph-based provenance analysis opens a vast range of opportunities for automated analysis, such as: reverse engineering workflows from scripts; optimizing scripts by either refactoring slow functions or running data mining algorithms to extract recurring execution patterns; identifying flaws in script execution; and showing the script evolution over time.

Acknowledgments. This work was supported in part by CNPq, FAPERJ, and the National Science Foundation (CNS-1229185, CNS-1153503, IIS-1142013).

References

1. Bochner, C., Gude, R., Schreiber, A.: A python library for provenance recording and querying. In: Freire, J., Koop, D., Moreau, L. (eds.) IPAW 2008. LNCS, vol. 5272, pp. 229–240. Springer, Heidelberg (2008)
2. Cheney, J., Ahamed, A., Acar, U.A.: Provenance as dependency analysis. Math. Struct. Comput. Sci. **21**, 1301–1337 (2011)
3. Davison, A.: Automated capture of experiment context for easier reproducibility in computational research. Comput. Sci. Eng. **14**(4), 48–56 (2012)
4. Diehl, S.: Software Visualization - Visualizing the Structure, Behaviour, and Evolution of Software. Springer, London (2007)
5. Freire, J., Koop, D., Santos, E., Silva, C.: Provenance for computational tasks: a survey. Comput. Sci. Eng. **10**(3), 11–21 (2008)
6. Frew, J., Metzger, D., Slaughter, P.: Automatic capture and reconstruction of computational provenance. Concurr. Comput. Pract. Exp. **20**(5), 485–496 (2008)
7. Gavish, M., Donoho, D.: A universal identifier for computational results. Procedia Comput. Sci. **4**, 637–647 (2011)
8. Guo, P.J., Seltzer, M.: BURRITO: wrapping your lab notebook in computational infrastructure. In: TaPP, p. 7 (2012)
9. van der Hoek, A.: Design-time product line architectures for any-time variability. Sci. Comput. Program. **53**(3), 285–304 (2004)

10. Huq, M.R., Apers, P.M.G., Wombacher, A.: ProvenanceCurious: a tool to infer data provenance from scripts. In: EDBT, pp. 765–768 (2013)
11. Koop, D., Freire, J., Silva, C.: Visual summaries for graph collections. In: 2013 IEEE Pacific Visualization Symposium (PacificVis), pp. 57–64 (2013)
12. Koop, D., Santos, E., Bauer, B., Troyer, M., Freire, J., Silva, C.T.: Bridging workflow and data provenance using strong links. In: Gertz, M., Ludäscher, B. (eds.) SSDBM 2010. LNCS, vol. 6187, pp. 397–415. Springer, Heidelberg (2010)
13. Koop, D., Scheidegger, C.E., Freire, J., Silva, C.T.: The provenance of workflow upgrades. In: McGuinness, D.L., Michaelis, J.R., Moreau, L. (eds.) IPAW 2010. LNCS, vol. 6378, pp. 2–16. Springer, Heidelberg (2010)
14. Macko, P., Seltzer, M.: Provenance map orbiter: interactive exploration of large provenance graphs. In: TaPP (2011)
15. Missier, P., Woodman, S., Hiden, H., Watson, P.: Provenance and data differencing for workflow reproducibility analysis. Concurr. Comput. Pract. Exp. (2013). doi:10.1002/cpe.3035
16. Mouallem, P., Barreto, R., Klasky, S., Podhorszki, N., Vouk, M.: Tracking files in the kepler provenance framework. In: Winslett, M. (ed.) SSDBM 2009. LNCS, vol. 5566, pp. 273–282. Springer, Heidelberg (2009)
17. Muniswamy-Reddy, K.K., Holland, D.A., Braun, U., Seltzer, M.: Provenance-aware storage systems. In: USENIX, p. 4 (2006)
18. Neves, V.C., Braganholo, V., Murta, L.: Implicit provenance gathering through configuration management. In: SE-CSE, pp. 92–95 (2013)
19. Tariq, D., Ali, M., Gehani, A.: Towards automated collection of application-level data provenance. In: TaPP, pp. 1–5 (2012)

LabelFlow: Exploiting Workflow Provenance to Surface Scientific Data Provenance

Pinar Alper[1]([✉]), Khalid Belhajjame[2], Carole A. Goble[1], and Pinar Karagoz[3]

[1] School of Computer Science, University of Manchester, Manchester, UK
alperp@cs.manchester.ac.uk
[2] Université Paris Dauphine, Paris, France
[3] Department of Computer Engineering,
Middle East Technical University, Ankara, Turkey

Abstract. Provenance traces captured by scientific workflows can be useful for designing, debugging and maintenance. However, our experience suggests that they are of limited use for reporting results, in part because traces do not comprise domain-specific annotations needed for explaining results, and the black-box nature of some workflow activities. We show that by basic mark-up of the data processing within activities and using a set of domain specific label generation functions, standard workflow provenance can be utilised as a platform for the labelling of data artefacts. These labels can in turn aid selection of data subsets and proxy for data descriptors for shared datasets.

Keywords: Provenance · Annotation · Scientific workflows

1 Introduction

Many fields of science are experiencing a proliferation in the sharing and re-use of scientific datasets [TA+11]. Widespread data-oriented science and data sharing necessitates principled data reporting regimes [TF+08] and richer metadata. In this context **"scientific data provenance"** is considered to be essential metadata that describes (1) **the experimental context**, in which data is generated, such as the scope of study, assumptions, experimental settings and descriptions of specialist resources or techniques adopted [TF+08], and (2) **the data's origins** in terms of primary datasets or source databases [TA+11].

Scientists go through a phase of **experiment reporting** prior to sharing datasets. During reporting they **select relevant data subsets** among the pool of all results obtained and **annotate data** to denote its scientific provenance using domain-specific vocabularies [TF+08]. A recent survey [TA+11] has shown that even though there is significant tool support for the collection and analysis of data, similar support does not exist for the organisation of results. Consequently scientists welcome any tool support for it.

Increasingly, scientific datasets are produced from entirely computational experiments. In many domains, Scientific Workflows have become a widespread

© Springer International Publishing Switzerland 2015
B. Ludäscher and B. Plale (Eds.): IPAW 2014, LNCS 8628, pp. 84–96, 2015.
DOI: 10.1007/978-3-319-16462-5_7

mechanism for specifying experiments as systematic and (re)runnable composi-tions of datasets and analysis tools [DF08]. Experiments organised as workflows are advantageous over adhoc analyses as they provide repeatability of compu-tation and traceability among results. Wide adoption of scientific workflows has fostered research on workflow provenance [DF08] with several provenance models and query mechanisms developed [Ge12, BC+12, MD+13, MLA+08]. Given their extensive provenance traces, at first glance one expects workflow-based exper-iments to be advantageous during **experiment reporting**. However, there is little use of workflow provenance during experiment reporting. This is due to: (1) workflow provenance being generic, implementation-oriented metadata [SSH08] that cannot stand-in for domain-specific descriptions expected during scientific data publishing; and (2) the established means of querying workflow provenance i.e. lineage traversal, can be an imprecise selection mechanism for scoping data subsets to be reported.

To this date, the approach to acquiring domain-specific annotations over workflow generated data has been either entirely manual [ZW+04] or partially-automated [MSZ+10]. Certain fixed characteristics at workflow description level are collected and then propagated to data generated by executions. This fixed metadata is useful for reporting but insufficient. Often experiments are reported based-on parametric information that is supplied at runtime via inputs. When one workflow execution is configured with multiple values of one parameter, results need to be annotated accordingly. This category of *dynamic information* offers significant utility in reporting yet it has received limited research attention. On the other hand, while manual annotation can be feasible for capturing fixed metadata, it is hard to scale for dynamic metadata.

Scientists invest significant time and effort into organising experiments as workflows. While this brings benefits when running the experiment, it has limited benefits for reporting. **We propose to bridge this gap and exploit workflow provenance to its full potential by treating it as a medium on which an automated data annotation (labelling) framework can be weaved.** The benefit of labels are twofold: (1) they have the potential to stand-in as data descriptors during publishing; and (2) they can be used for more precise scoping of data subsets to be reported.

We describe *Label*Flow, a semi-automated infrastructure for tracking domain specific provenance with *Data Labels*. We introduce a domain-independent process model comprised of four operators for the **in-situ generation** and **propaga-tion** of labels, predicated on basic information given in the form of semantic workflow annotations, called *Motifs*, that describe the data processing charac-teristic of workflow steps. We provide a practical algorithm for the generation of *Labelling Pipelines* out of motif-annotated scientific workflows, and provide an implementation where labelling pipelines are realised as functional programs. In prior work [AGB13] we proposed requirements and a preliminary approach; here we present a fully implemented architecture and report results on the impact of availability of labels to provenance queries. We start by introducing a sample real-world workflow and outline the provenance categories and queries for experiment reporting (Sect. 2). We outline the *Label*Flow architecture in Sect. 3 followed by details of the proposed solution, including Motif annotations (Sect. 3.1), the core model for labelling pipelines (Sect. 3.2), labels (Sect. 3.3) and labelling operators (Sect. 3.4). We review related work in Sect. 4, and conclude in Sect. 5.

2 Motivation

Figure 1 illustrates a workflow from astronomy[1] that takes as input a set of galaxy names ("list_cig_name"), and outputs extinction/reddening calculations per galaxy ("data_internal_extinction"), and galaxy details such as coordinates and morphology ("ra" "dec" "sesame" "logr25", and "leda_output"). The workflow starts by retrieving data, including coordinates, for each galaxy through a service based lookup from the Sesame astro-repository (Step-1- "SesameXML"). Coordinates are used to query the Visier Database to retrieve further data regarding galaxies (Step-2- "VII_237"). Galaxy morphology information is extracted from the Visier results, which is input together with coordinates into a local tool that computes galaxy extinction values (Step-3-"calculate_internal _extinction"). The scientifically significant activities in this workflow are the data retrievals and the local extinction calculation. The remaining activities are data adapters [GAB+14], a.k.a. shims, which are dedicated to the extraction of data, format transformation or moving data between the workflow environment and the file system. An important adapter in our example is the "Flatten_List" step, which bundles all input coordinates for all galaxies from Step-1 into a single output list for Step-2.

Workflow execution results in a set of intermediary and final data artefacts. For a single galaxy (e.g. M31, the Andromeda Galaxy) a total of 17 final results are generated at 6 output ports. The number of outputs increases linearly with the number of inputs. For a list of 6 galaxy names supplied as input, we get 20+ values for extinction and 100+ values for all results. This illustrates how workflows as automation tools proliferate data generation and makes apparent that manual annotation of data artefacts would quickly become a challenge for users.

The provenance landscape for workflow-generated data contains two categories of information

(i) *Generic:* Standard (Workflow) Provenance vocabularies make-up this category. They capture activities, input/output ports, activity instantiations, and data artefacts appearing at ports. Data influence and activity causality relations are also represented at this layer [Ge12,BC+12].

(ii) **Domain Specific:** Field-specific vocabularies for describing the scientific context and characteristics of data and experiments make up this category. The importance of domain-specific metadata has been acknowledged early-on in provenance research; 5 out of 9 of the Provenance Challenge queries [MLA+08] are based on restrictions on either data values or "annotations",

---

[1] http://www.myexperiment.org/workflows/2920.html.

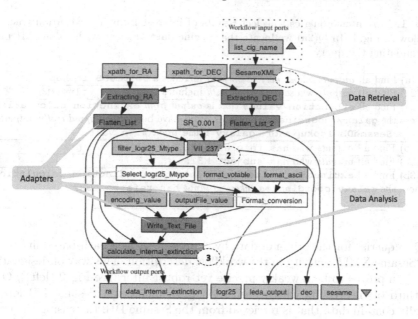

Fig. 1. Sample workflow from Astronomy developed by the Wf4Ever project.

which are "assumed" to exist. Domain specific annotations can further the categorised as containing `Static` or `Dynamic` metadata. The former identifies fixed/general domain types for activities or their inputs and outputs. E.g. Specifying that an activity is a SesameDB lookup, a parameter is a galaxy name. Dynamic metadata corresponds to attributes of data that can change from run to run. This information is often to be found innately but implicitly within data values, e.g. the galaxy name input parameter such as M31 or M33.

Let's now look at the state of the art in reporting with the *Lineage-Based Approach*, and compare with our proposed *Label-Based Approach*. In the former we only have generic workflow provenance to query, in the latter we employ *Label*Flow to obtain domain-specific annotations, which we later query.

Lineage-Based Data Selection: One can use workflow provenance to select data subsets by using lineage as a scoping mechanism. For instance, querying for results that are on the derivation path of a particular input artefact, or those whose derivation includes a particular activity. Table 1 presents three traditional lineage queries; Q1a, Q2a are adapted from [ZS+11], and Q3a is an adaptation of Provenance Challenge Query #6 [MLA+08]. Queries are font-highlighted to denote the different layers of provenance metadata needed to support them.

We analyse queries with respect to their **Contextual-Precision**, which we define as $\frac{\#of\textbf{Contextually-Accurate}results}{Total\#of results}$. We define **Contextual Accuracy** as the results actually belonging to the scope implied by the query (e.g. for Q1a the results that actually contain data that is retrieved from the Sesame database, or for Q2a the results that actually contain data belonging to galaxy M31).

Table 1. Provenance queries to select results of interest from the execution traces of workflow in Fig. 1. In Q(2a) we locate the specific data artefact with value M31 prior to formulating the query.

Lineage	Q(1a) Find all *outputs* whose *derivation path* includes a `SesameDB lookup`.
	Q(2a) Find all *outputs* whose *derivation path* includes *input* `with value M31.`see caption
	Q(3a) Find all **extinction values** that is *output from* **extinction calculation** where the **galaxy coordinates** *taken as input* have been *directly/indirectly outputted from* a **SesameDB lookup** with a **galaxy name** *input* `with value M31.`
Label	Q(1b) Find all *outputs* who has `referenceURI http://cds.u-strasbg.fr.`
	Q(2b) Find all *outputs* who has `subject M31.`
	Q(3b) Find all **extinction values** that is *output from* **extinction calculation** where the **galaxy coordinates** *taken as input* has `referenceURI http://cds.u-strasbg.fr` and has `subject M31.`

Q1a queries for the origin of data by expressing it as a path-based linkage to the "Sesame XML" activity in the workflow description. This way of designating the origin proves to be a weakly precise yet robust filter (see Fig. 2 (left)). Only one third of the results whose derivation path includes a Sesame DB lookup actually contain data that is retrieved from the Sesame DB. Increasing the number of galaxies in a workflow run does not diminish the precision of Q1a. **Q2a** defines a filter for results belonging to the Andromeda Galaxy by expressing it as a path-based linkage to the data artefact at the galaxy name input port with value "M31". While Q1a puts constraints on workflow description level entities, Q2a puts restrictions on run-time provenance-level entities. As depicted in Fig. 2 (right) the precision for Q2a quickly deteriorates. **Q3a** is a more elaborate query that combines the metadata requirements of Q1a and Q2a. Q3a is not robust against input data increase either. The fragility of queries that make use of dynamic elements (Q2a, Q3a) is due to the well-known Black-Box nature of workflow activities. For our case specifically, the "Flatten_List" step, which bundles all input coordinates for all galaxies into a single output list. At this point we lose fine-grained traceability between a specific galaxy name and the relevant data generated downstream in the workflow. As our example demonstrates, in the face of loss of fine-grained traceability, path-based querying of provenance becomes an ineffective index for reporting.

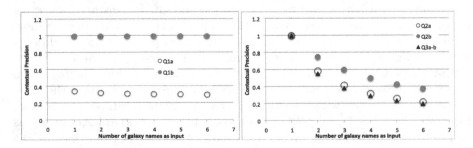

Fig. 2. Precision values for Q1 (left) and for Q2&Q3 (right) with respect to input size.

Annotation with *Label*Flow and Label-Based Selection: In order to employ *Label*Flow, as a pre-requisite we developed two simple functions that extract attributes (labels) for astronomical datasets from their XML based representation. We associated these functions with the "SesameXML" and "VII_237" activities, so that whenever these two data retrieval activities are used in a workflow they would have an associated labelling capability denoting the data's origin using an endpoint and its context i.e. the astronomical object it belongs to. We also semantically annotated data adaptation steps in our astro-workflow to give them basic transparency to denote whether inputs are carried-forward to (copied-to) outputs. Using this information *Label*Flow creates a labelling pipeline, which we use to decorate the runs of our workflow with labels. Labels have two potential uses, as descriptors during publishing and as data selection aides. In this work we explore the latter use of labels.

Table 1 also presents label-based data selections queries Q1b, Q2b and Q3b. In these we directly refer to the asserted origin (`has referenceURI`) and the asserted context (`has Subject`). Label-based queries Q1b and Q2b have higher precision then their lineage based counterparts (see Fig. 2), which can be explained as follows. First, lineage-based association is by-definition only a pseudo mechanism for denoting origin/context. By replacing lineage-based association with explicitly asserted attributes we gain in precision, as now only the data items that originate from the Sesame DB, and their local copies are returned to **Q1b**. Secondly, loss of fine-grained traceability also affects label-based query precision, see **Q2b** in Fig. 2 (right). While each item output from "SesameXML" bears the correct label denoting the associated galaxy, all items in the output of "Flatten_List" would bear a set of labels (for all galaxies), even though each contains the data of one. This time, however, *Label*Flow offers the possibility of asserting/recovering context in other data minting steps ("VII_237"); the labelling function associated with this step would exploit the raw data returned from the Visier DB and associate each result item with its context using a common attribute (`has subject`). In precision **Q3b** and Q3a are of equal capability in filtering (Fig. 2 (right)). This shows us that even though Q3b makes use of labels, it queries workflow results with reference to a particular blindspot (i.e. output of "Flatten_List") and therefore has precision performance equivalent to lineage-based queries. Thus, lineage-based queries represent the bottom-line (worst-case) precision for data scoping, where availability of labels offers the possibility of increased precision (at varying levels depending on existence and frequency of activities where fine-grain traceability is lost). In the remainder of the paper we describe the *Label*Flow infrastructure.

3   The *Label*Flow System

Figure 3 provides the overall architecture of our approach. We undertake labelling as an offline process, where we do not interfere with the established process of scientific workflow design (Step A1) and execution (Step A2). Workflow runs result in the generation of data artefacts and generic workflow provenance. These two make up our primary sources of information for obtaining and propagating domain-specific *Data Labels*. We perform labelling through latent processes informed by scientific workflow descriptions themselves enriched with semantic **Motif** annotations and associated **Labelling Functions**.

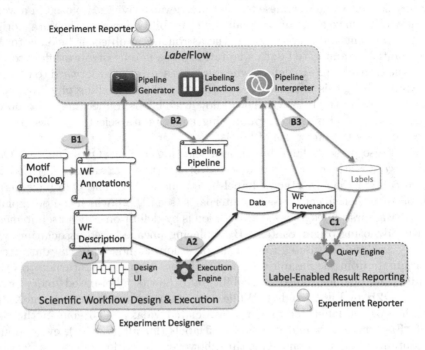

Fig. 3. Labelling System Architecture.

We operationalize the process model with **Labelling Pipelines**. Labels are opaque to the process model, as it out-sources their creation to external **Labelling Functions**. Using motif annotations (Step B1 in Fig. 3) and a repository of labelling functions we compile (Step B2) a labelling pipeline for a given scientific workflow. This pipeline is in-turn used to annotate the desired execution traces of that workflow with labels (Step B3). Once labels are generated they can be used in conjunction with generic workflow provenance metadata for the reporting of experimental results (Step C1).

3.1   Annotation of Workflow Activities with Motifs

In a previous empirical study [GAB+14] we inspected a corpus of 240 workflows from 4 systems and 10 domains in order to understand the nature of data processing in them. This resulted in a catalog of *Motifs*, a set of high-level abstractions for describing activity functionality. The analysis showed that a certain minority (30 %) group of activities perform the scientific heavy lifting in a workflow by minting data through analysis or retrievals. The remainder majority (70 %) are dedicated to data adaptation. A common characteristic of adapters, is that their computation is based on *value-copying* from inputs to the outputs. It follows then that we should seek labels for data artefacts that are generated by Data Minting activities, and grab hold of labels as data passes through (i.e. copied through) Data Preparation activities. These two categories of behaviour form the backbone of our labelling system. In Table 2 we list a subset of motifs with examples (including those from our astro-workflow as applicable) and corresponding labelling behaviour. Motifs are captured in an ontology, which we use to manually annotate activities. This basic annotation is in turn used to infer the data handling behaviour of each step. Annotation is finalised by collecting the particulars from the user; for value-copying, the source and sink ports, and for data minting the associated Labelling Function (if any) and the sink port to receive labels. Note that we scope our approach to scientific **dataflows**, i.e. those without any explicit control construct such as looping or branching. The pure dataflow model underpins several systems such as Taverna [MSRO+10], Galaxy[2] or Wings [GRK+11]. In others like Kepler [LAB+06] and Vistrails [MSFS11] pure dataflow model is widely adopted, while control-constructs are add-on modules or supplied in alternative design modes. We also assume that data is structured as Collections-Items, which is a ubiquitous structure for scientific workflow systems.

Table 2. Workflow motifs, Value copying and corresponding labelling behavior

Motif	src→snk	Example	Labelling
Data_Minting	$I \xrightarrow{m-1} O$	"SesameXML", "VII_237", "calculate_int_extinction"	Mint
Augmentation	$I \xrightarrow{m-1} O$	Adding a header to a CSV dataset	Propagate
Extraction	$I \xrightarrow{1-m} O$	"Select_logr25_Mtype", "'Extract_DEC&RA"	Propagate
Splitting	$I \xrightarrow{1-1} O$	Splitting a dataset by newline char	Propagate
Flattening	$I \xrightarrow{1-1} O$	"Flatten_List"	Propagate
Filter	$I \xrightarrow{1-1} O$	Filtering empty rows from a CSV	Propagate
Join	$I \xrightarrow{m-1} O$	Row by row dot product of two CSV tables	Propagate
Union	$I \xrightarrow{m-1} O$	Concatenating two CSV tables	Propagate

3.2 Labelling Pipelines

We provide a tool which takes as input a motif annotated workflow description w and produces a labelling pipeline Π_w for this workflow. Π_w could in turn be used to annotate data artefacts generated from all runs of w. A pipeline generator implements an algorithm based on the traversal of all dataflow paths in w. For each workflow element (i.e. activity or dataflow link) the tool checks the availability of motif annotations and label-flow continuity and accordingly places

---

[2] http://galaxyproject.org.

an operator into Π_w as a labelling proxy for that element. We note that this algorithm can operate with partial/missing annotations; in the case of missing motif annotations, the generator simply registers the current stack of connected labelling operators as a labelling sub-pipeline and resets. The algorithm initiates a new thread in the labelling pipeline whenever it encounters an activity that mints new data. To coordinate inter-operator communication among labelling operators we use simple *runs-after* type control tokens. The output of the *generator* tool is an intermediate representation for a labelling pipeline which is further expanded into a runnable form using the syntactic/macro expansion capabilities of a functional programming language.

The inputs to a particular execution of the labelling pipeline Π_w is the 6-tuple $\langle d, p, l, v, F_L, F_P \rangle$, where p, denotes the provenance trace of one run of workflow w, and d denotes the set of data artefacts generated during that run. The domain specific provenance represented with labels is accumulated in the label space l. v is the labelling vector that the system will take into account for label propagation. The system relies on sets of predefined functions, F_L for provisioning labels and for management of the label space (read-write) and F_P for querying generic workflow provenance.

3.3   Labels

A label is in effect a Label Instance that is defined with the triple $L_{ins} = \langle def, target, value \rangle$. def refers to the label's type, $target$ is the id of the data artefact, which the label describes, and $value$ is the actual annotation content carried by the label. Label definitions are triples of the form $L_{def} = \langle name, datatype, f_{agg} \rangle$. They have a unique $name$ and a $datatype$ designator. Labels can contain primitively typed information such as *Integer* or *String*. f_{agg} is the identifier for a function to be used when the system needs to aggregate multiple labels of this type. For the majority of labels, this element is *nil*, in which case the default aggregation function, i.e. *Union*, is used. A non-default case is, for example, the *spatialaggregation* function which computes the convex hull representing the overall spatial coverage of multiple datasets. Label definitions are grouped together in Label Vectors, $v = \langle name, \{L_{def}\} \rangle$. When used to configure the run of a pipeline Π_w, the vector sensitizes Π_w to the label types that it contains. Label and label vector definitions are to be made at the scientific investigation level, which spans multiple workflow descriptions.

3.4   Labelling Operators

Labelling pipelines are compositions of four labelling operators, namely *Mint*, *Propagate*, *Distribute* and *Generalize* (Fig. 4). In addition to input parameters, each operator accesses the provenance space, and depending on the labelling behaviour, accesses either the data artefacts (in case of *mint*) or the label space (others). Each operator has the side-effect of populating the label space. Operators return a boolean control token that is used for composing multiple operators into a labelling pipeline:

- *Mint* is a labelling proxy for those scientifically significant steps in the work-flow. *Mint* obtains labels by invoking the designated external labelling function; the labels are then associated with the data artefacts that fulfil the sink port and submitted to the label space. Minting is iterated for all invocations of the designated activity found in the provenance trace.
- *Propagate* is a labelling proxy for the value-copying Data Preparation steps in the workflow. Similar to mint, it is iterated for all invocations of the designated activity. *Propagate* clones labels describing the inputs at the source port and associates these clones with the outputs at the sink port.
- *Distribute* and *Generalize* are variants of propagation. While the former two are labelling proxies for activities, these are labelling proxies for dataflow links in the workflow, specifically those links with data structure depth mismatches between the two ends. In cases where the activity at one end of a dataflow link produces a collection, and the other end consumes an item, *Distribute* is responsible for propagating labels from the top-level collection to each item at specified depth. And vice-versa for *Generalize*.

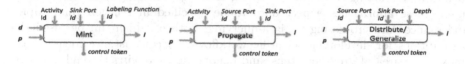

Fig. 4. Labelling Operator Signatures.

3.5 Implementation

The provenance and the label spaces are underpinned by RDF based meta-data. *Label*Flow can operate over standard PROV [Ge12] + Wfprov [BC+12] compliant provenance traces. Our provenance inquiry functions in the p space are implemented as Java methods. We implemented labelling operators as Java methods and labelling pipelines as Clojure programs that adhere to the dataflow paradigm[3], though in our case we *flow* control tokens among operators and the inter-operator communication regarding labels is done over the shared label space. The Label*Flow* system is agnostic to the inner workings of labelling functions. For our example from astronomy we had a simple local registry of labelling functions, which are Java classes adhering to a label generation interface.

4 Related Work

As mentioned previously, provenance annotation has so far been either entirely manual, or semi-automated with particular focus on static metadata [MSZ+10]. In [SSH08] authors describe the SPADE system where they highlight dynamic metadata, and they too address data artefacts as the source of this information.

---

[3] http://clojuredocs.org/clojure_core/clojure.core/future.

The authors propose "semantic provenance modules" to supply this metadata and claim modules can be integrated into workflows on-demand, though details of the integration are omitted. When compared to our work, this work is focused on devising an elaborate provenance ontology for one particular scientific domain, whereas ours is a domain-independent mechanism. Moreover the SPADE system requires altering the original scientific workflow to denote integration points, while ours is non-intrusive to the workflow design and execution process Finally SPADE does not address metadata propagation.

There is a large body of work on the provenance of database queries, which is recently revisited for its applicability to workflow provenance [AD+11,IC+, BL06]. These approaches propose white-box workflow activities that correspond to relational query operators. The benefit of white-box steps is that they allow full-transparency and enable fine-grained lineage, also making way for the tracking of cell-level value-copying and annotation propagation [BC+04]. Similarly, work on dependency analysis in programming languages has recently found applicability as a formal foundation for the tracking of Nested Relational Calculus query provenance [CAA07]. Such white-box transparency could be instrumental in developing workflow debugging or change tracking aids. On the other hand, these approaches expect data to be specified in relations and tuples, and reduce data-processing to data-querying; both of which can be restrictive assumptions for developing scientific workflows. In contrast, we focus on the unexplored area of grey-box steps, and denote value-copying through a rough-cut semantic annotation.

5   Conclusion

We described a semi-automated approach and an implemented architecture for the generation of Labels over data artefacts generated from runs of workflow based experiments. Labelling is performed through labelling pipelines, which use data artefacts as the main source of information for extracting domain-specific metadata and workflow provenance as a roadmap for association and propagation of labels with data. Pipelines are built up using four domain-independent labelling operators, which are agnostic to the contents of the domain-specific labels they carry around.

We argue that experiments organised as workflows make-up an ideal medium to capture and carry domain-specific provenance. Labels, i.e. carriers of this information, stand as a light-weight but controlled representation mechanism for metadata, which is a middle-ground between having no explicit metadata and having fully-fledged models that can represent complex/structured metadata. The benefit of labelling is two-fold: not only does it make implicit information explicit, but it also enables provenance queries that directly refer to scientific provenance/context rather than expressing context indirectly it in terms of derivation paths.

The cost involved in adapting our system is the manual annotation of workflow activities with motifs and developing labelling functions for the focal data generation points in workflows. These are one-time costs. Both motif annotations and labelling functions are highly reusable as most workflows are built by re-using building blocks pooled in module libraries or service registries. Consequently an annotation or a labelling proxy for a building block propagates to all workflows that the block is involved. When compared to workflow design, the cost of annotation is modest(as it amounts to single attribute setup per activity). Moreover motif annotation can be (semi)automated through the application of mining techniques to workflows and activity scripts [GCP13]. The re-usability of labelling functions can be maximised by developing metadata extraction utilities that operate over standardised scientific data formats.

Acknowledgements. The work has been supported in part by the award EP/G0262-38/1 myGrid: A Platform for e-Biology Renewal, and enabled by collaborations with the EU FP7 STREP 270192 Wf4Ever Advanced Workflow Preservation Technologies for Enhanced Science and EU FP7 283359 BioVel BioDiversity eLaboratory.

References

[AD+11] Amsterdamer, Y., Davidson, S.B., et al.: Putting lipstick on pig: Enabling database-style workflow provenance. PVLDB **5**(4), 346–357 (2011)

[AGB13] Alper, P., Goble, C., Belhajjame, K.: On assisting scientific data curation in collection-based dataflows using labels. In: WORKS 2013, pp. 7–16. ACM, New York (2013)

[BC+04] Bhagwat, D., Chiticariu, L., et al.: An annotation management system for relational databases. In: (e)Proceedings of the 13th VLDB Conference, pp. 900–911 (2004)

[BC+12] Belhajjame, K., Corcho, O., et al.: Workflow-centric research objects: First class citizens in scholarly discourse. In: Proceedings of Workshop on the Semantic Publishing (SePublica), Crete, Greece (2012)

[BL06] Bowers, S., Ludäscher, B.: A calculus for propagating semantic annotations through scientific workflow queries. In: Grust, T., Höpfner, H., Illarramendi, A., Jablonski, S., Fischer, F., Müller, S., Patranjan, P.-L., Sattler, K.-U., Spiliopoulou, M., Wijsen, J. (eds.) EDBT 2006. LNCS, vol. 4254, pp. 712–723. Springer, Heidelberg (2006)

[CAA07] Cheney, J., Ahmed, A., Acar, U.A.: Provenance as dependency analysis. In: Arenas, M. (ed.) DBPL 2007. LNCS, vol. 4797, pp. 138–152. Springer, Heidelberg (2007)

[DF08] Davidson, S., Freire, J.: Provenance and scientific workflows: challenges and opportunities. In: SIGMOD Conference, pp. 1345–1350 (2008)

[GAB+14] Garijo, D., Alper, P., Belhajjame, K., Corcho, O., Gil, Y., Goble, C.: Common motifs in scientific workflows: An empirical analysis. Future Gener. Comput. Syst. **36**, 338–351 (2014)

[GCP13] Ghoshal, D., Chauhan, A., Plale, B.: Static compiler analysis for workflow provenance. In: Proceedings of the 8th Workshop on Workflows in Support of Large-Scale Science, WORKS 2013, pp. 17–27. ACM, New York (2013)

[Ge12] Gil, Y., Miles, S., (eds.) A primer for the prov provenance model. In: World Wide Web Consortium (W3C) (2012)

[GRK+11] Gil, Y., Ratnakar, V., Kim, J., González-Calero, P.A., Groth, P.T., Moody, J., Deelman, E.: Wings: Intelligent workflow-based design of computational experiments. IEEE Intel. Syst. **26**(1), 62–72 (2011)

[IC+] Ikeda, R., Cho, J., et al.: Provenance-based debugging and drill-down in data-oriented workflows. In: ICDE 2012, Stanford InfoLab (2012)

[LAB+06] Ludäscher, B., Altintas, I., Berkley, C., Higgins, D., et al.: Scientific workflow management and the kepler system. Concurrency Comput. Pract. Exp. **18**(10), 1039–1065 (2006)

[MD+13] Missier, P., Dey, S., et al.: D-prov: extending the prov provenance model with workflow structure. In: Proceedings of the 5th USENIX Workshop on the Theory and Practice of Provenance, TaPP 2013, pp. 9:1–9:7 (2013)

[MLA+08] Moreau, L., Ludäscher, B., Altintas, I., et al.: The first provenance challenge. CCPE **20**(5), 409–418 (2008)

[MSFS11] Mates, P., Santos, E., Freire, J., Silva, C.T.: CrowdLabs: Social analysis and visualization for the sciences. In: Bayard Cushing, J., French, J., Bowers, S. (eds.) SSDBM 2011. LNCS, vol. 6809, pp. 555–564. Springer, Heidelberg (2011)

[MSRO+10] Missier, P., Soiland-Reyes, S., Owen, S., Tan, W., Nenadic, A., Dunlop, I., Williams, A., Oinn, T., Goble, C.: Taverna, reloaded. In: Gertz, M., Ludäscher, B. (eds.) SSDBM 2010. LNCS, vol. 6187, pp. 471–481. Springer, Heidelberg (2010)

[MSZ+10] Missier, P., Sahoo, S.S., Zhao, J., Goble, C., Sheth, A.: *Janus*: From Workflows to Semantic Provenance and Linked Open Data. In: McGuinness, D.L., Michaelis, J.R., Moreau, L. (eds.) IPAW 2010. LNCS, vol. 6378, pp. 129–141. Springer, Heidelberg (2010)

[SSH08] Sahoo, S.S., Sheth, A., Henson, C.: Semantic provenance for escience: Managing the deluge of scientific data. IEEE Internet Comput. **12**(4), 46–54 (2008)

[TA+11] Tenopir, C., Allard, S., et al.: Data sharing by scientists: Practices and perceptions. PLoS ONE **6**(6), e21101 (2011)

[TF+08] Taylor, C.F., Field, D., et al.: Promoting coherent minimum reporting guidelines for biological and biomedical investigations: the MIBBI project. Nat. Biotechnol. **26**(8), 889–896 (2008)

[ZS+11] Zhao, J., Sahoo, S.S., et al.: Extending semantic provenance into the web of data. IEEE Internet Comput. **15**(1), 40–48 (2011)

[ZW+04] Zhao, J., Wroe, C., Goble, C.A., Stevens, R., Quan, D., Greenwood, M.: Using semantic web technologies for representing E-science provenance. In: McIlraith, S.A., Plexousakis, D., van Harmelen, F. (eds.) ISWC 2004. LNCS, vol. 3298, pp. 92–106. Springer, Heidelberg (2004)

Auditing and Maintaining Provenance in Software Packages

Quan Pham[1]([⊠]), Tanu Malik[2], and Ian Foster[1,2]

[1] Department of Computer Science, The University of Chicago,
Chicago, IL 60637, USA
quanpt@cs.uchicago.edu
[2] Computation Institute, The University of Chicago, Chicago, IL 60637, USA
tanum@ci.uchicago.edu

Abstract. Science projects are increasingly investing in computational reproducibility. Constructing software pipelines to demonstrate reproducibility is also becoming increasingly common. To aid the process of constructing pipelines, science project members often adopt reproducible methods and tools. One such tool is CDE, which is a software packaging tool that encapsulates source code, datasets and environments. However, CDE does not include information about origins of dependencies. Consequently when multiple CDE packages are combined and merged to create a software pipeline, several issues arise requiring an author to manually verify compatibility of distributions, environment variables, software dependencies and compiler options. In this work, we propose software provenance to be included as part of CDE so that resulting provenance-included CDE packages can be easily used for creating software pipelines. We describe provenance attributes that must be included and how they can be efficiently stored in a light-weight CDE package. Furthermore, we show how a provenance in a package can be used for creating software pipelines and maintained as new packages are created. We experimentally evaluate the overhead of auditing and maintaining provenance and compare with heavy weight approaches for reproducibility such as virtualization. Our experiments indicate minimal overheads.

Keywords: Reproducibility · Software packaging tools · Software provenance · Tools and methods

1 Introduction

Computational reproducibility is a challenge, yet crucial for science. To meet the challenge, large-scale science projects are increasingly adhering to reproducibility guidelines. For instance, software associated with a publication is made available for download (see Figshare [20], RunMyCode [21], and Research Compendia [19]); but increasingly many science projects are making end-to-end software pipelines available. These pipelines are often for the larger scientific community, as in the case of Bio-Linux 5.0 [15], which is a bioinformatics virtual machine

© Springer International Publishing Switzerland 2015
B. Ludäscher and B. Plale (Eds.): IPAW 2014, LNCS 8628, pp. 97–109, 2015.
DOI: 10.1007/978-3-319-16462-5_8

that provides access to several pipelines for conducting next-generation sequence analysis, or sometimes to demonstrate project impacts as in the case of Swift Appliance [3], a virtual machine, which demonstrates crop simulation models using workflow systems.

To help projects adhere to these reproducibility guidelines, project members often adopt best practices and tools for developing and maintaining software so that their contributed software quickly becomes part of a pipeline. In this paper, we focus on software packaging tools. We describe how auditing and maintaining *software provenance* as part of a packaging tool can significantly help in building and deploying software pipelines. In particular, provenance can be helpful in cutting down manual effort involved in ensuring software compatibility, thus leading to improved administration of software pipelines.

A software pipeline consists of many individual software modules. Given the collaborative nature of science, it is not uncommon for modules to develop independently. Furthermore, a module itself may depend upon externally-developed libraries, which evolve independently. To ensure library compatibility, and avoid what is often called "dependency hell", a software module is often packaged together with specific versions of libraries that are known to work with it. In this way, contributing project members can ensure that their module will run on any target system regardless of the particular versions of library components that the target system might already have installed.

However, packaging software modules with associated dependencies, but without clearly identifying the origin of the dependencies, gives rise to a number of provenance-related questions, especially when constructing software pipelines. For instance, determining the environment under which a dependency was built or other dependencies which must be present for using a module, are questions that must be answered when combining packages for creating software pipelines. Similarly, if a new software package is released, then through dependency analysis it will be useful to know which packages of a pipeline can use it. If a new version of a library is released that contains security fixes, then it will be useful to know which pipelines or packages are vulnerable.

To answer such questions, we must be able to capture and determine the provenance of a software entity, i.e., capture and determine where it came from. Current package management systems do not provide a means to audit or maintain software provenance within it. We use CDE, a software packaging tool that creates a source code and data package while identifying all static and dynamic software dependencies. CDE has also been successfully shown to create software packages out of many development environments. Though CDE packages static and dynamic dependencies for an application, it does not store associated provenance.

The first contribution of this paper is to enhance CDE to include software provenance, i.e., provenance of shared libraries and binaries on which a program depends. We call this enhanced CDE as CDE-SP. We describe tools and methods to audit, store, and query this provenance in CDE-SP. We then describe a science project use case in which software reproducibility is a concern. Our second contribution is to show how provenance, audited and stored as part of

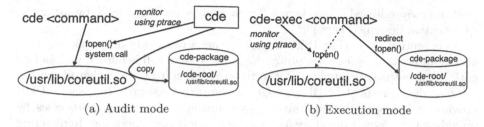

(a) Audit mode   (b) Execution mode

Fig. 1. CDE audit and execution modes

a CDE-SP package, can help in creating software pipelines for this use case. Finally, we show how provenance can be maintained as new packages are built during construction of software pipelines.

The remainder of the paper is structured as follows: We describe CDE, a software packaging tool that can identify and package program dependencies, in Sect. 2. Currently, CDE does not audit provenance of the program dependencies that it determines. In Sect. 3, we describe provenance that can be audited, stored, and queried in CDE-SP, resulting in a provenance-included package. In Sect. 4 we describe a science use case where provenance, included as part of software packages, can help in creating pipelines. In Sect. 5 we further enhance CDE-SP to enable it to maintain correct provenance as new packages are created. In Sect. 6, we conduct a thorough experimental evaluation to measure the overheads associated with auditing and maintaining provenance. Section 7 provides an overview of the related work in this area. We conclude in Sect. 8.

2   CDE: A Software Packaging Tool

The CDE tool [12,13] aims to easily create a package on a source resource and execute a program in that package on a target resource without any installation, configuration, or privilege permissions. It runs in two main modes: audit mode to create a CDE package, and execution mode to execute a program in a CDE package.

In audit mode (Fig. 1a), CDE uses the UNIX *ptrace* system call interposition to identify the code used by a running application (e.g., program binaries, libraries, scripts, data files, and environment variables), which it then records and combines to create a package. For example, when a process accesses a file or a library using the system call *fopen()*, CDE intercepts that syscall, extracts the file path parameter from the call, and makes a copy of the accessed file into a package directory, rooted at *cde-root* and consisting of all sub-directories and symbolic links of the original file's location.

The resulting package can be redistributed and run on another target machine, provided that the other machine has the same architecture (e.g. x86). The original CDE as available through [12,13] was limited to major Linux kernel versions (e.g. 2.6.x), but we have removed that restriction by adapting it for the newly released Linux kernel 3.0 as well as for Mac OS X by using the specification described here [2].

In execution mode (Fig. 1b), while executing a process from a package, CDE also monitors that process via *ptrace*. Each file system call is interrupted and its path argument is redirected to refer to the corresponding path of that file within the root directory of the CDE package on the target resource. In essence, CDE provides a lightweight virtualization environment to its running processes by providing the *cde-root* directory as a sandbox in a *chroot* operation. Redirecting all library dependency requests into this sandbox, CDE fools the target program into believing that it is executing on the original source machine [12]. It is to be noted that CDE binary only captures a single execution path, which is the execution path taken during run-time. If different execution paths need different types of dependencies, some dependencies may be left out. However, CDE does provide external scripts in its source code to find additional dependencies from strings inside binaries and libraries of captured packages.

3   CDE-SP: Software Provenance in CDE

The objective of auditing provenance is to capture additional details of the creation and origins of a library or a binary, such as the version of the compiler, the compilation options used, the exact set of libraries used for linking. This information must be gathered on a per environment basis so that it becomes easy to compile and create software pipelines.

Audit. CDE's audit feature identifies static and dynamic program dependencies. We instrument this feature to first determine a dependency tree, and then use UNIX utilities to store additional provenance information about each dependency. To create a dependency tree, process system calls are monitored that audit process name, owner, group, parent, host, creation time, command line, environment variables and the process binary's path. Whenever a process executes a file system call, a dependency of that process is recorded. In general, this dependency can be a data file or a shared library. We identify shared libraries using standard extensions, such as .so for system libraries and .jar for Java libraries, and create a dependency tree based on these libraries. Information about binaries and required shared libraries, such as version number, released version of shared libraries, and associated kernel distribution, is audited using UNIX commands *file, ldd, strings,* and *objdump*. By including these commands, we can obtain other static and dynamic dependencies, some of which are not audited by CDE during run-time. This set of commands is a more comprehensive way of obtaining dependencies comparing to CDE's external scripts. Current operating system distribution and user information is recorded from command *uname -a* and function *getpwuid(getuid())*.

Storage. Each package can store captured provenance to a relational database. Since this provenance will be useful for whatever target resource package is being used, we believe it is best to store this provenance within the package itself. We use LevelDB, a very fast and light-weight key-value storage library for storing provenance. To store provenance graphs that contain process-file and process-process edges, in a key-value store, we encode in the key the UNIX process identifier along with spawn time. The value is the file path or the process time. Table 1 describes the LevelDB schema for storing provenance graphs:

Table 1. LevelDB key-value pairs that store file and process provenance. Capital letter words are arguments.

Key	Value	Explanation
pid.PID1.exec.TIME	PID2	PID1 wasTriggeredBy PID2
pid.PID.[path, pwd, args]	VALUES	Other properties of PID
io.PID.action.IO.TIME	FILE(PATH)	PID wasGeneratedBy/wasUsedBy FILE(PATH)
meta.agent	USERNAME	User information
meta.machine	OSNAME	Operating system distribution

Query. LevelDB has a minimal API for querying. Instead of providing a rich provenance query interface, currently we implement a simple, light-weight query interface. The interface takes as input the program whose dependencies need to be retrieved. Using depth first search algorithm, a dependency tree in which the input program is the root is determined. The result is saved as a GraphViz file. Since the result may include multiple appearances of common files like those in */lib/*, */usr/lib/*, */usr/share/*, and */etc/* directories, the query interface also provides an exclusion option to remove uninteresting dependencies.

4 Using CDE-SP Packages to Create Software Pipelines

We describe a software pipeline through a use case. We then describe how CDE-SP packages can help to create the described software pipeline. The use case will also be used for experimental evaluation in Sect. 6.

4.1 Software Pipelines

Scientists with varying expertise at the Center for Robust Decision Making on Climate and Energy Policy (RDCEP) engage in open-source software development at their individual institutions, and rely primarily on Linux/Mac OS X environments. The Center often needs to merge its individual software modules to create software pipelines. We describe software modules being developed by three scientists, henceforth denoted as **A**lice, **B**ob, and **C**harlie, and the associated software pipeline that needs to be constructed.

- **A** measures and characterizes land usage and changes within it. She develops **data integration methods** to produce higher-resolution datasets depicting inferred land use over time. To develop the needed methods, her software environment consists of R, geo-based R libraries (raster, ggplot2, xtable, etc.), and specific versions of Linux packages (r-base v2.15, libgdal v1.10, libproj v4.8).

- **B** develops **computational models** for climate change impact analysis. He conducts model-based comparative analysis, and his software environment consists of **A**'s software modules to produce high-resolution datasets, and other Linux packages, including C++, Java, AMPL [11] modeling toolkits and libraries.

- **C** uses **A** and **B**'s software modules within **data-intensive computing methods** to run them in parallel. **C**'s scientific focus is the efficiency of distributed computing methods and his software environment is primarily Java and Python and its libraries on Linux.

- For the **Center**, the goal of their combined collaboration is to predict future yields of staple agricultural commodities given changes in the climate; changes that are expected to drive, and be influenced by, changes in land usage [9]. The Center curator's environment is Mac OS X and a basic Unix shell.

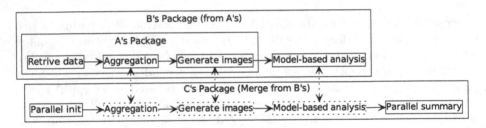

Fig. 2. Software packages of **A**, **B**, and **C**

Given the linear workflow of the science problem, it is often the case that **B** needs to rerun **A**'s software in his own environment. Instead of installing, this can simply be achieved if **A** shares a CDE package with **B**. However, if **B** attempts to create a software pipeline that includes **A**'s package and her software modules, then he needs to verify the provenance of each dependency included in **A** and her software. This is because a dependency with the same file path, but built on different Linux distributions (therefore different content), will conflict. In fact, if B creates a CDE package corresponding to this pipeline, one of the dependencies will be overwritten in the newly created package. By using the provenance-enabled CDE packages, which store md5 checksums of dependencies, such origins can be immediately verified, without manually tracking kernel distributions on which the dependency was built or communicating with the author of the software. Similarly, by checking versions of all dependencies within the package, **B** can document the compatibility of the newly created software pipeline.

As the use case demonstrates, **C** needs to use **A**'s and **B**'s packages, and the problem of dependency tracking, i.e., determining distributions and versions, given several dependencies and software environments, can increase significantly. In the Appendix we describe the magnitude of the dependency tracking problem if software development is undertaken in cloud-based environments.

5 Merging Provenance in CDE-SP

While provenance-included packages can eliminate much of the manual and tedious efforts of ensuring software compatibility, the downside is that provenance stores within a package need to be effectively maintained as software pipelines are themselves cast into new packages. Consider the Center's need for creating a software pipeline that satisfies reproducibility guidelines. To help the Center build this software pipeline, assume **A**, **B**, and **C** share their individual provenance-included packages. By exploring A, B and C's package provenance, the Center can examine all data and control dependencies among the contributing packages. The Center can then define a new experiment with steps using data and control dependencies from the three contributed packages, and create a new software package of this experiment. In particular, correct pathnames, attribution, etc., will need to be verified. We next describe how CDE-SP, with a $-m$ option, can be used to merge provenance from contributing packages.

In the typical CDE audit phase, file system binaries and libraries found in the path of program execution are copied to the *cde-root* directory. However, provenance may indicate two dependencies with the same path but emerging from different distributions or versions. In CDE-SP, these two files are stored in separate directories identified by a UUID, which is unique to the machine on which CDE-SP is executed. The UUID is the hash of the Mac address and the operating system. By creating this separate directory based on a UUID, files with the same paths but different origins can be maintained separately. Note that only files with differing content but the same path are maintained in separate UUID directories. Files with different paths can all still be in the same generic *cde-root* folder. We also include versioning of UUID directories so that they are copied and maintained correctly in new packages.

Because provenance informs that separate UUID based directories be created within a CDE-SP package, correspondingly, the modifications are needed in the LevelDB provenance store and the CDE-SP redirection mechanism. The LevelDB path in the value field needs to reflect the UUID directory where the dependency exists. The CDE redirection, which redirects all system calls to the *cde-root* directory, in CDE-SP needs to redirect to the appropriate UUID directory. This redirection can be tricky since it needs to know where the process is running. To enable correct redirection, CDE-SP with merge maintains a *current_root_id* pointer for each tracing process. This bookkeeping pointer helps in redirecting to the package root directory of the pointer in case the process forks other processes. Alternatively, if the process performs an *execve()* system call, or accesses a file, or changes directories, absolute paths are read and checked to determine if redirection is necessary.

Another issue when merging two packages is maintaining licensing information. While general licensing issues are outside the scope of this paper, the current CDE-SP maintains authorship of software modules during the merge process. When two packages are merged in their entirety, the authorship of a new package is the combined authorship of the contributing packages. However, when part of a contributing package is used to create a new package, then authorship must be validated from the provenance stored in the original package. To validate, CDE-SP generates the subgraph associated with the part of the package, and, using subgraph isomorphism, validates that it is indeed part of the original provenance graph.

The subgraph isomorphism (or matching) problem is NP-complete [22] leading to an exponential time algorithm. In our case, we compare file paths and names to determine if two provenance graphs are subgraph-isomorphic. In our implementation of VF2 subgraph-isomorphism algorithm [6], we reduce computation time by only matching provenance nodes of processes with the same path to their binary and working directory, and only matching provenance nodes of files with the same path. We believe that this implementation is sufficient for validating provenance subgraph isomorphism among lightweight packaging tools.

6   Experiment and Evaluation

The benefits of reproducibility can be hard to measure. In this Section, we describe the three experiments we conducted to determine the overall performance of CDE-SP.

1. We determined the performance of CDE-SP in: auditing performance overhead, disk storage increase, and provenance query runtime;
2. We determined the redirection overhead if multiple UUID-based directories are created in CDE-SP; and
3. We compared the lightweight virtualization approach of CDE-SP with Kameleon [10], a heavyweight virtualization approach used for reproducibility.

All experiments in this section are tested on an Ubuntu 12.04.3 LTS workstation with an 8 GBs RAM and 8-core Intel(R) processor clocking at 1600 MHz.

6.1   Audit Performance and Size Overhead in CDE-SP

In Table 2, we record execution times and disk usage of CDE and CDE-SP in auditing a software pipeline mentioned in Sect. 4.1. Both CDE-SP and CDE are set up for a pipeline with two applications: *Aggregation* and *Generate Image*. Each is repeated 10 times. The result shows approximately a 2.1 % slowdown of CDE-SP in comparison with CDE due to provenance capture. The result fits with our observation that the overhead is from *ptrace* which both CDE and CDE-SP rely on heavily to implement their capture capabilities. Additional functions that store provenance record to LevelDB database introduce negligible provenance capture overhead compared to 0–30% CDE virtualization overhead [12]. In this setup, CDE package uses 732 MB; while CDE-SP, in addition to the

Table 2. Increase in CDE-SP performance is negligible in comparison with CDE

	Create package	Execution	Disk usage	Provenance query
CDE	852.6 ± 2.4 (s)	568.8 ± 2.4 (s)	732 MB	
CDE-SP	870.5 ± 2.5 (s)	569.5 ± 1.8 (s)	732 MB + 236 kB	0.4 ± 0.03 (s)

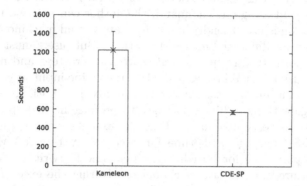

Fig. 3. Overhead when using CDE with Kameleon VM appliance

software package, creates a LevelDB database of size 236 kB (0.03 % increase) that contains approximately 12,000 key-value pairs.

To measure provenance query performance, we created a Python script to query the audited LevelDB provenance database and create a provenance graph of the experiment with common shared libraries filtered out. The Python script reads through approximately the 12,000 key-value pairs in 0.39 s to create a GraphViz script that can be converted to image or visualized later.

6.2 Redirection Overhead in CDE-SP

We also compared an execution of CDE package and CDE-SP package to measure the redirection overhead of CDE-SP. Using the packages created by the above experiment with two applications, *Aggregation* and *Generate Image*, we pipelined output of *Aggregation* to input of *Generate Image*, which requires CDE-SP to apply redirection among multiple CDE roots. The experiment showed 3 data files, as outputs of *Aggregation* package, were moved to *Generate Image* package. After the data was moved to the next package, the experiment was executed the same as in CDE. The result shows less than a 1 % slowdown of CDE-SP, which maybe due to initial loading of library dependencies in *Generate Image* package.

6.3 CDE-SP Vs Kameleon

In this experiment, we used the Kameleon engine to make a bare bone VM appliance that contains the content of a CDE-SP package corresponding to the software pipeline described in the use case (Sect. 4.1). The package content was copied directly to the root file system of the VM appliance. In terms of user software, the new VM appliance is close to a replica of the package, without any redundant installed software. We compared the two approaches qualitatively and quantitatively.

Qualitatively, the overhead of instantiating a VM is significant as compared to creating a CDE-SP package. In particular, for CDE-SP the user needs to specify input packages, and using one command, the author can create a new software package. Kameleon is user friendly and can create virtual machine appliances in different formats for different Linux distributions. But, users must provide self-written YAML-formatted recipes or self-written macrosteps and microsteps to generate customized virtual images. Based on the recipe input, it generates bash scripts to create an initial virtual image of a Linux distribution, and populates the initial image with more Linux packages to produce needed appliances.

Quantitatively, we compared the time for executing the software pipeline within a CDE-SP package with time for execution within a VM. Note that we do not compare time for initializing, since time for writing YAML scripts cannot be measured in the case of Kameleon. During the execution, CDE-SP redirected 2717 file-read system calls, 10 file-write system calls, 17 file-read-write system calls. Figure 3 shows that the Kameleon VM appliance slowed down the experiment significantly: approximately 200 % or more. This heavyweight VM overhead is substantial in comparison with the CDE-SP lightweight approach.

7   Related Work

Details about software have been included in provenance collected within workflow systems. For instance, Research Objects [4], packages scientific workflows with auxiliary information about workflows, including provenance information and metadata, such as the authors, the version. Our focus here is not limited to any specific workflow system.

Software packaging tools such as CDE [12,13] and Sumatra [8] can capture an execution environment in a lightweight fashion. Sumatra captures the environment at the programming level (Python), while CDE operates at the operating system level, and is thus more generic. Even at the system level, different tracing mechanisms can be used. At the user-space level, *ptrace* [1] is a common mechanism, whereas at the kernel-level, use of SystemTap [18] is more common. SystemTap, being kernel-based, has better performance compared to *ptrace* since it avoids context switching between the tracee (which is in the kernel) and the tracer (which is user space) [14]. However, from a reproducibility standpoint, SystemTap needs to run at a higher privilege level, i.e., it requires root access, creating a more restricted environment.

Virtual machine images (VMIs) provide a means of capturing the environment in a form that permits later replay of a computation. Kameleon [10] uses a bash script generator to create virtual images from scratch for any Linux distributions. Using recipes, users can generate customized virtual images with predefined software packages to run on different cloud computing service providers. We have compared our approach with creating VMIs for reproducibility.

Tools such as Provenance-to-Use (PTU) [17] and ReproZip [5] have demonstrated the advantages of including provenance in self-contained software packages. Currently, these tools include execution provenance and not software provenance. Finally, software provenance is an emerging area that uses Bertillonage metrics for finding software entities in large code repositories [7]. In this paper, we have described how software provenance can help in building packages that can satisfy reproducibility guidelines.

8   Conclusion

CDE is a software packaging tool that helps to encapsulate static and dynamic dependencies and environments associated with an application. However, CDE does not encapsulate provenance of the associated dependencies such as their build, version, compiler, and distribution. The lack of information about the origins of dependencies in a software package creates issues when constructing software pipelines from packages. In this paper, we have introduced CDE-SP, which can include software provenance as part of a software package. We have demonstrated how this provenance information can be used to build software pipelines. Finally, we have described how the CDE-SP can maintain provenance when used to construct software pipelines.

Acknowledgments. The authors would like to thank the following participants in the RDCEP Center, in particular, Neil Best, Joshua Elliott and Justin Wozniak at The University of Chicago, Columbia University, and Argonne National Laboratory for motivating our use case, and Allison Brizius for describing the Center's activities. This work is supported by NSF grant SES-0951576 and subcontract award under grant GEO-1343816.

Appendix

In our use case, **A**, **B**, and **C** develop open-source code and use publicly-available datasets. Their specified software environments, which may appear different, can be still overlapping. To demonstrate the magnitude of overlap, we assume that each developer uses the cloud for their research, which is not uncommon in today's projects, and chooses a different Linux distribution. Differences in the choice of linux distributions is also not surprising as the Linux Counter Distributions Report [16] indicates that there is no clean winner in terms of usage of Linux distributions, with no one distribution accounting for more than 30 %. Further, we limit software environments to refer to application binaries and libraries that are often overlapping and create conflicts.

If the two assumptions are sound, then the overlap in the environment, i.e., files which have the same path, but differing content, can be as high as 18 %. We calculate this by taking five Linux distributions with similar setup available on Amazon EC2. For each pair of machines, we calculate the number of files with the same path on two machines, and the number of files with the same path on two machines but having different md5 checksum. Table 3 shows that between any two machines, on average, 6.8 % of files have the same path but differ in content. In other words, these files are not interchangeable but depend on the underlying operating system.

Table 3. Ratio of different files having the same path in 5 popular AMIs. The denominator is number of files having the same path in two distributions, and the numerator is the number of files with the same path but different md5 checksum. Ommited are manual pages in */usr/share/* directory.

	RH	SUSE	U12	U13
Amz	5498/23 k	3184/11 k	1203/5.4 k	1819/5.5 k
RH		3861/12 k	1654/6.6 k	2223/6.3 k
SUSE			1245/3.9 k	2085/6.4 k
U12				8226/24 k

References

1. *ptrace*(2) - Linux man page. http://linux.die.net/man/2/ptrace
2. Replacing *ptrace()*. http://uninformed.org/index.cgi?v=4&a=3&p=14
3. Swift appliance at science clouds. http://scienceclouds.org/appliances/swift-appliance/
4. Belhajjame, K., Corcho, O., et al.: Workflow-centric research objects: First class citizens in scholarly discourse. In: Proceedings of Workshop on the Semantic Publishing (SePublica), Crete, Greece (2012)
5. Chirigati, F., Shasha, D., Freire, J.: ReproZip: using provenance to support computational reproducibility. In: USENIX Workshop on the Theory and Practice of Provenance, TaPP 2013 (2013)
6. Cordella, L., Foggia, P., Sansone, C., Vento, M.: A (sub)graph isomorphism algorithm for matching large graphs. IEEE Trans. Pattern Anal. Mach. Intell. **26**(10), 1367–1372 (2004)
7. Davies, J., German, D.M., Godfrey, M.W., Hindle, A.: Software bertillonage. Empirical Softw. Engg. **18**(6), 1125–1155 (2013)
8. Davison, A.P.: Automated capture of experiment context for easier reproducibility in computational research. Comput. Sci. Eng. **14**, 48–56 (2012)
9. Elliott, J., et al.: Constraints and potentials of future irrigation water availability on agricultural production under climate change. In: Proceedings of the National Academy of Sciences (2013)
10. Emeras, J., Richard, O., Bzeznik, B.: Reconstructing the software environment of an experiment with kameleon (2011)
11. Fourer, R., Gay, D.M., Kernighan, B.W.: AMPL: A Mathematical Programming Language. ATT Bell Laboratories, Murray Hill (1987)
12. Guo, P.: CDE: Run any linux application on-demand without installation. Technical. report, USENIX Association, Boston, Massachusetts (2011)
13. Guo, P.J., Engler, D.: CDE: Using System Call Interposition to Automatically Create Portable Software Packages. USENIX Association, Portland (2011)

14. Keniston, J., Mavinakayanahalli, A., Panchamukhi, P., Prasad, V.: Ptrace, utrace, uprobes: Lightweight, dynamic tracing of user apps. In: Linux Symposium (2007)
15. Krampis, K., et al.: Cloud BioLinux: pre-configured and on-demand bioinformatics computing for the genomics community. BMC Bioinf. **13**(1), 42 (2012)
16. Löhner, A.: Lico-Project information (2012)
17. Pham, Q., Malik, T., Foster, I.: Using provenance for repeatability. In: USENIX Workshop on the Theory and Practice of Provenance (2013)
18. Prasad, V., Cohen, W., Eigler, F., Hunt, M., Keniston, J., Chen, B.: Locating system problems using dynamic instrumentation (2005)
19. Seiler, J.: Research compendia: Connecting computation to publication (2013)
20. Singh, J.: FigShare. J. Pharmacol. Pharmacotherapeutics **2**(2), 138–139 (2011)
21. Stodden, V., Hurlin, C., Perignon, C.: RunMyCode.Org: a novel dissemination and collaboration platform for executing published computational results (2012)
22. Wegener, I.: Complexity Theory Exploring the Limits of Efficient Algorithms. Springer, Berlin (2005)

Security and Privacy Implications
of Provenance

An Analytical Survey of Provenance Sanitization

James Cheney[✉] and Roly Perera

School of Informatics, University of Edinburgh, Edinburgh, UK
{jcheney,rperera}@inf.ed.ac.uk

Abstract. Security is likely to be a critical factor in the future adoption of provenance technology, because of the risk of inadvertent disclosure of sensitive information. In this survey paper we review the state of the art in secure provenance, considering mechanisms for controlling access, and the extent to which these mechanisms preserve provenance integrity. We examine seven systems or approaches, comparing features and identifying areas for future work.

1 Introduction

Automatically associating data with metadata describing its provenance has emerged as an important requirement in databases, scientific computing, and other domains that place a premium on reproducibility, accountability or trust [27]. Providing such metadata typically involves instrumenting a system with monitoring or logging that tracks how results depend on inputs and on other, perhaps untrustworthy, sources.

Publishing the entire provenance record associated with a computation is not always feasible or desirable. Disclosing certain information may violate security, privacy, or need-to-know policies, or expose sensitive intellectual property. Sometimes the complete provenance record may be too detailed for the intended audience, or may leak irrelevant implementation detail. But simply omitting some of the provenance information may leave it unable to certify the origins of the data product.

We refer to the general problem of ensuring that provenance solutions satisfy not only disclosure requirements but also security or privacy requirements as the problem of *provenance sanitization* or *provenance abstraction*. A number of approaches to provenance sanitization have been proposed recently [3,8,15, 16,18], sometimes under other names such as *provenance views* or *provenance redaction*. These techniques have been developed mainly for scientific workflow systems, where provenance is viewed as a directed acyclic graph, as in the Open Provenance Model [28].

Existing approaches have several elements in common. Typically, an *obfuscation policy* specifies the aspects of the provenance which are to be hidden. A *disclosure policy* may additionally specify that certain other aspects of the provenance are to remain visible. *Sanitization* then involves transforming the provenance graph to obtain a view which satisfies both the obfuscation and the disclosure policies.

B. Ludäscher and B. Plale (Eds.): IPAW 2014, LNCS 8628, pp. 113–126, 2015.
DOI: 10.1007/978-3-319-16462-5_9

Few of the existing systems have been formally studied, and the security guarantees they actually provide are unclear. Some do provide formal guarantees, but are narrow in applicability or have other shortcomings. Moreover, many systems provide some form of security or confidentiality without considering the impact on the causal or explanatory role of provenance. In this paper we review the state of the art in provenance sanitization by reviewing seven systems or approaches: ZOOM [2,13], security views [8], surrogates [3], ProPub [18], provenance views [15,16], provenance abstraction [26], and provenance redaction [7].

2   Related Work

The relationship between security and provenance has been considered in several survey or vision papers [4,20,23,25]. This paper focuses narrowly on provenance sanitization via graph transformations; here we briefly mention some related topics.

Formal foundations. Chong [11] gave an early definition of provenance-related security policies. Cheney [9] subsequently generalized this approach to notions of *disclosure* and *obfuscation* with respect to a query Q on the underlying provenance, and a view P of the provenance. Obfuscation is similar to (non-quantitative) *opacity* in computer security [1], and means that P does not allow the user to determine whether the underlying provenance satisfies Q. Disclosure means that P preserves Q-equivalence.

Secure provenance for evolving data. Provenance tracking is an especially critical issue for data that changes over time [6], for which provenance can be hard to recover after the fact. Work in this area to date includes tamper-resistant provenance for databases [30], use of cryptographic techniques to ensure integrity of document version history [21], and database audit log sanitization [22].

3   Background Concepts and Terminology

The solutions surveyed in Sect. 4 mainly target scientific workflow systems, with similar notions of provenance; we review some common concepts here. Some acquaintance with basic graph theory will be useful. For more background on scientific workflow provenance, we refer the reader to Davidson and Freire [14].

Workflow systems and provenance graphs. A *workflow system*, or simply *workflow*, is a directed graph capturing the high-level structure of a software-based business process or scientific process. Nodes represent software components called *modules*, or *tasks*. Edges represent links, or *data channels*, connecting modules. Sometimes modules are considered to have input and output *ports* to which data channels are connected. Figure 1a shows a simple workflow with modules m_1 to m_6.

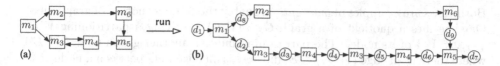

Fig. 1. Cyclic workflow, plus bipartite provenance graph for a possible run

Node labels are typically used to identify modules. Iterative processes can be modelled by cycles, if permitted, or via a built-in construct for iteration. Workflow systems often support other coordination patterns such as conditional branching and synchronisation which are beyond scope of the systems considered here. Some permit *composite* modules, i.e. modules that contain other modules.

A *provenance graph* is a directed, acyclic graph (DAG) recording the causal history of a data product. Often such a graph represents the (coarse-grained) *execution* of a software system, such as a workflow; more generally, provenance graphs can describe ad hoc processes or collaborations involving both human and software components. The nodes of the graph represent participants, actions and intermediate artifacts.

Figure 1b shows a provenance graph that captures one possible execution of the workflow in Fig. 1a. The rectangular nodes, or *activities*, represent invocations of modules; the circular nodes d_1 to d_9, sometimes called *entities*, record data values passed between modules. Moreover activities yield entities, and entities feed into activities; a graph that is partitioned in this way is called *bipartite*. Bipartiteness is just one of many possible design choices for graph-structured provenance; for example, one could add $d_1, \ldots, d_9$ as labels to the edges instead of using special nodes.

When a provenance graph represents a run of an iterative process, each module invocation must give rise to a distinct node, to maintain acyclicity. If necessary additional tags on the node label can be used to distinguish invocations of the same module.

Sanitizing provenance graphs. The goal of provenance sanitization is to derive a *sanitized view* which hides or abstracts sensitive details of a provenance graph, whilst preserving some of its disclosure properties. Typically one wants the view itself to be a well-formed provenance graph. Figure 2 below illustrates a simple provenance graph with two examples of views. On the right, tasks c_1 and c_2 have been abstracted into a single task c_3; on the left, entities d_2 and d_4 and intermediate task c_2 have been abstracted into a single entity d_5.

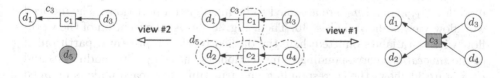

Fig. 2. Two possible views of a provenance graph

Both views are examples of *quotients*, arguably the simplest notion of graph view. One specifies a quotient of a graph $G = (V, E)$ by giving a partitioning $V' = \{V_1, \ldots, V_n\}$ of its nodes. The partitioning induces another graph $G' = (V', E')$ where there is an edge $(V_i, V_j) \in E'$ iff there is an edge in G between a node of V_i and a node of V_j, for any $i \neq j$. In Fig. 2 the dotted border labeled c_3 determines a partitioning if we consider each of the remaining nodes to inhabit a singleton partition; the dotted border labeled d_5 determines a different partitioning, under a similar assumption.

Quotients are natural forms of provenance view as they preserve *paths*, which represent relationships of direct or indirect dependency between nodes. If paths are preserved then related nodes are mapped to related nodes in the view; in other words, every dependency in the original graph gives rise to a dependency between the corresponding view nodes. Quotients preserve paths but not edges; for example the edges (d_4, c_2) and (c_2, d_2) have no counterpart in view #2 because all three nodes are mapped to d_5. Indeed edge-preservation, or *homomorphism*, is a stronger property than we usually require for provenance sanitization, where dependency is assumed to be reflexive and transitive.

It can also be important to consider whether paths are *reflected*: whether nodes are related in the view *only if* there exist related nodes in the original graph which map to those nodes in the view. This too can be understood in terms of dependency, since it means that every reported dependency arises from a dependency between corresponding nodes in the original graph. Quotients do not in general reflect paths, because they coarsen the dependency relation: in view #1, for example, d_1 now appears to depend on d_4, and d_2 on d_3. This can be problematic if it violates cardinality constraints, such as a requirement that every artifact be generated by at most one activity [29].

4   Survey of Techniques for Provenance Sanitization

In the ZOOM system of **Biton, Cohen-Boulakia and Davidson** [2,13], the user obtains a provenance view by first defining an abstract workflow view. A ZOOM workflow is a directed graph of atomic modules; a provenance graph is a DAG of invocations with edges labeled with runtime values. A workflow view is a quotienting which partitions the system into composite modules; for a given run of the workflow, the corresponding "quotient run" can then be obtained automatically by deriving invocations of each composite module from the invocations of its constituent modules.

Figure 3 illustrates the ZOOM approach. In Fig. 3a we see the original workflow with the partitioning identified by dashed borders labeled c_2 and c_3. The modules m_1, m_2 and m_5 are assumed to be in singleton partitions. The induced workflow view is shown in Fig. 3b. Then, Fig. 3c shows an execution of the workflow with data labels omitted; here the dashed borders represent a partitioning of the *invocations* corresponding to invocations of the composite modules c_2 and c_3. Figure 3d shows the corresponding quotient run where each node is mapped to its equivalence class.

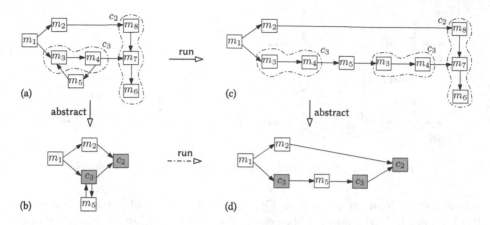

Fig. 3. ZOOM: deriving a provenance view from a workflow view

ZOOM is not overtly motivated by security, but its views can be seen as abstracting away uninteresting parts of the graph while ensuring user-identified "relevant" parts remain visible. ZOOM is unique in respecting the semantic relationship between program and provenance, as alluded to by the dotted run arrow relating Fig. 3b and d. Moreover being able to derive provenance views from *ex post facto* modularisations of a workflow is extremely powerful. However, it seems unlikely that their method for doing so (sketched only briefly in the papers) will generalise to workflows with non-trivial control flow or settings where submodules are shared by composite modules. In [13], most of the focus is on workflow views instead, in particular a method for deriving workflow views that preserve and reflect certain structural properties of the workflow, given a user-specified set of modules that are of interest.

The **security views** of **Chebotko, Chang, Lu, Fotouhi and Yang** [8] provide both access control and abstraction for scientific workflow provenance. Their workflows are DAGs with additional structure to model hierarchical tasks; the data channels of a composite task are those of its constituent tasks that cross the boundary of the composite task, relating composite tasks to the partitions of a quotient view. However, composite tasks are fixed features of the workflow rather than on-the-fly abstractions as in ZOOM, above. Being acyclic, workflows are unable to represent iteration.

To obtain a security view, one first specifies the accessibility of the various tasks and data channels, marking each element as accessible or inaccessible. Inheritance rules define the accessibility of an element if it is not given explicitly. Access control can be specified down to the level of individual ports; consistency constraints ensure that (for example) a data value inaccessible on one port is not accessible via another port. The access specification is then used to derive a provenance view from which inaccessible data values, tasks and channels have been removed.

Figure 4a shows a run of a hierarchical workflow with two levels of composite task; both data nodes and ports have been elided for brevity. A node written as

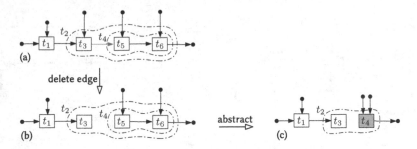

Fig. 4. Security views: combining abstraction with access control

• indicates an input or output. In Fig. 4b, the data channel between t_3 and t_5 has been deleted to conform to the access specification. Although dummy nodes, similar to the *surrogates* of Blaustein et al. below [3], may be added to the view to preserve well-formedness constraints, more general integrity requirements are not considered. For example once the edge between t_3 and t_5 has been deleted, the view no longer preserves dependencies, and so its ability to provide a full account of the output is compromised. Access control can however be combined with quotienting. In Fig. 4c the composite module t_4 has been abstracted to a single node with two inputs, preserving the dependency structure of Fig. 4b, even though the latter view is unsound.

Blaustein, Chapman, Seligman, Allen and Rosenthal [3] present an approach based on *surrogates*. They define a *protected account* of a graph G to be any graph G', along with a path-preserving function from the nodes of G' to the nodes of G. Since by definition every path in the view has an image in the original graph, a protected account necessarily reflects dependencies, but in general does not preserve them. Surrogates are a mechanism for publishing dependency information in a way that still protects sensitive nodes and edges.

Figure 5a, adapted from [3], shows a typical graph with sensitive nodes and edges in red. Figure 5b shows a protected account where e has been deleted and f replaced by a surrogate f', shown with a dotted border, that hides its sensitive data (perhaps its identity). The view in Fig. 5c hides two more edges, breaking the indirect dependency between c and g. This is repaired in Fig. 5d by a surrogate edge (dotted arrow).

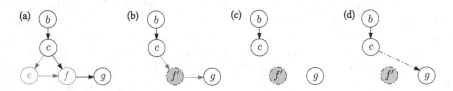

Fig. 5. Surrogates: provenance graph, plus three protected accounts (Color figure online)

Blaustein et al.'s approach has three components: user privileges, which allow the graph provider to control graph access down to the level of individual ports; an algorithm for protecting graphs by deleting nodes and edges and adding surrogates; and metrics for analyzing disclosure and obfuscation properties of the resulting graph. For a given set of user privileges, their algorithm purportedly obtains a protected account which is "maximally informative", according to a utility metric derived from the proportion of G-paths retained in G' plus the similarity of each node in G' to its counterpart in G. However definitions given are rather informal, and the theorems lack proofs, making this claim hard to evaluate.

Even when a protected account satisfies a particular obfuscation policy, an attacker may still be able to infer the original graph G from G'. To study this, Blaustein et al. introduce the notion of *opacity*, a measure of the difficulty of inferring an edge in G that is not present in G', given a user-supplied model of the attacker. (The notion of opacity in the security literature [1] is somewhat different.)

The ProPub framework of **Dey, Zinn and Ludäscher** [18], based on Datalog, provides what the authors refer to as "policy-aware" provenance sanitization. A provenance query is expressed as a set of Datalog facts, asserting that the provenance for certain data items is to be disclosed, plus additional requirements relating to sanitization and disclosure. ProPub works directly with a provenance graph, which may not have been derived from an underlying workflow. A sanitization requirement might assert that certain data associated with a particular node is to be erased, that several nodes are to be abstracted into a single node, or that some nodes are to be deleted; a disclosure constraint might insist that a specific node is always retained in the view. In addition there will usually be global policies which hold across all queries (for example to outlaw "false dependencies" of the kind illustrated earlier in Fig. 2), as well as the usual well-formedness conditions such as acyclicity or bipartiteness.

A unique feature of ProPub is its ability to detect conflicts in the sanitization and disclosure requirements and to assist with their resolution. When conflicts arise, ProPub uses a ranking scheme and various auto-correction strategies to resolve them, with the user also able to intervene to withdraw or modify a constraint in the light of the conflicts. For example in Fig. 6, adapted from [18], a naïve abstraction of three nodes into a single node c_4 violates both acyclicity and bipartiteness:

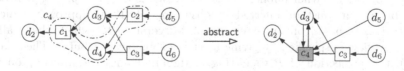

Fig. 6. ProPub: conflict detection

In this case a possible resolution would be to include d_3 into the abstraction as well, removing the cycle and restoring bipartiteness. Should applying a correction induce other conflicts, the process of conflict resolution continues. Only when a conflict-free variant of the query is obtained can a final sanitized view be derived. Any constraints rescinded during conflict resolution are reported alongside the sanitized view, providing a certain level of "meta-provenance", also a unique feature amongst the systems considered here. For example, it might record that a spurious dependency was tolerated in order to accommodate an abstraction. ProPub's logical foundation also means that the final view is guaranteed to have the chosen disclosure and security properties.

Davidson et al. [15,16] tackle a rather different problem with **provenance views**. Workflows are modelled as directed acyclic multigraphs (graphs with potentially more than one edge between any two nodes). Edges are labeled with identifiers called *attributes* which identify the port that the edge starts from; because workflows are acyclic, the semantics of a workflow can be given as a relation R over the set of all attributes, where each tuple consists of the data values that arise during a possible execution. (Equivalently, one can consider each tuple to be a labeling function assigning data values to ports.) In Fig. 7 below, adapted from [15], the workflow consists of three modules computing Boolean functions. Port a_4 of m_1 is consumed by both m_2 and m_3. The relation R for this particular workflow in shown in the middle of Fig. 7. Effectively R is the natural join $R_1 \bowtie R_2 \bowtie R_3$ of the relations R_1, R_2 and R_3 capturing the *extension* (input-output mapping) of the modules individually.

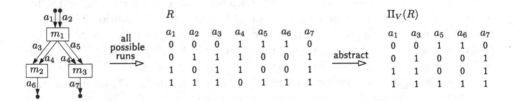

Fig. 7. Provenance views: hiding functional behaviour

Rather than hiding or abstracting parts of a particular run, Davidson et al. are interested in hiding the extension of a sensitive module m_i, namely the relation R_i, regardless of how many different executions the user observes. They classify modules as either public, whose behaviour is known *a priori*, or private, whose behaviour must be inferred by observing R. Their approach, which is quantitative, is based on an extension of ℓ-diversity [24] which they call Γ-*privacy*. A view is specified by giving a set V of visible attributes. The relation $\Pi_V(R)$, the projection of R to V (Fig. 7, right), defines the information that is publicly visible through V. For any positive natural number Γ, a private module is Γ-*private* with respect to V if for each input, the number of possible outputs from that module consistent with $\Pi_V(R)$ is greater than Γ. With only this information, an attacker is unable to predict the output of the module for a given input with probability greater than $1/\Gamma$.

The first paper [15] studies some specific cases, including standalone private modules, multiple private modules, and heterogeneous workflows with a mixture of private and public modules where public modules can be "privatized" by renaming, so that their functional behaviour is no longer known. They show that standalone Γ-privacy is composable in a workflow consisting only of private modules. The authors also study the problem of finding minimum-cost views, given a cost function stating the penalty of being denied access to hidden attributes. The second paper [16] studies a more general solution for heterogeneous workflows, which involves *propagating* hiding, i.e. hiding attributes of public modules if they might disclose information about hidden attributes of private modules. They present a composability result generalizing the one for the all-private setting, to *single-predecessor* (that is, tree-like) workflows.

The privacy problem studied by Davidson et al. is interesting, but their work so far has a number of drawbacks. In particular, the PTIME bounds for the algorithms for mixed workflows [16] assume a fixed domain size, which in turn means that the size of relation R is treated as a constant. If we take the domain size d and number of attributes a into account, then the size of R is $O(d^a)$, so treating it as a constant may not be realistic. Moreover, it is also not always clear how to choose sensible values of Γ. For example, with a domain of 1024×1024, 8-bit grayscale images, Γ may need to be much higher than 10^6 to provide meaningful privacy, because changing a single grayscale pixel does not hide much information. (This criticism also pertains to other possibilistic definitions of security properties, such opacity [1] and obfuscation [9].) Techniques from quantitative information flow security [12], quantitative opacity [5] or differential privacy [19] may be relevant here.

The **provenance abstraction** approach of **Missier, Bryans, Gamble, Curcin and Danger** [26], implemented as ProvAbs, is based on graph quotienting and finding partionings that satisfy both security needs and well-formedness constraints. Their provenance graphs follow the PROV model [29] and its associated constraints specification [10]. First, Missier et al. consider simple bipartite provenance graphs with node types representing activities and entities, and define three basic graph operations pclose, extend and replace. Intuitively, pclose takes a subgraph which is a candidate for replacement, and grows it until it is convex (there are no paths that lead out of the subgraph and back in again); extend further grows the subgraph until both its "input" nodes and its "output" nodes are homogeneous with respect to node type; and replace contracts such subgraphs to single nodes and adjusts edges to preserve paths.

Figure 8, adapted from [26], illustrates extend and replace. In Fig. 8a, the user selects activity a_2 and entity e_3 for abstraction. Replacing these two nodes by either an activity or an entity whilst preserving paths would violate bipartiteness. In Fig. 8b, extend is used to grow the target subgraph to include e_4, so that the output nodes of the target subgraph are uniformly entities. Replacing the

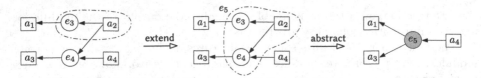

Fig. 8. ProvAbs: growing a partition so that abstraction preserves bipartiteness

subgraph by a single abstract entity e_5 in Fig. 8c is now valid, although it coarsens the (transitive) dependencies by introducing a path between a_4 and a_1.

Having shown how these transformations can be used to preserve basic validity constraints, Missier et al. go on to consider graphs which incorporate the PROV agent node type and associated relations such as attribution and delegation. They consider three cases of increasing sophistication. Grouping a homogeneous set of agents into a single abstract agent is relatively straightforward. Grouping agents and entities together is trickier; the type of the target abstract node (entity or agent) must be specified, and in order to maintain the type-correctness of certain relations between actions and agents (waw, "was associated with") and between entities and agents (wat, "was attributed to"), the subgraph to be abstracted must made larger. Finally, grouping arbitrary node types together presents the additional difficulty of agent-to-agent delegation edges (abo, "acted on behalf of"), which require similar treatment.

Like ProPub, a key feature of ProvAbs is that transformations operate directly on the provenance graph, and are thus more suited to situations where there is no underlying workflow. Missier et al. claim that their system avoids introducing spurious dependencies between nodes. However, their views are quotients, which in general over-approximate dependencies, so technically this claim is only correct for provenance applications where dependency is not required to be transitive.

The work of **Cadenhead, Khadilkar, Kantarcioglu and Thuraisingham** [7] on **provenance redaction** is also based on graph rewriting. Their provenance graphs are tripartite and conform to the Open Provenance Model's labeled DAG format [28]. "Redacting", or sanitizing, such a graph has two phases. First, the sensitive region G_Q (typically a single node or a path between two nodes) of the original graph G is isolated using a graph query Q. Then, this region of the graph is transformed according to an obfuscation policy expressed as rewrite rules. A rewrite rule has two components: a production rule $r : L \to R$, where L is matched against subgraphs of G_Q, plus an *embedding* specification, which determines how edges are to be connected to R once it has replaced L. The rewrites involve graph operations such as vertex contraction, edge contraction, path contraction and node relabeling.

In Fig. 9, adapted from [7], hexagons represent agents, rectangles represent processes, and circles represent artifacts. In the left graph, the gray triangle indicates an area of the graph that was previously redacted. On the right, a further subgraph is redacted by contracting the the wcb ("was controlled by")

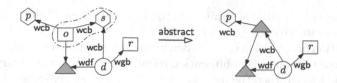

Fig. 9. Provenance redaction: abstraction by edge contraction

edge relating a heart operation o to the surgeon s who carried out the operation, and replacing the two nodes by another gray triangle.

Cadenhead et al.'s work is implementation-focused. Several formal definitions are given but not always made use of, and neither are their provenance or disclosure properties analyzed. One issue they do not appear to address, in contrast for example to Missier et al. (above), is preservation of basic well-formedness properties of the provenance graph. While edge contraction (as a particular kind of quotient) preserves dependencies, the interaction with tripartiness is potentially problematic. For example in the view in Fig. 9, the new triangle has both an incoming *and* an outgoing wcb edge, because it subsumes both an agent and a process. Moreover, as the authors themselves point out, the obfuscation policy is only applied to a subgraph G_Q of the original graph G. Sensitive information available elsewhere in G will not be subject to the policy. Information flow techniques [17] may be relevant here.

5   Conclusions and Future Directions

We conclude our survey with a brief feature comparison, summarised in Table 1. The column headings refer to broad feature areas (discussed in more detail below); ● indicates reasonably comprehensive support for that feature, ○ little or no support, and ◐ somewhere in between. Necessarily this is a somewhat simplistic assessment.

Integrity. We divide integrity features into basic integrity maintenance (**Int**) and integrity of causal or dependency structure (**Dep**). Even systems that make some effort to preserve the latter, such as provenance redaction, may in so doing

Table 1. Feature comparison for the approaches surveyed

System	Int	Dep	Acc	Qry	Sem	Form	Conf	Meta
ZOOM [2,13]	◐	●	◐	○	◐	○	○	○
Security views [8]	◐	◐	●	○	○	○	◐	○
Surrogates [3]	○	◐	●	○	○	○	◐	○
ProPub [18]	◐	◐	●	●	○	●	●	◐
Provenance views [15,16]	○	◐	◐	◐	◐	●	○	○
ProvAbs [26]	●	●	●	◐	○	○	◐	○
Provenance redaction [7]	◐	●	●	●	○	○	○	○

violate low-level integrity constraints. In the future it seems likely that users will take low-level integrity for granted.

Preservation or reflection of dependency structure is more challenging because of the inherent tensions with obfuscation requirements. When arbitrary nodes or edges can be deleted, then the user may be responsible for repairing the damage, as with security views or surrogates. ProPub offers greater automation through conflict detection; ProvAbs and provenance redaction make safer (if simplistic) assumptions, by working mainly with quotient views.

Sanitization. Sanitization features range from explicit fine-grained access control (**Acc**), which all systems provide in some form or another, to query-based abstraction (**Qry**), as offered by ProPub and provenance redaction. Query-based systems typically subsume fine-grained access control, via fine-grained queries.

Formal and semantic properties. Few of the surveyed systems consider the problem of relating provenance views to the semantics of the underlying system (**Sem**). Instead, they operate directly on provenance graphs, without regard to how the graph was created. This is flexible, but means one cannot easily treat the provenance view as an (abstracted) account of how something was computed. ZOOM stands out in this respect, in relating provenance views to workflow views for simple kinds of workflow. On the other hand, this is a hard problem to solve in a general way.

Few existing systems provide formal guarantees of obfuscation or disclosure properties (**Form**). ProPub has the advantage of a solid logical foundation. The Γ-privacy of provenance views is a formal notion of (quantitative) opacity, but the goal is somewhat different from the other systems considered.

Conflict detection and resolution. As mentioned, ProPub stands out in being able to automatically detect conflicts between obfuscation and disclosure requirements (**Conf**), thanks to its logic-based approach. It is also the only system which makes conflict resolution an explicit and persistent part of the process, providing a certain level of "meta-provenance" for the sanitization process (**Meta**). If provenance security techniques are widely adopted, it seems likely that how provenance is manipulated to hide or reveal information will itself often be the point of interest (cf. "provenance of provenance" [29]).

Undoubtedly, controlling access to sensitive provenance metadata is of growing importance, and moreover we sometimes simply want to deliver provenance information at a particular level of detail. However, as the summary above highlights, current methods for provenance sanitization are immature. Future effort should focus on semantics, formal guarantees, and techniques for detecting and resolving conflicting policies.

Acknowledgments. We are grateful to Jeremy Bryans, Brian Gamble, and Paolo Missier for comments on this paper. Effort sponsored by the Air Force Office of Scientific Research, Air Force Material Command, USAF, under grant number FA8655-13-1-3006. The U.S. Government and University of Edinburgh are authorized to reproduce and distribute reprints for their purposes notwithstanding any copyright notation thereon.

References

1. Bailliage, R.D., Mazaré, L.: Using unification for opacity properties. In: Proceedings of WITS 2004, pp. 165–176 (2004)
2. Biton, O., Cohen-Boulakia, S., Davidson, S.B., Hara, C.S.: Querying and managing provenance through user views in scientific workflows. In: ICDE, pp. 1072–1081. IEEE (2008)
3. Blaustein, B.T., Chapman, A., Seligman, L., Allen, M.D., Rosenthal, A.: Surrogate parenthood: protected and informative graphs. PVLDB 4(8), 518–527 (2011)
4. Braun, U., Shinnar, A., Seltzer, M.: Securing provenance. In: Proceedings of the 3rd Conference on Hot Topics in Security, pp. 4:1–4:5 (2008)
5. Bryans, J.W., Koutny, M., Mu, C.: Towards quantitative analysis of opacity. In: Palamidessi, C., Ryan, M.D. (eds.) TGC 2012. LNCS, vol. 8191, pp. 145–163. Springer, Heidelberg (2013)
6. Buneman, P., Chapman, A.P., Cheney, J.: Provenance management in curated databases. In: SIGMOD 2006, pp. 539–550 (2006)
7. Cadenhead, T., Khadilkar, V., Kantarcioglu, M., Thuraisingham, B.: Transforming provenance using redaction. In: SACMAT, pp. 93–102. ACM, New York (2011)
8. Chebotko, A., Chang, S., Lu, S., Fotouhi, F., Yang, P.: Scientific workflow provenance querying with security views. In: WAIM 2008, pp. 349–356 (2008)
9. Cheney, J.: A formal framework for provenance security. In: CSF, pp. 281–293. IEEE (2011)
10. Cheney, J., Missier, P., Moreau, L. (eds.) De Nies, T.: Constraints of the PROV data model. W3C recommendation, W3C, April 2013
11. Chong, S.: Towards semantics for provenance security. In: Cheney, J. (ed.) TaPP 2009. USENIX (2009)
12. Clark, D., Hunt, S., Malacaria, P.: Quantitative analysis of the leakage of confidential data. Electron. Notes Theor. Comput. Sci. 59(3), 238–251 (2002). QAPL 2001
13. Cohen-Boulakia, S., Biton, O., Cohen, S., Davidson, S.: Addressing the provenance challenge using zoom. Concurr. Comput. Pract. Exp. 20(5), 497–506 (2008)
14. Davidson, S.B., Freire, J.: Provenance and scientific workflows: challenges and opportunities. In: Proceedings of SIGMOD 2008, pp. 1345–1350. ACM, New York, (2008)
15. Davidson, S.B., Khanna, S., Milo, T., Panigrahi, D., Roy, S.: Provenance views for module privacy. In: PODS, pp. 175–186 (2011)
16. Davidson, S.B., Milo, T., Roy, S.: A propagation model for provenance views of public/private workflows. In: ICDT, pp. 165–176. ACM, New York (2013)
17. Denning, D.E., Denning, P.J.: Certification of programs for secure information flow. Commun. ACM 20(7), 504–513 (1977)
18. Dey, S.C., Zinn, D., Ludäscher, B.: PROPUB: towards a declarative approach for publishing customized, policy-aware provenance. In: Bayard Cushing, J., French, J., Bowers, S. (eds.) SSDBM 2011. LNCS, vol. 6809, pp. 225–243. Springer, Heidelberg (2011)
19. Dwork, C.: Differential privacy. In: Bugliesi, M., Preneel, B., Sassone, V., Wegener, I. (eds.) ICALP 2006, Part II. LNCS, vol. 4052, pp. 1–12. Springer, Heidelberg (2006)
20. Hasan, R., Sion, R., Winslett, M.: Introducing secure provenance: problems and challenges. In: Proceedings of StorageSS 2007, pp. 13–18. ACM, New York (2007)

21. Hasan, R., Sion, R., Winslett, M.: Preventing history forgery with secure provenance. Trans. Storage **5**, 12:1–12:43 (2009)
22. Lu, W., Miklau, G., Immerman, N.: Auditing a database under retention policies. VLDB J. **22**(2), 203–228 (2013)
23. Lyle, J., Martin, A.: Trusted computing and provenance: better together. In: Proceedings of TAPP 2010. USENIX Association, Berkeley (2010)
24. Machanavajjhala, A., Kifer, D., Gehrke, J., Venkitasubramaniam, M.: L-diversity: Privacy beyond k-anonymity. ACM Trans. Knowl. Discov. Data **1**(1) Article 3 (2007)
25. Martin, A., Lyle, J., Namilkuo, C.: Provenance as a security control. In: Proceedings of TaPP 2012, pp. 3–3. USENIX Association, Berkeley (2012)
26. Missier, P., Bryans, J., Gamble, C., Curcin, V., Danger, R.: Provenance graph abstraction by node grouping. Technical report CS-TR-1393, Newcastle University (2013)
27. Moreau, L.: The foundations for provenance on the web. Found. Trends in Web Sci. **2**(2–3), 99–241 (2010)
28. Moreau, L., Clifford, B., Freire, J., Futrelle, J., Gil, Y., Groth, P., Kwasnikowska, N., Miles, S., Missier, P., Myers, J., Plale, B., Simmhan, Y., Stephan, E., Van den Bussche, J.: The OPM core specification (v1.1). Future Gener. Comput. Syst. **27**(6), 743–756 (2011)
29. Moreau, L., Missier, P. (eds.): PROV-DM: The PROV Data Model. W3C Recommendation REC-prov-dm-20130430 (2013)
30. Zhang, J., Chapman, A., LeFevre, K.: Do you know where your data's been? – tamper-evident database provenance. In: Jonker, W., Petković, M. (eds.) SDM 2009. LNCS, vol. 5776, pp. 17–32. Springer, Heidelberg (2009)

A Provenance-Based Policy Control Framework for Cloud Services

Mufajjul Ali[1](✉) and Luc Moreau[2]

[1] Orange Labs, London, UK
mufajjul.ali@orange.com
[2] University of Southampton, Southampton, UK

Abstract. In the context of software, provenance holds the key to retaining a mirror instance of the lifespan of a service, which can be replayed/reproduced from the beginning. This entails the nature of invocations that took place, how/where the data were created, modified, updated and the user's engagement with the service. With such an encyclopedia of information, it opens up a diversity of value-added features (compliance control, accountability) that can improve the usability of a service.

In this paper, we extend our previous work on the provenance-based policy language (cProvl) and model (cProv) by proposing a preliminary policy control framework. The framework provides the necessary building blocks for integrating and developing services that are able to generate and use provenance data for provenance-based compliance control, which runs on a XACML engine. We demonstrate the capability of the framework by applying it to a service case, and conduct benchmarks to determine its scalability and performance.

Keywords: Provenance · XACML · cProv · Prov · cProvl · Share · Cloud

1 Introduction

Cloud computing is built on top of many existing technologies, to support features such as the dynamic scaling, resource pooling, pay-per usage and on-demand self-services. While cloud computing adoption is gaining momentum in the industry, the compliance and accountability remain its main Achilles heel [1]. One approach to addressing this problem is through the use of provenance [2]. Provenance is a well understood area in art and digital-libraries, where lineage, pedigree and source plays a major role in understanding how things have been derived, and in determining the collection's authenticity and value [3]. Provenance helps in answering questions such as: What processes were involved in transforming the data? Did the processes conform to all necessary regulations? Where in the actual physical location within the cloud has the execution of data taken place? Answering these questions are pivotal to achieving compliance in the cloud environment.

© Springer International Publishing Switzerland 2015
B. Ludäscher and B. Plale (Eds.): IPAW 2014, LNCS 8628, pp. 127–138, 2015.
DOI: 10.1007/978-3-319-16462-5_10

In additional to provenance, a policy control mechanism is required to define the compliance requirements, and to be acted upon if a violation occurs. XACML [4], an industry wide standard is deployed by many organizations as standard policy-based control for their services. Organizations are looking to migrate their existing services to the cloud. Having the ability to use the existing policy control would minimize the cost of migration, reduce deployment effort, and mitigating the risk of using unproven technology. Its architecture is modular and provides scope for extensibility. However, it does not cater for provenance data.

In our previous work [5], we have defined a provenance ontology that extends the Prov model [6] for cloud-based services, and a provenance-based policy language that can be mapped to the XACML policy language. This allows us to express questions and conditions in the form of policies, and execute them using the ontology via the extended XACML engine.

The contributions of this paper are as follows: First, we propose a policy control framework that leverages on the XACML architecture and the Prov standard for industrial cloud-based applications. Secondly, the framework is integrated with a cloud-based service (a Telco's file sharing service) to support its compliance requirements. Finally, we perform benchmarks on the framework's integration with the service to evaluate its scalability and performance.

2   A Telco Service

ConfidenShare is a cloud service developed by a Telco Operator for the sharing of sensitive and non-sensitive information such as a file, meeting data and other data with users within the cloud environment. It uses Proxy re-encryption [7], a cryptographic technique that allows the sharing of all or part of user's data with one or more parties. ConfidenShare is interoperable with many existing cloud providers, and can meet varying country-specific cloud strategies. While the file sharing mechanism is secure, it does not have the necessary means of declaring constraints, capturing requirements and compliance control for them.

2.1   Service Requirements

Files are typically categorized as 'confidential', 'restricted' or 'general'.

A 'confidential' file is the most restricted and only the originator (creator of the document) is allowed to initiate the share.

A 'restricted' file, is where an originator can share with one or more recipients. Any changes or modifications can only be shared with the originator and recipients of the original document only.

A 'general' file can be shared with any users, and there are no explicit restrictions on the re-sharing. A further restriction can be added to the 'general' category to indicate if the file shared is modifiable, if it isn't it can only be shared unmodified.

Any user no longer registered with the service, all traceable files associated with that user cannot be shared, and should be removed. This is in accordance to the "EU:Right to erasure" legislation [8]. Unless explicit permission has been given by the user to allow the retention of data they have already shared with other users.

In all cases the provenance of the documents are intact. From the service requirements, we can derive policies such as:

Policy 1 - If a file (fileA) is marked as 'confidential', only the originator is allowed to share it with another user (userB), re-sharing by userB is not allowed.

The provenance data contains information related to when the file was created, by whom, where, and other information that can be used to determine if it is in compliance with this policy or not.

Policy 2 - If a user (userA) is 'removed' from the service, any shared files (file X) by this user cannot be shared further (userB).

When a user is deleted, by law, all the data associated with the user must be deleted, this includes all the shared files. Provenance data can be used to check for the origin of a file. If the originator of the file is no longer with the system, then any derived or shared copy of the file can be identified from the provenance data and prevent further shares.

In order to fulfill these requirements, the following is necessary:

- Integration of the provenance capabilities to the 'ConfidenShare' service. The generated provenance data can be used to check for compliance breaches, which are fundamental to service level agreements.
- Declaration of requirements as policies, which are to run in a compliance control engine to determine and act upon the compliance status (this will require the generated provenance data).

2.2   Background

A number of provenance-based frameworks have been proposed [9,10]. Kepler is a provenance framework designed to work with workflow management for collecting, and processing of provenance data. It provides three APIs: recording, query and management for handling such task, as well as algorithms for tracking and finding files. While their solution works well for workflows, it is not generic enough [9]. Karma is also a workflow-based framework [11] similar to Kepler, but does not have the additional processing algorithms and neither incorporates any support for provenance-based policy control.

Tsai, W.-T. et al. [12] discusses issues related to the data provenance in SOA; focusing on the security, reliability and integrity of the data. They also propose a SOA data-provenance framework [13], which is a more advanced version proposed earlier by Rajbhandari, S et al. [14]. This framework is based on the non-standard provenance model, and entails functionalities such as multiple data provenance classification (minimal provenance, time-based, event-based, etc.), data collection (actor-based and time-based), dynamic analysis (security policy checking service (SPEC), integration estimation service) and others. The checking source SPEC appears to have some degree of correlation with our work.

However, no information is supplied in relation to the language used, supported features, limitations, and how it operates on the provenance data.

Aldeco-Perez, R *et al.* [3] proposes a provenance-based compliance framework, based on the Open Provenance Model. The framework provides a processing view (represented as a provenance graph for a specific execution time) and usage policy definition (UPD). It uses the UPD to validate against the processing view for compliance. The framework lacks the integration with the commercial applications and policy standard such as XACML.

K.K. Muniswamy-Reddy *et al.* [15,16] aims to address automation of provenance collection, by proposing three protocols for storing provenance for their existing cloud service. The provenance data is collected using their existing system called PASS (Provenance aware storage system) [17]. Any objects stored in the system automatically extracts the provenance data related to it, for example a system call read, write, etc. However their solution is proprietary.

In regards to policy, Cheney, J. [18] gives a formal model for security control for provenance, and Martin, A *et al.* [19] provides pertinent details of the applicability of provenance as a security control. PAPEL [20] is a provenance-based policy language which attempts to integrate with XACML with limited expressibility on the provenance data.

C. Dai *et al.* [18], proposes a confidence policy compliance query evaluation, that restricts or grant based on a certain confidence level. However the policy language is fairly restricted.

Much of these works are complementary to our previous work [5], on the provenance-based policy language, but they lack any real mapping and integration with the commercial standard such the Prov and XACML. Our focus is on using standardised policy language and model to be used in commercial applications.

3   Policy Control Framework

It is imperative for the framework to provide ease of integration of the provenance model cProv and policy language (cProvl). In order to support the provenance-based compliance control, with the existing and new commercial cloud-based services. For this purpose, we have leveraged two industrial standards: Prov and XACML architecture, that forms the backbone of the framework's stacks (Fig. 1).

3.1   Client Side Stack

The client stack handles operations such as the integration and generation of provenance data, as well as the request for provenance-based compliance control. More concretely, it is structured as a six layered stack (left image of Fig. 1).

Layer 1 - Defines the actual integration with a service. This is where one or more services are modified to provide provenance capability (this has been applied to the ConfidenShare service (Sect. 2)).

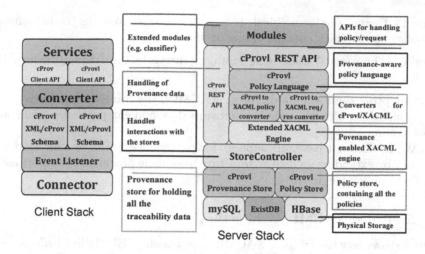

Fig. 1. Framework Stacks

Layer 2 - Provides two APIs (provenance and policy) that assist the generation of the provenance data, and declaration of a request for compliance control.

Layer 3 - Defines a list of converters (native to XML provenance and cProvl XML policy request).

Layer 4 - Provides the underlying schemas for cProv provenance model and cProvl policy request for their XML representations.

Layer 5 - Handles the generated provenance statements via the event handler, statements are placed in a temporary queue for permanent storage.

Layer 6 - Transfers the provenance statements to permanent storage and sends the policy request to the policy controller.

3.2   Server Side Stack

The server side stack defines operations for storing, querying and updating the provenance store. For compliance control, it provides the mechanism for handling policy requests, translation and execution in the extended XACML policy engine.
   It contains five layers (right image of Fig. 1).

Layer 1 - Builds modules for extending functionalities, such as a classifier (not discussed in this paper).

Layer 2 - Provides the server side integration. It has two core APIs (cProv REST API and cProvl REST API). One for handling the provenance data and the other for compliance control. This layer also supplies converters (cProvl to XACML, and XACML to cProvl) for interacting with the XACML engine.

Layer 3 - Provides the mechanism for interfacing with the provenance and policy store.

Layer 4 - Defines the hierarchical storage structure. It contains the provenance and policy store, which consists of one or more services.

Layer 5 - The actual underlying storage (currently the framework uses the exist DB).

By adopting these standards (prov, XACML), the framework is likely to be more compatible with the existing software development processes, tools and infrastructure.

XACML does not have any support for provenance, we have addressed this deficiency by extending its core architecture to provide provenance support using our cProvl policy language.

3.3   Extended XACML Architecture

Figure 2 shows how the five core XACML components: PEP (Policy Enforcement Point), PDP (Policy Decision Point), context handler, PAP (Policy Administration Point) and PIP (Policy Information Point) [4] were extended to support the *provenance-based compliance control.*

PAP (writes XACML policies and makes then available to PDP) module has been extended to allow the creation of cProvl policies, and provides a mapping from cProvl policies to XACML policies, as well as providing storage for these policies.

The PEP (handles the initial incoming service specific request typically from an application) module has been extended to cater for a service request to be translated into cProvl request and stored in the policy store with its provenance. The service response is treated in the same manner.

The context handler is responsible for converting a service request into an XACML request. We provide the support for a cProvl request to be translated into an XACML request. The request is then transferred to the PDP module.

The PDP module determines the outcome of a request. We have introduced new functions to accommodate the handling of provenance data (used by the translated XACML polices). Before making a decision, it may request the context handler for additional attributes via the PIP module (in our case, attribute references to provenance statements).

The PIP module has been extended to interface with the provenance store. It returns the necessary statements requested by the PDP module for decision making.

The context handler receives an XACML response from the PDP module. We have also added the support for an XACML response translated to a cProvl response (stored in the policy store), which is then sent to the PEP module. The PEP translates it to service specific response and enforces the control, i.e. Permit/Deny (detailed mapping is discussed in our previous paper [5]).

To our knowledge, this is the only framework that enables ease of integration of the extended Prov provenance model with the XACML architecture for cloud-based services. The benefit we can see in using this framework is that only the high level APIs can be utilised without the developers requiring knowledge

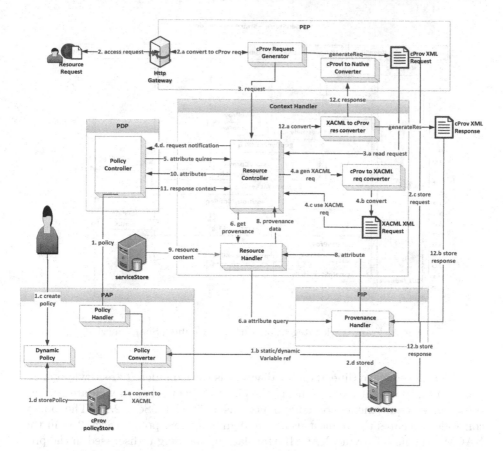

Fig. 2. XACML Extended Architecture to Support Provenance

of the underlying complexity of extended XACML architecture or the provenance model. This can save integration and development time, is less prone to errors, and minimizes the integration complexities, which ultimately will allow developers to focus their efforts on the business logic.

4 Framework Service Integration

We have successfully integrated the framework with the ConfidenShare service (Sect. 2). The service is able to generate provenance data, and apply provenance-based control.

The sequence diagram (Fig. 3) demonstrates the interactions between the framework's components with the service. It shows a user, Bob, invoking a resource share request on the ConfidenShare web client (line 1–3). The client (using cProv client API) generates provenance data for this invocation and interacts with the 'ProvenanceHandler' for translating it to XML Prov elements, then storing it using the cProv server API (line 4–8).

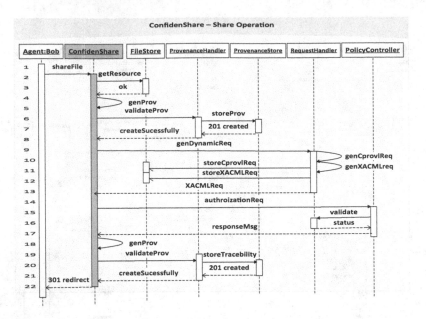

Fig. 3. Framework Integration with the ConfidenShare Service

The next sequence (line 9) on the diagram is the ConfidenShare service generating and initiating a request (using the cProvl Client API) to validate against the service requirements for compliance (as defined in Sect. 2.1). The policy controller executes the request using the defined cProvl policy (Sect. 2.1) in the XACML engine (cProvl to XACML translation/mapping is discussed in the previous paper [5]) (line 14–16). If the response is granted, then the resource share is permitted, and the provenance record is updated (line 17–22).

An example of a dynamic request using the Client Stack (cProvl Client API) for a share request is as follows:

```
// service provenance-based control request integration
dpr.constructRequest(session.get(SESSION_USER_NAME), false, filename.getName(), false,
    null, 'a-share', true, null); //generates a cProvl request (see below)
```

This example can be read as a 'ConfidenShare' session user ('Bob') is requesting for authorization to share a file (document1). This request gets automatically translated into an cProvl request, as follows.

```
<cprovl:PolicyRequest ....> <cprovl:Agent isRef="false"prov:id="confidenshare:ag-Bob"/>
    <cprovl:Entity prov:id="confidenshare:e-document1">
        <cprovl:reqField>cprovd:Resource</cprovl:reqField>
        <cprovl:fieldValue isRef="false">confidenshare:e-document1 </cprovl:fieldValue>
    </cprovl:Entity> ...
</cprovl:PolicyRequest>
```

An XACML equivalent of this request is as follows.

```
<Request xmlns="urn:oasis:names:tc:xacml:3.0:core:schema:wd-17 ... CombinedDecision="false">
  <Attributes Category="urn:oasis:names:tc:xacml:1.0:subject-category:access-subject">
    <Attribute ... AttributeId="urn:oasis:names:tc:xacml:3.0:subject-id">
      <AttributeValue DataType="urn:oasis:names:tc:xacml:3.0:data-type:xpathExpression"
      XPathCategory="urn:oasis:names:tc:xacml:1.0:subject-category:access-subject">ex:ag-Bob
      </AttributeValue> </Attribute> ...
  </Attributes>...
</Request>
```

This request is used by the extended XACML engine to determine if it is compliant with the defined policies (Sect. 2.1) using the 'ConfidenShare' service's provenance data.

By making use of the APIs, major alterations to the service and business logic were avoided when integrating the framework with the ConfidenShare service. This will ultimately increase the level of trust using provenance-based compliance control in order to empower the user to verify the compliance of SLAs of cloud-based services.

5   Evaluation of Performance

Following is an evaluation of our integration of the framework with the ConfidensShare service in terms of performance and scalability. Our interest is in the provenance model, compliance control engine and policy statements. The machine used is an Intel (R) Core (TM) i7-2820QM CPU @2.30 GHZ, with 6Gb of RAM and 600Gb of disk space.

Hypothesis 1 (Service Statements). *The integration of the cProv provenance model with the 'ConfidenShare' service generates and stores provenance data at a relatively constant time in relation to the running of the service.*

Method. We generate and store the provenance statements using the cProv client API, and cProv REST API. Policy one requires a minimum of 10 statements to execute, while 20 statements for policy two. This process is repeated 1000 times and added to the existing provenance graph. This produces two graphs of 10,000 and 20,000 statements. The time it takes between the creation and storage of statements are recorded as a unit of 10 statements in the first graph and 20 in the second (resulting in 2000 measurements).

Analysis. Figure 4 shows a good correlation between the provenance entries (generation & insertion) and the time. For every statement, on average, it required 34.371 ms. On average per unit it took 314 ms in graph one and 746 ms in graph two. This indicates the provenance store performance for both policies are linear and in theory the store is scalable. The 34.371 ms overhead for provenance integration is favorable for the 'ConfidenShare' service.

Hypothesis 2 (Compliance Control). *The cProvl policies related to the 'ConfidenShare' runs in a XACML engine to support compliance control. It is likely to add some overhead costs relative to the number of provenance statements that are required in the policy execution.*

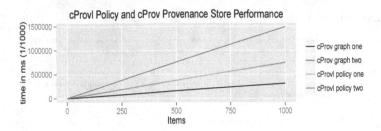

Fig. 4. Policy and Provenance Store Result

Method. We use the static cProvl policy one and two of the ConfidenShare service (Sect. 2). The requests for policies are generated dynamically using cProvl client API, which are then translated into an XACML equivalent and executed in a extended XACML engine. The engine uses the provenance data obtained based on the previous method to evaluate each policy. This process is repeated 1000 times and the start/finish times are recorded.

Analysis. From Fig. 4, we can also see policy one's execution took on average time of 731.99 ms (386.37 ms without prov generation/storage time) per execution and for policy two it took 1265.22 ms (518.77 without cProv). The addition of the provenance compliance control almost doubles the overhead cost. This may be due to the complex architecture (see Fig. 2), however, the performance is still relatively good.

Hypothesis 3 (Policy Statements). *The number of statements within a policy determines the execution time. Target statements are likely to take less time to execute compared to the conditional statements, but both should have a relatively constant execution time.*

Method. Policy one(Sect. 2) contains four targets and three conditional statements (see our previous paper [5] for further explanation). *A new policy statement (resource related) is added incrementally* to the existing policy per execution. This process is repeated 100 times, first with conditional statements, and then with target statements. The time it takes to execute a policy, from the request to the response and excluding the policy update time, is recorded. A total of 200 measurements (100 target statements and 100 conditional statements).

Analysis. As it can be seen from Fig. 5, with each addition of a policy statement, there is proportional increase in the time (30 ms) it takes to execute the policy, which is linear. The condition statements take longer to execute than the target. This is as expected because they are multi-valued and contain dynamic variable references, whereas targets are typically single valued statements.

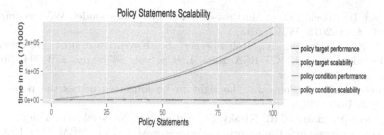

Fig. 5. Policy Statements Scalability Result

6   Conclusion

In this paper, we have presented a provenance-aware policy control framework that provides client and server stacks for integrating provenance model and provenance-based compliance control seamlessly.

We have successfully integrated the framework with the 'ConfidenShare' service, and have conducted few benchmarks. The results show a good linear relationship between the generation and storage of prov statements with an average of 34.3 ms per statement. The integration of the policy language adds around 0.9 s. Both, in theory, are scalable. In regards to policy statements, with each additional statement, the execution time increases by around 30 ms.

We can conclude from the benchmark results, the integration of the framework with the 'ConfidenShare', can add up to 2 s to support compliance based control (with two policies), which is reasonable and encouraging. However, for a commercial deployment, we would need to take into account the network lag, bandwidth, distribution of service components, and other factors to get a true value of the overhead cost of adopting provenance based policy control [21].

Acknowledgments. The first author would like to thank Rafel Uddin, Kashif Chawdhry, Tansir Ahmed and other members of Orange Labs for their support.

References

1. Pearson, S.: Toward accountability in the cloud. IEEE Internet Comput. **15**, 64–69 (2011)
2. Weitzner, D.J., Abelson, H., Berners-Lee, T., Feigenbaum, J., Hendler, J., Sussman, G.J.: Information accountability. Commun. ACM **51**, 82–87 (2008)
3. Aldeco-Perez, R., Moreau, L.: Information accountability supported by a provenance-based compliance framework (2009)
4. Rissanen, E.: Extensible access control markup language (xacml) version 3.0. (2010). http://docs.oasis-open.org/xacml/3.0/xacml-3.0-core-spec-cs-01-en.pdf
5. Ali, M., Moreau, L.: A provenance-aware policy language (cprovl) and a data traceability model (cprov) for the cloud. In: 2013 Third International Conference on Cloud and Green Computing (CGC), pp. 479–486 (2013)

6. Moreau, L., Missier, P., et al.: Prov-dm: The prov data model. W3c recommendation 30 April 2013, W3C (2013)
7. Ateniese, G., Benson, K., Hohenberger, S.: Key-private proxy re-encryption. In: Fischlin, M. (ed.) CT-RSA 2009. LNCS, vol. 5473, pp. 279–294. Springer, Heidelberg (2009)
8. Ambrose, M.L., Ausloos, J.: The right to be forgotten across the pond. J. Inf. Policy 3, 1–23 (2013)
9. Mouallem, P., Barreto, R., Klasky, S., Podhorszki, N., Vouk, M.: Tracking files in the Kepler provenance framework. In: Winslett, M. (ed.) SSDBM 2009. LNCS, vol. 5566, pp. 273–282. Springer, Heidelberg (2009)
10. Simmhan, Y.L., Plale, B., Gannon, D., Marru, S.: Performance evaluation of the karma provenance framework for scientific workflows. In: Moreau, L., Foster, I. (eds.) IPAW 2006. LNCS, vol. 4145, pp. 222–236. Springer, Heidelberg (2006)
11. Simmhan, Y., Plale, B., Gannon, D.: A framework for collecting provenance in data-centric scientific workflows. In: International Conference on Web Services, ICWS '06, pp. 427–436 (2006)
12. Tsai, W., Wei, X., Chen, Y., Paul, R., Chung, J.Y., Zhang, D.: Data provenance in soa: security, reliability, and integrity. Serv. Oriented Comput. Appl. 1, 223–247 (2007)
13. Tsai, W.T., Wei, X., Zhang, D., Paul, R., Chen, Y., Chung, J.Y.: A new soa data-provenance framework. In: Eighth International Symposium on Autonomous Decentralized Systems, ISADS '07, pp. 105–112 (2007)
14. Rajbhandari, S., Walker, D.: Incorporating provenance in service oriented architecture. In: International Conference on Next Generation Web Services Practices, NWeSP 2006, pp. 33–40 (2006)
15. Muniswamy-Reddy, K.K., Macko, P., Seltzer, M.: Making a cloud provenance-aware. In: First Workshop on on Theory and Practice of Provenance. TAPP'09, pp. 12:1–12:10. USENIX Association, Berkeley (2009)
16. Muniswamy-Reddy, K.K., Macko, P., Seltzer, M.: Provenance for the cloud. In: Proceedings of the 8th USENIX Conference on File and Storage Technologies. FAST'10, pp. 15–14. USENIX Association, Berkeley (2010)
17. Seltzer, M., Muniswamy-Reddy, K., Holland, D., Braun, U., Ledlie, J.: Provenance-aware storage systems. In: Proceedings of the USENIX Annual Technical Conference (USENIX06) (2006)
18. Cheney, J.: A formal framework for provenance security. In: 2011 IEEE 24th Computer Security Foundations Symposium (CSF), pp. 281–293 (2011)
19. Martin, A., Lyle, J., Namilkuo, C.: Provenance as a security control. TaPP. USENIX (2012)
20. Ringelstein, C., Staab, S.: PAPEL: a language and model for provenance-aware policy definition and execution. In: Hull, R., Mendling, J., Tai, S. (eds.) BPM 2010. LNCS, vol. 6336, pp. 195–210. Springer, Heidelberg (2010)
21. Hsu, P.F., Ray, S., Li-Hsieh, Y.Y.: Examining cloud computing adoption intention, pricing mechanism, and deployment model. Int. J. Inf. Manage. 34, 474–488 (2014)

Applying Provenance to Protect Attribution in Distributed Computational Scientific Experiments

Luiz M.R. Gadelha Jr.[1]([✉]) and Marta Mattoso[2]

[1] National Laboratory for Scientific Computing, Petrópolis, Brazil
lgadelha@lncc.br
[2] Federal University of Rio de Janeiro, Rio de Janeiro, Brazil
marta@cos.ufrj.br

Abstract. The automation of large scale computational scientific experiments can be accomplished with the use of scientific workflow management systems, which allow for the definition of their activities and data dependencies. The manual analysis of the data resulting from their execution is burdensome, due to the usually large amounts of information. Provenance systems can be used to support this task since they gather details about the design and execution of these experiments. However, provenance information disclosure can also be seen as a threat to correct attribution, if the proper security mechanisms are not in place to protect it. In this article, we address the problem of providing adequate security controls for protecting provenance information taking into account requirements that are specific to e-Science. Kairos, a provenance security architecture, is proposed to protect both prospective and retrospective provenance, in order to reduce the risk of intellectual property disputes in computational scientific experiments.

1 Introduction

Provenance allows for the precise description of how a computational scientific experiment was set up, and what happened during its execution. It also makes it easier to reproduce an experiment for the purpose of verification. New scientific results may be derived from the analysis of an experiment, which may produce valuable intellectual property. Therefore, this ease of reproducibility can also be seen as a threat to intellectual property, if the proper security mechanisms are not in place to protect provenance information. This article follows the computer security terminology used by Anderson [3]. An *entity* can be defined as a person, a computer system or an organization. *Secrecy* can be defined as the property of access to some information being limited to a number of entities. Particular cases of secrecy are *confidentiality*, when a group of entities can limit access to some information they share, and *privacy*, when an entity is able to limit access to some information it knows. *Integrity* is the property of preventing unauthorized or accidental modifications to some information. *Authenticity* is the assurance of identity of an entity in a communication. A *threat* is a possible event that may

B. Ludäscher and B. Plale (Eds.): IPAW 2014, LNCS 8628, pp. 139–151, 2015.
DOI: 10.1007/978-3-319-16462-5_11

compromise the protection of a system. A *vulnerability* is property of a system that, in conjunction with a threat, may cause a system to be compromised. An *adversary* can be defined as an entity that seeks to exploit some vulnerability. One needs to identify threats, vulnerabilities and the potential damage to provenance information, and to propose mechanisms to reduce or eliminate the risk of these vulnerabilities being explored. The lack of adequate security controls may also lead to vulnerabilities that can cause provenance information being accessed without permission, or being modified intentionally or accidentally. Many scientific communities, such as the life sciences, are sensitive to security issues, so the absence of appropriate security controls may prevent wider adoption of provenance systems in production environments in these areas. Kairos is not as relevant, but still can be applied, in *Open Science*, where all the steps in a scientific experiment are publicly accessible during its execution and often open to participation. In this case, intellectual property protection is usually not a concern due to the transparency of this methodology. The main objective of this work is to address the problem of providing adequate security controls for protecting the authorship of computational scientific experiments, taking into account the requirements that are specific to e-Science. These requirements include, as we describe later in this article, being able to share scientific workflow provenance without loosing control on intellectual property. The early steps in the life cycle of a computational experiment, such as the design phase, are critical in the production of intellectual property since it is typically where the hypothesis of the experiment is defined. In previous work, we have defined Kairos [12], a security architecture for protecting the authorship of computational scientific experiments by securing retrospective provenance information. However it lacked mechanisms for protecting prospective provenance information. In this work, we improve Kairos by including such mechanisms, allowing for security controls to be applied at an earlier stage of the computational experiment, the design phase, for protecting hypothesis formulation. Applying security controls in this phase is more effective since it is less vulnerable to attacks that are typical of distributed environments used in the execution phase of the experiment. A combination of digital signatures and cryptographic timestamps [16] are used to build verifiable assertions on authorship and temporal information about the computational experiment.

This work has the following contributions: a threat model for provenance in e-Science; a new version of Kairos comprising extended security support to different phases of the experiment; an evaluation with the proposed techniques using a real application with provenance records from the Swift system [26]; and an overhead analysis of the security controls implemented in this new version of Kairos.

The remainder of this article is organized as follows. In Sect. 2, we review related work in this subject. In Sect. 3, we present security requirements for provenance systems in the context of e-Science, and describe a threat model for them. In Sect. 4, we extend Kairos [12] by implementing the proposed techniques as an extension of MTCProv [15], a provenance management system for many-task computing. In Sect. 5, we evaluate the implementation both in terms of

additional storage space required and execution time. Finally, in Sect. 6, we close
with some concluding remarks.

2   Related Work

Provenance security is a relatively recent research issue [7,10,17,22,25,27], found
in different areas such as scientific workflows, databases, and storage systems.
There are cases in which the subject of provenance data may lead to privacy
concerns [10]. Intellectual property issues are also frequently mentioned in the
literature about provenance systems [18], a clear indication that provenance
information is a valuable information asset that must be protected. The most
common approach for protecting provenance is to use access control mechanisms to prevent unauthorized access to this information [5,20,21]. This can be
seen as an approach that targets the protection of confidentiality and privacy.
Tan et al. [25] observed that access control is a provenance security requirement and that digital signatures can be used attribution and integrity. Hasan,
Sion and Winslett [17] also target confidentiality of provenance records, they
use asymmetric cryptography to achieve it and integrity is also obtained with
the use of digital signatures. Dai et al. [9] presented an approach that allows
for evaluating data trustworthiness from provenance information before using
it as input to scientific workflows that are often time consuming. Qian et al.
[22] introduce a method for building *editable signatures*, where multiple parties
sign data records in a chained process to assure their trustworthiness. These
approaches focus on assurance mechanisms for provenance information one gets
from third parties. Our work, on the other hand, focuses on protecting provenance information that one owns and wants to share. The main contribution
of this work is the evaluation of security threats to attribution in provenance
systems in the context of e-Science and the proposition of security controls for
protection against these threats. As far as we know, no other work provides protection of computational experiment attribution with the same flexibility as in
the new version of Kairos, allowing for provenance information sharing at the
same time. To our knowledge, none of these approaches found in related work
propose security controls for protecting temporal information, a critical aspect
in asserting attribution as we argue in Sect. 3. Instead, most of them target
controlling access to provenance information. A fundamental limitation of these
approaches is that they restrict scientific collaboration. Due to concerns about
correct attribution, scientists usually start sharing their experiment descriptions
and data more openly only when their results are published in some academic
journal or conference. By protecting the integrity and authenticity of temporal
information, along with authenticity of authorship through digital signatures in
different phases of a computational experiment, the approach proposed in the
new version of Kairos, provenance information can be shared and disseminated
earlier with less concern with respect to maintenance of correct attribution. In
securing log files and audit trails [23] one is concerned with preserving integrity
with the purpose of, for instance, chronologically reproducing an attack. However, differently from Kairos, verifiable assertion of the time-stamp of each event

is not taken into account, which is a requirement in protecting attribution and intellectual property.

3   Security Requirements for Provenance Systems

Scientific research pursues the generation of knowledge [4], which often involves going through the steps of formulating a question, generating a hypothesis, making a prediction, performing an experiment, and analyzing its outcome. If the analysis confirms the hypothesis, one can say that new scientific knowledge was generated as a product. A computational scientific experiment follows a similar knowledge derivation process, in which provenance information supports its analysis phase. Therefore, one can say that provenance information is one the most important information assets for a scientist. In Fig. 1, we describe a model for provenance management systems upon which we analyze security threats. It fits the definition of provenance management system commonly found in surveys about provenance [6]. Provenance may be classified as *prospective*, when it is captured during the workflow design phase and it describes its activities and data dependencies, or as *retrospective*, when it is captured during the workflow execution phase and it describes activity executions and data artifacts generated. This information is used by the scientific workflow management system (SWMS) to plan the execution of the scientific workflow and submit its application components for execution on computational resources. A provenance management system is given by a provenance collection service, a provenance database, and a provenance access service. The provenance collection service gathers prospective and retrospective provenance information and stores it in the provenance database. In our threat model, we are assuming that provenance information is gathered at the workflow level. The provenance access service provides a browsing or querying interface to the provenance database, where users can retrieve provenance information for computational experiment analysis.

Our main objective in this section is to identify threats to the confidentiality, integrity, authenticity, and availability of provenance information. As far as we know, this is the first work to identify these threats and their relationship to intellectual property protection adapted to e-Science. The methodology used follows commonly used steps for modeling threats [24]. First one needs to identify the main information assets of computational scientific experiments. Then, one needs to attribute a value to each of these assets. Next, one needs to identify existing threats to these assets and their likelyhood of materializing as attacks. For each of these threats, the potential loss in case of a successful attack needs to be evaluated as well as the cost of the respective security controls. Finally, depending on the relation between potential loss and cost of security control, one needs to decide whether to accept a risk or to establish protective mechanisms. This risk analysis procedure should be periodically repeated for refinement and for taking emerging threats into consideration. In e-Science, experiments are performed using computational models to simulate phenomena. Therefore all artifacts involved in applying the scientific method *in silico* can be considered

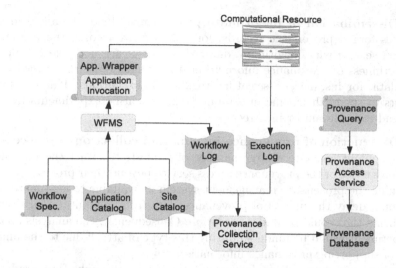

Fig. 1. Provenance management system model (modified from [15]).

as important information assets. This includes its input and output data sets, and all related provenance information. Next, we explore scenarios that illustrate threats to these assets.

{S1} Illegitimate claim of attribution. An adversary is able to intercept network communication between the site from which a scientist submits his or her scientific workflow for execution and the site hosting computational resources that will execute its component applications. If the adversary is able to retrieve retrospective provenance records he/she might be able to infer both the intent and results of the computational scientific experiment. The adversary might obtain the same information if he/she is able, for instance, to obtain privileged administrative rights either in the remote computational resources. Using the provenance records, the adversary might be able reproduce the computational experiment. With knowledge of the intent and the results of the computational experiment, and by having reproduced it, the adversary can eventually claim its attribution before the original author.

{S2} Unauthorized access to private data. If proper access control is not in place in the provenance database, or if network communication is not secured, an adversary might have access to private data manipulated by a scientific computational experiment. For instance, patient data in biomedical workflows. This might legal action because of adequate security controls not being used while manipulating private data.

{S3} Intentional modification of provenance records. An adversary could modify provenance records to mislead the scientist during the analysis of a computational scientific experiment. As a consequence, experiments that had a relevant outcome might be disregarded. The opposite situation is also possible, where one might spend time in experiments that did not produce valuable results.

{S4} Dissemination of illegitimate provenance data. An adversary disseminates forged provenance records, for instance, by feeding the provenance collection service with illegitimate data. If scientists are not able to infer the trustworthiness of provenance information, they might reuse this forged provenance data, for instance, in scientific workflow re-executions. This can induce scientists to spend their time in computational scientific experiments that will likely lead to irrelevant or incorrect results.

{S5} Obstruction of provenance information collection and access. An adversary might generate a large number of requests to either the provenance collection service or the provenance access service beyond their processing capacity, turning the provenance management system unavailable to legitimate users. This would delay the upload of provenance data from computational scientific experiments that could be under execution. Consequently, the analysis phase of the experiment would be hindered during this type of attack due to the unavailability of supporting provenance information.

Provenance records are analogous to laboratory notebooks from traditional scientific experiments. They record the plan of an experiment, its initial parameters, and its outcome. Many scientific institutions maintain guidelines [1] for protecting any resulting intellectual property, observing that the laboratory notebook is one of the most important elements in the process of applying for a patent, where one should prove that the work that lead to some result was performed before the work of anyone else that could claim the same result. One of the guidelines is that notes should be signed and dated and not modified afterwards. In the same manner, provenance records about computational scientific experiments should be protected with appropriate security controls that enable one to assert by whom and when an experiment was performed, and that its provenance records were not modified afterwards. Therefore, to prevent scenario {S1} from happening, security controls that prevent illegitimate claims of attribution are an important security requirement for provenance systems. A combination of digital signatures and cryptographic timestamps [16] were used in the Kairos [12] security architecture for provenance systems to protect retrospective provenance, which we extend in this work to also cover prospective provenance. Since digital signatures also protects the integrity of provenance records, Kairos also prevents scenario {S3} from happening. Preventing scenario {S2} is a concern when personal data is manipulated [10], which is not the predominant case in e-Science. Also, personal data manipulated by scientific workflows is not as important to the scientist as an asset as information that leads to knowledge generation, which is the primary goal in scientific research. Therefore, scenario {S1} has a higher potential damage than scenario {S2}. Both scenarios {S4} and {S5} may lead a scientist to loose significant time by either being unable to access provenance information required for experiment analysis or by consuming data that might not be valid, leading to incorrect results [9,22]. In both of these situations, scientists are often able to detect and correct the problems by either blocking the source of attack and re-establishing availability or by identifying and discarding untrustworthy data sources. Hence, we see both scenarios {S4} and {S5} as less threatening than scenario {S1}, placing the protection of attribution of computational scientific experiments as a security requirement that should be given high priority. In the next section, we present security controls for preventing this particular scenario.

4   Protecting Attribution in Distributed Scientific Workflows

In order to protect intellectual property, Kairos provides tools given by the combined use of digital signatures and the TSP [16] to securely determine the author of provenance assertions and the date in which they were created. The secure time-stamping process involves computing a hash value of the provenance record, which is sent to the Time-Stamping Authority [16] (TSA). The TSA appends to the hash the current date, obtained from a trustworthy source of time. This pair is digitally signed, which requires access to the private key of the TSA, resulting in a *time-stamp receipt*. The time-stamp receipt is sent to the user and can be used to prove the date of creation of the provenance record. This can be done by verifying the date contained in the digital receipt and the digital signature of the TSA, which requires access to the public key of the TSA. We use the notation $\mathsf{Sign}(\langle object \rangle, \langle credential \rangle)$ to indicate the resulting object of a digital signature operation over object $\langle object \rangle$ using credential $\langle credential \rangle$, which consists of computing the hash value of $\langle object \rangle$ and encrypting it with the private key associated to $\langle credential \rangle$; and $\mathsf{TSP}(\langle object \rangle)$ to indicate the digital receipt that results from applying the TSP to object $\langle object \rangle$ which results in a time-stamp receipt, as described in Sect. 1. To also prove authorship of a provenance record, we add a digital signature performed by the scientist. This allows for the verification of both authorship and date of creation of the provenance record. This was proposed in our previous work for protecting retrospective provenance records [12]. However, this process was still susceptible to attacks since retrospective provenance records are usually generated on remote computational resources during the execution of component activities of a scientific workflow. These records can still be vulnerable to network or privileged user attacks from the time they are generated on remote computational resources to the time one applies the security techniques described. Our approach for mitigating this threat consists of extending Kairos to also protect prospective provenance, which is usually generated at the beginning of the computational scientific experiment life cycle, before anything is sent to remote computational resources. The procedure $\mathsf{Sign\text{-}and\text{-}Time\text{-}stamp}(\mathcal{P}, \mathcal{C})$, for digitally signing and time-stamping a provenance trace $\mathcal{P}$ using a credential $\mathcal{C}$ and a TSA, consists of computing $\mathcal{S} = \mathsf{Sign}(\mathcal{P}, \mathcal{C})$; and then computing $\mathcal{T} = \mathsf{TSP}(\mathcal{S})$. Finally $\mathcal{S}$ and $\mathcal{T}$ are stored in the provenance database.

In Table 1, we present the Kairos protocol, for applying the Sign-and-Time-stamp to both the prospective and retrospective provenance traces of a scientific workflow execution run_i, denoted by $\mathcal{P}_{\mathrm{prospective}}(run_i)$ and $\mathcal{P}_{\mathrm{retrospective}}(run_i)$ respectively. The same protocol is illustrated in Fig. 2 using corresponding steps.

The pair of objects produced by the protocol in the Sign-and-Time-stamp steps will be called a *secure provenance receipt*, or $\mathcal{SP}$-receipt.

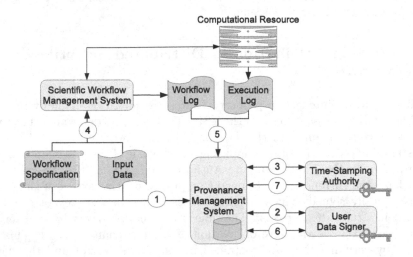

Fig. 2. Kairos: procedure overview.

Table 1. Description of the Kairos protocol.

Step 1. Store $\mathcal{P}_{\text{prospective}}(\text{run}_i)$ in the provenance database;
Steps 2 and 3. Sign-and-Time-stamp$(\mathcal{P}_{\text{prospective}}(\text{run}_i), \mathcal{C})$;
Step 4. Execute scientific workflow;
Step 5. Store $\mathcal{P}_{\text{retrospective}}(\text{run}_i)$ in the provenance database;
Steps 6 and 7. Sign-and-Time-stamp$(\mathcal{P}_{\text{retrospective}}(\text{run}_i), \mathcal{C})$;

An auditor can verify the $\mathcal{SP}$-receipt produced by the protocol using the public keys of both the user and the TSA. To verify the time-stamp receipt one needs to apply the encryption function to the digital signature performed by the TSA using its public key and compare the result with the hash value of the concatenation of the time-stamp and the object produced by the digital signature performed by the user. If they match, the time-stamp receipt is valid. To verify the digital signature performed by the user, the process is analogous and uses the public key of the user instead. A complete validation would also verify the digital signatures in the digital certificates used in the process. These certificates usually form a chain and the validation is completed when one reaches a trusted certificate authority.

Next, we discuss how the protocol can support the preservation of the correct attribution of a computational experiment. Suppose a user is the first one to run a scientific workflow on a remote computational resource, with some specification and input data sets, and follows the Kairos security protocol. Therefore, he or she gets an SP-receipt as result. Now suppose an adversary was able to compromise a computational resource and obtain both the prospective and retrospective provenance traces. If the adversary tries to claim the authorship of the computational scientific experiment, the user can challenge him or her to present an SP-receipt with an earlier time-stamp for prospective provenance. Since the prospective provenance trace was generated and time-stamped before submitting the scientific workflow for execution to the computational resource, the adversary would only be able to access this trace if the submitting host was also compromised. This is less likely to happen since the submitting host is often not shared with other users. Therefore, it is unlikely that the adversary would be able to forge an SP-receipt containing an earlier time-stamp that the one contained in SP-receipt of the user. The portion of the SP-receipt related to the retrospective provenance trace can be useful, for instance, when claiming a patent based on the outcome of the computational experiment, since detailed description of experiment execution and its respective temporal information are critical steps in this process.

The cryptographic data stored in MTCProv by Kairos enables queries involving security aspects of provenance to be answered. Given a dataset produced by a scientific workflow, one can securely determine all the individuals that were involved in the production of a particular scientific dataset. Such query can be answered, for instance, by traversing the provenance graph recursively to determine ancestral processes and datasets, and gathering respective name-value annotations containing digital signatures. One can also, given several provenance traces describing the generation of the same scientific dataset, securely verify which one was the earliest. This can be done, for instance, by retrieving name-value annotations associated to the respective executions containing time-stamping receipts and selecting the earliest one. One important aspect of the answers to these queries is that they are verifiable with cryptographic techniques if one has access to the respective public keys of either the TSA or the author of a digital signature. With these tools, one can more easily assert the *what*, *who*, and *when* of a computational scientific experiment, essential in any patenting process.

5   Implementation and Evaluation

The experiments with the proposed protocol are based on Swift [26], a parallel scripting system that allows for managing many-task scientific workflows. Swift generates provenance traces in its log files, and this information can be exported to a relational database using a data model [15] similar to PROV [19]. Therefore, the techniques presented in this work are also applicable to provenance information represented using these standards. MTCProv [15] is the provenance management component of Swift. It has a query interface with built-in procedures that supports commonly used provenance queries [13,14]. We implemented a prototype of Kairos in the Python programming language as a wrapper that interacts with cryptographic functions of the OpenSSL library [2], Swift and MTCProv. The implementation uses cryptographic functions of the OpenSSL cryptographic toolkit: the `smime` function can be used for the digital signatures and the `ts` function can be used to both execute the TSP and to implement a TSA. The digital signatures and time-stamp receipts generated by the prototype described above are stored as name-value pair annotations associated to the respective scientific workflow execution in the provenance database.

To evaluate the impact of Kairos, we used a a ray-tracing workflow, `c-ray.swift`, that generates a number of scene definitions, invokes a ray-tracing application to render them, and converts the resulting image frames into a video. For each number of iterations, five executions were performed for gathering the storage space and execution time statistics. The evaluation was performed in an environment consisting of a submission host with a six-core Intel Xeon E7540 processor, where Swift was executed, and a remote multi-processed host with two 12-core AMD Opteron 6238 processors, where the computationally demanding application components of the workflow were executed. To scale the execution of the workflow, Swift is able to execute multiple ray-tracing tasks in parallel in this remote multi-processed host using the SSH execution provider. The TSA was installed in the submission host and we included a pause with a random duration between 100 and 400 ms before submitting each time-stamping request, in order to simulate the cost of communication with a remote TSA. In Fig. 3, we plot the extra amount of storage space and execution time required by Kairos.

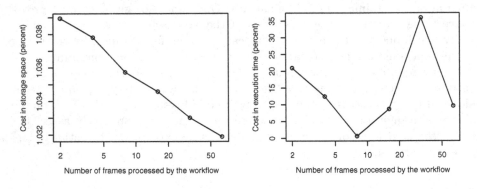

Fig. 3. Impact of Kairos in terms of storage space and execution time.

Since the time-stamp receipt is computed from a hash value, which has a fixed size, it will also have approximately fixed size, apart from minor variations due to padding. The size of digital signature performed with the `smime` tool, grows very slowly when compared to the size of the provenance trace. Therefore, as one can observe in Fig. 3, the size of digital signatures and time-stamp receipts becomes proportionally smaller as the size of the workflow grows. As mentioned in the previous section, the current prototype also stores the original objects that

were signed, in addition to the digital signatures, with the purpose of enabling
signature verification. To preserve the validity of an SP-receipt, the respective
original provenance trace should not be modified. The management of cryptographic data could be improved in Kairos by using cryptographic standards
that have better support for managing both digital signatures and time-stamp
receipts, such as XAdES [8]. The time to execute both the timestamp protocol
and the digital signature procedure depend on the size of the provenance trace,
since a hash value needs to be computed from its content. For the 64-step execution of the workflow, the retrospective trace has about 803 KB in size and it
takes about 35 ms to digitally sign and time-stamp it on the submission host.
Therefore, one can observe in Fig. 3 that the impact in terms of execution time is
smaller than other factors, such as the scheduling heuristics used by the execution provider and the staging-in and staging-out of files between the submission
and the multi-processed host. In the current implementation of Kairos, the granularity used for applying the security controls is at the provenance trace level.
One could alternatively use a finer-grained granularity at the provenance assertion level, however the impact in terms of space would be considerably higher.
Consider, for instance, the 64-step execution of the workflow. It is given by 6403
provenance assertions, with an average size of 124 bytes. The cryptographic data
associated to the digital signatures and time-stamping receipts has an average
size of 3.3 KB per assertion, since it must contain also information about the
credentials used. This results in 20.6 MB of cryptographic data in comparison
to the total provenance trace size of 803 KB, a 26-fold increase. However, the
need of fine-grained protection is diminished by the application of the security
controls to the prospective provenance information prior to the execution of the
scientific workflow.

6   Conclusion

In this work, we survey and analyze security requirements for provenance management systems. We propose that the main information asset of these systems is
given by provenance traces describing the intellectual process of a computational
scientific experiment, which require appropriate security controls for protection. This information is particularly vulnerable in current e-Science infrastructures since they often are transferred to third-party computational resources
which scientists have little control of. Therefore, we have extended Kairos [12],
which secures the authorship and temporal information of computational scientific experiments, to also protect prospective provenance and implemented it as
part of MTCProv [15], a provenance management system for many-task computing. We describe useful queries that can be answered by MTCProv using
the information generated by these security controls and stored in its relational
database. The security controls implemented are essential to any claim of intellectual property, where individuals need to present evidence that they were the
first ones to obtain some scientific result. The improvements implemented in
Kairos, relative to the version presented in [12], allow for better protection of

correct authorship attribution since it applies the proposed security controls also to prospective provenance information at the design phase of the computational scientific experiment life cycle. The hypothesis of the experiment is typically defined at this stage, which makes it critical in applying security controls for protecting intellectual property. At this stage the information is much less exposed to attacks commonly found in remote and distributed computational resources, where retrospective provenance is gathered. We also presented an evaluation of the impact of the proposed techniques in terms of storage space required and execution time, concluding that it is relatively small when they are applied at the provenance trace level of granularity. As in GSI [11], the security controls used in Kairos are based on common public key infrastructure techniques, where certificate authorities are trusted to digitally sign and publish, in the form of digital certificates, public keys associated to users. Therefore, Kairos should be relatively straightforward to integrate to existing grid computing infrastructures, where many large scale computational scientific experiments are performed.

Acknowledgment. This work is partially funded by CNPq and FAPERJ.

References

1. Guidelines for Maintaining a Lab Notebook. Los Alamos National Laboratory (2014)
2. OpenSSL (2014). http://www.openssl.org
3. Anderson, R.: Security Engineering: A Guide to Building Dependable Distributed Systems, 2nd edn. Wiley, New York (2008)
4. Booth, W.C., Colomb, G.G., Williams, J.M.: The Craft of Research, 3rd edn. University of Chicago Press, Chicago (2008)
5. Braun, U., Shinnar, A., Seltzer, M.: Securing provenance. In: Proceedings of the 3rd Conference on Hot Topics in Security, pp. 4:1–4:5. USENIX, Berkeley (2008)
6. Carata, L., Akoush, S., Balakrishnan, N., Bytheway, T., Sohan, R., Selter, M., Hopper, A.: A primer on provenance. Commun. ACM **57**(5), 52–60 (2014)
7. Chebotko, A., Lu, S., Chang, S., Fotouhi, F., Yang, P.: Secure abstraction views for scientific workflow provenance querying. IEEE Trans. Serv. Comput. **3**(4), 322–337 (2010)
8. Cruellas, J., Karlinger, G., Pinkas, D., Ross, J.: XML advanced electronic signatures (XAdES) (2003). http://www.w3.org/tr/xades
9. Dai, C., Lin, D., Bertino, E., Kantarcioglu, M.: An approach to evaluate data trustworthiness based on data provenance. In: Jonker, W., Petković, M. (eds.) SDM 2008. LNCS, vol. 5159, pp. 82–98. Springer, Heidelberg (2008)
10. Davidson, S.B., Khanna, S., Milo, T., Panigrahi, D., Roy, S.: Provenance views for module privacy. In: Proceedings of ACM PODS 2011, pp. 175–186. ACM (2011)
11. Foster, I., Kesselman, C., Tsudik, G., Tuecke, S.: A security architecture for computational grids. In: Proceedings of ACM CCS 1998, CCS 1998, pp. 83–92. ACM, New York (1998)
12. Gadelha, L., Mattoso, M.: Kairos: an architecture for securing authorship and temporal information of provenance data in grid-enabled workflow management systems. In: IEEE Fourth International Conference on eScience (e-Science 2008), pp. 597–602. IEEE (2008)

13. Gadelha, L., Mattoso, M., Wilde, M., Foster, I.: Provenance query patterns for many-task scientific computing. In: Proceedings of the 3rd USENIX Workshop on Theory and Applications of Provenance, TaPP 2011 (2011)
14. Gadelha, L., Wilde, M., Mattoso, M., Foster, I.: Exploring provenance in high performance scientific computing. In: Proceedings of the First Annual Workshop on High Performance Computing Meets Databases, HPCDB 2011, pp. 17–20. ACM, New York (2011)
15. Gadelha, L., Wilde, M., Mattoso, M., Foster, I.: MTCProv: a practical provenance query framework for many-task scientific computing. Distrib. Parallel Databases **30**(5–6), 351–370 (2012)
16. Haber, S., Stornetta, W.: How to time-stamp a digital document. J. Cryptol. **3**(2), 99–111 (1991)
17. Hasan, R., Sion, R., Winslett, M.: Preventing history forgery with secure provenance. ACM Trans. Storage **5**(4), 12:1–12:43 (2009)
18. Miles, S., Groth, P., Branco, M., Moreau, L.: The requirements of recording and using provenance in e-science. J. Grid Comput. **5**(1), 1–25 (2007)
19. Moreau, L., Groth, P.: Provenance: an introduction to PROV. Synth. Lect. Semant. Web: Theory Technol. **3**(4), 1–129 (2013)
20. Nagappan, M., Vouk, M.A.: A model for sharing of confidential provenance information in a query based system. In: Freire, J., Koop, D., Moreau, L. (eds.) IPAW 2008. LNCS, vol. 5272, pp. 62–69. Springer, Heidelberg (2008)
21. Ni, Q., Xu, S., Bertino, E., Sandhu, R., Han, W.: An access control language for a general provenance model. In: Jonker, W., Petković, M. (eds.) SDM 2009. LNCS, vol. 5776, pp. 68–88. Springer, Heidelberg (2009)
22. Qian, H., Xu, S.: Non-interactive editable signatures for assured data provenance. In: Proceedings of ACM CODASPY 2011, pp. 145–156. ACM, New York (2011)
23. Schneier, B., Kelsey, J.: Secure audit logs to support computer forensics. ACM Trans. Inf. Syst. Secur. **2**(2), 159–176 (1999)
24. Swiderski, F., Snyder, W.: Threat Modeling. Microsoft Press, Redmond (2004)
25. Tan, V., Groth, P.T., Miles, S., Jiang, S., Munroe, S.J., Tsasakou, S., Moreau, L.: Security issues in a SOA-based provenance system. In: Moreau, L., Foster, I. (eds.) IPAW 2006. LNCS, vol. 4145, pp. 203–211. Springer, Heidelberg (2006)
26. Wilde, M., Hategan, M., Wozniak, J.M., Clifford, B., Katz, D.S., Foster, I.: Swift: a language for distributed parallel scripting. Parallel Comput. **37**(9), 633–652 (2011)
27. Xu, S., Ni, Q., Bertino, E., Sandhu, R.: A characterization of the problem of secure provenance management. In: Proceedings IEEE International Conference on Intelligence and Security Informatics (ISI 2009), p. 314 (2009)

Provenance Discovery and Data Reproducibility

Looking Inside the Black-Box: Capturing Data Provenance Using Dynamic Instrumentation

Manolis Stamatogiannakis$^{(\boxtimes)}$, Paul Groth, and Herbert Bos

VU University Amsterdam, Amsterdam, The Netherlands
{manolis.stamatogiannakis,p.t.groth,h.j.bos}@vu.nl

Abstract. Knowing the provenance of a data item helps in ascertaining its trustworthiness. Various approaches have been proposed to track or infer data provenance. However, these approaches either treat an executing program as a *black-box*, limiting the fidelity of the captured provenance, or require developers to modify the program to make it provenance-aware. In this paper, we introduce DataTracker, a new approach to capturing data provenance based on *taint tracking*, a technique widely used in the security and reverse engineering fields. Our system is able to identify data provenance relations through dynamic instrumentation of unmodified binaries, without requiring access to, or knowledge of, their source code. Hence, we can track provenance for a variety of well-known applications. Because DataTracker looks inside the executing program, it captures high-fidelity and accurate data provenance.

Keywords: Data provenance · Dynamic · Taint analysis · Taint tracking · PROV

1 Introduction

Provenance is a "record that describes the people, institutions, entities, and activities involved in producing, influencing, or delivering a piece of data or a thing" [26]. This record can be analyzed to understand if data was produced according to regulations, understand the decision making procedure behind the generation of data, used in debugging complex scientific programs, or used to make trust calculations [25].

Given the need for an explicit record to analyze, the community has studied a variety of ways to record or capture data provenance ranging from modifying applications, to explicitly recording provenance, to reconstructing provenance from the computational environment. In designing a provenance capture system, one must make a trade-off between the *fidelity* of the captured provenance (i.e. how accurate the provenance is) and the *effort* on the part of application developers and/or users to make a system provenance-aware.

In this work, we introduce DataTracker, a new system for capturing provenance that practically eliminates the effort of making an application provenance-aware while still producing *high-fidelity provenance*. Analogous to high-fidelity sound, we use this term to refer to provenance information with minimal amounts

© Springer International Publishing Switzerland 2015
B. Ludäscher and B. Plale (Eds.): IPAW 2014, LNCS 8628, pp. 155–167, 2015.
DOI: 10.1007/978-3-319-16462-5_12

of noise (false-positives) and distortion (misrepresentation of existing relations). DataTracker offers both these qualities as it *(a)* eliminates a large number of false-positives by tracking how data are actually used, and *(b)* is able to capture provenance at the byte-level. Our system is based on *dynamic taint analysis* (DTA), a method popular with the security research community, allowing our system to leverage already available infrastructure. It can track data provenance for a wide-variety of unmodified binaries ranging from small command line utilities to full-fledged editors like vim. Moreover, unlike other systems that can be used to capture high fidelity provenance, DataTracker does not require knowledge of the application semantics. Concretely, the contributions of this paper are:

1. A system, DataTracker[1], to transparently capture data provenance of unmodified binaries based on DTA.
2. An evaluation of the system that shows high-fidelity provenance capture on small inspectable programs.
3. Case studies of provenance capture for well-known applications.

The rest of the paper is organized as follows. Section 2 discusses previous work on capturing provenance and introduces dynamic binary instrumentation and taint analysis, the techniques we use to implement DataTracker. In Sect. 3 we present the architecture of our system and detail its implementation. Next, in Sect. 4 we evaluate the provenance produced by it. We use both simple programs that address cases that are not adequately handled by the state of the art, as well as real applications. Finally, in Sect. 5 we discuss some of the aspects of DataTracker, highlighting possible follow-up work.

2   Background and Related Work

2.1   Capturing Provenance

Provenance has been widely studied in the database [5], distributed systems [31] and e-science communities [9]. For a comprehensive overview of the field, we refer the reader to Moreau [24]. Furthermore, Cheney et al. [5] and Simmhan et al. [30] provide specialized reviews for databases and e-science respectively. Here, we focus on systems for provenance capture.

We classify provenance capture approaches on a spectrum in terms of how much intervention they require to make an application provenance-aware. By intervention, we mean the modifications of a program or computational environment to capture provenance. Typically, the more intervention required the higher fidelity of provenance and the greater the required effort is.

At the most detailed level are systems modified to be provenance-aware. For example, Trio DBMS [35] extends a relational database system to cope with uncertain data and provenance. Frameworks for modifying programs to record provenance information have also been proposed [20,23].

---

[1] The source code of DataTracker is available on: http://github.com/m000/dtracker.

An alternative take to provenance-awareness is the use of middleware to wrap applications and components. The provenance is generated by the middleware after inspection of the inputs and outputs of the wrapped components. This approach is popular with the scientific workflow community and includes systems such as Taverna [29], VisTrails [11], Kepler [2] and Wings [17]. Other middleware-based systems like Karma [31] are not tied to a workflow system, but instead tap into the communication stack to capture provenance.

It has also been proposed to capture provenance by exploiting the mechanisms offered by the operating system to trace the activities of programs. Such systems include TREC [34], ES3 [12] and the work of Gessiou et al. [13]. All these systems operate in user-space and don't require special privileges. A slightly different approach is taken by PASS [14], which has been implemented as a Linux kernel extension. From this vantage point, PASS is able to capture provenance from multiple processes at once. The fidelity of the provenance captured by these systems is comparable, as they all retrieve and use similar information (albeit using different mechanisms) and all of them treat traced programs as *black boxes* without tracking how data are actually processed. We consider our system to be an extension of these approaches to support higher fidelity provenance. From them, DataTracker is mostly related to Gessiou's et al. system, in the sense that both use dynamic binary instrumentation.

Finally, newer work [21,28] does not use a-priori instrumentation but attempts to reconstruct provenance directly from data. Without primary access to the actual provenance, this approach will always suffer from lower fidelity.

2.2 Dynamic Instrumentation and Taint Analysis

Dynamic Instrumentation: DataTracker applies Dynamic Instrumentation on the executing programs using the Intel Pin [19] framework. Pin allows monitoring and interacting with an executing program using a rich API and provides the base platform for the implementation of *Dynamic Taint Analysis* (discussed next). We picked Pin over similar *Dynamic Binary Instrumentation* (DBI) platforms [3,27] because it is considered the easiest to work with while providing high performance without the need for much manual tinkering. Instrumentation techniques which require modification or recompilation of the instrumented programs [18,33] were precluded.

Dynamic Taint Analysis: Pioneered by Denning in the 70s [10], the idea of tracking the flow of data though a program is all but new. The technique has remained relevant through the years and has been implemented on different levels, ranging from source code [22], to interpreters[2], to full emulators [1,8]. Its most common applications are in the field of security and intrusion detection [1,7]. However, until now, it hasn't been used for capturing provenance.

When data flow tracking is applied at runtime, it is generally called Dynamic Flow Tracking or, equivalently, *Dynamic Taint Analysis* (DTA). The term *taint* refers to the metadata associated with each tracked piece of data. A short and

---

[2] E.g. Perl taint mode: http://perldoc.perl.org/perlsec.html#Taint-mode.

concise definition of DTA has been given by Kemerlis et al. [16] as: "the process of accurately tracking the flow of selected data throughout the execution of a program or system". The four elements that are define a DTA implementation are: *(a)* the *taint type*, which encapsulates the semantics tracked for each piece of data; *(b)* the *taint sources*, i.e. locations where new taint marks are applied; *(c)* the *taint sinks*, i.e. locations where the propagated taint marks are checked or logged; *(d)* a set of *propagation policies* that define how that taint marks are handled during program execution.

Given the effectiveness of DTA, recently much research has been done on reusable DTA frameworks. This was largely made possible by the maturing of dynamic binary instrumentation platforms (see above). Dytan [6] uses the Intel Pin [19] DBI framework and provides much flexibility for configuring taint sources and propagation policies. Additionally, it offers some support for implicit data flows (see Sect. 5). DTA++[15] by Kang et al. focuses on the efficient handling of such implicit flows in benign programs.

A more recent effort (also based on Intel Pin) which emphasizes on performance is libdft [16]. To achieve superior performance, libdft consciously sacrifices some flexibility by supporting only bit or byte sized taint marks and omitting any support for implicit data flows. DataTracker is based on libdft, however we opted to use a modified version which adds support for arbitrary taint marks.

3 System

The architecture of DataTracker is illustrated in Fig. 1a. Colored blocks represent the additional components required for capturing provenance information in PROV format from unmodified applications. The darker blocks are those specifically developed for DataTracker. Due to Pin's architecture, application and instrumentation code appear as a single process to the OS and share the same address space. This means that instrumentation code has access to all of the application data and can intercept system-calls made by the application.

3.1 Modifications to Libdft

A fundamental requirement of DataTracker is the ability to use richer taint marks than those offered by the original libdft. Libdft has been carefully optimized with security applications in mind. For such applications, it has been argued that byte-sized taint marks are large enough for the current crop of security applications based on DTA [6]. So, libdft has limited the size of supported taint marks to either 1b or 1B, which allows for optimizing the taint propagation logic and reducing the memory requirements.

However, the requirements for DTA-based provenance applications are quite different. In this case, the default byte-sized taint marks of libdft just do not provide enough fidelity. In order to accommodate for the higher fidelity we need, we opted to use a modified version of libdft developed at our lab[3]. The modified

---

[3] Source code available on: https://git.cs.vu.nl/r.vermeulen/libdft.

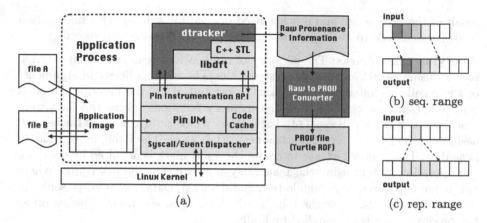

Fig. 1. DataTracker architecture (a) and taint ranges (b, c).

version shares much code with the original, however the taint mark type and propagation logic can be configured to match the application needs.

For DataTracker, the taint marks associated with each memory location are modeled as set of two-tuples: $\{\langle \texttt{ufd0:offset0}\rangle, \langle \texttt{ufd1:offset1}\rangle, \ldots\}$. Each of these tuples is 64bit long, and uniquely identifies an offset in a file[4]. The first half of each tuple is a *unique file descriptor* (UFD) which identifies a file during an application session. The second half represents the *offset* of the data within the file mapped to the UFD. Unlike file descriptors provided by the OS, UFDs increase monotonically and are not recycled after closing a file. Thus, they enable us to tell apart data which outlive the file descriptor they were read from. UFDs are only used internally and are resolved back to filenames during the conversion to PROV.

3.2   The `dtracker` Pin Tool and Converter

The `dtracker` pin tool is the core component of DataTracker. It implements the following functionality: *(a)* identifying when taint should be applied; *(b)* properly setting taint marks on data; *(c)* logging raw provenance information.

Identification of data to taint: When an instrumented program accesses a file for the first time, `dtracker` intercepts the `open()` system call and invokes its *UFD mapper* sub-component. The mapper checks whether the file descriptor returned by `open()` should be watched for input/output operations in order to respectively assign/log taint marks. This check is necessary in order to avoid applying taint on data that are either of no interest or highly unlikely to end-up in the application output. Examples of such files are shared libraries, UI icons, etc. The mapper includes heuristics to identify such files. If the mapper determines that the file descriptor should be watched, it will create a new UFD mapping for it. Additionally, it will check whether the file was created as a

---

[4] For simplicity, we prefer the term *"file"* over the more accurate *"file-like resource"*.

result of the system call and if it has been opened for writing. This information is logged and used to avoid generating false `prov:wasGeneratedBy` records.

Applying taint marks: The majority of applications read data from external sources using `read()` and `mmap2()` system calls. The return values and arguments of these calls are intercepted by DataTracker and, if the file descriptor used is watched, taint marks are set on the memory locations where the data were read into. E.g. for a call `read(fd, buf, size)` which returns n, DataTracker will assign `tags[buf+i]` ← ⟨`ufd[fd]:offset+i`⟩, $\forall i \in [0, n)$. The handling of `mmap2()` is similar. The required `offset` to create the taint mark is acquired by querying the operating system using the `lseek()` system call. For file descriptors where this is not supported (e.g. pseudo-terminal devices), DataTracker keeps separate read/write counters. After the taint marks have been set, their propagation as the program executes is handled by libdft.

Raw provenance logging and aggregation: While some pieces of raw provenance are logged by the instrumentation code attached to `open()`, the bulk of logging happens when `write()` and `munmap()` are called. A naive approach for this logging would be to just loop through written buffer and log one entry per tainted memory location. This strategy would easily result in very large log files. Logging large amount of data to disk would also slow-down the execution of the application. To avoid these issues and produce more compact and meaningful output, `dtracker` includes a simple aggregator for the logged taint marks which condenses logged information into two types of *taint ranges*: *(a) Sequence ranges* (Fig. 1b), which occur when the same sequence of consecutive taint marks appears both in the input and the output; *(b) Repetition ranges* (Fig. 1c), which occur when consecutive output bytes are all marked with the same taint mark. From the supported ranges the most common is the first, which naturally occurs whenever data are moved or copied by the application.

Raw output to PROV converter: In order to be able to use existing tools to further process the produced provenance, DataTracker provides a converter from its own raw format to PROV-O, the RDF serialization of PROV. While the bulk of the conversions are simple transformations, the converter script also needs to maintain some internal state, in order to avoid producing false-positives in some specific cases (e.g. false `prov:wasGeneratedBy` triples).

4   Evaluation

We carry out a two part evaluation. In the first part, we examine simple baseline programs with transparent and inspectable functionality. The goal is to demonstrate specific cases where our system is able to improve on the quality of produced provenance and produce less false-positives than existing approaches. In the second part, we focus on well-know applications and show how Data-Tracker can be used to extract useful provenance information from them without

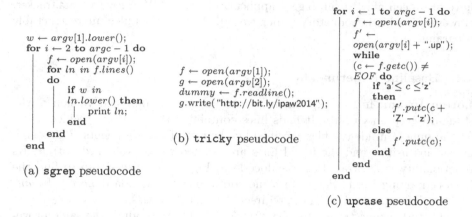

```
w ← argv[1].lower();
for i ← 2 to argc − 1 do
    f ← open(argv[i]);
    for ln in f.lines()
    do
        if w in
        ln.lower() then
            print ln;
        end
    end
end
```

(a) **sgrep** pseudocode

```
f ← open(argv[1]);
g ← open(argv[2]);
dummy ← f.readline();
g.write("http://bit.ly/ipaw2014");
```

(b) **tricky** pseudocode

```
for i ← 1 to argc − 1 do
    f ← open(argv[i]);
    f' ←
    open(argv[i] + ".up");
    while
    (c ← f.getc()) ≠
    EOF do
        if 'a' ≤ c ≤ 'z'
        then
            f'.putc(c +
            'Z' − 'z');
        else
            f'.putc(c);
        end
    end
end
```

(c) **upcase** pseudocode

Fig. 2. Pseudocode for baseline programs.

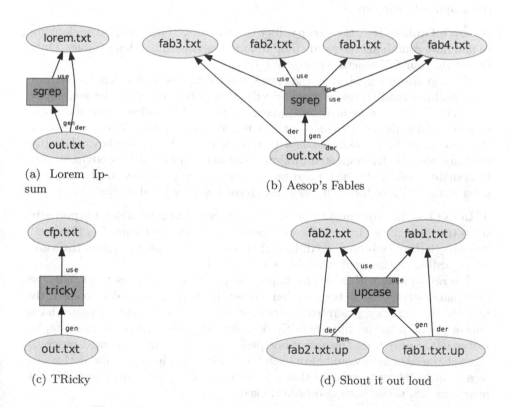

(a) Lorem Ipsum

(b) Aesop's Fables

(c) TRicky

(d) Shout it out loud

Fig. 3. Output from baseline experiments with DataTracker.

requiring modifications. We use the diagrammatic convention of PROV[5]. We have also been able to run bigger applications like AbiWord with DataTracker. However, in this introductory paper we will focus on simpler, more tractable programs.

4.1 Baseline Experiments

Lorem Ipsum: In this experiment, we use `sgrep`, a simplified version of the standard `grep` unix utility. It finds lines containing the word w specified as its first argument inside the files specified by the rest of the arguments. The search is case-insensitive and the found lines are printed to the standard output. Its functionality is illustrated as pseudocode in Fig. 2a. We use `sgrep` to find the lines containing word *"dolor"* in a file containing the standard *Lorem Ipsum*[6] passage. The standard output is redirected to file *"out.txt"*.

This test demonstrates that DataTracker is able to produce the same provenance graph as those of techniques like [12–14]. In Fig. 3a we can see that Data-Tracker correctly produces the expected usage and derivation edges. Our system also produces byte level provenance information, which has been omitted from the graph for saving space.

Aesop's Fables: Here, the `sgrep` utility is again used. This time, we are looking to find lines containing the word *"lion"* in four files containing Aesop fables. Only two of the four fables actually involve a lion.

We can see in Fig. 3b that DataTracker correctly identifies that the output contains lines (and therefore was derived) from only two out of the four input files. This is an improvement over systems like [12–14], which would have also produced false derivation edges for the remaining two files. The reason that DataTracker is able to eliminate these false positives, is that it goes beyond simply tracking how the instrumented program exchanges data with its environment. It actually looks inside the program, a *provenance black box* until now, and determines which of the exchanged data have been used and where.

TRicky: For this experiment, we use a utility called `tricky` which purportedly scans the input file for urls, and writes them to the specified output file. However, it seems that we've been tricked! In reality, the program always prints the same url regardless of the input it reads, as shown in Fig. 2b.

We ran `tricky` with a call for papers as input that happens to include the exact same string that `tricky` has hardcoded. DataTracker was able to correctly identify that `tricky` generated the output file but its contents actually have nothing to do with the input file (Fig. 3c). Similarly with the previous example, systems that only trace the operations performed by the instrumented program but not the data used would have been tricked into producing a false derivation edge. But in this case, systems that infer provenance by applying content-based heuristics [28] would have also been tricked.

---

[5] http://www.w3.org/2011/prov/wiki/Diagrams.

[6] A common placeholder text which has been used by typesetters since the 1500s.

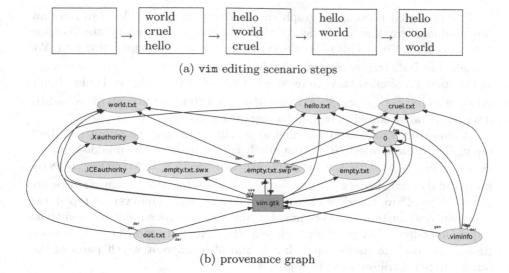

(a) vim editing scenario steps

(b) provenance graph

Fig. 4. Case study – vim editor.

Shout it out loud: In this final baseline experiment, we use a utility called upcase. This program opens the files specified as arguments and produces one output file for each of them with its contents in uppercase. The pseudocode of upcase is shown in Fig. 2c.

This experiment is simply a verification that DataTracker is able to identify the correct derivation edges in the case of multiple inputs and outputs. The generated graph is depicted in Fig. 3d. For upcase and N input files, other systems would have produced a graph with $N \times N$ edges. Such a result is too vague to be of practical use. With the use of heuristics, the quality of this result could be improved. However, with DataTracker we don't have to resort to heuristics that may fail in other cases.

4.2   Case Studies

In this section we will present the provenance produced by DataTracker when instrumenting two well-known applications: vim editor and Python.

vim editor: We used vim to run the following editing scenario (illustrated in Fig. 4a):

1. Open *empty.txt* with vim.
2. Read *world.txt*, *cruel.txt*, and *hello.txt* into the buffer.
3. Move contents of *hello.txt* to the top of the buffer.
4. Remove contents of *cruel.txt* from the buffer.
5. Type the word *"cool"* in the buffer.
6. Write the buffer to *out.txt* and quit.

The produced provenance graph can is shown in Fig. 4b. We can see that the produced graph is much denser than the ones produced by the baseline programs of Sect. 4.1. This is because vim opens numerous supporting files. We can see that DataTracker correctly didn't produce an $out.txt \xleftarrow{der} cruel.txt$ edge, as the contents of *cruel.txt* were removed in step 3 of the scenario. It also didn't produce an $out.txt \xleftarrow{der} .empty.txt.swp$ edge, even though the contents of *out.txt* were temporarily stored in *.empty.txt.swp* during the session.

Additionally, our system was able to capture provenance attributed to user input. The node labeled "0" in the graph corresponds to the pseudo-terminal device which is used by the program. We can see that DataTracker correctly produced derivation edges $out.txt \xleftarrow{der} 0$ and $0 \xleftarrow{der} 0$ for it: the former represents the word "cool" we typed, while the latter denotes that whatever we typed was also displayed on the pseudo-terminal. Capturing the user input has remained largely unaddressed by previous work (e.g. [34]). Not only can DataTracker trace provenance back to user's input, but it can also pinpoint which parts of the output were contributed by the user.

Python scripts: We used DataTracker to capture the provenance produced by some simple Python scripts in order to test how it performs with interpreted languages. Due to limited space, we will only briefly present our findings. DataTracker was able to produce correct provenance graphs on the file granularity. However, the provenance of some byte ranges was not captured correctly. This can be attributed to *implicit flows*, discussed in Sect. 5.

5   Discussion

The use of DTA allows for tracking of high-fidelity provenance. Following, we discuss some shortcomings of this technique as well as avenues for future work.

Capturing implicit provenance: A noteworthy deficiency of DTA is that it cannot easily track *implicit information flows*. An implicit information flow between variables x and y occurs when the value of y is set from a variable/constant z but the execution of the assignment is determined by the value of x. This matches cases like conditional assignments (e.g. if (x) then y=0; else y=1;) or assignment through lookup tables (e.g. int v[] = {1, 2, 3}; y = v[x];). In DTA implementations like libdft [16], where taint marks propagate only through operations directly involving a tainted location, these cases will not result in propagation of taint from x to y. This problem had already been noted by Denning [10] in her seminal work. The provenance relations that occur as a result of implicit flows are called *implicit provenance*.

Attempting to track implicit flows may result in *over-tainting* and a high number of false-positive, especially when using DTA to analyze malware [32]. For tracking taint through implicit flows in benign programs, Kang et al. propose DTA++ [15]. Their approach uses an offline analysis phase to identify locations where implicit flows occur and cause loss of taint. This is consistent with Cavallaro's observations [4]. However, when using DTA to capture provenance we can safely assume that our programs are benign. So, in principle, techniques like DTA++ could be retrofitted to DataTracker to improve its recall on the retrieved implicit provenance relations.

Performance: While performance is acceptable on most command-line programs, issues do exist. E.g. the use of large taint marks may result in increased memory usage. The extent of this effect depends on how much tainted data are used at once. It can be alleviated by attaching to the application after its launch, reducing the amount of un-needed taint applied. We plan to quantitatively study this effect and investigate optimizations to lessen it. Another issue is that DTA is particularly slow when instrumenting interpreted programs (see Sect. 4.2). This is because it treats interpreted programs as data and applies taint to them. Investigation of possible solutions to this problem is an area of future work.

6   Conclusions

We have presented DataTracker, a novel system for capturing provenance from unmodified binaries based on Dynamic Taint Analysis and implemented using Dynamic Instrumentation. DataTracker advances the state of the art by not treating executing programs as *black-boxes*, inferring provenance by how they interact with their environment, but instead dynamically tracking the flow of data through their internals, capturing high-fidelity provenance along the way. We have shown that DataTracker is able to generate *accurate provenance* in cases where state-of-the-art techniques would have produced false-positives. It is also capable of capturing *user interaction provenance* and generating *high-fidelity provenance* for individual byte ranges within files.

References

1. Bosman, E., Slowinska, A., Bos, H.: Minemu: the world's fastest taint tracker. In: Sommer, R., Balzarotti, D., Maier, G. (eds.) RAID 2011. LNCS, vol. 6961, pp. 1–20. Springer, Heidelberg (2011)
2. Bowers, S., McPhillips, T.M., Ludaescher, B.: Provenance in collection-oriented scientific workflows. Concurr. Comput. Pract. Exper. **20**(5), 519–529 (2008)
3. Bruening, D.L.: Efficient, transparent, and comprehensive runtime code manipulation. Ph.D. thesis, MIT, Cambridge, MA, USA (2004)
4. Cavallaro, L., Saxena, P., Sekar, R.: On the limits of information flow techniques for malware analysis and containment. In: Zamboni, D. (ed.) DIMVA 2008. LNCS, vol. 5137, pp. 143–163. Springer, Heidelberg (2008)
5. Cheney, J., Chiticariu, L., Tan, W.C.: Provenance in databases: why, how, and where. Found. Trends Databases **1**(4), 379–474 (2009)
6. Clause, J., Li, W., Orso, A.: Dytan: a generic dynamic taint analysis framework. In: Proceedings of ISSTA 2007, London, UK (2007)
7. Costa, M., Crowcroft, J., Castro, M., Rowstron, A., Zhou, L., Zhang, L., Barham, P.: Vigilante: end-to-end containment of internet worm epidemics. ACM TOCS **26**(4), 1–68 (2008)

8. Crandall, J.R., Chong, F.T.: Minos: control data attack prevention orthogonal to memory model. In: Proceedings of MICRO 37, Portland, OR, USA (2004)
9. Davidson, S.B., Freire, J.: Provenance and scientific workflows: challenges and opportunities. In: Proceedings of SIGMOD 2008, Vancouver, Canada (2008)
10. Denning, D.E., Denning, P.J.: Certification of programs for secure information flow. Commun. ACM **20**(7), 504–513 (1977)
11. Freire, J.-L., Silva, C.T., Callahan, S.P., Santos, E., Scheidegger, C.E., Vo, H.T.: Managing rapidly-evolving scientific workflows. In: Moreau, L., Foster, I. (eds.) IPAW 2006. LNCS, vol. 4145, pp. 10–18. Springer, Heidelberg (2006)
12. Frew, J., Metzger, D., Slaughter, P.: Automatic capture and reconstruction of computational provenance. Concurr. Comput. Pract. Exper. **20**(5), 485–496 (2008)
13. Gessiou, E., Pappas, V., Athanasopoulos, E., Keromytis, A.D., Ioannidis, S.: Towards a universal data provenance framework using dynamic instrumentation. In: Gritzalis, D., Furnell, S., Theoharidou, M. (eds.) SEC 2012. IFIP AICT, vol. 376, pp. 103–114. Springer, Heidelberg (2012)
14. Holland, D.A., Seltzer, M.I., Braun, U., Muniswamy-Reddy, K.K.: PASSing the provenance challenge. Concurr. Comput. Pract. Exper. **20**(5), 531–540 (2008)
15. Kang, M.G., McCamant, S., Poosankam, P., Song, D.: DTA++: dynamic taint analysis with targeted control-flow propagation. In: Proceedings of NDSS 2011, San Diego, CA, USA (2011)
16. Kemerlis, V.P., Portokalidis, G., Jee, K., Keromytis, A.D.: libdft: Practical dynamic data flow tracking for commodity systems. In: Proceedings of VEE 2012, London, UK (2012)
17. Kim, J., Deelman, E., Gil, Y., Mehta, G., Ratnakar, V.: Provenance trails in the wings-pegasus system. Concurr. Comput. Pract. Exper. **20**(5), 587–597 (2008)
18. Lattner, C., Adve, V.: LLVM: a compilation framework for lifelong program analysis & transformation. In: Proceedings of CGO 2004, Palo Alto, CA, USA (2004)
19. Luk, C.K., Cohn, R., Muth, R., Patil, H., Klauser, A., Lowney, G., Wallace, S., Reddi, V.J., Hazelwood, K.: Pin: building customized program analysis tools with dynamic instrumentation. In: Proceedings of PLDI 2005, Chicago, IL, USA (2005)
20. Macko, P., Seltzer, M.: A General-purpose provenance library. In: Proceedings of USENIX TaPP 2012, Boston, MA, USA (2012)
21. Magliacane, S.: Reconstructing provenance. In: Cudré-Mauroux, P., et al. (eds.) ISWC 2012, Part II. LNCS, vol. 7650, pp. 399–406. Springer, Heidelberg (2012)
22. McCamant, S., Ernst, M.D.: Quantitative information-flow tracking for C and related languages. Technical report, MIT-CSAIL-TR-2006-076, MIT, Cambridge, MA, USA (2006)
23. Miles, S., Groth, P., Munroe, S., Moreau, L.: PrIMe: a methodology for developing provenance-aware applications. ACM TOSEM **20**(3), 8:1–8:42 (2009)
24. Moreau, L.: The foundations for provenance on the web. Found. Trends Web Sci. **2**(2–3), 99–241 (2010)
25. Moreau, L., Groth, P.: Provenance: an introduction to PROV. Synth. Lect. Semant. Web: Theory Technol. **3**(4) (2013)
26. Moreau, L., Missier, P.: PROV-DM: The PROV Data Model. Recommendation REC-prov-dm-20130430, W3C (2013)
27. Nethercote, N., Seward, J.: Valgrind: a framework for heavyweight dynamic binary instrumentation. In: Proceedings of PLDI 2007, San Diego, CA, USA (2007)
28. De Nies, T., Coppens, S., Van Deursen, D., Mannens, E., Van de Walle, R.: Automatic discovery of high-level provenance using semantic similarity. In: Groth, P., Frew, J. (eds.) IPAW 2012. LNCS, vol. 7525, pp. 97–110. Springer, Heidelberg (2012)

29. Oinn, T., Greenwood, M., et al.: Taverna: lessons in creating a workflow environment for the life sciences. Concurr. Comput. Pract. Exper. **18**(10), 1067–1100 (2006)
30. Simmhan, Y.L., Plale, B., Gannon, D.: A survey of data provenance in e-science. SIGMOD Rec. **34**(3), 31–36 (2005)
31. Simmhan, Y.L., Plale, B., Gannon, D.: Karma2: provenance management for data driven workflows. Int. J. Web Serv. Res. **5**(2), 1–22 (2008)
32. Slowinska, A., Bos, H.: Pointless tainting?: evaluating the practicality of pointer tainting. In: Proceedings of EuroSys 2009, Nuremberg, Germany (2009)
33. Srivastava, A., Eustace, A.: ATOM: a system for building customized program analysis tools. In: Proceedings of PLDI 1994, Orlando, FL, USA (1994)
34. Vahdat, A., Anderson, T.: Transparent result caching. In: Proceedings of USENIX ATC 1998, New Orleans, LA, USA (1998)
35. Widom, J.: Trio a system for data uncertainty and lineage. In: Aggarwal, C.C. (ed.) Managing and Mining Uncertain Data, vol. 35. Springer, New York (2009)

Generating Scientific Documentation for Computational Experiments Using Provenance

Adianto Wibisono[1,2]([✉]), Peter Bloem[1], Gerben K.D. de Vries[1], Paul Groth[2], Adam Belloum[1], and Marian Bubak[1,3]

[1] System and Network Engineering Group, Informatics Institute,
University of Amsterdam, Amsterdam, The Netherlands
{a.wibisono,p.bloem,g.k.d.devries,a.z.s.belloum}@uva.nl, bubak@agh.edu.pl
[2] VU University Amsterdam, Amsterdam, The Netherlands
pgroth@vu.nl
[3] Department of Computer Science, AGH Krakow, Kraków, Poland

Abstract. Electronic notebooks are a common mechanism for scientists to document and investigate their work. With the advent of tools such as IPython Notebooks and Knitr, these notebooks allow code and data to be mixed together and published online. However, these approaches assume that all work is done in the same notebook environment. In this work, we look at generating notebook documentation from multi-environment workflows by using provenance represented in the W3C PROV model.

Specifically, using PROV generated from the Ducktape workflow system, we are able to generate IPython notebooks that include results tables, provenance visualizations as well as references to the software and datasets used. The notebooks are interactive and editable, so that the user can explore and analyze the results of the experiment without re-running the workflow.

We identify specific extensions to PROV necessary for facilitating documentation generation. To evaluate, we recreate the documentation website for a paper which won the Open Science Award at the ECML/ PKDD 2013 machine learning conference. We show that the documentation produced automatically by our system provides more detail and greater experimental insight than the original hand-crafted documentation. Our approach bridges the gap between user friendly notebook documentation and provenance generated by distributed heterogeneous components.

1 Introduction

Common approaches to computational experimentation[1] span a spectrum. On one side, we find quick, informative experiments intended for fast iteration. These often involve a single researcher, working on consumer-scale hardware, and can

---

[1] In this paper, we will call an experiment which can be run entirely *in silico* (i.e. as a computer program) a *computational experiment*.

© Springer International Publishing Switzerland 2015
B. Ludäscher and B. Plale (Eds.): IPAW 2014, LNCS 8628, pp. 168–179, 2015.
DOI: 10.1007/978-3-319-16462-5_13

take as little as a few minutes to run. The aim is to get quick results to inform further experiments and to build towards larger results in an iterative manner. The environment that is used for this type of experimentation is usually designed around quick iteration, and quick inspection of results: MATLAB, R, or a simple UNIX command line. More recently, this is often done within interactive notebook environments such as IPython notebooks [1], Knitr [2] or Mathematica [3].

On the other side of the spectrum we find large-scale experimentation. Well-prepared, thoroughly designed experiments, intended to run for long amounts of time on powerful hardware. These experiments are often implemented by scientific programmers, separate from the researchers designing the experiment. The chosen environment is often a workflow system [4], providing features like monitoring of execution, robustness against hardware failure and provenance tracking. The downside is that each experiment must be carefully prepared, and purpose-written for the workflow system.

Experimentation usually starts with quick iterations in an interactive system, and progresses towards the more robust environments as the experiments become more involved, often at the expense of a re-implementation step as the code is ported to a more robust environment. At the larger scales, iterations invariably become slower.

Finally, once results have been produced that are expected to be fit for publication, the researchers must translate and summarize their approach to allow for peer-review, reproduction and reuse. The ideal is to publish the datasets, the code and to provide instructions for reproducing the experiment. In the small-scale iterative end of the spectrum, this can be very cumbersome: gathering unversioned code, unstructured datasets and documenting all idiosyncratic steps required to execute it. In the large-scale end, experiments tend to be more structured, as enforced by the workflow system, but the description of the workflow is still tied to the workflow platform. Even a provenance trace, which is intended to illustrate the source of the results, can be difficult to interpret in its raw form.

1.1   Main Idea

In this paper, we present a concept for generating notebook documentation for computational experiments from provenance information. Our approach aims to retain some of the iteration speed of the small-scale experimentation at the large-scale end of the spectrum. This documentation generation process is built on three ideas.

1. After a large-scale experiment has finished, many questions raised by its output can, theoretically, be answered without re-running the experiment. Unfortunately, these questions were not the ones which the experiment was originally designed to answer, so the required data was not collected during the run. Output representing as much information about the original run as possible can help to postpone the need for a new run of a (redesigned) experiment.

2. While provenance is often seen as a kind of semantically annotated log file—helping for keeping track of the origins of data, and for finding answers in the case of unforeseen errors—a complete provenance trace will actually contain all information about a run of a computational experiment: all data produced, and the semantic links between them [5]. Any output required from the experiment, such as tables, graphs and statistical analysis, can be reconstructed from the provenance trace.

3. A semantically annotated representation of a run of an experiment (such as a provenance trace) allows us to make intelligent guesses at default modes of reporting. Thus, we can automatically create reasonable scientific documentation; reporting not only the results of the experiment, but a human-readable representation of how the results emerged: which datasets were used, where they can be found, what code was used, using which versions and in what configuration. An interactive environment allows the researcher to tweak this documentation to filter out less relevant information.

In short, we propose to put provenance at the heart of computational experimentation, rather than the sidelines, to combine the best of both worlds. A large-scale experiment is run on a workflow system, producing mainly a provenance trace. This trace is then loaded into an interactive environment, allowing a researcher to investigate the questions that inspired the experiment, and any further questions that these results raise. The researcher can filter, plot and analyze the results at length, with much greater depth than a non-semantic output, such as a CSV file, could offer. Only when all information produced by the original run is exhausted, does a new experiment need to be started.

When the time comes for the results to be shared, e.g. via a publication, the provenance trace provides all required information. All that is needed is a means to convert it to human readable form. The semantic annotations allow us to create reasonable default documentation, while anybody interested in the experiment can load the provenance trace into an interactive system and study the details.

1.2   Contributions

Interactive notebooks provide both a good format for presenting default documentation and an interactive environment to study experimental results. The proof-of-concept implementation presented in this paper uses provenance, in the W3C PROV-O [6] format, generated by our own workflow system Ducktape[2], to automatically create IPython notebooks. We chose IPython Notebooks as this system is becoming widely used in data processing. Additionally, they provide a web-based environment, independent of the underlying language. This means that future versions of our system could also support R, Julia and other programming languages. Our notebooks have result tables and graphs, visualization of the provenance and links to the software and datasets used. Furthermore, they

---

[2] http://github.com/Data2semantics/ducktape.

are interactive and editable, so that the user can explore and analyze the results of the experiment without re-running the workflow. As a running example use-case, we take the documentation web-page that won the Open Science Award at the ECML/PKDD 2013 machine learning conference.

The rest of this paper is structured as follows. In the next section, we discuss related work. Section 3 describes our proof-of-concept implementation. The final section contains conclusions and directions for future research.

2   Related Work

A key part of related work is in the area of workflow systems. Often, these systems provide accessible documentation to the end user through graphical representations of the workflow. Additionally, they attach detailed provenance information to those workflows [7]. Our work is different in that we build a notebook style representation directly from the provenance.

Other existing papers also explore and derive insight from scientific workflow provenance, with different goals than ours. Work by Biton et al. [8] lets users define views based on relevant workflow parts that determines how a possibly large workflow provenance graph can be explored. The high level query languages for provenance: QLP [9] and OPQL [10], can be used for interactive querying and visualization. Both views simplify provenance results and allow exploration of scientific workflow provenance at the graph level.

Close to our work is that of Gibson et al. [11], on creating an interactive environment where provenance is stored. We see our work as complementary as one can see the generation of the workflows as similar to generating a notebook. Deep [12], an executable document environment that generates scientific results dynamically and interactively, also records the provenance for these results in the document. In this system, provenance is exposed to users via an interface that provides them with an alternative way of navigating the executable document.

Burrito [13] is a system that uses a combination of provenance tracking and user interface constructs for notes to help generate a lab notebook. Our approach shares their motivation but focuses instead documenting distributed computational workflows using provenance. Similarly, Scientific Application Middleware [14] combines information coming from both lab notebooks but also distributed computational components to create documentation for experiments. Our work adds to this vision by connecting to widely used interactive (computational) notebook environments.

The idea of using provenance as a singular result of workflow execution shares some aims with the idea of *Research Objects* [15]. This is a construct that aims to replace the traditional paper article as the main unit of scientific publication. A research object is a package of not just the research results, but also all artifacts used to create them, such as datasets, code and provenance. Within the research object, the provenance is seen as a feature to facilitate auditing. In our approach, we see the provenance as the key entry point: it should not just be used to audit the experiments, but also to aggregate results and to perform statistical analyses. Our perspective does not change or replace the use of Research Objects, but suggests that the provenance could be used as its central component, tying together the other contents of the package.

3   Proof-of-Concept

The proof-of-concept implementation for our documentation generation approach consists of three components: a workflow system, workflow provenance and generating notebooks from provenance. We first introduce a running example that will illustrate these three components and then we describe the components themselves.

3.1   Running Example

The webpage[3] for the paper *A fast approximation of the Weisfeiler Lehman graph kernel for RDF data* [16] won one of the two Open Science Awards at ECML/PKDD 2013, the conference where it was published. On the page, links to software libraries, datasets and the original source code are provided, as well as instructions on how to run the experiments using the provided material. The datasets are available online, via figshare.com, and the code is stored in a git repository, at github.com. We have recreated two partial experiments in the ECML/PKDD 2013 paper [16] for our proof-of-concept. We use these experiments as running examples below. Note that we do not recreate the full set of experiments in the paper. However, the recreated parts are a representative subset, since we cover both a classification experiment and a runtime experiment.

In the classification experiment a number of graph kernels for RDF data are tested on an affiliation prediction task. The goal in this task is to predict affiliations for persons in the dataset. Three different kernels are tested, each for a number of parameter settings. These kernels are combined with a Support Vector Machine (SVM) to perform prediction. To reduce randomness, the experiment is repeated 10 times, with different random seeds.

The runtime experiment uses the same graph kernels and dataset, but this time the kernels are computed for different fractions of that dataset to investigate the runtime performance of the different kernels. The most computationally intensive settings for the kernels are used. For each dataset fraction, the computation is performed 10 times (on 10 random subsets).

3.2   Workflow System: Ducktape

Ducktape is a light-weight workflow system developed in the context of the Data2Semantics[4] project. This project provides essential semantic infrastructure for e-science and focuses on how to share, publish, access, analyze, interpret

---

[3] http://www.data2semantics.org/publications/ecmlpkdd-2013/.
[4] http://www.data2semantics.org.

and reuse scientific data. Ducktape is designed to compose experiments using components developed within the project. By using an annotation approach, we keep the system light-weight and impose little additional effort for a scientist to use his existing code in our environment.

Ducktape uses computational modules, which are annotated pieces of codes, typically classes. The annotations indicate what the inputs and outputs of the module are and what the main computation routine is. Currently, Java, Python and command line scripts are supported.

A Ducktape workflow is described in a simple data flow format represented in YAML (YAML Ain't Markup Language) [17], which contains a list of modules and specifications of each of the modules' input data. Figure 1 shows part of the workflow description for the affiliation prediction experiment. Module inputs can either be raw data type values, i.e. integers, doubles and strings, or data produced by other modules within the same workflow (e.g. Fig. 1, line 17, 20, 22).

Module input fields in the YAML workflow description can be supplied with lists of inputs of the same type, to allow for parameter sweeps (Fig. 1, line 23). Ducktape allows users to specify whether they want input lists to be consumed in a pair-wise manner or whether the full Cartesian product between the lists should be used in the parameter sweep. Furthermore, there are keywords to indicate whether certain inputs represent datasets (Fig. 1, line 10), what module outputs should be considered experimental results (Fig. 1, line 25) and for which input parameter we want to aggregate results (Fig. 1, line 26).

3.3 Provenance: W3C PROV

Whenever a workflow is executed, Ducktape automatically generates the provenance that captures this execution in the W3C PROV-O [6] format.[5] Table 1 shows how the different elements of a Ducktape workflow map to the concepts in W3C PROV. The main concepts from W3C PROV that we use are prov:Activity and prov:Entity and their connecting relations: prov:used and prov:wasGeneratedBy. Essentially, a workflow leads to a bipartite graph with alternating nodes of prov:Activity and prov:Entity.

Modules are prov:Activitys and inputs and outputs are prov:Entitys. We model this by creating a class dt-rsc:ModuleName[6] with the name of the module for all modules. Each dt-rsc:ModuleName is rdfs:subClassOf of prov:Activity. Every instance of a module executed during the run of the workflow is an rdf:type of its corresponding dt-rsc:ModuleName. We do the same for the inputs and outputs, introducing a dt-rsc:InputName or dt-rsc:OutputName for each input and output, which are rdfs:subClassOf of prov:Entity. Each input/output instance is an rdf:type of its corresponding dt-rsc:InputName/OutputName. Outputs that are inputs of another module have one unique URI. For example, the specific instance of 'seed' with

---

[5] We note other serializations of PROV [18] can also be supported.
[6] dt-rsc is a shorthand for: http://prov.data2semantics.org/resource/ducktape/.

```
1    workflow:
2        name: "Affiliation Prediction Experiment IPAW 2014"
3        modules:
4        - module:
5            name: RDFDataSet
6            source: d2s.RDFDataSetModule
7            inputs:
8                filename: "http://.../aifb_fixed_complete.n3"
9                ...
10           datasets: filename
11       ...
12       - module:
13           name: Experiment
14           source: d2s.SingleGraphKernelExperimentModule
15           inputs:
16               matrix:
17                   - reference: RDFWLSubTreeKernel.matrix
18                   ...
19               target:
20                   reference: AffiliationDataSet.target
21               parms:
22                   reference: LibSVMParms.parameters
23               seed: [1,2,3,4,5,6,7,8,9,10]
24               folds: 5
25           results: [accuracy, f1]
26           aggregators: seed
```

Fig. 1. Example of YAML workflow description from the affiliation prediction experiment. The full workflow is not shown.

value '1' in the module 'Experiment' in Fig. 1, line 23, would be of type dt-rsc:Experiment/seed/[7] which is an rdfs:subClassOf of prov:Entity.

Each module (dt-rsc:ModuleName) is associated with a prov:Agent, which represent the specific Ducktape engine used for execution (i.e. the machine(s) and version), and a prov:Plan, the specific YAML workflow file.

Optionally, inputs can also be a dt-voc:Dataset[8], if they refer to a dataset (e.g. by a URL) or a dt-voc:Aggregator, if they determine how to aggregate experiment outputs based on this input. Outputs can have the dt-voc:resultOf predicate that links them to the workflow (i.e. prov:Plan), if they should be considered the results of that workflow. These optional concepts are added when they are specified in the YAML workflow file.

Furthermore, we also add the software artifact dependencies that we know that are used during execution to the provenance. This is done by creating URI for each artifact and adding it to the prov:Plan via a new property dt-voc:-usesArtifact. Currently, we manage our dependencies and execute our workflows

---

[7] There can be multiple inputs/outputs with the same name, so the module name is also included in this URI.

[8] dt-voc is a shorthand for: http://prov.data2semantics.org/vocab/ducktape/.

Table 1. Mapping of ducktape elements to W3C PROV

Ducktape	W3C PROV	Optional
Ducktape engine	prov:Agent	
Workflow description	prov:Plan	
Module instance	prov:Activity	
Input	prov:Entity	dt-voc:Dataset, dt-voc:Aggregator
Output	prov:Entity	dt-voc:resultOf

using Maven[9], thus each artifact furthermore has the properties: dt-voc: hasArtifactId, dt-voc:hasGroupId and dt-voc:hasVersion.

3.4   Notebook Generation

Based on the generated provenance, draft IPython notebooks are created. There are two types of notebook drafts: an overview notebook with general workflow execution information and a more detailed notebook at the workflow module level.

The overview notebook contains general information about the workflow plan, software artifacts and datasets used. A summary of the Ducktape modules instantiated during the experiment and inline provenance visualization generated using Prov-O-Viz [19][10] is also included in this overview notebook to give intuitive insight into the overall workflow execution. This notebook is illustrated in Figs. 2 and 3.

The detailed notebook draft describes individual module execution results. Users have access to the module input parameters and execution results through default Python code snippets injected into the notebook. The code snippets are generated by performing SPARQL queries on the workflow provenance graph. By using these snippets, users can manipulate how they view the module parameters and execution results.

We use the existing Python Data Analysis library (Pandas)[11] in the code snippets, to allow users to play with and change the view on their results. Essentially, what the user has here is a data analysis view of each individual module in workflow execution. By default we provide tables of relevant input and outputs for each individual module which users can change by tweaking the injected Python code.

For modules that have input data marked as dt-voc:Aggregator, we provide a pivot table, which aggregates the outputs that are dt-voc:resultOf, grouping by the other input parameters. The default form of aggregation is computing the mean value, however this can be easily changed by editing the code snippet.

---

[9] http://maven.apache.org/.
[10] http://provoviz.org.
[11] pandas.pydata.org.

Overview Report

Software

Agent : ducktape on: wongiseng-note, versionID: 6847885952040544661

http://prov.data2semantics.org/resource/ducktape/ducktape/wongiseng-note/6847885952040544661

Plan : Affiliation Prediction Runtime Experiment IPAW 2014, date: Thu May 15 09:40:44 CEST 2014

http://prov.data2semantics.org/resources/workflow/s.%Project/%mustard/%mustard-experiment/%workflow.yaml/cfba9416:d4e5ba554d8a5908f1083054e

Libraries

Out [5] :

GroupID	ArtifactID	Version
data2semantics	ducktape	0.0.1-SNAPSHOT
data2semantics	mustard	0.0.1-SNAPSHOT

Modules

Out [6] :

Module	Instances
RDFDataSet	1
RDFIntersectionSubTreeKernel	10
RDFIntersectionPartialSubTreeKernel	10
AffiliationDataSet	10
RDFWLSubTreeKernel	10

Datasets

Out [7] :

Module	Dataset	Value
RDFDataSet	filename	http://files.figshare.com/1118822/aifb_fixed_complete.n3

Fig. 2. Overview report for the runtime experiment, part 1.

Provenance Visualization

Out [8] :

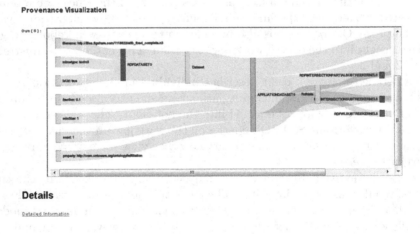

Details

Detailed Information

Fig. 3. Overview report for the runtime experiment, part 2.

An example of this aggregation is given in Fig. 4, where the results accuracy and F1 are aggregated over the seed input parameter.

In summary, the notebooks for the classification[12] and the runtime[13] experiments contain the following information: a list of datasets, a list of software artifacts, provenance visualization and detailed result tables. This is significantly

---

[12] Available here: http://j.mp/ecml-notebook.
[13] Available here: http://j.mp/runtime-notebook.

Result for module Experiment

In [23]:
```
pt = pivot_table(df, rows= ['Aggregator','parent0'])
pt
```
Out[23]:

Aggregator	parent0	accuracy	f1
0	AffiliationDataSet0 LibSVMParms0 RDFWLSubTreeKernel0	0.865537	0.811191
1	AffiliationDataSet0 LibSVMParms0 RDFWLSubTreeKernel1	0.811299	0.747912
2	AffiliationDataSet0 LibSVMParms0 RDFWLSubTreeKernel10	0.863277	0.824467
3	AffiliationDataSet0 LibSVMParms0 RDFWLSubTreeKernel11	0.822599	0.766933
4	AffiliationDataSet0 LibSVMParms0 RDFIntersectionSubTreeKernel0	0.829379	0.747343
5	AffiliationDataSet0 LibSVMParms0 RDFIntersectionSubTreeKernel1	0.825989	0.752534
6	AffiliationDataSet0 LibSVMParms0 RDFIntersectionSubTreeKernel2	0.809040	0.730443
7	AffiliationDataSet0 LibSVMParms0 RDFIntersectionSubTreeKernel3	0.787571	0.703818
8	AffiliationDataSet0 LibSVMParms0 RDFIntersectionPartialSubTreeKernel0	0.762712	0.661025
9	AffiliationDataSet0 LibSVMParms0 RDFIntersectionPartialSubTreeKernel1	0.748023	0.655392
10	AffiliationDataSet0 LibSVMParms0 RDFIntersectionPartialSubTreeKernel2	0.685876	0.541612
11	AffiliationDataSet0 LibSVMParms0 RDFIntersectionPartialSubTreeKernel3	0.560452	0.366949
12	AffiliationDataSet0 LibSVMParms0 RDFWLSubTreeKernel2	0.853107	0.810756
13	AffiliationDataSet0 LibSVMParms0 RDFWLSubTreeKernel3	0.850847	0.818110
14	AffiliationDataSet0 LibSVMParms0 RDFWLSubTreeKernel4	0.865537	0.811191
15	AffiliationDataSet0 LibSVMParms0 RDFWLSubTreeKernel5	0.811299	0.747912
16	AffiliationDataSet0 LibSVMParms0 RDFWLSubTreeKernel6	0.861017	0.824743
17	AffiliationDataSet0 LibSVMParms0 RDFWLSubTreeKernel7	0.838418	0.766040
18	AffiliationDataSet0 LibSVMParms0 RDFWLSubTreeKernel8	0.865537	0.811191
19	AffiliationDataSet0 LibSVMParms0 RDFWLSubTreeKernel9	0.811299	0.747912

20 rows × 2 columns

Fig. 4. Part of the detailed notebook for the affiliation prediction experiment which shows a table for the Experiment module.

more information than the original webpage and the notebooks can easily be extended by hand, both by changing the tables and adding more explanatory text[14]. Currently, the notebooks lack instructions on how to re-execute the experiments, this can be partly solved by adding instructions that explain how to use the datasets and artifacts. However, in future work we would like to add automatic re-execution of the workflow from the notebook, all the ingredients are already there.

4   Conclusions and Future Work

We have described an approach for automatic generation of scientific documentation for computational experiments. This is approach is based on the idea of placing provenance at the heart of such experiments, using it as the main output, not just as a way to trace the execution of a workflow. Interactive notebooks provide a way to explore the results and its provenance and are an ideal starting point for creating documentation for the experiments.

We have created a proof-of-concept implementation to automatically generate IPython notebooks from provenance created by workflows run using our Ducktape platform. These notebooks aggregate the main results and components of an experiment. This automatically generated draft documentation provides

---

[14] Note that the used artifacts are different from the original version, and that the samples above are static views requiring a local IPython environment to edit.

more information and insight then a hand-crafted documentation page for a machine learning paper that won an Open Science Award.

While our proof-of-concept uses a specific workflow system and a specific interactive platform to load and analyze the provenance, the approach is transferable to other workflow systems and interactive environments. Indeed, most PROV serializations can be represented as a more human-friendly notebook. Central to this conception is the notion that provenance can be a true interface between the execution of an experiment and the analysis of its results.

Another outcome of this work is confirmation of the importance of connecting interactive notebook environments and provenance. By using the IPython Notebook environment, we were able to benefit significantly from the variety of tools within that community, including notebook visualization (using the nbviewer app) and analytics. We believe that the connection between notebooks in general and distributed provenance generation is an area that the community should look at in more detail as there are a number of areas of interest. For instance, one may investigate the issue of maintaining the provenance of live results streamed to notebook environment, encapsulating provenance within a notebook or tracking provenance of interactive sessions.

Beyond investigating these larger themes, there are a number of concrete extensions to the environment we intend to make. First, the current configuration does not allow us to directly re-run the experiments from within the notebooks. We aim to implement such a feature to further improve reproducibility. Furthermore, while we can create links to software artifacts that were used, it would be even nicer to link to the actual source code for these artifacts, if that is available. Therefore, we plan to investigate how to integrate with methods such as GIT2Prov [20] to connect from execution to the source code. Furthermore, we are also investigating what additional visualizations we can embed to make the documentation richer.

Acknowledgments. We thank the reviewers and Rinke Hoekstra for their useful feedbacks and discussion. This publication was supported by the Dutch national program COMMIT.

References

1. Pérez, F., Granger, B.E.: IPython: a system for interactive scientific computing. Comput. Sci. Eng. **9**(3), 21–29 (2007)
2. Xie, Y.: Knitr: a general-purpose package for dynamic report generation in R. R Package Version **1**(7) (2013)
3. Wolfram, S.: The Mathematica Book, vol. 221. Wolfram Media Champaign, Illinois (1996)
4. Gil, Y., Deelman, E., Ellisman, M., Fahringer, T., Fox, G., Gannon, D., Goble, C., Livny, M., Moreau, L., Myers, J.: Examining the challenges of scientific workflows. IEEE Comput. **40**(12), 26–34 (2007)
5. Moreau, L.: Provenance-based reproducibility in the semantic web. Web Semant. Sci. Serv. Agents World Wide Web **9**(2), 202–221 (2011)

6. Lebo, T., Sahoo, S., McGuinness, D., Belhajjame, K., Corsar, D., et al.: Prov-o: The prov ontology. W3C Recommendation. World Wide Web Consortium (2013)
7. Davidson, S., Ludaescher, B., McPhillips, T., Freire, J.: Provenance in scientific workflow systems. Bull. Tech. Comm. Data Eng. **30**(4), 44–50 (2007)
8. Biton, O., Cohen-Boulakia, S., Davidson, S.B., Hara, C.S.: Querying and managing provenance through user views in scientific workflows. In: Proceedings of the 24th International Conference on Data Engineering, ICDE 2008, pp. 1072–1081 (2008)
9. Anand, M., Bowers, S., Ludascher, B.: Provenance browser: displaying and querying scientific workflow provenance graphs. In: 2010 IEEE 26th International Conference on Data Engineering (ICDE), pp. 1201–1204, March 2010
10. Lim, C., Lu, S., Chebotko, A., Fotouhi, F., Kashlev, A.: OPQL: querying scientific workflow provenance at the graph level. Data Knowl. Eng. **88**, 37–59 (2013)
11. Gibson, A., Gamble, M., Wolstencroft, K., Oinn, T., Goble, C., Belhajjame, K., Missier, P.: The data playground: an intuitive workflow specification environment. Future Gener. Comput. Syst. **25**(4), 453–459 (2009)
12. Yang, H., Michaelides, D.T., Charlton, C., Browne, W.J., Moreau, L.: DEEP: a provenance-aware executable document system. In: Groth, P., Frew, J. (eds.) IPAW 2012. LNCS, vol. 7525, pp. 24–38. Springer, Heidelberg (2012)
13. Guo, P.J., Seltzer, M.: Burrito: Wrapping your lab notebook in computational infrastructure. In: Proceedings of the 4th USENIX Workshop on the Theory and Practice of Provenance, TaPP 2012. USENIX Association, Berkeley (2012)
14. Myers, J.D., Chappell, A., Elder, M., Geist, A., Schwidder, J.: Re-integrating the research record. Comput. Sci. Eng. **5**(3), 44–50 (2003)
15. Bechhofer, S., De Roure, D., Gamble, M., Goble, C., Buchan, I.: Research objects: towards exchange and reuse of digital knowledge. In: The Future of the Web for Collaborative Science (2010)
16. de Vries, G.K.D.: A fast approximation of the Weisfeiler-Lehman graph kernel for RDF data. In: Blockeel, H., Kersting, K., Nijssen, S., Železný, F. (eds.) ECML PKDD 2013, Part I. LNCS (LNAI), vol. 8188, pp. 606–621. Springer, Heidelberg (2013)
17. Ben-Kiki, O., Evans, C., Ingerson, B.: Yaml ain't markup language (yaml) version 1.1. Working Draft 2008–05 11 (2001)
18. Moreau, L., Groth, P.: Provenance: an introduction to prov. Synth. Lect. Semant. Web: Theory Technol. **3**(4), 1–129 (2013)
19. Hoekstra, R., Groth, P.: PROV-O-Viz - understanding the role of activities in provenance. In: Ludäscher, B., Plale, B. (eds.) IPAW 2014. LNCS, vol. 8628, pp. 215–220. Springer, Heidelberg (2014)
20. De Nies, T., Magliacane, S., Verborgh, R., Coppens, S., Groth, P., Mannens, E., Van de Walle, R.: Git2prov: exposing version control system content as w3c prov. In: Posters & Demonstrations Track within the 12th International Semantic Web Conference (ISWC-2013), CEUR-WS, pp. 125–128 (2013)

Computing Location-Based Lineage from Workflow Specifications to Optimize Provenance Queries

Saumen Dey[1(✉)], Sven Köhler[1], Shawn Bowers[2], and Bertram Ludäscher[1]

[1] Department of Computer Science, University of California, Davis, Davis, USA
scdey@ucdavis.edu
[2] Department of Computer Science, Gonzaga University, Spokane, USA

Abstract. We present a location-based approach for executing provenance lineage queries that significantly reduces query execution cost without incurring additional storage costs. The key idea of our approach is to exploit the fact that provenance graphs resemble the workflow graphs that generated them and that many workflow computation models assume workflow steps have statically defined data consumption-production (i.e., data input-output) rates. We describe a new lineage computation technique that uses the structure of workflow specifications together with consumption-production rates to pre-compute (i.e., to forecast) the access paths of all dependent data items prior to workflow execution. We also present experimental results showing that our approach can significantly out perform traditional data lineage query techniques.

1 Introduction

Scientific workflow systems are increasingly used to automate data processing, analysis, and visualization steps [1]. These systems typically capture the processing history (i.e., the provenance) of all steps involved in a workflow run and store this information as a provenance graph [2,3]. Provenance graphs can be used for a number of purposes including: (i) to help explain how input data is processed to produce output data products; (ii) to help debug workflow designs by identifying processes responsible for workflow failure and detecting workflow steps that were affected; and (iii) to help in the reproduction of data products, e.g., by recording the steps involved in a workflow run (along with their corresponding parameter settings).

Each of these examples require the ability to determine how a data product (or workflow step) depends on input data (or other workflow steps), e.g., by posing queries over provenance graphs. In these cases, provenance queries return subgraphs of the given provenance graph [4], where the subgraph is often referred to as the *lineage* of the data products in question. Answering such queries requires recursion, making lineage queries potentially expensive to execute [5]. In particular, if E is the set of edges in the provenance graph, these queries may require as many as $|E|$ recursive steps (i.e., traversals of dependency edges).

© Springer International Publishing Switzerland 2015
B. Ludäscher and B. Plale (Eds.): IPAW 2014, LNCS 8628, pp. 180–193, 2015.
DOI: 10.1007/978-3-319-16462-5_14

A better approach is to use semi-naive evaluation [6], where the number of traversals is bounded by the diameter k of the provenance graph with $k < |E|$ in typical cases. An alternative to employing recursion is to compute and store the transitive closure of edges in the provenance graph [4,5]. Because the transitive closure can be computed once and reused for all lineage queries over the graph, the time complexity required to compute the closure is often not a concern (since the cost can be aggregated). Using the transitive closure, if V is set of nodes in the provenance graph, the time to evaluate a lineage query is $\mathcal{O}(log|V|)$ with storage cost $\mathcal{O}(|V|^2)$. Thus, for large provenance graphs, the recursive approach is space efficient, but not time efficient, whereas computing transitive closures is time efficient, but not space efficient. In this paper, we propose a new technique called *location-based lineage* for answering provenance queries that is both time and space efficient.

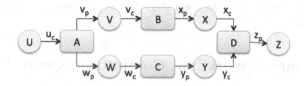

Fig. 1. An example workflow consisting of actors (rectangles), data containers (circles), and data flow edges annotated with consumption-production rates.

The main idea behind location-based lineage is to exploit the fact that a workflow specification provides a blue print (or "schema") for the provenance graphs that they generate. The constraints imposed on provenance graphs by a workflow specification arise from both the structure of the workflow as well as the underlying computational model used by a workflow engine during workflow execution. As a simple example, consider the workflow specification in Fig. 1, where U through Z denote dataflow channels and A through D denote processing steps (i.e., actors). Based on the structure of the workflow, a data product on channel X (output by an invocation of B) may be dependent on a data product (input by the invocation of B) on channel Y, but cannot depend on a data product, e.g., on channel W. The constraints imposed by workflow computation models define the general order in which actors can be invoked as well as the number of data items that can be consumed and produced by each actor invocation. For instance, many workflow systems model actors as simple function calls that take a fixed number of arguments, i.e., input values, and return a fixed number of output values (e.g., VisTrails [7]). The synchronous dataflow (SDF) computation model [8] extends this by allowing workflow designers to specify the number of data items an actor needs on each input channel for the actor to be invoked, and the number of outputs produced on each channel by an invocation. Data items are buffered on channels until the needed number of items are received by an actor.[1] Many of the scientific workflows developed in Kepler use the SDF model of computation (e.g., see [9,10]).

Location-based lineage uses the structure of the workflow graph together with the data consumption and production rates to precompute data dependency information prior to workflow execution. In particular, we provide an algorithm to compute the location of data consumed and produced by actors within channels statically (before workflow execution) and show how this information can be used to more efficiently answer lineage queries.

Paper Organization. Section 2 describes the general workflow, computation, and provenance models we assume for location-based lineage. Section 3 presents our approach for computing lineage queries for various workflow patterns and actor types. Section 4 describes the overall algorithm for computing location-based lineage. Section 5 explains the experiments we performed to validate our technique and analyzes the results. In Sect. 6, we discuss the recent efforts toward finding efficient lineage computation and finally in Sect. 7, we conclude with future directions.

2 Preliminaries: Workflow, Computation, and Provenance Models

Here we briefly describe the assumptions made concerning workflow graphs, provenance graphs, and workflow execution in our location-based lineage approach.

Workflow Model. We assume a workflow specification $W = (V, E)$ can be represented as a directed graph whose nodes $V = A \cup C$ are partitioned into *actors* A and *containers* C (e.g., see Fig. 1). Actors represent computational entities that can be executed (i.e., invoked). Each invocation of an actor can consume and produce data *tokens* representing either primitive or structured values or references to external data products (e.g., a file). Containers represent buffers (often implemented as FIFO queues) that can hold data tokens during communication between actors. The edges of a workflow graph $E = In \cup Out$ are either *input* edges $In \subseteq C \times A$ or *output* edges $Out \subseteq A \times C$. Actors can consume tokens from one or more containers and can produce tokens on one or more containers. Additionally, we assume input and output edges are annotated with token *consumption* and *production rates*, respectively. A consumption rate is a positive integer that specifies the number of input tokens needed to invoke an actor, and similarly, a production rate is a positive integer that specifies the number of output tokens generated by one invocation of an actor.

Computation Model. We make similar assumptions concerning workflow execution as used in the synchronous dataflow (SDF) model. In particular, actors can be invoked when their required number of input tokens on each channel

---

[1] Petri net based models, although not typically used for scientific workflow systems, also have similar constraints represented through edge multiplicities.

become available. Figure 1 is an example SDF workflow in which actor A can be invoked when u_c tokens in container U are available resulting in v_p and w_p tokens being output to containers V and W, respectively. For many actors (e.g., those representing simple function calls) the consumption-production rates will be 1 for each input and output. We also make a distinction between stateful and stateless actors. In particular, a stateful actor maintains one or more data tokens across its invocations within a workflow run and uses these tokens (i.e., the state) to compute output values. We consider two variants of stateful actors: (1) an invocation consumes all tokens that one or more of its previous invocations received, and (2) each invocation maintains a constant number of tokens that were consumed by its most recent invocation. Finally, to enable lineage queries based on specific data values we assume that as a workflow is executed, the contents of each container are persisted.

Provenance Model. We assume provenance graphs that generally follow the Open Provenance Model [11] in which provenance information can be represented as a directed graph $P = (V, E)$ whose nodes $V = D \cup I$ represent either data tokens D or actor invocations I and whose edges $E = \mathit{Used} \cup \mathit{GenBy}$ are either used edges $\mathit{Used} \subseteq I \times D$ or generated-by edges $\mathit{GenBy} \subseteq D \times I$. An used edge $(i, d_1) \in E$ implies that an invocation i consumed token d_1 as input, while a generated-by edge $(d_2, i) \in E$ implies that a token d_2 was output by i. In this case we say that d_2 depended on d_1 (i.e., d_2 is part of d_1's lineage). The complete set of data tokens, used, and generated-by edges that led to (i.e., that lie on a path to) a data token d denote the lineage of d. We use the following auxiliary relation to compute the data dependencies.

$$\mathtt{ddep}(D_1, D_2) :- \mathtt{genBy}(D_1, I), \mathtt{used}(I, D_2).$$

The $\mathtt{ddep}(D_1, D_2)$ relation specifies that the data D_1 depends on the data D_2. Additionally, given the workflow graph W that produced the provenance graph P, where A and C are the actors and containers of W, respectively, we assume the relation $\mathit{invoc} \subseteq I \times A$ connects each invocation $i \in I$ with its corresponding actor $a \in A$ and the relation $\mathit{loc} \subseteq D \times C \times L$ connects each data token $d \in D$ to its corresponding container $c \in C$ such that d is located at position $l \in L$ in c's persistent queue.

3 Precomputing Dependency Tables

Given a workflow W and a provenance graph P, we statically compute the lineage of all data tokens in three steps. The first step dependenciescontainers using the following Datalog rules.

$$\mathtt{cdep}(C_1, C_2) :- \mathtt{out}(P, C_1), \mathtt{in}(C_2, P).$$
$$\mathtt{cdep}^*(C_1, C_2) :- \mathtt{cdep}(C_1, C_2).$$
$$\mathtt{cdep}^*(C_1, C_2) :- \mathtt{cdep}(C_1, C), \mathtt{cdep}^*(C, C_2).$$

The relation cdep*(C_1, C_2) captures all the containers C_2 on which the container C_1 depends, i.e., some token in C_1 may be derived either directly or transitively from tokens in C_2. We call C_2 the container dependency of each token in C_1. Note that while all tokens in a container C_1 have the same set of container dependencies, they may depend on different tokens within those containers.

The second step computes the positions of all the tokens in all container dependencies C_2 on which a token at position l in container C_1 depends by using the consumption and production rates. The result of this step is a relation

$$\text{dependency}(D, C_1, L, C_2, L_S, L_E)$$

where D is a data token in container C_1 at position L that depends on the tokens in container C_2 starting at position L_S and ending at position L_E. We describe how this relation is computed in the rest of this section and in Sect. 4. Finally, the third step uses the dependency relation to answer lineage queries, which is also further described in Sect. 4. The result of this step is a (virtual) relation

$$\text{lineage}(D_1, D_2, D_3)$$

where data tokens D_2 and D_3 form a dependency edge that lies on the lineage path of D_1. Thus, ddep(D_1, D_2), ddep(D_1, D_3), and ddep(D_2, D_3) hold such that given a specific token d, lineage(d, D_2, D_3) gives the set of dependency (ddep(D_2, D_3)) edges that represent the lineage of d.

The following definitions are used to compute the dependency and lineage information. We assume below that x is a container dependency of y and that $y[k]$ denotes the kth position in y.

- $end_x(y[k])$ is the last position in x that the token at $y[k]$ depends.
- $width_{xy}$ is the number of consecutive positions in x that tokens in y depend on.
- $start_x(y[k])$ is the first position in x that the token at $y[k]$ depends on such that $start_x(y[k]) = end_x(y[k]) - width_{xy} + 1$.
- $dep_x(y[k])$ is the sequence of positions in x that the token at $y[k]$ depends on such that $dep_x(y[k]) = [start_x(y[k]), start_x(y[k]) + 1, \ldots, end_x(y[k])]$.

The rest of this section describes how to compute $end_i(j[k])$ and $width_{ij}$ for various types of actors and workflow patterns. The $start_i(j[k])$ is then computed using $end_i(j[k])$ and $width_{ij}$.

Stateless Actors. Consider the actor B in Fig. 1 (which we assume here is stateless). An invocation of B consumes v_c tokens from container V and produces x_p tokens in container X. Let's assume that we want to know the dependencies of the kth token in X on the tokens in V. To do so, we need to know the invocation of B that produced the kth token in X as well as all of the tokens from V that were consumed. Since in each invocation, B outputs x_p tokens into X, $\lceil \frac{k}{x_p} \rceil$ is the invocation during which the kth token was produced in X and as B consumes v_c tokens from V per invocation, $end_v(x[k]) = v_c * \lceil \frac{k}{x_p} \rceil$ and $width_{vx} = v_c$. Thus, tokens from positions $start_v(x[k])$ through $end_v(x[k])$ in V were consumed to produce the kth token in X.

Now, let's assume that we want to know the dependencies of the kth token in container X on the tokens in container U in Fig. 1 (again, assuming A is stateless). To do so, we first compute $end_v(x[k])$ and $width_{vx}$ as above and then use these two values to compute $end_u(x[k])$ and $width_{ux}$, where $end_u(x[k]) = u_c * \lceil \frac{end_v(x[k])}{v_p} \rceil$ and $width_{ux} = u_c * \lceil \frac{width_{vx}}{v_p} \rceil$. We extend this approach to a chain of n actors, where we want to know the dependencies of the kth token in the jth container on the tokens in the ith container. We use the following formulas to compute $end_i(j[k])$ and $width_{ij}$.

$$end_i(j[k]) = \begin{cases} i_c * \lceil \frac{end_{i+1}(j[k])}{(i+1)_p} \rceil & \text{if } j > i+1 \\ i_c * \lceil \frac{k}{j_p} \rceil & \text{if } j = i+1 \end{cases}$$

$$width_{i,j} = \begin{cases} i_c * \lceil \frac{width_{i+1,j}}{(i+1)_p} \rceil & \text{if } j > i+1 \\ i_c & \text{if } j = i+1 \end{cases}$$

Feedback Loops. A workflow has a feedback loop if there is a cycle among the actors and containers as shown in Fig. 2(a) and (b). In Fig. 2(a), actor A is connected to container X with consumption and production rates x_c and x_p, respectively. To prevent deadlock[2], x_c tokens are initially provided in X before invocations are started. In this case, tokens from $(x_c + 1)^{th}$ through $(2 * x_c)^{th}$ positions in X, which are generated during the 1st invocation of A, will depend on the first x_c tokens in X. Subsequently, the pth set of x_c tokens in X, which were generated during the $(p-1)^{th}$ invocation of A, will depend on the $(p-1)^{th}$ set of x_c tokens in X. Thus, any token generated during the pth invocation will depend on the 1st through $x_c * (p - 1)$ tokens in X. Using this idea we compute $end_x(x[k])$ as shown below. Here $width_{xx} = end_x(x[k])$, i.e., $start_x(x[k]) = 1$.

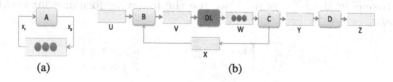

(a)   (b)

Fig. 2. Two example workflows containing feedback loops.

$$end_x(x[k]) = \begin{cases} x_c * (\lceil \frac{k}{x_p} \rceil - 1) & \text{if } k > x_p \\ 0 & \text{otherwise} \end{cases}$$

---

[2] Actors in a feedback loop would be in deadlock as an actor in the loop would expect input tokens in its input ports. But, all actors in the loop expects the same and thus, it would get into a deadlock [8].

In Fig. 2(b), a *SimpleDelay* (*DL*) actor is used to avoid deadlock and we assume that W is the starting container into which DL initially outputs n tokens, where $2 * w_c > n >= w_c$ [8]. Here, containers V, W, and X are contained in a workflow loop. Now assume we want to know the dependencies of the kth token in the jth container on the tokens in the ith container. In this case, if the jth container depends on all of the containers in the loop, we use the following formula to compute $end_i(j[k])$. Here $width_{ij} = end_i(j[k])$, i.e., $start_i(j[k]) = 1$.

$$end_i(j[k]) = \begin{cases} i_c * \lceil \frac{end_{i+1}(j[k]) - n}{(i+1)_p} \rceil & \text{if } i+1 \text{ is the starting container, e.g., } W \\ i_c * \lceil \frac{end_{i+1}(j[k])}{(i+1)_p} \rceil & \text{if } i+1 \text{ is not the starting container} \\ 0 & \text{if } k <= n \text{ and } i+1 \text{ is the starting container} \end{cases}$$

If the jth container does not depend on any of the containers in the loop, e.g., if we want to know $end_y(z[k])$ in Fig. 2(b), then we use the formulas discussed above for stateless actors.

Stateful Actors. Stateful actors vary based on how they buffer and pass tokens from one invocation to the next. As discussed above, we consider two variations: (1) *Fixed Buffering*, and (2) *Dynamic Buffering*. Let's assume actor A is a *Fixed Buffering* actor with an input container X and an output container Y such that during any invocation, A consumes x_c tokens from X and produces y_p tokens into Y. When an invocation starts, actor A first fills the buffer by consuming x_c tokens per invocation and once the buffer is full, in subsequent invocations it removes x_c tokens from the buffer (i.e., the queue) consuming x_c new tokens, while keeping the buffer size at x_s. Thus, to know the dependencies of the kth token in Y on the tokens in X, we compute $end_x(y[k])$ and $width_{xy}$, where $end_x(y[k]) = x_c * \lceil \frac{k}{y_p} \rceil$ and $\lceil \frac{k}{y_p} \rceil$ is the invocation during which the kth token was generated. Similarly, $width_{xy} = x_s$ if the buffer is full, otherwise $width_{xy} = x_c * \lceil \frac{k}{y_p} \rceil$. Thus, given a chain of actors, to compute the dependencies of the kth token in the jth container on the tokens in the ith container, we use the following formulas for $end_i(j[k])$ and $width_{ij}$.

$$end_i(j[k]) = \begin{cases} i_c * \lceil \frac{end_{i+1}(j[k])}{(i+1)_p} \rceil & \text{if } j > i+1 \\ i_c * \lceil \frac{k}{j_p} \rceil & \text{if } j = i+1 \end{cases}$$

$$width_{i,j} = \begin{cases} i_c * \lceil \frac{width_{i+1,j}}{(i+1)_p} \rceil + i_s - i_c & \text{if } \lceil \frac{i_s}{i_c} \rceil \leq \lceil \frac{end_{i+1}(j[k])}{(i+1)_p} \rceil - \lceil \frac{width_{i+1,j}}{(i+1)_p} \rceil + 1 \\ i_c * \lceil \frac{end_{i+1}(j[k])}{(i+1)_p} \rceil & \text{Otherwise} \end{cases}$$

If an actor instead uses *Dynamic Buffering*, it will consume all of its buffered tokens in each of its previous invocations. Note that the dependency computation for this type of actor is exactly the same as with feedback loops with a single actor as discussed above.

Example. We now show (by example) how to use the formulas discussed in this section. Consider the example workflow shown in Fig. 1 and assume that all the

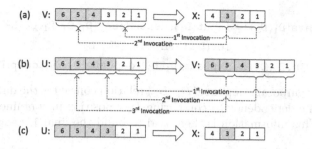

Fig. 3. This is partial execution details of the workflow in Fig. 1. In (a), and (b) we show partial invocation details of actors B, and A respectively. In (c) we show the relationship among U and X channel, which are transitively dependent.

actors are stateless. Assume we want to know the dependencies of the 3rd token in container X, i.e., on which all tokens in containers V and U the 3rd token in container X depends. We use the cdep*(C_1, C_2) to find out that any token in X depends on tokens in V and U. First, we find the dependencies of $x[3]$ on the tokens in V. Here, $x_p = 2$, $k = 3$, and $v_c = 3$ using the stateless actor formulas from which we get $end_v(x[k]) = 6$ and $weight_{vx} = 3$. That is, the token at $x[3]$ depends on the tokens at $v[4]$, $v[5]$, and $v[6]$, as shown in Fig. 3(a). These dependencies are captured in the dependency relation as dependency($id, x, 3, v, 4, 6$), where id is assumed to be the token identifier for $x[3]$. Second, we need to find the dependencies of $v[4]$, $v[5]$, and $v[6]$ on the tokens in U. Here, $v_p = 2$, $k = 6$, and $u_c = 2$ and thus we get $end_u(v[k]) = 6$ and $weight_{uv} = 4$. Then $v[4]$, $v[5]$, and $v[6]$ tokens depend on the $u[3]$, $u[4]$, $u[5]$, and $u[6]$ tokens, which is shown in Fig. 3(b). These dependencies are captured in the dependency relation as dependency($id, x, 3, u, 3, 6$).

In Sect. 4, we discuss how to compute the lineage relation once all the dependency tuples have been obtained.

4   Querying Lineage Using Dependency Tables

Our approach allows users to ask for the lineage of one or more data tokens within a single query. Here we assume that each of the data tokens D_1 from which lineage should be computed is stored in a relation input(D_1). From dependency($D_1, C_1, L_1, C_2, L_S, L_E$), we know that D_1 is a data token in container C_1 at position L_1 and that it depends on the tokens in container C_2 starting at position L_S and ending at position L_E. We also assume a relation loc(D_2, C_2, L_2) that captures the tokens stored within each container during workflow execution such that a token D_2 was stored in container C_2 at location L_2. Given these relations, we use the following Datalog rules to compute the lineage relation.

$$\text{depData}(D_1, D_2) :- \text{input}(D_1), \text{dependency}(D_1, C_1, L_1, C_2, L_S, L_E),$$
$$\text{loc}(D_2, C_2, L_2), L_2 \geq L_S, L_2 \leq L_E.$$
$$\text{lineage}(D_1, D_2, D_3) :- \text{depData}(D_1, D_2), \text{depData}(D_1, D_3), \text{ddep}(D_2, D_3).$$

As shown, the temporary $\text{depData}(D_1, D_2)$ relation computes the data tokens D_2 that D_1 has as a dependency by comparing D_2's position in container C_2 against L_S and L_E. This information is then used to build the final $\text{lineage}(D_1, D_2, D_3)$ relation.

To better understand the performance of our location-based lineage technique we compare its runtime and space requirements to lineage computation techniques based on the semi-naive query evaluation approach and the approach of directly storing the transitive dependency closure. We briefly describe these two techniques below.

Semi-Naive Query Evaluation. First, we query the $\text{ddep}(D_1, D_2)$ relation to find the tokens D_2, on which D_1 directly depends. Then, we compute the "transitive" dependencies of D_1 in rounds, where in each round we find new reachable data tokens. The $\text{dep}(D_1, D_2, D_3, J)$ relation captures the reachable token D_3 along with the token D_2 from which D_3 is reachable from D_1. Here, J is the round number with at most N rounds, where N is the diameter of the data dependency graph (based on the $\text{ddep}(D_1, D_2)$ relation). This approach is implemented using the following Datalog rules and further details can be found in [6].

$$\text{delta}(D_1, D_2, D_3, I) :- \text{ddep}(D_1, D_3), I = 1, \text{input}(D_1), D_2 = D_1.$$
$$\text{newDep}(D_1, D_2, D_3, J) :- \text{delta}(D_1, D_2, D, I), \text{ddep}(D, D_3), J = I + 1.$$
$$\text{delta}(D_1, D_2, D_3, J) :- \text{newDep}(D_1, D_2, D_3, J), \neg \text{dep}(D_1, D_2, D_3, I), I = J - 1.$$
$$\text{dep}(D_1, D_2, D_3, J) :- \text{delta}(D_1, D_2, D_3, J).$$
$$\text{lineage}(D_1, D_2, D_3) :- \text{dep}(D_1, D_2, D_3, \_).$$

Transitive Closure Based Query Evaluation. In this approach, the transitive closure of data dependencies is first computed and stored. Once stored, all subsequent lineage queries are answered directly from the closure. The following Datalog rules demonstrate the approach where the transitive closure of the $\text{ddep}(D_1, D_2)$ is stored in the $\text{ddep}^*(D_1, D_2)$ relation. Then, the $\text{lineage}(D_1, D_2, D_3)$ relation is computed using the $\text{ddep}^*(D_1, D_2)$ and $\text{ddep}(D_1, D_2)$ relations.

$$\text{ddep}^*(D_1, D_2) :- \text{ddep}(D_1, D_2).$$
$$\text{ddep}^*(D_1, D_2) :- \text{ddep}(D_1, D), \text{ddep}^*(D, D_2).$$
$$\text{lineage}(D_1, D_2, D_3) :- \text{input}(D_1), \text{ddep}^*(D_1, D_2), \text{ddep}^*(D_1, D_3), \text{ddep}(D_2, D_3).$$

5   Experiments and Results

Experiment Setup. We used three workflow patterns as shown in Fig. 4 to evaluate our *location-based lineage (LBL)* computation technique against the

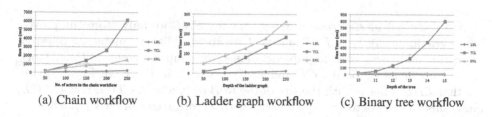

(a) Chain.   (b) Ladder graph   (c) Binary tree

Fig. 4. Different workflow patterns we used in our experiments.

two natural choices *Semi-Naive Query Evaluation (SNL)* and *Transitive Closure Based Query Evaluation (TCL)*[3]. In all our experiments, the workflow specification and provenance graphs were generated for all three workflows using the respective models presented in Sect. 2. We generated provenance graphs for first workflow shown in Fig. 4(a), which forms a *chain* pattern, with 30 tokens in the first container, all the actors with three invocations, and with both the consumption and production rates equal to10 for all containers, while varying the number of actors in the chain. Similarly, for the second workflow shown in Fig. 4(b), which forms a *ladder graph* pattern, we assumed only one token for both the initial containers and assumed both the consumption and production rates equal to 1 for all containers, and we generated the provenance graphs by varying the number of actors in the graph. For the third workflow shown in Fig. 4(c), which forms a *binary tree* pattern, we assumed only one token to the initial container and assumed both the consumption and production rates to be 1 for all the containers, and generated provenance graphs by varying the height of the tree.

For all three lineage querying techniques, i.e., *LBL*, *SNL*, and *TCL*, discussed in this paper, we persist the provenance graph. In addition, for *LBL* we compute and persiste the dependency$(D, C_1, L, C_2, L_S, L_E)$, and loc$(D, C, L)$ relations and for *TCL* we compute and persist the ddep$^*(D_1, D_2)$ relation.

We then evaluated lineage queries using the algorithms discussed in Sect. 4, where we ran all the queries 100 times and took an average query time.

(a) Chain workflow   (b) Ladder graph workflow   (c) Binary tree workflow

Fig. 5. Comparisons of run times of computing lineage.

Analysis. When we review the chart in Fig. 5(a), we see that as the size of the workflow grow, i.e., the number of actors grow, *SNL* outperforms *TCL*.

---

[3] we introduce these acronyms to be used in the charts presenting the results in Figs. 5 and 6.

This is because of the high growth rate of the ddep*(D_1, D_2) relation for TCL
over the size of the workflow. In Fig. 5(b), TCL outperforms SNL. There are
two reasons, (i) number of iterations for SNL, which is directly proportional
to the size of the graph, and (ii) growth in data volume, which is not high in
this case as both consumption and productions are 1. Thus, the growth in data
volume of the ddep*(D_1, D_2) relation for TCL is not significant. Now, in case
the containers have higher consumption of productions rates as in the case of
Fig. 5(a), SNL would eventually outperform TCL. In Fig. 5(c), we find TCL to
be non-linear, where as both SNL and LBL are linear with very low slopes.
This is because of the properties of a binary tree. From any given leaf node,
to find its lineage, SNL needs the number of iterations equal to the height of
the binary tree and in each iteration, SNL only find one new edge, whereas
the volume of the ddep*(D_1, D_2) relation for TCL is large, which be seen in
Fig. 6(c). In all three charts in Fig. 5, we see that LBL to be linear with very
low slopes and we observed that as the size of workflow and the consumption
and production rates grows, LBL scales better compare to TCL and SNL. Here,
the observations are (i) when the consumption and production rates grows, the
volume of ddep*(D_1, D_2) relation grows rapidly adversely impacting TCL, but
does not impact LBL, and (ii) when the size of the workflow grows, the number
of rounds for SNL grows, which impacts its performance, without impacting
LBL.

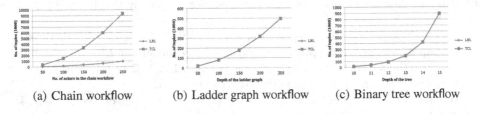

(a) Chain workflow   (b) Ladder graph workflow   (c) Binary tree workflow

Fig. 6. Comparisons of additional space requirements of computing lineage

We discussed in *Experiment Setup* that for SNL we only store the provenance graph, but for both TCL and LBL we store additional metadata towards
improving efficiencies of lineage queries. Thus, we compare these additional storage requirements by both TCL and LBL as shown in Fig. 6. In Fig. 6(a), we
see that LBL is linear with the size of the workflow, whereas TCL is not. TCL
maintains all pairs of token dependencies with a storage cost of $\mathcal{O}(|V|^2)$, whereas
LBL maintains only one record for all the dependencies for a token to all tokens
of another container with a storage cost of $\mathcal{O}(|V| * k)$, where $|V|$ and k are the
number of tokens and the number of containers respectively, with $|V| \gg k$.
Now, in case there is only one token in a container then storage requirements of
both LBL and TCL become same. This is the reason why in Fig. 6(b) and (c)
the space requirements for both LBL and TCL are same.

Thus, these experiments show that LBL outperforms the traditional lineage querying techniques and is more scalable both in query time and additional space requirements.

6   Related Work

The problem of efficiently evaluating lineage queries has been an active area of research and many approaches have been introduced. Heinis et al. [5] proposed an extension to tree-based interval encoding that supports DAGs. As part of this approach, a DAG representing provenance information is converted to a (compressed) tree structure. While this can improve query execution time (based on using interval encodings), the storage cost can significantly increase since shared portions of the graph are copied in the corresponding tree structure. Both [5] and LBL support lineage for all tokens, where only LBL is both space and time efficient.

The Zoom*UserView by Biton et al. [12] allows users to specify the relevant parts of a workflow, customize both the workflow and provenance based on that specification, and then query the reduced provenance graph based on a "virtual" workflow. Missier et al. [13] developed an efficient and scalable algorithm for querying fine-grained lineage information by exploiting the model of computation used in the Taverna workflow system [14]. LBL is similar to [13] as both techniques are exploiting the constraints of models of computation, but, LBL (i) precomputes lineage even before the execution of the workflow by forecasting the sizes of the input containers and later adjusts the lineage with the actual sizes, and (ii) enables lineage for all the tokens and thus expands the use of provenance, e.g., for focused data analysis where only input dependencies of an output is needed, and debugging where dependencies on the intermediate tokens are also needed.

Trio [15] and GridDB [16] use recursive query evaluation on a collection-based data model to answer lineage queries. Both [15,16] support lineage for all tokens as LBL does, but, LBL is time efficient while incurring very little additional space cost.

7   Conclusion and Future Work

Lineage information plays a key role in helping users understand and reuse data generated by scientific workflow systems. Many applications of provenance within these systems rely on being able to easily pose and efficiently answer lineage queries, which for data-intensive workflows require evaluation techniques that are both time and space efficient. While semi-naive query evaluation is generally space efficient, it may result in slow query execution time, whereas computing and storing transitive closures can result in faster query execution time at the cost of increased storage space. In this paper, we have developed a new location-based lineage approach that is both space and time efficient. Our approach exploits information available in workflow specifications, in particular, container dependency information and the consumption-production rate constraints used in many workflow systems. Our experimental results demonstrate that the location-based lineage technique is both efficient and scalable for various types of workflow patterns and results in both faster query evaluation time and lower storage space requirements than using semi-naive query evaluation and storing transitive closures. As future work, we are currently extending the location-based approach presented here to support more complex data structures (e.g., collections of data tokens) that are increasingly being developed for more general dataflow frameworks.

Acknowledgments. Supported in part by NSF ACI-0830944 and IIS-1118088.

References

1. Gil, Y., Deelman, E., Ellisman, M., Fahringer, T., Fox, G., Gannon, D., Goble, C., Livny, M., Moreau, L., Myers, J.: Examining the challenges of scientific workflows. Computer **40**(12), 24–32 (2007)
2. Davidson, S.B., Boulakia, S.C., Eyal, A., Ludäscher, B., McPhillips, T.M., Bowers, S., Anand, M.K., Freire, J.: Provenance in scientific workflow systems. IEEE Data Eng. Bull. **30**(4), 44–50 (2007)
3. Miles, S., Deelman, E., Groth, P., Vahi, K., Mehta, G., Moreau, L.: Connecting scientific data to scientific experiments with provenance. In: Proceedings of the IEEE International Conference on e-Science and Grid Computing, pp. 179–186 (2007)
4. Anand, M.K., Bowers, S., Ludäscher, B.: Techniques for efficiently querying scientific workflow provenance graphs. In: EDBT, pp. 287–298 (2010)
5. Heinis, T., Alonso, G.: Efficient lineage tracking for scientific workflows. In: Proceedings of the 2008 ACM SIGMOD International Conference on Management of Data, pp. 1007–1018. ACM (2008)
6. Abiteboul, S., Hull, R., Vianu, V.: Foundations of Databases, vol. 8. Addison-Wesley, Reading (1995)
7. Koop, D., Freire, J., Silva, C.T.: Enabling Reproducible Science with VisTrails. CoRR abs/1309.1784 (2013)
8. Lee, E.A., Messerschmitt, D.G.: Synchronous data flow. Proc. IEEE **75**(9), 1235–1245 (1987)
9. Sun, S., Chen, J., Li, W., Altintas, I., Lin, A.W., Peltier, S., Stocks, K., Allen, E.E., Ellisman, M.H., Grethe, J.S., Wooley, J.C.: Community cyberinfrastructure for advanced microbial ecology research and analysis: the CAMERA resource. Nucleic Acids Res. **39**, 546–551 (2011)
10. Altintas, I., Wang, J., Crawl, D., Li, W.: Challenges and approaches for distributed workflow-driven analysis of large-scale biological data: vision paper. In: EDBT/ICDT Workshops, pp. 73–78 (2012)
11. Moreau, L., Clifford, B., Freire, J., Futrelle, J., Gil, Y., Groth, P., Kwasnikowska, N., Miles, S., Missier, P., Myers, J., Plale, B., Simmhan, Y., Stephan, E., den Bussche, J.V.: The open provenance model core specification (v1.1). Future Gener. Comput. Syst. **27**(6), 743–756 (2011)
12. Biton, O., Cohen-Boulakia, S., Davidson, S.: Zoom* userviews: querying relevant provenance in workflow systems. In: Proceedings of the 33rd International Conference on Very Large Data Bases, pp. 1366–1369. VLDB Endowment (2007)

13. Missier, P., Paton, N.W., Belhajjame, K.: Fine-grained and efficient lineage querying of collection-based workflow provenance. In: EDBT, pp. 299–310 (2010)
14. Turi, D., Missier, P., Goble, C., De Roure, D., Oinn, T.: Taverna workflows: syntax and semantics. In: International e-Science and Grid Computing Conference, pp. 441–448 (2007)
15. Benjelloun, O., Sarma, A.D., Halevy, A., Theobald, M., Widom, J.: Databases with uncertainty and lineage. VLDB J. **17**(2), 243–264 (2008)
16. Liu, D.T., Franklin, M.J.: GridDB: a data-centric overlay for scientific grids. In: Proceedings of the Thirtieth International Conference on Very Large Data Bases, vol. 30, pp. 600–611. VLDB Endowment (2004)

System Demonstrations

Interrogating Capabilities of IoT Devices

Stanislav Beran, Edoardo Pignotti$^{(\boxtimes)}$, and Peter Edwards

Computing Science and dot.rural Digital Economy Hub, University of Aberdeen,
Aberdeen AB24 5UA, UK
{s.beran,e.pignotti,p.edwards}@abdn.ac.uk

Abstract. In this demo we present the *Trusted Tiny Things* system that
can be used to interrogate Internet of Things (IoT) devices and present
users with information about their characteristics and capabilities. The
system consists of a mobile application used to retrieve information about
IoT devices supported by RESTful web services. In order to infer IoT
device capabilities our services perform reasoning over the provenance
of devices characterised using an extension of the PROV-O ontology.
In this demo we illustrate the use of the system with two distinct IoT
devices: an NFC tag used at bus stops to provide a means to access
real-time bus timetables, and a blackbox device installed into vehicles
by insurance companies to track driving behaviour.

Keywords: Internet of things · Provenance · Transparency

1 Introduction

The *Trusted Tiny Things project*[1] is exploring how semantic technologies can
make Internet of Things (IoT) devices more transparent to users. IoT devices
now routinely gather, analyse and manipulate data from their surroundings;
they are also capable of exchanging such data with other devices and services
by means of M2M (Machine to Machine) communications. The need for transparency in the IoT domain is seen as crucial in order to ensure the legitimacy
of activities performed by devices, but also to increase security and privacy [1].
Certain operations associated with IoT devices may be deemed undesirable by
users (e.g. third-party data sharing, consumption of personal data), and therefore users should be made aware of such capabilities. In this paper we argue
that by publishing information about IoT devices such as manufacturer, owner,
device type) according to the linked data principles [2] and by capturing their
provenance (e.g. services, owners, organisations, etc.), it is possible to make
capabilities of IoT devices more transparent.

We are investigating these issues via two user scenarios. The first of these
explores the use of NFC tags attached to timetables at bus stops in Aberdeenshire, UK. A user with an NFC enabled phone can scan such tags to access a

---

[1] This research is supported by the UK Research Councils' Digital Economy IT
as a Utility Network+ (EP/K003569/1) and the dot.rural Digital Economy Hub
(EP/G066051/1).

B. Ludäscher and B. Plale (Eds.): IPAW 2014, LNCS 8628, pp. 197–202, 2015.
DOI: 10.1007/978-3-319-16462-5_15

real-time bus timetable via the phone's web browser. Users may expect that the service is operated by Aberdeenshire Council, but in fact it is run by an external IT solutions provider. As part of offering the service, this third party organisation collects data from the smartphone (e.g. IP address, type of smartphone device). Our second user scenario investigates the use of in-car blackboxes, which are being installed into vehicles by insurance companies. These devices are used to track driver's behaviour in order to tailor insurance premiums to individuals. The devices continuously collect data (e.g. GPS location, acceleration, driving patterns, etc.) and connect to a third party service that collects the data on behalf of the insurance company. In this scenario the service could change over time. For example, a new organisation (e.g. a car manufacturer analysing engine management data) could be allowed to use the data generated by the sensors.

2   Semantic Framework

In order to inform the design of a semantic framework for IoT devices we have conducted three participatory design events involving a total of 14 participants with different technological backgrounds. Participants were asked to discuss issues surrounding the capabilities of IoT devices. Questions were posed such as: *What do you think are the capabilities of this device?* and *What kind of capabilities would you want to be aware of before interacting with this kind of device?*. We have developed an OWL ontology[2] (illustrated in Fig. 1) to link physical entities (*iota:PhysicalEntity*) with their IoT components (*iota:Device*[3]) using concepts derived from a model created as part of the Internet of Things Architecture (IoTa) project[4]. This allows us to identify those IoT devices and their virtual representations (*iota:VirtualEntity*) so we can analyse their characteristics and capabilities. The PROV-O [3] ontology is used as an upper ontology and allows us to characterise entities (data), activities (device processes and operations) and agents (either software or physical) associated with IoT devices and supporting services. For example, we can associate a particular device activity (e.g. location sensing) to the agent that initiated the operation (e.g. insurance company). Using PROV-O allows queries to be formulated such as: Who initiated the action? What entities have been used? When was a particular action executed? However, PROV-O on its own cannot answer questions such as: Why and for what purpose were the data used? Is the data confidential?

Guided by user requirements we have designed an ontology to support inferences about device capabilities using provenance described according to the PROV-O and IoTa ontology. We created a lightweight ontological model called T3[5] that provides annotations over provenance records. Using this model, we

---

[2] http://t3.abdn.ac.uk/ontologies/iota.owl.
[3] An artefact that provides an interface between the digital world and the physical world.
[4] http://www.iot-a.eu.
[5] http://t3.abdn.ac.uk/ontologies/t3.owl.

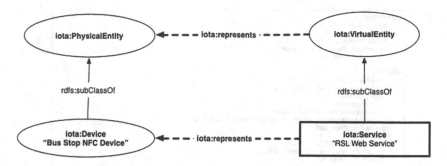

Fig. 1. An extract of the iota ontology representing relationships between a virtual entities and a physical entities in the internet of things

are able to annotate the qualified usage class (*prov:Usage*) with *ttt:purpose* to describe why a particular entity (data) is used by a specific activity.

When managing provenance of IoT devices it is not always possible to instrument devices and services to generate information about their usage and operation (retrospective provenance). In some cases, manufacturers can provide information on how devices are intended to operate (prospective provenance). In our framework we therefore make provision for both kinds of provenance. Our framework is also capable of distinguishing between direct capabilities (activities performed onboard the device) and indirect capabilities (activities performed by associated devices or services).

In order to infer the capabilities of IoT devices using our ontological framework we can associate rules to specific classes of *ttt:Capability*. We make use of the SPIN ontology[6] to support the use of SPARQL to specify rules and logical constraints necessary to reason about capabilities. The SPIN ontology allows SPARQL queries to be represented in RDF and associated to classes in an ontology using a pre-defined *spin:rule* property that can be used to specify inference rules using SPARQL CONSTRUCT, DELETE and INSERT statements. Figure 2 (top box) shows an example of such a rule for the *ttt:DataConsumption* class. The rule is designed to traverse a PROV-O provenance graph starting from an instance of an *iota:Device* and to identify activities that have used or generated entities classified as personal data. Once such activities have been identified the rule specifies how an annotation about the data consumption capability is generated, including a link to the agent responsible for the activity and the specific purpose. In this ontology we have also specified two rules that are used to determine what provenance has been used to infer a specific device capability. These rules make use of the *ttt:Follows* qualified relationship to distinguish between prospective and retrospective provenance and are illustrated in Fig. 2 (bottom left and bottom right boxes).

Participants during our design exercises highlighted the need to provide contact information about agents (individuals or organisations) responsible for

---

[6] http://spinrdf.org/spin.html.

```
CONSTRUCT {
    _:b0 a :DataConsumption .
    _:b0 :consumes ?data .
    _:b0 :consumer ?agent .
    _:b0 :purpose ?purposeDescription .
    ?this :isCapableOf _:b0 .
}
WHERE {
    ?virtualentity iota:represents ?this .
    ?activity (prov:qualifiedUsage)+ ?usage .
    ?usage prov:entity ?data .
    ?data a :PersonalData .
    ?usage :purpose ?purposeDescription .
    ?activity (prov:wasAssociatedWith)+/prov:actedOnBehalfOf ?agent .
    ?agent a foaf:Organization .
    NOT EXISTS {
        ?this :isCapableOf ?capability .
        ?capability :purpose ?purposeDescription .
        ?capability :consumer ?agent .
        ?capability :consumes ?data .
    } .
}
```

```
CONSTRUCT {
    ?device :prospectiveCapability ?capability .
}
WHERE {
    ?device prov:wasAttributedTo ?agent .
    ?agent :qualifiedFollow ?follow .
    ?follow :shouldGenerate ?bundle .
    ?device :isCapableOf ?capability .
    ?capability :consumes ?data .
    ?bundle :contains ?data .
    NOT EXISTS {
        ?device :prospectiveCapability ?capability .
    } .
}
```

```
CONSTRUCT {
    ?device :retrospectiverCapability ?capability .
}
WHERE {
    ?device prov:wasAttributedTo ?agent .
    ?bundle a prov:Bundle .
    ?bundle prov:wasAttributedTo ?agent .
    ?device :isCapableOf ?capability .
    ?capability :consumes ?data .
    ?bundle :contains ?data .
    NOT EXISTS {
        ?device :retrospectiveCapability ?capability .
    } .
}
```

Fig. 2. Example of device capability inference rule (top box) and two rules used to distinguish between prospective and retrospective provenance (bottom left and bottom right boxes).

certain devices and therefore we use the FOAF[7] ontology. The class *foaf: Organization* is defined as a subclass of *prov:Agent*. Figure 3 presents a visualisation of the device capabilities in a mobile app and the respective sample provenance graph taken from the bus stop scenario.

3   The Trusted Tiny Things System

In order to support our semantic framework we have developed a software infrastructure (see Fig. 4) that can be used to query, update and register IoT devices and to notify the user of any changes in the capabilities of a particular device. We store device data in an OpenRDF Sesame[8] triplestore. Additionally, we utilize a MySQL database server to store smartphone IDs (used to identify users) and accepted device capabilities. Our framework is composed of five core services, which are responsible for registering devices to our system, updating and synchronizing the provenance record, providing access to information, reasoning over the provenance record to infer capabilities, and notifying users about changes in device provenance. In order for a user to interact with the system, we have implemented an Android mobile application (Fig. 3), that is able to query

---

[7] http://www.foaf-project.org/.
[8] http://www.openrdf.org.

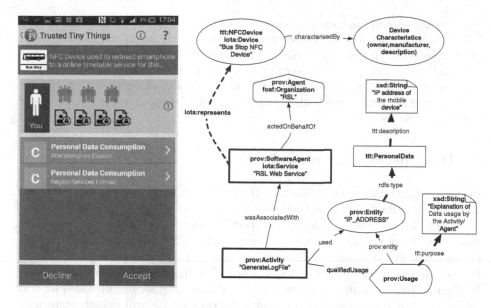

Fig. 3. Smartphone app showing the capabilities of a bus stop NFC tag (left) and an extract of the supporting provenance (right).

and visualise capabilities of IoT devices registered in our system and to notify users of changes in the provenance record. The application can be downloaded from the Google Play Store[9].

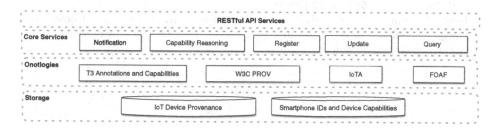

Fig. 4. Trusted Tiny Things System Architecture

The provenance-based approach for determining the capabilities of a device has certain advantages over similar compliance-based alternatives. In Google Play, for example, users are presented with a list of access permissions based on the capabilities of the app being installed. These permissions are determined only by the functionalities implemented in the app (e.g. use of the GPS sensor) disregarding how and why information is used and by whom. However, by using

---

[9] https://play.google.com/store/apps/details?id=uk.ac.abdn.t3.trustedtinythings.

a provenance-based approach, it is possible to define capabilities in terms of how information has been used. Moreover, the Google Play approach notifies users of changes only when a new version of the app is pushed into the store. In our approach, such changes are determined using the provenance record which is independent from new versions of applications, devices or services (e.g. change in the server infrastructure with regards to manipulation of user's data triggers notification to user).

4   Demonstration Content

In the demonstration we will illustrate the behaviour of the system using the two scenarios described above. In the Bus Stop scenario we will highlight the capabilities of the NFC device based on prospective provenance. A short presentation video of this scenario can be viewed at our Trusted Tiny Things website[10]. In the car blackbox scenario we will demonstrate how retrospective provenance is used to infer the capabilities of the telemetry box. Finally, we will showcase our notification service by changing the way that the insurance service operates (it will begin to share sensor data with car manufacturers). We will demonstrate how our system would detect the change and infer new capabilities associated with this change (i.e. confidential data is now shared with a third-party company).

References

1. Weber, R.H., Weber, R.: Internet of Things. Springer, New York (2010)
2. Bizer, C., Heath, T., Berners-Lee, T.: Linked data-the story so far. Int. J. Semant. Web Inform. Syst. **5**(3), 1–22 (2009)
3. Lebo, T., Sahoo, S., McGuinness, D., Belhajjame, K., Cheney, J., Corsar, D., Garijo, D., Soiland-Reyes, S., Zednik, S., Zhao, J.: Prov-o: The prov ontology. W3C Recommendation, 30 April 2013

---

[10] http://t3.abdn.ac.uk.

A Lightweight Provenance Pingback and Query Service for Web Publications

Tom De Nies[1]([✉]), Robert Meusel[2], Dominique Ritze[2],
Kai Eckert[2], Anastasia Dimou[1], Laurens De Vocht[1],
Ruben Verborgh[1], Erik Mannens[1], and Rik Van de Walle[1]

[1] Ghent University - iMinds - Multimedia Lab, Ghent, Belgium
{tom.denies,anastasia.dimou,laurens.devocht,
ruben.verborgh,erik.mannens,rik.vandewalle}@ugent.be
[2] Research Group Data and Web Science,
University of Mannheim, Mannheim, Germany
{robert,dominique,kai}@informatik.uni-mannheim.de

Abstract. Web resources, such as publications, datasets, pictures and others can be directly linked to their provenance data, as described in the specification about Provenance Access and Query (PROV-AQ) by the W3C. On its own, this approach places all responsibility with the publisher of the resource, who hopefully maintains and publishes provenance information. In reality, however, most publishers lack incentives to publish the provenance of resources, even if the owner would like such information to be published. Currently, it is very intricate to link existing resources to new provenance information, either provided by the owner or a third party. In this paper, we present a solution for this problem by implementing a lightweight, read/write provenance query service, integrated with a pingback mechanism, following the PROV-AQ recommendation.

1 Introduction

Provenance is an essential part of trust and value assessment of web content, as it describes everything involved in producing this content. The PROV-AQ document [KGM+13] describes several options to access provenance:

- providing a *link header* in the HTTP response of the resource
- providing a *link element* in its HTML representation
- providing a `prov:has_provenance` *relation* in its RDF representation

In all these cases, however, the representation of the resource is directly linked to its corresponding provenance, so that only the publisher of the resource is in control of which provenance information is provided. This type of *"packaged"* solution gives rise to multiple issues, particularly when the owner of the resource is not in control of the publication process. In this paper, we will focus on the domain of *scientific publishing* since it is a striking example showing this

© Springer International Publishing Switzerland 2015
B. Ludäscher and B. Plale (Eds.): IPAW 2014, LNCS 8628, pp. 203–208, 2015.
DOI: 10.1007/978-3-319-16462-5_16

characteristic. Furthermore, the need of providing additional provenance information in this domain has long been identified [DF08, ZGSB04].

In the domain of scientific publishing, the resource (usually a PDF document) is published by the publisher, whereas its provenance (e.g. datasets, processes, and/or software used) is generally controlled by the author. Besides provenance information created at publication time, additional information such as pointers to corrections or derivations – forward-links in the provenance chain – should be added to enhance the value and the trustworthiness of the resource. The process of most publishers is currently not designed for this kind of updates, as they do not include information about the creation process at all. For example, an empirical study for economics journals shows that of all 141 considered journals, over 70 % do not have any policy dealing with the data used in the journal publications [Vla13].

While general approaches to store and query workflow provenance have been introduced, c.f. [DWW+11, DMMM11, GJM+06], these solutions date from before the publication of the W3C PROV standard, and/or constitute highly customized architectures. Additionally, in these solutions, the responsibility for publishing the provenance still lies either with the author or publisher, with no method to establish a *pingback* or *backlink* to the other party. Despite the PROV-AQ description [KGM+13] and the possibility to apply basic technologies, to the best of our knowledge a lightweight, distributed solution has not been implemented yet.

A possible, fully distributed solution to this problem is the concept of *provenance pingback*, as introduced in PROV-AQ. Provenance pingback enables the establishment of forward-links, e.g. to get to know which resources are based on a certain resource or who makes use of the resource. This solution, however, also highly relies on the goodwill and technological know-how of publishers to provide a pingback URI. Additionally, this would require the publishers to implement a management system aiding in the decision of which provenance is accepted to be published with the associated resource(s). These facts justify the clear need for a *lightweight* and *flexible* solution, in the form of an independent service. An independent service has the advantage that it does not rely on the cooperation of the publishers and enables all authors to use this service. The distributed nature of the Semantic Web makes this technically possible. Such a service needs to allow the storage and retrieval of provenance links for published resources, thereby enriching them with information that is otherwise hard to expose. PROV-AQ defines a mechanism for this concept, named *provenance query services*.

In the following, we introduce our implementation of such a service targeted at the domain of scientific publishing (Sect. 2). Further, we show the advantages of our solution in this application domain (Sect. 3). We discuss the presented approach within Sect. 4 and finish the paper with the conclusion.

2   Lightweight Distributed Provenance Service

We propose a lightweight, RESTful web service for linking resources published on the Web with their provenance information. The solution allows pushing and querying of provenance information. This way, a seamless integration with existing publication management systems, such as *Research Gate*, *Mendeley*, *Google Scholar*, etc., is achieved. Figure 1 shows the process diagram of our service.[1] If possible, the publisher should support a provenance service by linking to it using a *pingback URI* and *provenance query service URI* as specified in PROV-AQ, but this is not a strict prerequisite. Note that in Fig. 1, both these URIs are represented by the prov_service_uri.

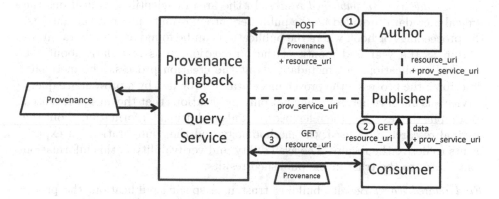

Fig. 1. The process diagram of our provenance pingback and query service.

1. An author **POST**s provenance about a published resource, identified by the resource_uri, to a service, identified by the prov_service_uri. Both, the resource_uri and the prov_service_uri are forwarded to the publisher.
2. A consumer requests (**GET**) the publication with the resource_uri at the publisher and gets the data about the publication resp. the publication itself. Ideally (but not necessarily), the publisher of the resource provides the whole service as a *pingback URI*. This way, whenever consumers access the resource through the publisher, they are provided with the proper prov_service_uri, at which the provenance can be found. Note that if the publisher does not provide a prov_service_uri, this does not prevent the author from posting his/her provenance to a service of his/her choice (e.g., where provenance of the same domain is collected). We briefly elaborate on alternatives in Sect. 4.
3. With both, the prov_service_uri and the resource_uri, the consumer GETs all additional provenance information of the resource provided by the author. Using the PROV Data Model allows users to provide and retrieve provenance of the resource as a whole, as well as the provenance of certain sub-parts of the publication, such as data, code, etc.

---

[1] A live demonstration of this service can be accessed at http://git2prov.org/prov-pings.

3   Application Domain

Application domains that illustrate the merit of provenance query services include, but are not limited to: online news, blogs, digital books, code repositories, and data sets. In the following, we describe use cases that illustrate the different benefits provided by such a query service in our chosen domain of *scientific publications*:

Increase the trust in published results: In the area of scientific publications the typical metadata provided by the publishers are information about the authors, the proceedings or book where the publication can be found and temporal information as the year and month of the publication. It is metadata about the finalized publication, not metadata about the creation process. The metadata describing the process – the provenance data, as provided by a provenance query service – is much richer, revealing not only publications that the author has used to compile the text, i.e., the references, but also additional information about the original research data used, the methodology and the configurations of experiments to derive the results. The availability and verifyability of this information contributes to the trust in the published results.

Find related work: Beyond building trust in a specific publication, the provenance data also helps to identify *related work*, in this case work that uses the same original data or the same method. Results obtained on the same data are much more comparable. Applications of the same method on different data can demonstrate the general applicability of an approach. Contradicting interpretations of data can be found simply by the fact that both interpret the same data. Currently, information about original data can only be derived by reading the publications, which make it very time consuming or even practically impossible to find all relevant publications. With proper provenance data, this becomes trivial. To support this use case, our service specifically supports the submission of links between publications and used datasets by third parties, e.g. by an (semi-) automated process as described by Boland et al. [BREM12].

Update and link to future work: Although the authors as well as the publishers are making huge efforts to create a final, perfect and error-free version of a publication, it happens that published results are superseeded by future work, not to mention actual corrections in the case of errors identified after the publication. Minor updates of applied methods, adoptions to newer datasets or application versions, as well as errors in the code, dataset and process happen more often than not. Even when the additions to existing work lead to a new publication, it is not trivial to find this newer publication. Smaller corrections, however, often do not even result in a proper new publication and an author has no reasonable way to add something to already published work. A provenance query service including the capacity of a pingback overcomes these problems, as the author is able to point to a newer, updated version of a publication. Such forward links in the provenance chain are not limited to the original author, in fact everyone can indicate that a later work builds on top of the publication.

4 Discussion and Future Work

To realize the full potential of our approach, there are a number of considerations to be made for its integration.

The first issue to be considered is the *author verification & curation*. When a third party provides provenance information of a resource, this provenance might be inaccurate or even harmful when used to assess the trustworthiness of the resource. In order to prevent this, a form of verification should be deployed by the author upon the submission of provenance information. An already practiced solution, which is also applicable for scientific publications, is the approval of the email address which is usually associated with the publications of an author. This mechanism is exemplarily used by *Google Scholar*. Alternatively, an authorship claiming mechanism similar to http://authorclaim.org could be implemented. Here, authors of information linked to provenance can claim ownership of the published provenance as well.

Another issue is the tracking of *provenance of the provenance*. Within a system where anyone can make claims about any resource, keeping track of the origin of submitted information and the evolution is crucial. Possible mechanisms to overcome this, can be found in version control systems, from which the provenance information can then be extracted using a mapping service such as Git2PROV [DNMV+13]. A similar mapping could also support the resolution of the *provenance authoring* issues. Needles to say, that such a service needs an user-friendly way to specify provenance information, otherwise the obstacle of getting started will prevent authors and publishers to adapt the service.

At last, the question remains what happens when the publisher does not play along and refuses to publish the link to a provenance service. A single, global provenance service is neither realistic nor desirable. Whereas a peer-to-peer communication between provenance services could be a possibility, a more straight-forward solution would be a registry for provenance services or a dedicated search engine functioning as main entry point to provenance information. The investigation of all these issues remains future work.

5 Conclusion

We have shown that the wide-spread provision of provenance query services will be a useful addition to the Web. We illustrated this by implementing such a service for the domain of online (scientific) publications, where it has important implications regarding discoverability and reproducibility. Provenance information can not only increase the trust in the published results, it also allows the retrieval of publications that share parts of their provenance, most importantly publications that use the same research data. The same holds for future publications that build on current ones.

We believe these services will form an essential step towards a distributed Web of publications, where the provenance provides the silk to make it sustainable and trustable.

Acknowledgments. The research activities in this paper were funded by Ghent University, iMinds (by the Flemish Government), the IWT Flanders, the FWO-Flanders, and the European Union.

References

[BREM12] Boland, K., Ritze, D., Eckert, K., Mathiak, B.: Identifying references to datasets in publications. In: Zaphiris, P., Buchanan, G., Rasmussen, E., Loizides, F. (eds.) TPDL 2012. LNCS, vol. 7489, pp. 150–161. Springer, Heidelberg (2012)

[DF08] Davidson, S.B., Freire, J.: Provenance and scientific workflows: challenges and opportunities. In: Proceedings of the International Conference on Management of Data (SIGMOD), pp. 1345–1350. ACM, New York (2008)

[DMMM11] Ding, L., Michaelis, J., McCusker, J., McGuinness, D.L.: Linked provenance data: a semantic Web-based approach to interoperable workflow traces. Future Gener. Comput. Syst. **27**(6), 797–805 (2011)

[DNMV+13] De Nies, T., Magliacane, S., Verborgh, R., Coppens, S., Groth, P., Mannens, E., Van de Walle, R.: Git2PROV: exposing version control system content as W3C PROV. In: Proceedings of the Posters & Demonstrations Track within the12th International Semantic Web Conference (ISWC), pp. 125–128. CEUR-WS, Aachen (2013)

[DWW+11] Dalman, T., Weitzel, M., Wiechert, W., Freisleben, B., Noh, K.: An online provenance service for distributed metabolic flux analysis workflows. In: Proceedings of the 9th European Conference on Web Services (ECOWS), pp. 91–98. IEEE Computer Society, Washington, DC (2011)

[GJM+06] Groth, P., Jiang, S., Miles, S., Munroe, S., Tan, V., Tsasakou, S., Moreau, L.: An Architecture for Provenance Systems. Technical report, University of Southampton, February 2006

[KGM+13] Klyne, G., Groth, P., Moreau, L., Hartig, O., Simmhan, Y., Myers, J., Lebo, T., Belhajjame, K., Miles, S.: PROV-AQ: Provenance Access and Query, W3C (2013)

[Vla13] Vlaeminck, S.: Data management in scholarly journals and possible roles for libraries-some insights from edawax. Liber Quart. J. Assoc. Eur. Res. Libr. 23(1), 48–79 (2013)

[ZGSB04] Zhao, J., Goble, C.A., Stevens, R., Bechhofer, S.: Semantically linking and browsing provenance logs for e-science. In: Bouzeghoub, M., Goble, C.A., Kashyap, V., Spaccapietra, S. (eds.) ICSNW 2004. LNCS, vol. 3226, pp. 158–176. Springer, Heidelberg (2004)

Provenance-Based Searching and Ranking for Scientific Workflows

Víctor Cuevas-Vicenttín[1]($\boxtimes$), Bertram Ludäscher[1], and Paolo Missier[2]

[1] Department of Computer Science, University of California at Davis,
One Shields Avenue, Davis, CA 95616, USA
victorcuevasv@gmail.com, ludaesch@ucdavis.edu
[2] School of Computing Science, Newcastle University, Claremont Tower 9.08,
Newcastle upon Tyne NE17RU, UK
paolo.missier@ncl.ac.uk

Abstract. We present PBase, a scientific workflow provenance repository that supports declarative graph queries and keyword-based graph searching, complemented with ranking capabilities taking into consideration authority and quality of service criteria. Given the widespread use of scientific workflow systems and the increasing support and relevance of provenance as part of their functionality, the challenge arises to enable scientists to use provenance for the discovery of experiments, programs, and data of interest. PBase aims to satisfy this requirement while also presenting to the user a customized graphical user interface that greatly facilitates the exploration of the repository and the visualization of results.

Keywords: Provenance · Scientific workflows · Graph keyword search · Quality of service · Ranking

1 Introduction

Scientific workflow management systems (SWMSs) offer numerous advantages for computational experiments exploiting scientific data. Through a friendly user interface, the various tasks comprising an experiment can be associated with concrete computational actors (e.g. Web Services, scripts, etc.) and organized in a pipeline, which can be easily modified and shared. Furthermore, the execution environment of the SWMS often offers capabilities such as fault tolerance, distributed execution, and scalability. An additional capability of modern SWMSs is to automatically record the context and events associated with the execution of a workflow, resulting in a trace that represents the retrospective provenance of the associated data products.

Much effort has been devoted to modeling scientific workflow provenance and enabling its capture in SWMSs. In addition, graph querying techniques and their related declarative query languages have been successfully applied to provenance data, enabling its close examination for purposes such as debugging or attribution. We consider an scenario in which scientists are interested in discovering

© Springer International Publishing Switzerland 2015
B. Ludäscher and B. Plale (Eds.): IPAW 2014, LNCS 8628, pp. 209–214, 2015.
DOI: 10.1007/978-3-319-16462-5_17

high quality experiments, programs, and data from third parties related to their research. In this scenario, as users of a scientific workflow provenance repository, they are first likely to want to interact with the system via simple keyword searches that bring ranked results, and then possibly through a sophisticated declarative query language that yields exact results.

Therefore we introduce PBase, a scientific workflow provenance repository that enables, besides declarative queries, searching and ranking under various criteria and at different granularities. Concretely, users can search annotated workflows and traces based on criteria that apply globally to entire workflows and traces, or individually to their component actors and data products. Result items can be obtained not only if they contain the associated keywords but also if they are related to items that contain them. The criteria or facets under consideration include quality of service and authority metrics computed from the provided traces, to which additional information sources can be incorporated as well. These features are supported by a custom GUI that facilitates the visualization of workflows, their associated traces, and the search and query results.

2 Provenance-Based Searching for Scientific Workflows

PBase adopts the ProvONE[1] model which represents workflows (prospective provenance) and execution traces (retrospective provenance) in a generic manner aiming to cover the majority of SWMSs. ProvONE is serialized in an OWL 2 ontology and data instances are represented in RDF. Searching and ranking in the PBase repository is performed by keyword searches complemented by authority and quality of service criteria, which we briefly describe next.

2.1 Authority

We adopt the ObjectRank [HHP08] metric, which is applied in three variants that in turn can be combined to yield an overall ranking.

Global ObjectRank represents the overall importance of a node in a way similar to PageRank. This metric captures, for instance, that a data item that is used in important experiments may be regarded as important, whereas an ordinary experiment that uses important data may itself not be important. However, while PageRank is computed uniformly based on the links between web pages, ObjectRank is computed taking into consideration the semantics of the relations between entities. This occurs as specified by the authority transfer schema graph, which through weights established by domain experts, specifies the flow of authority across the data entities in an adjustable manner. An example authority transfer schema graph is depicted in Fig. 1 for our domain of concern.

To find entities relevant for a particular keyword query, the keyword-specific ObjectRank metric is also calculated for all keywords subject to a threshold value. In this manner nodes that do not contain the keywords but are relevant

---

[1] http://purl.org/provone.

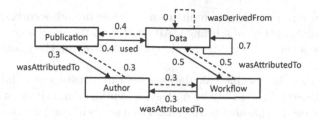

Fig. 1. Example authority transfer schema graph

for the query can be found and ranked. Finally, an inverse ObjectRank metric captures the specificity of results, placing a stronger constraint on matching the keywords of the query for cases in which the user is interested in a specific type of experiment, for example, rather than those related to a particular area. These keyword-specific metrics are computed for the most important annotated elements of both workflows and traces, i.e., actors and their executions and data items. If multiple traces are associated with a workflow, these can yield different values for a given query, due to possible missing nodes in some traces in the case of failures, for example. Collections of workflows and traces can be ranked based on the resulting values of its constituent nodes.

Furthermore, a global graph is constructed from traces to generate the ObjectRank values, whenever it is possible to identify that data generated from one workflow is used in another. This "stitching" of traces is currently limited to unique identifiers, future work involves developing alternative methods in the absence of such identifiers, by analyzing metadata, for example. If additional provenance information is available about the workflows and data, it can be incorporated into the global graph. For example, information about publications and authors as depicted in Fig. 1. Note that although the global graph is constructed from provenance information, it can be configured in various ways as required by domain experts.

2.2   Quality of Service

Numerous criteria of this type are applicable to the individual programs and data associated with workflows and their traces, the individual metrics in turn can be aggregated to assess the quality of the entire workflow, even before it is executed. In PBase we adopt the framework introduced in [CMSA04] which takes into consideration: time, cost, and reliability. The execution time is usually specified by timestamps in provenance traces, although not detailed in terms of setup and remote invocation duration, for example. We assume given measures of cost, which can be related to computational resources use or monetary cost. Reliability follows from measuring the number of times a given actor failed during its execution, which is normally inferable from traces.

The manner in which the individual metrics are aggregated for complete workflows depends on the different constructs present in the workflow as well as on the metric type. For instance, for parallel execution, the execution time of the parallel execution construct built from multiple branches corresponds to the maximum execution time of a branch. Alternatively, the reliability of a workflow built from a sequence of actors is calculated by multiplying the reliability metrics of the individual actors.

Table 1 shows the specific calculations for time, cost, and reliability (T, C, and R respectively) if we denote by c_{ij} the sequential composition of components c_i and c_j; whereas the parallel composition of a series of components c_i delimited by an *and-split* operator a and an *and-join* operator b is denoted by c_{ab}.

Table 1. Example quality of service metrics calculations

Sequential execution	Parallel execution
$T(c_{ij}) = T(c_i) + T(c_j)$	$T(c_{ab}) = max_{i \in \{1..n\}}\{T(c_i)\}$
$C(c_{ij}) = C(c_i) + C(c_j)$	$C(c_{ab}) = \sum_{i \in \{1..n\}} C(c_i)$
$R(c_{ij}) = R(c_i) * R(c_j)$	$R(c_{ab}) = \prod_{i \in \{1..n\}} R(c_i)$

3   Demonstration and Implementation

The aforementioned search criteria can be applied to the PBase repository via a GUI (see Fig. 2) that facilitates the visualization of workflows and their corresponding traces, as well as of the resulting metrics on their nodes. Keyword queries can be issued either for workflows or traces through their corresponding panels. The ranked results can be browsed over and at any time the workflow corresponding to a trace (or vice versa) can be visualized side by side. The nodes forming part of a result are also highlighted analogously and the various metrics associated with each node can be visualized by overlays next to the nodes, while global ranking lists are presented in a pop-up window.

Furthermore, it may be the case that the user is interested in a particular node, and wants to know which nodes are reachable from it (i.e. its lineage), then she can select the node and the reachable nodes are highlighted. This is done efficiently on the client side with the use of a tree cover encoding [ABJ89]. We also offer the capability to evaluate SPARQL queries on workflows and traces and visualize their results, as described in [CKL+14], which however describes an earlier version of our repository that did not include any searching and ranking functionality.

The system is implemented following a three-tier architecture, in which the user interacts with the system through a Web GUI that employs the mxGraph library for graph visualization in combination with the YUI JavaScript framework. The application logic is organized into various components that run as a Java application on the Tomcat server. Some of these components expose a series of Restful Web services that enable the interaction with the client. Communication takes place using the JSON data format. The data is stored in the TDB RDF triplestore of the Jena framework.

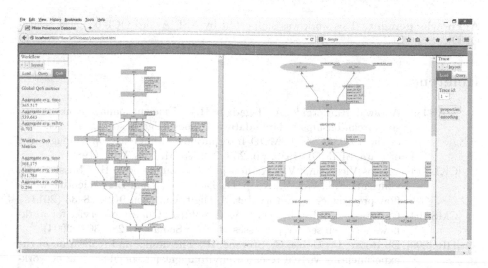

Fig. 2. Graphical user interface of PBase

Currently, for testing and demonstration purposes we have created a synthetic dataset of workflows and their corresponding traces obtained via simulation, which are stored in accordance to the ProvONE model. These workflows correspond to series-parallel graphs generated randomly. Quality of service values are assigned randomly as well during the simulation process, which takes possible failures into consideration. Annotations to describe actors, data, and additional entities were obtained from myExperiment and ProgrammableWeb for example domains and are processed with the Lucene Java library.

4   Future Work

In regards to keyword relevance ranking for collections of workflows and their corresponding traces, currently we simply compute the average ranking of nodes above a certain threshold. Future work involves more sophisticated ranking techniques and exploring top-k result retrieval techniques. We also plan to incorporate quality of service metrics aggregation for various workflow models. Presently the graph algorithms run on custom Java code, future work involves exploring high performance graph libraries as well as graph distributed computing frameworks.

5   Related Work

The use of authority metrics such as ObjectRank for provenance is explored in [IHFG12], which however focuses on a generic computing framework rather than a repository. The computation of aggregate quality of service metrics has received significant attention for business processes, for example in [YDGBn+12]. Our approach aims to enable the use of techniques developed through research to enhance some of the functionality present in systems such as myExperiment [DRGS09].

Acknowledgement. This work was supported by NSF Award OCI–0830944 (Data-ONE).

References

[ABJ89]   Agrawal, R., Borgida, A., Jagadish, H.V.: Efficient management of transitive relationships in large data and knowledge bases. In: Proceedings of the 1989 ACM SIGMOD International Conference on Management of Data, SIGMOD 1989, pp. 253–262. ACM, New York (1989)

[CKL+14]   Cuevas-Vicenttín, V., Kianmajd, P., Ludäscher, B., Missier, P., Chirigati, F.S., Wei, Y., Koop, D., Dey, S.C.: The PBase scientific workflow provenance repository. Int. J. Digit. Curation **9**(2), 28–38 (2014)

[CMSA04]   Cardoso, J., Miller, J., Sheth, A., Arnold, J.: Quality of service for workflows and web service processes. J. Web Seman. **1**, 281–308 (2004)

[DRGS09]   De Roure, D., Goble, C., Stevens, R.: The design and realisation of the experimentmy virtual research environment for social sharing of workflows. Future Gener. Comput. Syst. **25**(5), 561–567 (2009)

[HHP08]   Hristidis, V., Hwang, H., Papakonstantinou, Y.: Authority-based keyword search in databases. ACM Trans. Database Syst. **33**(1), 1:1–1:40 (2008)

[IHFG12]   Ives, Z.G., Haeberlen, A., Feng, T., Gatterbauer, W.: Querying provenance for ranking and recommending. In: Proceedings of the 4th USENIX Conference on Theory and Practice of Provenance, TaPP 2012, p. 9. USENIX Association, Berkeley (2012)

[YDGBn+12] Yang, Y., Dumas, M., García-Bañuelos, L., Polyvyanyy, A., Zhang, L.: Generalized aggregate quality of service computation for composite services. J. Syst. Softw. **85**(8), 1818–1830 (2012)

PROV-O-Viz - Understanding the Role of Activities in Provenance

Rinke Hoekstra[1,2(✉)] and Paul Groth[1]

[1] Network Institute, VU University Amsterdam,
Amsterdam, The Netherlands
{rinke.hoekstra,p.t.groth}@vu.nl
[2] Faculty of Law, University of Amsterdam, Amsterdam, The Netherlands

Abstract. This paper presents PROV-O-Viz, a Web-based visualization tool for PROV-based provenance traces coming from various sources, that leverages Sankey Diagrams to reflect the flow of information through activities. We briefly discuss the advantages of this approach compared to other provenance visualization tools. PROV-O-Viz has already been used to visualize provenance traces generated by very different applications.

Keywords: Provenance · Visualization · Sankey · Information flow · Linked data · Reusability

1 Introduction

Understanding data provenance (the origin or source of data) is a critical facilitator for data quality, trust, reproducibility, compliance and debugging of complex computational systems [1]. In 2013, the World Wide Web consortium released the W3C PROV standards that enable the interchange of provenance between systems [2]. These standards are becoming increasingly implemented [3].

Given the wealth of provenance information available, techniques are needed to help users navigate and investigate this information space. Several works have focused on the visualization or provenance using a number of presentation paradigms including networks, data flow graphs, and radial layouts [4,5], https://provenance.ecs.soton.ac.uk/vis/.

Here, we focus on a visualization approach to identify important activities within a provenance graph and link those activities together. Additionally, our aim is to show how this approach can be useful in an uncontrolled setting, i.e. for PROV coming from multiple environments, generated through the execution of diverse and potentially undefined tasks or workflows. To do so, we demonstrate a Sankey Diagram based visualization of PROV and apply that visualization to multiple provenance traces originating from multiple environments, machine learning experiments, version control systems (GitHub), and scientific workflows originating from different workflow systems. The demonstration is available at http://provoviz.org.

© Springer International Publishing Switzerland 2015
B. Ludäscher and B. Plale (Eds.): IPAW 2014, LNCS 8628, pp. 215–220, 2015.
DOI: 10.1007/978-3-319-16462-5_18

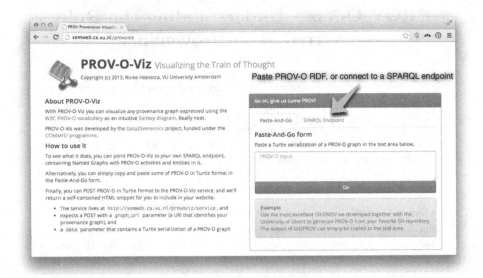

Fig. 1. Add PROV-O by pasting text, or by connecting to a SPARQL endpoint.

2   Sankey Diagrams

Our approach adopts Sankey Diagrams, which visualize the magnitude of flow within in a network. Sankey diagrams are particularly helpful in locating choke points or other places that aggregate flow. Specifically, we view a provenance graph as a network of activities where data flows through and between activities. Our aim then is to provide a view that allows us to:

1. determine important activities based on data flow; and
2. understand how data flows through a selected activity.

In a standard, directed acyclic graph (DAG) rendering, this flow gets easily lost in a large network. Other layouts, for example radial layouts, focus on the interconnectivity of data or activities. Furthermore, other layout approaches do not leverage the temporal ordering inherent in provenance graphs.

3   PROV-O-Viz

PROV-O-Viz is a web-based PROV visualization tool that leverages Sankey Diagrams and adds a number of provenance specific features. PROV-O-Viz uses the PROV-O RDF serialization of PROV. Figures 1 and 2 show a screenshots of PROV-O-Viz where we highlight these features:

1. Import of PROV data from both plain text and published data (i.e. available at a URL)

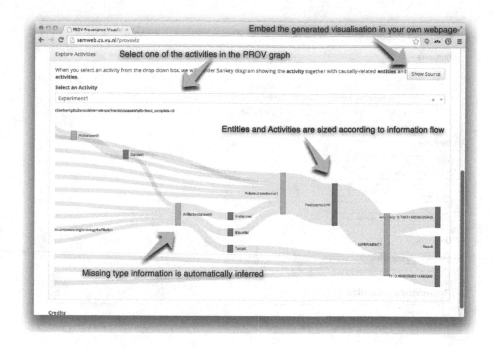

Fig. 2. Visualization of a provenance trace generated by Ducktape.

2. Focus on particular activities within a provenance diagram, by selecting them from a dropdown box.
3. Highlight data flows in and out of activities within the diagram,; the width of the box indicates the amount of information flowing through the activity.
4. Leverage reasoning to fill out missing information within a provenance graph.

Additionally, we allow provenance graphs to be embedded directly within web pages. This allows provenance visualizations to be included directly with other web applications. Furthermore, this visualization is self contained. Once the provenance is rendered there is no need to call to the server. For example, in LinkItUp ([7], http://linkitup.data2semantics.org), an application to enrich the content of data with metadata, PROV-O-Viz is used to display the provenance of how the application enriches data with this extra data. Thus, users understand how the application makes its suggestions. (We will also demonstrate this capability.)

3.1   Evaluation

We evaluated the visualization capabilities of PROV-O-Viz by using it to inspect PROV data coming from four different sources. First of all, the provenance traces of scientific workflows executed through the Taverna and WINGS workflow systems, that are made available as part of the Wf4Ever ProvBench benchmark.[1]

---

[1] See https://github.com/provbench/Wf4Ever-PROV/.

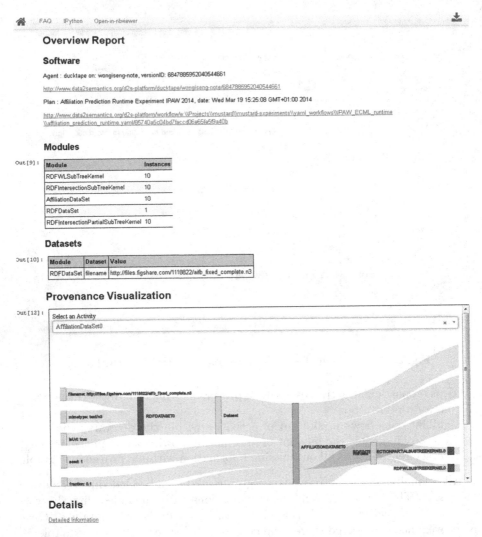

Fig. 3. Overview report of a runtime experiment, generated by Ducktape [6].

The Taverna PROV traces do not explicitly provide the *type* of events and activities that many visualizations rely on. PROV-O-Viz automatically infers these types by applying reasoning over the PROV-O schema definitions. Even though some of these datasets are relatively large, focusing on the ego graph of information dependencies flowing through the selected activity allows the visualization to remain manageable. At the moment, however, PROV-O-Viz generates a visualization for the ego graph centered around every activity. This means that for provenance traces that contain very many connected activities, the process of generating the Sankey diagram may take a long time. After the diagrams have been built, the visualization will be very responsive. Embedded PROV-O-Viz diagrams are already generated, and therefore do not suffer from this potential performance hit. The next version will feature a more responsive user interface, that keeps users up-to-date as to the progress made in generating the visualizations.

The Ducktape platform[2] is another such scientific workflow system that is focused on Machine Learning tasks. The visualization in Fig. 2 is based on the provenance of one of the steps in a Machine Learning pipeline. Ducktape can generate interactive reports of workflow execution that embeds a visualization of its provenance trace [6]. See Fig. 3 for a screenshot of such a report.

The LinkItUp[3] system for enriching metadata for datasets stored in the Figshare.com scientific data publishing platform, stores all enrichment activities performed by users as part of a provenance trace. This provenance trace can be inspected from within the application through a call to the PROV-O-Viz API.

Git2PROV is a web service that can convert Git version histories to a provenance trace expressed in various PROV compliant syntaxes.[4] Every commit is represented as a PROV activity. Visualizing these graphs can be even more challenging than those of the workflow systems because version commit histories are tree-shaped, and highly connected: they all originate from the same initial commit. Workflow systems can produce large graphs, but oftentimes these are in fact multiple separate graphs for runs against multiple files.

4   Conclusion

In this demonstration, we show how generic visualization tools can be used to interrogate provenance coming from multiple different applications. This provides evidence that provenance can provide added value without domain specific extensions. In future work we will focus on the ability to generate entity-centric diagrams, a browsing feature, allowing users to click through the various parts of the provenance graph. We are furthermore considering the implementation a more efficient method for calculating the information flow, e.g. based on centrality measures based on current flow in an electrical network [8].

Acknowledgements. This work was funded under the Dutch national programme COMMIT.

References

1. Freire, J., Bonnet, P., Shasha, D.: Computational reproducibility: state-of-the-art, challenges, and database research opportunities. In: Proceedings of the 2012 ACM SIGMOD International Conference on Management of Data. SIGMOD '12, pp. 593–596. ACM, New York (2012)

---

[2] See https://github.com/Data2Semantics/ducktape.
[3] See http://linkitup.data2semantics.org.
[4] See http://git2prov.org.

2. Groth, P., Moreau, L.: PROV overview: An overview of the prov family of documents. Technical report, W3C (2013)
3. Huynh, T.D., Groth, P., Zednik, S.: Prov implementation report. Technical report, W3C (2013)
4. Borkin, M.A., Yeh, C.S., Boyd, M., Macko, P., Gajos, K.Z., Seltzer, M., Pfister, H.: Evaluation of filesystem provenance visualization tools. IEEE Trans. Visual Comput. Graphics 19(12), 2476–2485 (2013)
5. Meyer, B., Prohaska, S., Hege, H.C.: Provenance visualization and usage. Technical report (2009)
6. Wibisono, A., Bloem, P., de Vries, G.K., Groth, P., Belloum, A., Bubak, M.: Generating scientific documentation for computational experiments using provenance. In: Proceedings of IPAW 2014 (2014)
7. Hoekstra, R., Groth, P.: Linkitup: link discovery for research data. In: Discovery Informatics: AI Takes a Science-Centered View on Big Data, AAAI Fall Symposium Series (2013)
8. Brandes, U., Fleischer, D.: Centrality measures based on current flow. In: Diekert, V., Durand, B. (eds.) STACS 2005. LNCS, vol. 3404, pp. 533–544. Springer, Heidelberg (2005)

Joint IPAW/TaPP Poster Session

The Aspect-Oriented Architecture of the CAPS Framework for Capturing, Analyzing and Archiving Provenance Data

Peer C. Brauer, Florian Fittkau, and Wilhelm Hasselbring[✉]

Software Engineering Group, Kiel University, Kiel, Germany
{pcb,ffi,wha}@informatik.uni-kiel.de

With aspect-oriented programming techniques, modularity may be achieved via separating cross-cutting concerns. Data provenance can be considered as a cross-cutting concern: code for collecting provenance data is usually scattered across various places in a software system. Aspect-oriented programming allows to seamlessly integrate cross-cutting concerns into existing software applications without interference with the original system.

Following this approach, CAPS[1] is a framework to weave provenance-capturing mechanisms into existing Java applications, which are not yet provenance aware. The CAPS framework employs AspectJ [5],[2] the Kieker framework [4, 7],[3] the Java Management Extensions JMX,[4] and some Java security mechanisms to automatically collect the provenance information. Woven inside the application as a minimal-invasive integration of the provenance capturing mechanisms, CAPS monitors the execution of the software. Whenever a data set is processed, CAPS creates the corresponding provenance graph entry. The graph itself is stored in an integrated provenance archive build on top of the Neo4j graph database.[5] CAPS is implemented and evaluated in the context of the PubFlow workflow system for semi-automatic research data publication [2]. In particular, workflow-generated provenance data is automatically gathered via CAPS, without mixing program logic with provenance mechanisms.

For deployment, CAPS provides a GWT-based web interface,[6] which allows the user to upload his own scientific Java applications to the CAPS runtime environment. While uploading the application, the user has to provide basic information about the application and its runtime environment. These include:

- the deployment type of the application (e.g., web based, Java archive),
- virtual machine parameters,
- application parameters and
- the URL of an existing CAPS Provenance Archive instance in case of stand-alone applications.

---

[1] CAPS stands for **C**apturing and **A**rchiving **P**rovenance in **S**cientific workflows.
[2] http://eclipse.org/aspectj/.
[3] http://kieker-monitoring.net/.
[4] http://docs.oracle.com/javase/tutorial/jmx/.
[5] http://www.neo4j.org/.
[6] http://www.gwtproject.org/.

© Springer International Publishing Switzerland 2015
B. Ludäscher and B. Plale (Eds.): IPAW 2014, LNCS 8628, pp. 223–225, 2015.
DOI: 10.1007/978-3-319-16462-5_19

Based on the provided information, CAPS suggests so-called application profiles for the application to be deployed. A profile contains a predefined selection of aspects and Kieker monitoring probes, that are applicable to the type of the given application. CAPS also provides profiles for Java-based workflow systems such as jBPM.[7] The user can refine the suggested profile or switch to another profile that collects more detailed information profile.

After selection of the profile to be applied to the application, CAPS creates a runtime configuration based on the provided information. After the creation of the profile, the user may check the configuration via a profiling run.

If the user chooses to initiate a profiling run, the system starts the application and displays the provenance information, captured by CAPS. This provides the user the opportunity to check, whether all relevant aspects of the system are under surveillance, and whether the monitoring level should be increased or decreased. The user can repeat this process to optimize the provenance trace produced by CAPS.

CAPS uses the Java sandbox security mechanism to intercept I/O and network calls.[8] We employ these components by weaving our monitoring probes directly into those methods that are responsible for checking the applications' calls against the JVM security constrains. CAPS also alters the configuration of the JVM for the client application which always activates the sandbox, whenever the application starts. It also obtains additional basic runtime information about the client application by querying the JMX interface.

Next, the user has to decide, whether the application should be exported as a standalone application, such that it can be used without CAPS, or whether the application should be added to the CAPS application library. For standalone applications, CAPS creates a so-called CAPS connector and embeds it into the application. The connector is responsible for connecting the application to the CAPS server, so the provenance data created by the application can be analyzed and archived.

To extract the provenance information from the collected monitoring data, CAPS utilizes the existing data analysis functionality of the Kieker framework, i.e. the analysis framework and the Kieker WebGUI [3].

CAPS provides specific Kieker filters, that can be used to filter the provenance data from the stream of monitoring records. These filters is described in [1]. CAPS comes with predefined analysis components, and offers the user to create her own analysis components. Predefined analyses are, for example, available for creating the PROV-O[9] provenance graph or for reconstructing workflows in scientific workflow environments.

To store the provenance information collected by the framework, CAPS uses an integrated provenance archive. The archive is built on top of the Eclipse

---

[7] http://www.jboss.org/jbpm.

[8] http://docs.oracle.com/javase/7/docs/technotes/guides/security/spec/
security-spec.doc1.html.

[9] http://www.w3.org/TR/prov-o/.

Modeling Framework Project (EMF),[10] the Google Web Toolkit (GWT)[11] the PubFlow Graphframework,[12] and Neo4j. It was a result of the W3C call for implementations of the PROV-O data model.[13] The provenance archive is developed based on an extended version of the PROV-DM [6], implemented with the Eclipse Modeling Framework. We made small additions to the PROV-DM model, such that we can store some additional information, like execution time stamps and user roles. However, we keep our model compatible to the original W3C PROV-DM. As persistence layer for our provenance archive we chose a Neo4j graph database. This offers the advantage of benefiting from the specific graph algorithms provided by the database engine. To store our EMF model in the graph database we are currently building a new persistence layer based on neo4emf,[14] a framework that allows mapping an EMF model to a Neo4j database.

References

1. Brauer, P.C., Hasselbring, W.: Capturing provenance information with a workflow monitoring extension for the Kieker framework. In: Proceedings of the 3rd International Workshop on Semantic Web in Provenance Management, CEUR-WS, May 2012. http://eprints.uni-kiel.de/19636/
2. Brauer, P.C., Hasselbring, W.: PubFlow: a scientific data publication framework for marine science. In: Proceedings of the International Conference on Marine Data and Information Systems (IMDIS 2013), vol. 54, pp. 29–31, September 2013. http://eprints.uni-kiel.de/22399/
3. Ehmke, N.C.: Everything in sight: Kieker's WebGUI in action. In: Proceedings of the Symposium on Software Performance: Joint Kieker/Palladio Days 2013, pp. 11–19. CEUR-WS, Nov 2013. http://eprints.uni-kiel.de/22528/
4. van Hoorn, A., Waller, J., Hasselbring, W.: Kieker: A framework for application performance monitoring and dynamic software analysis. In: Proceedings of the 3rd joint ACM/SPEC International Conference on Performance Engineering (ICPE 2012), pp. 247–248. ACM, April 2012. http://eprints.uni-kiel.de/14418/
5. Kiczales, G., Hilsdale, E., Hugunin, J., Kersten, M., Palm, J., Griswold, W.G.: An overview of aspectJ. In: Lindskov Knudsen, J. (ed.) ECOOP 2001. LNCS, vol. 2072, p. 327. Springer, Heidelberg (2001)
6. Moreau, L., Missier, P.: PROV-DM: The prov data model. Technical report, World Wide Web Consortium (2013)
7. Rohr, M., van Hoorn, A., Matevska, J., Sommer, N., Stoever, L., Giesecke, S., Hasselbring, W.: Kieker: Continuous monitoring and on demand visualization of Java software behavior. In: Proceedings of the IASTED International Conference on Software Engineering 2008 (SE'08), pp. 80–85, Feb 2008

---

[10] http://www.eclipse.org/modeling/emf/.
[11] http://www.gwtproject.org/.
[12] http://www.pubflow.uni-kiel.de/en/the-framework/the-graphframework.
[13] http://www.w3.org/TR/2013/NOTE-prov-implementations-20130430/.
[14] http://neo4emf.com/.

Improving Workflow Design Using Abstract Provenance Graphs

Tianhong Song[1]([✉]), Saumen Dey[1], Shawn Bowers[2], and Bertram Ludäscher[1]

[1] Department of Computer Science, University of California, Davis, Davis, USA
thsong@ucdavis.edu
[2] Department of Computer Science, Gonzaga University, Spokane, USA

1 Introduction and Motivation

A scientific workflow consists of a series of structured activities and computations that arise in scientific problem-solving. Recent work [7] has demonstrated that collection-oriented modelling and design (COMAD) [3] leads to simpler and more robust workflow design. In COMAD, for example, each actor is wrapped with a well defined configuration that hides the low level complexities of "wiring" processes together with respective data sources. On the other hand, some dataflow details (e.g., fine-grained data dependency information) are hidden in the workflow graph that the user may construct an erroneous or unoptimized workflow due to lack of information. Such problems are difficult to detect before workflow execution. Hence, configuring, maintaining and designing a collection-oriented workflow is sometimes challenging and time-consuming, in addition, large-scale workflows often tend to run for long time, therefore, error free and optimized workflow design is always desired.

Several approaches have been developed to detect and resolve workflow design issues in order to improve the correctness and efficiency of workflows, e.g., based on graph traversal [4], graph reduction [5], and graph refactoring [2]. Similar work has been done in the domain of Business Process Management [1] and Process-aware Information Systems [6]. However, much less work focuses on collection-oriented workflows. In previous work [8] *abstract provenance graphs* (APGs) have been proposed as a means to detect workflow design issues. APGs summarize all possible concrete provenance graphs and are computed prior to workflow execution via a static analysis technique, where fine-grained dependency information can be found.

Here, we extend this approach and illustrate how fine-grained data-oriented APGs can be used to improve workflow design by graph querying and pattern matching. Specifically, we propose to improve the state-of-the-art of workflow design and analysis and report on this ongoing work on both of the following fronts by employing abstract provenance information to: (1) Detect design problems. We show a declarative approach that workflow analysis can be performed by specifying and applying a set of queries and properties on APGs to detect design problems. (2) Improve workflow design. We propose to exploit APGs to derive a more parallel workflow structure prior to execution and to discover other optimization opportunities.

© Springer International Publishing Switzerland 2015
B. Ludäscher and B. Plale (Eds.): IPAW 2014, LNCS 8628, pp. 226–228, 2015.
DOI: 10.1007/978-3-319-16462-5_20

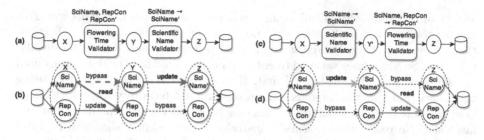

Fig. 1. Example workflow with actor configurations (a) and its inferred APG (b) showing fine-grained data dependencies. Highlighted edges reveal *read-before-updated (RBU)* pattern matching the query (read^{-1}.bypass*.update), indicating a design problem. Example workflow without the same problem (c) and its inferred APG (d).

We use data curation workflows as an example to showcase our work. A data curation workflow consists of several actors (processes) representing data validation tasks and connections among them indicating how the data flows. The data stream flowing among actors consists of a set of records (collections), each record contains a set of attribute-value pairs and each value is a concrete data item (e.g. scientific name). Each actor in a data curation workflow reads a data stream and validates and updates certain data items ("update") which may use other data items as references ("read") and the remaining (irrelevant) data items will be automatically transported bypassing the actor ("bypass").

2 Our Approach and Example

After an APG is constructed, design problems can be detected by checking whether the graph violates certain rules or constraints. Some of the problems can be recognized as graph patterns, e.g., certain type of edge cannot occur after another type. In this way, these problematic patterns can be discovered using graph queries. If the result of certain query is empty, this indicates a certain pattern is not present in the graph. So the corresponding workflow does not have this type of problem, otherwise, the workflow has this problem. Then we can inform the user about the design problems and suggest ways to fix them.

APGs can also be used to improve workflow design. Instead of constraints, optimization opportunities can be discovered by graph queries. If the result of a query is not empty, this indicates certain type of optimization opportunity has not been fully exploited. In addition, after the corresponding workflow has been improved, the same query can be applied again to check whether this type of opportunity has been fully exploited or not.

As the first prototype, we have identified some example constraints and optimization opportunities that can be discovered by Regular Path Query. Here, we show an example constraint called "No read-before-update". An example data curation workflow with two actors is shown in Fig. 1(a) where the "Scientific Name Validator" in the workflow validates "SciName" and the "Flowering Time

Validator" validates "RepCon" using "SciName" as a reference. This workflow has a problem that if "SciName" is not valid in the original input collection, then "Flowering Time Validator" may yield incorrect result due to the invalid reference. So sometimes we need to enforce a constraint that the data items used as references should be validated first. If we query the APG in Fig. 1(b) using this query read^{-1}.bypass*.update^1, the result will not be empty since "SciName" is read before it is validated. So we can conclude that the example workflow violates the "No read-before-update" constraint. The workflow shown in Fig. 1(c) doesn't have this issue (the order of actors is different), then if we apply the same query on the inferred APG in Fig. 1(d), the result is empty. Also, queries can be used to check whether a problematic workflow has been fixed or not.

Acknowledgements. Supported in part by NSF DBI-0960535 and ACI-0830944.

References

1. Brogi, A., Corfini, S., Popescu, R.: Semantics-based composition-oriented discovery of web services. ACM Trans. Internet Technol. (TOIT) **8**(4), 19:1–19:39 (2008)
2. Cohen-Boulakia, S., Chen, J., Missier, P., Goble, C., Williams, A.R., Froidevaux, C.: Distilling structure in Taverna scientific workflows: a refactoring approach. BMC Bioinform. **15**(Suppl. 1), S12 (2014)
3. McPhillips, T., Bowers, S., Zinn, D., Ludäscher, B.: Scientific workflow design for mere mortals. Future Gener. Comput. Syst. **25**(5), 541–551 (2009)
4. Meda, H.S., Sen, A.K., Bagchi, A.: On detecting data flow errors in workflows. J. Data Inf. Qual. (JDIQ) **2**(1), 4 (2010)
5. Sadiq, W., Orlowska, M.E.: Analyzing process models using graph reduction techniques. Inf. Syst. **25**(2), 117–134 (2000)
6. Weber, B., Reichert, M., Rinderle-Ma, S.: Change patterns and change support features-enhancing flexibility in process-aware information systems. Data Knowl. Eng. **66**(3), 438–466 (2008)
7. Zinn, D.: Modeling and Optimization of Scientific Workflows. Ph.D. thesis, UC Davis, Davis, California (2010)
8. Zinn, D., Ludäscher, B.: Abstract provenance graphs: anticipating and exploiting schema-level data provenance. In: McGuinness, D.L., Michaelis, J.R., Moreau, L. (eds.) IPAW 2010. LNCS, vol. 6378, pp. 206–215. Springer, Heidelberg (2010)

---

[1] Reversed read edge followed by an update edge with zero or more bypass edges in-between.

Early Discovery of Tomato Foliage Diseases Based on Data Provenance and Pattern Recognition

Diogo Nunes[1], Carlos Werly[1], Gizelle Kupac Vianna[1],
and Sérgio Manuel Serra da Cruz[1,2,3(✉)]

[1] UFRRJ – Universidade Federal Rural do Rio de Janeiro, Seropédica, RJ, Brazil
{diogo_c_nunes, carlos_werly, kupac, serra}@ufrrj.br
[2] PPGMMC/UFRRJ – Programa de Pós Graduação Modelagem Matemática e
Computacional, Seropédica, RJ, Brazil
[3] PET-SI/UFRRJ – Programa de Educação Tutorial-Sistemas de Informação,
Seropédica, RJ, Brazil

Abstract. This work presents an approach focused in enhancing the quality of tomato crops. We are developing and using low cost computational strategies to support early detection of the late blight. Our approach consorts tomatoes cultivars in an experimental field with inexpensive computer-aided resources based on Web and Android mobile tools in which workers collect scouting data and annotations and take images about the state of the crop, and in image filtering techniques and pattern recognition to detect foliage diseases on tomatoes images. In this study, we use provenance metadata about field observations, images and farmers' annotations as well, to improve the efficiency and accuracy of the patterns recognition algorithms. Our identification method achieved a hit rate of 94.12 %, using a reduced set of digital images of the tomato crops.

Keywords: Provenance · Pattern recognition · Neural networks

1 Introduction

Side by side with a very competitive agribusiness, Brazil have a dynamic and diversified family agriculture, composed by 4.3 million small agricultural establishments, responsible for the production of very important products. This diversity at production gives a huge economic value for the Brazilian agriculture, which nowadays experiments a strong rhythm of growth at its productivity [1]. In 2013, it contributed approximately with 6 % of Brazil's Gross National Product [2]. Thus there are real key benefits in ensuring the quality of data used by farmers, smallholder and agronomists to support activities such as monitoring permanent or temporary crops, and planning for sustainable development.

Among the temporary crops with very expressive value of production are the tomatoes. Tomatoes are climacteric soft skin fruits, highly susceptible to diseases and contamination, mainly through injured skin or damaged tissues during the plantation stage [3]. The indiscriminate use of pesticides in tomato crops brings serious problems

© Springer International Publishing Switzerland 2015
B. Ludäscher and B. Plale (Eds.): IPAW 2014, LNCS 8628, pp. 229–231, 2015.
DOI: 10.1007/978-3-319-16462-5_21

to human health and to environment. Last but not least, smallholders may lack the resources to comply the increasingly strict standards of food safety, as customer traceability needs, safety verification and inventory control, mainly because they do not have full access to computer-based systems that alert, detect or predict the occurrence of diseases. Such facilities may aid smallholders and farmers to reduce the chemical management of tomato diseases, to grow their income levels and to deliver healthier products. This research presents an approach focused in enhancing the quality of tomatoes crops based on provenance annotations and neural networks.

2   Materials and Methods

We are developing a loosely coupled distributed system that uses low cost computational strategies to support early detection of the late blight [4], the commonest tomato disease in Brazil. Late blight is severe and results in losses to tomato crops, especially in colder and wet periods of the year. The disease is visually recognized by the appearance of dark spots on tomato leaves, whose blotches vary from brown or gray to pale green, often located at the edges of the tomato leaves [3, 4].

Our approach consorts real field data from 66 different genotypes of tomatoes cultivars (plant varieties produced by breeding, grown under the principles of organic agriculture in a controlled experimental field) with inexpensive computer-aided resources based on:

(i) *Android-based mobile tools* in which smallholders may collect scouting data attributes for pests such as the occurrence of weeds, insects and diseases. They could also collect common annotations about the crop status and other environmental information, take georeferenced photos about the infected (or suspected) tomato stems and leaves, with a built-in camera. The tools would also manage the collected data and provenance annotations;

(ii) *Image filtering techniques and pattern recognition based on Multilayer Perceptron neural networks* to detect late blight on tomatoes images. Once acquired, these scouting data, annotations and images are transferred from the mobile devices to a base station that hosts the Web application and an Internet connection. To ensure that the data collected in the field have a good level of quality, the dataset is pre-processed with the objective to produce higher quality data. The processor checks the missing or erroneous data and annotations, the outliers and the quality of the images before performing pattern recognition algorithms. The Web application allows users to investigate rectified faulty data and annotate datasets with provenance to reduce error propagation on long-term evaluations. Besides, it is designed to allow the creation of analytical reports to empower smallholder and farmers, allowing them to: visualize the spreading of late blight on the field; reduce chemical sprayings; send or receive reports and image samples to agronomist professional services.

3   Foliage Disease Pattern Recognition

In this study, we use provenance annotations about field observations, to improve the efficiency and accuracy of patterns recognition algorithms, previously developed by our research group [5, 6]. The pattern recognition algorithm performs the following steps: first, it reduces the definition of the colored images about 70 % in order to speed the performance of further procedures; second, the reduced colored image is converted to black and white images; third, the reduced color images are used to generate novel images, containing only red, green and black pixels. Over the images created by the previous steps, we conduct a counting of pixels from different color bands. These counters are then stored in a repository that contains the absolute number of pixels of each color. Next, data are normalized, generating a new repository of those variables. Finally, the variables are evaluated to recognize the pattern of late blight disease, more specifically; the recognition used techniques of MLP neural networks [7].

4   Conclusion

Our foliage diseases identification approach achieved a hit rate of 94.12 %, using a reduced set of digital images and annotations about the tomato crops. The main role of provenance in our research is to ensure food safety, consumer protection and to offer opportunities to smallholders to run their operations more productively. The software tools were designed to use low cost apparatus and to guarantee the ease of use, because smallholders have little room for error and little expertise in digital processing with sophisticated programs.

Acknowledgements. We are grateful by the financial support provided by FAPERJ (E-26/112.588/2012 and E-26/110.928/2013 and FNDE-MEC-SeSU.

References

1. IBGE - Brazil in Figures (2013). http://biblioteca.ibge.gov.br/visualizacao/periodicos/2/bn_2013_v21.pdf
2. IBGE - Contas Nacionais Trimestrais Indicadores de Volume e Valores Correntes. (2013) http://ftpibge.gov.br/Contas_Nacionais/Contas_Nacionais_Trimestrais/Fasciculo_Indicadores_IBGE/pib-vol-val_201304caderno.pdf
3. Nakano, O.: As pragas das hortaliças: seu controle e o selo verde. Horticultura Brasileira, Vol. 17, n.1 UnB (1999)
4. Correa, F.M., Bueno Filho, J.S.S., Carmo, M.G.F.: Comparison of three diagrammatic keys for the quantification of late blight in tomato leaves. Plant Pathol. **58**, 1128–1133 (2009)
5. Vianna, G.K., Cruz, S.M.S.: Análise Inteligente de Imagens Digitais no Monitoramento da Requeima em Tomateiros. Anais do IX Congresso Brasileiro de Agroinformática. Cuiabá, MT (2013)
6. Cruz, S.M.S., Campos, M.L.M., Mattoso, M.: Towards a taxonomy of provenance in scientific workflow management systems. In: Proceedings of the SERVICES 2009 Congress, pp. 259–266, Los Angeles (2009)
7. Bishop, C.M.: Neural Networks for Pattern Recognition. Oxford University Press, New York (1995)

Provenance in Open Data Entity-Centric Aggregation

Fausto Giunghiglia and Moaz Reyad[✉]

Department of Information Engineering and Computer Science,
University of Trento, Trento, Italy
{fausto,reyad}@disi.unitn.it
http://www.disi.unitn.it

1 Motivation and goals

Recently an increasing number of open data catalogs appear on the Web [1]. These catalogs contain data that represents real world entities and their attributes. Data can be imported from several catalogs to build web services; hence there is a need to trace the source of each entity and attribute value in a way that handles also the possible conflicts between attribute values coming from overlapping sources [2]. For open data, source tracing requires capturing both the provenance [3] of the attribute values and the identity links [4] between entities. Moreover, resolving the conflicts manually becomes harder with the increasing size of data.

We propose a source tracing module that extends any existing import process by making it tracing-aware. The source tracing module contains three tools: authority, provenance and evidence. Authority provides rules for overriding attribute values, provenance specifies the source of an attribute value and evidence provides identity links between entities.

2 Problem

The problem of tracing sources is studied with respect to an import process that takes an open data catalog and extracts entities and their attribute values from its contents. The extracted entities and attribute values are imported into a database called *entity base*.

A common category of the open data repositories is the DCAT catalog. DCAT[1] (Data Catalog Vocabulary) is an RDF vocabulary for describing datasets in a data catalog. A DCAT catalog can have one or more datasets, a dataset can have one or more distributions. DCAT catalogs exist within a Web-based system called CKAN. CKAN[2] (Comprehensive Knowledge Archive Network) is a dataset distribution system. Datasets are distributed as packages. Each package has one or more resource groups, and each resource group has one or more resources.

---

[1] http://www.w3.org/TR/vocab-dcat/.
[2] http://ckan.org.

© Springer International Publishing Switzerland 2015
B. Ludäscher and B. Plale (Eds.): IPAW 2014, LNCS 8628, pp. 232–234, 2015.
DOI: 10.1007/978-3-319-16462-5_22

Open data catalogs contain data that represents objects from the real world. We refer to real world objects that are of enough importance to be given a name as *entities*. An example for entities is Italy. There are different *entity types*, such as Locations. Italy is an entity of type Location. The type of entity gives the list of *attribute definitions* that can be assigned to an entity of this type. Location entities may have the attribute Area which holds the value of the total area of the location. The values of the attribute definitions for a specific entity are called *attribute values*.

The entity base is populated with entities through an import process which can be, for instance, a generic work flow for importing any dataset or a custom procedure for importing a specific dataset. We consider any import process that has the following three aspects:

1. Partiality: The import process may take a partial input.
2. Overlap: Imported data may be disjoint or overlapped with existing entities and attribute values in the entity base.
3. Multiple Imports: The import process may run multiple times on the same catalog.

3   Our Approach

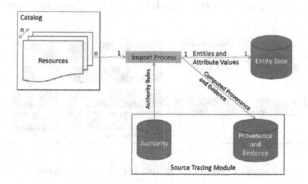

Fig. 1. Extending an import process with the source tracing module

We propose a source tracing module that extends any existing import process by making it tracing-aware (see Fig. 1). The source tracing module contains three tools: authority, provenance and evidence.

3.1   Authority

Authority is a meta-attribute of an element (entity type, an attribute definition, an entity or an attribute value) that provides a connection between the element and the resource which has the authority to create or update it. Authority is specified through a set of authority rules. An authority rule is a relation between a resource and one or more elements which is called the scope, with a ranking value that is called the priority.

The scope specifies the set of elements that are affected by an authority rule. We support four ordered levels of authority scope: (1) entity type, (2) a set of entities, (3) attribute definition and (4) attribute value. The three aspects of the import process (partiality, overlap and multiple imports) can happen at any scope. The priority is a ranking value that is assigned to order if multiple sources are given authority for the same scope. This ranking is a total order. Authority should be defined for each element. Its purpose is to help in finding a winning resource if there is a conflict between two resources in an attribute value.

3.2 Provenance and Evidence

An import process runs on an external resource and extracts entities and their attribute values from it. Before creating or updating the entities and their attribute values in the entity base, a tracing-aware import process creates a graph of elements between the external source and the entity base. This graph is shown in Fig. 2. The ultimate goal of this graph is to trace the sources of each element in the entity base. The graph is connected to the entity base through provenance and evidence. Provenance is a meta-attribute that specifies the source of an attribute value; while evidence is an attribute that links an entity with another external entity which represents the same real world object.

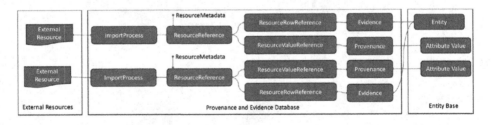

Fig. 2. Provenance graph for the entity base

References

1. Braunschweig, K., Eberius, J., Thiele, M., Lehner, W.: The state of open data limits of current open data platforms (2012)
2. Bleiholder, J., Naumann, F.: Data fusion. ACM Comput. Surv. **41**(1), 1:1–1:41 (2009)
3. Moreau, L., Groth, P.T.: Provenance: An Introduction to PROV. Synthesis Lectures on the Semantic Web: Theory and Technology. Morgan & Claypool, San Rafael (2013)
4. Halpin, H., Place, B.: When owl:sameas isn't the same: An analysis of identity links on the semantic web. In: Linked Data on the Web (LDOW) (2010)

Enhancing Provenance Representation with Knowledge Based on NFR Conceptual Modeling: A Softgoal Catalog Approach

Sérgio Manuel Serra da Cruz[1,2,3](✉) and André Luiz de Castro Leal[1]

[1] UFRRJ – Universidade Federal Rural do Rio de Janeiro, Seropédica, RJ, Brazil
[2] PPGMMC/UFRRJ – Programa de Pós Graduação em Modelagem Matemática
e Computacional, Seropédica, RJ, Brazil
[3] PET-SI/UFRRJ – Programa de Educação Tutorial - Sistemas de Informação,
Seropédica, RJ, Brazil
andrecastr@gmail.com, serra@ufrrj.br

Abstract. This work explores the organization of the provenance as a catalog of non-functional requirement (NFR). It considers provenance as a quality factor that should be incorporated since the early stages of software development as softgoals. The aim of this research is to introduce a systematic approach to design a provenance catalog using consolidated software engineering techniques. The study is an effort to depict provenance as patterns supported by Softgoal Interdependency Graphs (SIG) and Goal-Question-Operationalization method (GQO), a reusable framework that makes explicit characterization, decomposition, relationships and operationalization of elements that can be satisfied during the software design.

Keywords: Provenance · Non-functional requirements · Softgoal catalog · NFR patterns

1 Introduction

In Software Engineering (SE), one kind of requirement is called non-functional requirement. NFR is difficult to capture, organize, reuse and test; therefore, they are usually evaluated subjectively. NFR are known as constraints or quality requirements [1, 2] and are treated as *softgoals* [3]; they are targets that do not need to be addressed in an absolutely way but in a good enough sense [6]. The systematic treatment for NFR in early stages of software development may introduce positive contributions and increase software quality. The conceptual modeling for quality considering *provenance* as NFR is still underexplored either in the SE or Database domains. This is important because the quality achieved by data provenance has a clear proximity with software traceability. Both subjects are considered hot topics, offering potential benefits to data management and software development respectively.

Traceability and *provenance* handling consists of storing metadata that enables to reconstruct these chains of operations at different levels of abstraction. Due to the similarities between traceability and provenance [12], we advocate that the provenance

© Springer International Publishing Switzerland 2015
B. Ludäscher and B. Plale (Eds.): IPAW 2014, LNCS 8628, pp. 235–238, 2015.
DOI: 10.1007/978-3-319-16462-5_23

can also be considered as NFR in software development. There several representations of provenance focused on data [4, 7–9] and very few works of provenance focused on the software process [12, 13]. Data provenance authors use taxonomies, recommendations or ontologies to describe the elements involved in the conceptualization, classification and hierarchical structure of distinct kinds of provenance metadata. However, our research, differently from related works propose a new approach based on reusable catalogs (conceptual models) not only to represent provenance as a quality factor, but also to aid reducing the gap between software specification, its operationalizations and the diversity of data provenance descriptors generated by its execution.

The aim of this work is to present the steps to map provenance as NFR catalogs, using a systematic approach based on NFR framework [5], NFR patterns [6] and NRF catalogs [5, 10]. The NFR framework and the NFR patterns provide a solid theoretical foundation for treating NFR, with appropriate representation schemas and rules. In particular, the NFR pattern focuses on the reuse of NFR knowledge [3, 5]. NFR patterns may be decomposed to create/compose more precise and unambiguous patterns to build larger ones or be instantiated to create occurrence patterns using existing ones as templates.

2 Modeling Provenance as a NFR Catalog

Our proposal is one of the first to represent provenance as a quality factor within a catalog based on NFR framework and NFR patterns. We stress that the modeling effort is not a simple representation based on hierarchies of provenance or data provenance standards. Just the contrary, The NFR catalog was modeled taking into account the decomposition of softgoals to be addressed or achieved by (business or scientific) systems that require different kinds of provenance. Besides, our contribution also exposes the links and impacts between the software softgoals. We introduce a novel perception of provenance, describing it as a quality that must be satisfied to enhance the software traceability, enabling the construction of verifiable chains of operations in software systems to produce pieces of data with higher quality and embedded with data provenance descriptors.

The development of a Provenance NFR Catalog used several patterns defined by Supakkul et al. [6]: (i) *Objective Patterns* used to capture the definition of NFRs in terms of specific (soft)goals to be achieved; (ii) *Problem Patterns* captured knowledge of problems or obstacles to achieve goals; (iii) *Alternatives Patterns* (operationalizations) used to capture different means, solutions, and requirements mappings; (iv) *Selection Patterns* used to choose the best alternative considering their side-effects. To elaborate the provenance NFR Catalog we defined a set of three modeling steps.

First Step - The conceptual model was conceived to follow the Objective Pattern. The result is a Provenance SIG (not depicted here due to space restrictions). An SIG is a graph that shows two elements of Objective Patterns. First element is the Identification Pattern, where Provenance is modeled as the root of the graph. The second element is the Decomposition Pattern with relations, like 'Capturable', 'Classifiable' were presented. Such relations were based on the provenance taxonomy proposed by Cruz et al. [7].

The Provenance SIG was focused on the positive or negative contribution of the relations represented by links of the type HELP, HURT, BREAK and MAKE and also decompositions, operationalizations and argumentations represented by the links OR/AND [5].

Second Step - In this step we defined three patterns: GrupoIdentification, Questions and Alternatives. The definition of such categories is important because they help designers to define the questions and further select the operationalizations during the software development process. After these definitions, it was possible specify the QuestionIdentification [10] and combine them with the GroupIdentification. The questions were answered according to the list of operationalizations for the softgoals (Alternative Patterns). Their impact on other NFR softgoals (previously defined in the SIG graph) were evaluated and then linked with questions as alternative responses. The operationalizations were represented at the lowest level of the SIG graph as leafs associated with NFR softgoals by contribution links of the type ANSWER.

Third Step - After defining the above mentioned patterns; it was possible to use SE standardized document like GQO [10] to organize and represent the knowledge achieved by the previous steps. The result of such effort was a conceptual model with the knowledge about provenance in a framework that can be used in (business or scientific) systems or even be shared, reused and evolved by third-party.

3   Conclusion

In this work, we introduce an original proposal about treating provenance of software development as a quality factor of (business or scientific) systems. Our research provides systematic approach based on conceptual modeling to represent provenance as NFR. We stress that our study is supported by consolidated methods of SE that do not substitute, but may compliment, traditional data provenance standards and specifications. We also agree with [11, 14] on the need for further empirical research on the use of NFRs and SIG during requirements engineering. As future work, we will expand the catalog through larger number of softgoals and operationalizations and evaluate it in different domains.

Acknowledgements. We are grateful by the financial support provided by FAPERJ (E-26/112.588/2012 and E-26/110.928/2013 and FNDE-MEC-SeSU.

References

1. Sommerville, I., Sawyer, P., Viller, S.: Viewpoints for requirements elicitation: a practical approach, In: 3rd IEEE International Conference on Requirements Engineering, pp. 74–81 (1998)
2. Abran, A., Bourque, P., Dupuis, R., MooreDonald, J.W.: SWEBOK: Guide to the Software Engineering Body of Knowledge. IEEE Press, Piscataway (2004)

3. Chung, L.: Non-functional requirements. Department of Computer Science, The University of Texas at Dallas. http://www.utd.edu/~chung/RE/NFR-18-4-on-1.pdf
4. Simmhan, Y., Plale, B., Gannon, D.: A survey of data provenance in e-science. SIGMOD Rec. **34**(3), 31–36 (2005)
5. Chung, L., Nixon, B.A., Yu, E., Mylopoulos, J.: Non-functional Requirements in Software Engineering. Kluwer Academic Publishers, Boston (1999)
6. Supakkul, S., Hill, T., Chung, L., Than, T.T., Leite, J.C.S.P.: An NFR pattern approach to dealing with NFRs. In.: 18th IEEE International Requirements Engineering Conference, Sydney, vol. 18. pp. 179–188 (2010)
7. Cruz, S.M.S., Campos, M.L.M., Mattoso, M.: Towards a taxonomy of provenance in scientific workflow management systems. In: Proceedings of the SERVICES 2009 Congress, pp. 259–266. Los Angeles (2009)
8. Zhao, J. Bizer, C. Gil, Y. Missier, P.. Sahoo S.: Provenance requirements for the next version of RDF. In: Proceedings of the W3C Workshop - RDF Next Steps, Palo Alto (2010)
9. Moreau, L.: The foundations for provenance on the web. Found. Trends Web Sci. **2**, 99–241 (2010)
10. Serrano, M., Leite, J.C.S.P.: Capturing transparency-related requirements patterns through argumentation. In: 1st International. Workshop on Requirements Patterns (RePa), pp. 32–41 (2011)
11. Leal, A.L.C., Sousa, H.P., Leite, J.C.S.P.: Modelo orientado à meta para estabelecer relações de contribuição mútua entre Proveniência, Transparência e Confiança. In: XVII Workshop on Requirements Engineering (WER14), Pucón, Chile (2014). (in portuguese)
12. Asuncion, H.U., Asuncion, A.U., Taylor, R.N.: Software traceability with topic modeling. In: 32nd International Conference on Software Engineering (ICSE), pp. 95–104. Cape Town (2010)
13. Barbero, M., Didonet, M., Del Fabro, J.B.: Traceability and provenance issues in global model management. In: 3rd ECMDA-Traceability Workshop (2007)
14. Leal, A.L.C., Cruz, S.M.S.: Transparência em Experimentos Científicos Apoiados Em Proveniência: Uma Perspectiva para Workflows Científicos Transparentes. In: 2nd WTRANS-SBSI (2014)

Provenance Storage, Querying, and Visualization in PBase

Víctor Cuevas-Vicenttín[1]([✉]), Parisa Kianmajd[1], Bertram Ludäscher[1],
Paolo Missier[2], Fernando Chirigati[3], Yaxing Wei[4], David Koop[3],
and Saumen Dey[1]

[1] University of California at Davis, Davis, USA
{victorcuevasv,parisa.kianmajd}@gmail.com
ludaesch@ucdavis.edu
[2] Newcastle University, Newcastle upon Tyne, UK
Paolo.Missier@ncl.ac.uk
[3] New York University, New York, USA
{fchirigati,dakoop}@nyu.edu
[4] Oak Ridge National Laboratory, Oak Ridge, USA
weiy@ornl.gov

Abstract. We present PBase, a repository for scientific workflows and their corresponding provenance information that facilitates the sharing of experiments among the scientific community. PBase is interoperable since it uses ProvONE, a standard provenance model for scientific workflows. Workflows and traces are stored in RDF, and with the support of SPARQL and the tree cover encoding, the repository provides a scalable infrastructure for querying the provenance data. Furthermore, through its user interface, it is possible to: visualize workflows and execution traces; visualize reachability relations within these traces; issue SPARQL queries; and visualize query results.

Keywords: PBase · ProvONE · Scientific workflows · Provenance repository

1 Introduction

In the past few years, scientific workflows have been often used to define and execute a range of experiments. As science is collaborative, the need arises for a repository that allows multiple users to store and query scientific workflow provenance information. Additionally, such a repository must be interoperable, in the sense that workflow traces may come from different systems, and scalable as the number and the size of traces grow, providing an efficient query evaluation.

This paper presents PBase [CKL+14], which addresses three main key points: facilitate the *sharing* of scientific workflows and their corresponding execution traces among the scientific community; allow *user interaction* so that users can further explore the repository data; and provide both sharing and interaction in an *interoperable* and *scalable* manner. Our repository achieves these goals by:

© Springer International Publishing Switzerland 2015
B. Ludäscher and B. Plale (Eds.): IPAW 2014, LNCS 8628, pp. 239–241, 2015.
DOI: 10.1007/978-3-319-16462-5_24

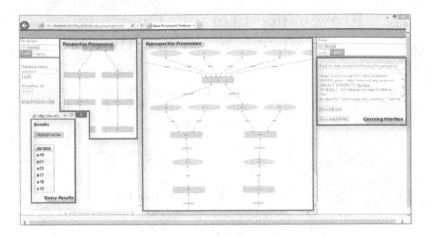

Fig. 1. The PBase Web GUI and its main components.

(i) making use of ProvONE [Dat14a], a standard provenance model that brings the advantages of the emerging W3C PROV standard [W3C13] and that addresses the interoperability challenge; (ii) defining a representative set of queries, identified in collaboration with climate scientists, that characterizes the required functionality and user interaction; and (iii) providing a scalable infrastructure based on TDB, the RDF triplestore of the Jena Framework[1] that supports SPARQL, an expressive query language, and its efficient evaluation. PBase also incorporates the tree cover encoding proposed by Agrawal et al. [ABJ89] to improve the performance of reachability queries.

To the best of our knowledge, PBase is the first repository to address all the aforementioned challenges.

2   PBase Features

Interoperability. PBase uses ProvONE [Dat14a] to represent both prospective provenance (i.e. workflow specifications) and retrospective provenance (i.e. execution traces). ProvONE is an extension of the W3C PROV [W3C13] standard and it is specified through an ontology serialized in OWL-2. Its goal is to be expressive enough to cover most workflow models used by different scientific workflow management systems, which allows PBase to work in an interoperable manner.

User Interaction. An essential feature for a provenance repository is to *visualize* a workflow and its various execution traces. PBase uses a Web GUI for this purpose (see Fig. 1). Furthermore, in collaboration with climate scientists, we have identified a series of queries, specified in SPARQL, that are representative for the functionalities that they require (such queries are available in [Dat14b]). As users may not be familiar with SPARQL, PBase also allows these queries to

---

[1] http://jena.apache.org/.

be issued from the GUI interface through their textual description. When the results of a query are generated, besides presenting them in a text representation, the provenance nodes corresponding to the results are highlighted. To see the lineage of a particular node in a workflow or trace, users can select this node and use the option to highlight its ancestors and descendants.

Scalability. We adopt RDF to store workflows and execution traces—in particular, we use TDB from the Jena Framework. As an example, XML traces from VisTrails[2] can be uploaded through the Web and they are automatically translated into ProvONE RDF and stored in TDB. As mentioned before, PBase uses SPARQL to issue queries in the repository, which allows for an expressive and efficient evaluation. The tree cover encoding [ABJ89] is also implemented: it enables determining reachability relations between nodes by simply comparing integer range intervals, thus avoiding more costly graph explorations and enhancing the performance of PBase.

3 Conclusion

We have presented PBase, a repository for scientific workflows and their corresponding execution traces. It can be regarded as a step towards a repository supporting sophisticated provenance querying and analytics over a large collection of traces. PBase was developed in the context of DataONE[3], a large scale and federated data infrastructure serving the Earth Sciences community, and our ultimate goal is to incorporate it into this infrastructure.

Acknowledgments. The authors thank: members of the DataONE Provenance Working Group, for helping in the specification of PBase; and members of the DataONE EVA Working Group, for their collaboration. This work was supported by NSF Award OCI-0830944 (DataONE).

References

[ABJ89] Agrawal, R., Borgida, A., Jagadish, H.V.: Efficient management of transitive relationships in large data and knowledge bases. In: Proceedings of the 1989 ACM SIGMOD International Conference on Management of Data, SIGMOD 1989, pp. 253–262. ACM, New York (1989)

[CKL+14] Cuevas-Vicenttín, V., Kianmajd, P., Ludäscher, B., Missier, P., Chirigati, F.S., Wei, Y., Koop, D., Dey, S.C.: The PBase scientific workflow provenance repository. Int. J. Digit. Curation 9(2), 28–38 (2014)

[Dat14a] DataONE Provenance Working Group. ProvONE: A PROV Extension Data Model for Scientific Workflow Provenance (2014). http://purl.org/provone

[Dat14b] DataONE Provenance Working Group. The ProvONE Scientific Workflow Provenance Dataset (2014). http://purl.org/provone/provbench

[W3C13] W3C Provenance Working Group. PROV Overview (2013). http://www.w3.org/TR/2013/NOTE-prov-overview-20130430/

---

[2] http://www.vistrails.org/.

[3] http://www.dataone.org/.

Engineering Choices
for Open World Provenance

M. David Allen[⊠], Adriane Chapman, and Barbara Blaustein

The MITRE Corporation, Mclean, USA
{dmallen, achapman, bblaustein}@mitre.org

Abstract. This work outlines engineering decisions required to support a provenance system in an open world where systems are not under any common control and use many different technologies. Real U.S. government applications have shown us the need for specialized identity techniques, flexible storage, scalability testing, protection of sensitive information, and customizable provenance queries. We analyze tradeoffs for approaches to each area, focusing more on maintaining graph connectivity and breadth of capture, rather than on fine-grained/detailed capture as in other works. We implement each technique in the PLUS system, test its real-time efficiency, and describe the results.

Keywords: Provenance · Lineage · Pedigree · System engineering

1 Introduction

All provenance systems to this point have been applied to "closed world" systems. As described in [12], a closed world system contains at least one of the following properties: The underlying application or systems are known in advance and provenance enabled; a provenance administrator has administrative privileges for the systems and applications in use; or full knowledge of either the data or processes is known in advance. These assumptions work very well for scientific applications [5, 15, 19, 27, 30], within relational databases [9, 14], and for specific applications [15]. However, the world of large-scale enterprises, as typified by our U.S. government sponsors, is much messier.

Our users typically operate in environments that involve computations distributed across personnel and systems in very large enterprises. Their interests usually do not lie with replication of results or very fine-grained provenance, but with more general queries whose purpose is to help users build trust that a particular dataset is appropriate for their use. Government sponsors are trying to exploit available assets from other government groups, so most users who wish to use novel datasets will eventually need to investigate the provenance of that information to determine its suitability for the mission at hand. In Sects. 2–6, we describe system design research that is required for functioning open-world provenance systems. Section 7 evaluates each proposed technique. We discuss related work and conclude in Sects. 8 and 9 respectively.

© Springer International Publishing Switzerland 2015
B. Ludäscher and B. Plale (Eds.): IPAW 2014, LNCS 8628, pp. 242–253, 2015.
DOI: 10.1007/978-3-319-16462-5_25

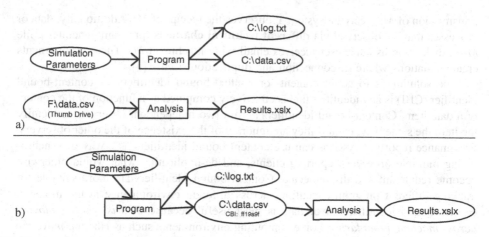

Fig. 1. (a) Two independent but related provenance graphs. (b) The correct provenance graph with the same data artifact from both graphs correctly identified.

2 Identity

The PROV Data Model [20, 28] uses URLs/URIs as identifiers for most things. If two entities have the same identifier then they are considered equal. We concur with this definition, but we have a frequent need to establish a common identifier that can be computed no matter what system/user/environment/organization is involved in the manipulation of the artifact. Figure 1 motivates the need for extensive identity capabilities in any open-world provenance system. A set of simulation parameters are given to a program that produces CSV data as an output (with a log). Days later, that CSV file is sent via a thumb drive or other unobservable method to a different user in another organization, across several network boundaries. That file is then saved to the user's hard disk and run through a separate analysis process. Figure 1(a) shows what can happen without an identification technique to establish common identity of data or process nodes in a provenance graph. An identification technique is fundamental, because we must concede that observing every provenance link without exception is unlikely. Our strategy, then, is to determine ways of identifying or "tagging" data in a way that will persist wherever and however the data might travel outside of our ability to observe it, resulting in a graph like that shown in Fig. 1(b).

Imposing an artifact naming or URI convention on provenance capture will not work in wide collaborations, and essentially no assumptions can be placed on the storage or transmission method of the data. Over a distributed system, it is entirely possible to see several, unrelated "Hello World Output.txt" files. Name, file size, owner, or other related metadata is useful to capture, but does not provide a sound basis for identification. Content does provide a basis: across many systems, the same file can be copied and the name changed, but the underlying information is the same: Alice's MyNotes.docx is the same as Bob's AliceNotes.docx in content.

When capturing and reporting provenance in complex environments, there may be **multiple, independent observations of the same thing** (sending system observes transmission of *M;* receiving system Y observes the receipt of *M*). Additionally, data or processes may be observed via **different technical channels** (program generates a file *M* on disk; months later, user receives email with attachment *M*). These requirements create situations where disconnection and duplication occurs [4].

The solution is to adopt content- or context-bound identifiers. A content-bound identifier (CBI) is any identifier that is effectively computed as a function of the content of a data item. Content-bound identifiers permit two independent observers to identify the item the same way, even if they are ignorant of the existence of the other observers. Provenance reporting systems can use content-bound identifiers as a way of synchronizing multiple observers/reporting clients, and de-duplicating what would otherwise become redundant and disconnected. Context-bound identifiers are more suitable for tracking different program executions across different environments; at the moment, content-bound identification of data is most useful because data *is what is moving across machine boundaries*. Some computing environments such as Hadoop *move the processing to the data* because of data volumes. Invocations can be de-duplicated with context-bound identifiers; unfortunately unlike *content*-bound identifiers, what constitutes a good context-bound identifier will be different depending on the underlying computational system.

In the example above, we must establish that the file named data.csv and the thumbdrive data are the same document, as shown in Fig. 1(b). Using content-bound identifiers, all parties that touch the file will compute the same CBI, thus providing the proof that the provenance graphs are indeed joined.

There are many available options for cryptographic hash functions; most have some suitability for content-bound identifiers. This section is not an exhaustive review, but just a brief look at two very common functions, along with their pros and cons. MD5, first published in 1992, produces 128-bit digests (hashes), while SHA256 is an instance of the SHA-2 cryptographic hash function that produces 256-bit digests.

Hash functions for provenance identity should be evaluated in terms of three aspects: performance (data volume hashed in a given period of time), resistance to collision (likelihood that two different data items would have the same digest), and size (how much data the digest contains). In terms of these tradeoffs, SHA-256 is larger, more robust/resistant to collisions, and slower than MD5 (see Sect. 7.1). MD5 is discouraged for cryptographic applications [29] yet is still in wide use in environments where collisions are not a primary concern.

3   Storage

There are several options for storing provenance information. These include: relational [5, 6, 31]; flat file [23]; bound to the data itself [17]; graph-based [13, 18, 25]. These storage options are not mutually exclusive. It is possible to take information from a database, output provenance for a particular file and bind it to the data. However, the choice of which storage strategy to use for a provenance management system depends on factors including: technology required by provenance-using applications; directives and mandates; provenance information required (the required usage of the provenance information will dictate the style in which it is stored); network architecture (transmission between different enclaves can be problematic, or even impossible); trust architecture (with many different government partners, trust issues may dictate that provenance needs to be hosted in a particular place, or not combined with other sources). At various times in our research system, PLUS, we have used relational databases, flat files, XML, and graph databases to store provenance.

XML: XML and other hierarchical document formats such as JSON and BSON are workable solutions, but an imperfect fit; the data model behind XML and JSON is fundamentally a tree, although XML languages that support directed graphs (i.e. GraphML) can help. XML is well-suited to expressing a subset of provenance graphs and data structures, but to express the full range of directed graphs, implementers will either fall back on the use of "pointers" (e.g. XML ID/IDREF) or data duplication within the document to express directed graphs without tree assumptions. In other words, the underlying model gets messy. In our experience, XML is useful as an interchange format, but not as a storage format because it complicates query.

Relational: For several years, our software used MySQL and PostgreSQL as a storage layer, providing us with extensive experience on the pros and cons of relational storage for provenance. Relational databases are attractive because of their wide adoption and mature tooling. We found, though, that the RDMBS made path-associative query extremely difficult. Storing provenance in an RDBMS typically involves a table of nodes and a table of edges. These designs are excellent for bulk query that does not require much edge traversal ("Fetch all provenance owned by Bob"), but tend to be very poor at path-associative queries ("Fetch all provenance that is between 2 and 5 steps downstream of X"). Path-associative queries typically end up being translated as dynamically constructed, variably recursive SQL queries that join nodes to edges. RDMBS rapidly pushes developers down the path of re-implementing basic graph techniques the RDBMS does not provide (e.g. shortest path algorithms) rather than exploiting known good implementations.

Graph DBs: Our findings over time have indicated that general purpose graph databases (such as Neo4J or, in principle, RDF triple stores) are by far the best fit for provenance, for two simple compelling reasons: (1) the graph model under the hood of a graph database is fundamentally a match for the core of provenance (a directed graph), and (2) graph databases will typically provide graph-oriented query languages (such as Cypher within Neo4J, or perhaps SPARQL within RDF triple stores) which greatly facilitate provenance queries. The negative aspect of graph databases is that because they are "naturally indexed" by relationships/edges, they do not perform as well on bulk queries mentioned above. While such bulk queries do have important uses, the most interesting and powerful provenance queries (see Sect. 8) typically are path-associative. This style of query emphasizes the strengths of graph query languages; an emphasis which plays to many of the weaknesses of other languages.

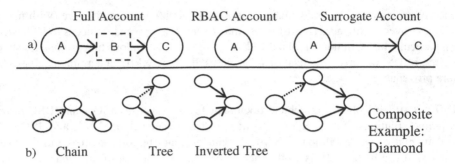

Fig. 2. (a) Example of provenance graph protection using surrogates. (b) Sample motif graphs.

4 Protection

Our US government sponsors are particularly concerned about protection of provenance information. Many times, materials and methods are more protected and sensitive than the resulting information. At a minimum, we must apply classic access control techniques to the provenance information [26]. However, classic access controls break provenance graphs. If a single node or edge within the provenance graph cannot be shown, then the provenance graph may be severely truncated. Consider the chain graph shown in Fig. 2(a). If the process B is sensitive and restricted, then the provenance graph showing descendants of A will only consist of A, instead of the richer graph. To this end, we have created surrogates as described in [10], in which we guarantee that protected nodes and edges will not be shown, but the utility of the graph is maximized by inserted surrogate nodes and edges.

The model we have adopted calls for permitting the attachment of various "privilege classes" to individual provenance nodes; users who attempt to access node information must demonstrate that they belong to the correct privilege class. Our notion of a privilege class is meant to subsume what we might otherwise refer to as a "role" or an "attribute" and, as such, the model is suitably general so that it can describe RBAC or ABAC. If users possess the right privilege classes, access is provided as normal. But if they do not, the surrogate algorithm seeks to provide access to as much information as possible, subject to user-configurable policies.

5 Testing

There have been previous efforts at creating provenance flows for testing. Of particular interest is the ProvBench effort [7] and the Provenance Challenge [1, 21]. ProvBench aims to distribute annotated provenance flows so that both the provenance and the intent of the overall workflow are understood within the dataset. We wish to exercise the system to ensure that it can work over any size or shape provenance graph in order to ensure all algorithms can function over bushy or sparse graphs. We do not claim that the generators discussed create provenance similar to the real observations; we target generators sufficiently tunable that they can mimic any form.

Motif Generators: We began with the observation that any provenance graph of any size and shape can be described as a conjunction of a set of smaller graph "primitives" or "motifs". Figure 2(b) shows the set of possible motifs that are generated by a motif generator. We built a motif generator that permits users to generate any number of randomly chosen motifs, with tunable connection parameters. In the most simple case, a motif generator might choose 100 random motifs; it would then choose a random node from within each motif and link it to a randomly chosen node from the next motif. Note that complex motifs such as a "diamond shape" can be created by joining simpler motifs (a tree, with an inverted tree).

Graph Simulation: Our graph simulator, DAGAholic, focuses on guaranteeing certain properties of the generated graph, including its size and edges, but does not generate any particular shape. DAGAholic is given parameters including number of nodes, proportions of data vs. invocations in the graph, and so on. Users specify a graph connectivity, which is the probability that a given node will be connected to something downstream in the provenance graph; 0.25 indicates that 25 % of nodes in the resulting graph will have an outbound provenance relationship. DAGAholic also has a rich set of options for protecting graphs. Because the determination to create a specific edge is based on a random number, the graphs, while generally conforming to the sparse/bushy objective, will be individually distinct.

Table 1. Examples of "canned queries released with PLUS"

Query	Description
Trace Taint Sources	Find all upstream "nodes marked as "tainted" or "corrupted" to determine quality of present information
Chain of Custody	Whose hands has this data passed through?
Time Span	The oldest item, the newest, and the time span between them
Distinct Sources	Number of distinct upstream sources: e.g., is this analysis based on five independent reports, or just one?

6 Output

We provide basic access to all provenance graphs via the Cypher query language, provided by Neo4J, to permit arbitrary query against stored provenance. Most users do not want to interact with the provenance graph or write queries. Instead, they have a goal such as checking the fitness for use of a particular item. One of our most common access patterns, then, is to establish the user's "fitness parameters" for information; for example, "I'm only interested in data less than 30 days old, which was processed by the Air Force, and went through System X". These parameters are then encoded as a set of pre-canned, but keyword-customizable, provenance queries [11]. Canned queries can then be arranged into dashboards for users which answer their questions, but do not require technical knowledge of provenance or query. Table 1 shows examples of canned queries currently packaged within PLUS, which can be combined into custom fitness assessments for new users.

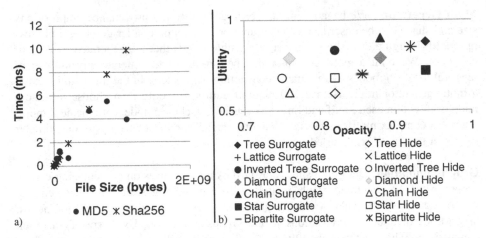

Fig. 3. (a) The time required to use hashing to generate a file identity using either MD5 or Sha256. (b) The tradeoff in utility for hiding or surrogating several sample graphs.

7 Implementation and Evaluation

Each problem discussed has been addressed within the PLUS system.[1] In this section, we use PLUS to demonstrate tradeoffs for these techniques and to illuminate the final system design decisions within PLUS.

7.1 Identity

Hashing is useful to define identity for artifacts from many different systems. In order to show that system performance is not unduly affected by incorporating hashing as an identifier, we created several data artifacts, of varying sizes, and ran them through each hashing function. Figure 3(a) shows the results; it only costs a few milliseconds on even the largest files. We also observe through these runs that the average memory size is 0 kB and the maximal memory size is between 2768 kB and 2928 kB, likely at process startup. Thus, we believe that using the hash value as an identifier is an acceptable method for identity, because its computational cost is low, and its memory requirements are small and fixed, irrespective of the input size. Because of concerns discussed earlier about compromises to MD5, we generally recommend the more secure and adopted SHA-2 algorithm, computing 256 bit hashes.

7.2 Storage

Using commercially available systems, such as MySQL and Neo4 J, the speed of each system is acceptable for a wide range of queries, but there are substantial performance

---

[1] https://github.com/plus-provenance/plus.

differences between different types of queries. Instead of comparing performance directly, we look at how easy or hard it is to perform operations specific to provenance. In order to provide an estimate on ease, we measure the lines of code required to create the functionality within the system, with either a relational or graph database backend. "Source lines of code" is unavoidably a coarse measure; in some cases minor differences may be accounted for by issues such as indentation style, volume of comments, and so on. These numbers are presented as our concrete implementation experience, and to provide a rough sense of the difficulty of implementation. We would expect alternative implementations to encounter the same set of issues we present in the discussion.

Our measures exclude the number of lines of code necessary for translating graph nodes into provenance objects (taking properties from the DB and putting them into java objects). In many applications, this serialization/deserialization of objects between the database and the object model is largely housekeeping work. Table 2 shows the lines of source code required for each storage implementation within PLUS.

Table 2. A snapshot of the code base required to support provenance manipulation.

Function	Description	Neo4j	MySQL
Load Graph from DB	Building database queries, iterating through results, returning a provenance collection consisting of nodes, edges, non-provenance edges, and actors	141	538
Trace Chain of Custody	Tracing through an entire provenance graph from some starting point, and extracting an ordered list of all owners of all data in the graph	85	638
Get Indirect Sources of Taint	Examine a particular provenance node and determine, at any distance upstream from the current node, if there is a marking indicating that one of its ancestors is "tainted" (e.g. has a problem, or is based on bad information as asserted by a user)	40	606
Arbitrary Graph Query	The ability for the user to formulate an arbitrary read-only query to traverse provenance graphs, returning any computable subset of provenance information	50	N/A

When loading a graph from a database, the resulting provenance collections form the basis of data presented to the user visually, and sent to other systems as reports. As a necessary prerequisite for so many other operations, loading a graph is probably the most common operation that a provenance system will do. In Neo4j, we use a traversal framework; the traverser does all of the work, and as the nodes and edges are returned, they are turned into provenance objects and added to a result collection. In MySQL, the traverser is custom-implemented code, essentially an iterator which fetches and joins nodes and edges. These issues apply to implementations that trace chains of custody and get indirect sources of taint.

Because data must be fetched via SQL when using MySQL, it is extremely difficult to implement arbitrary graph queries. With natively supported graph query languages

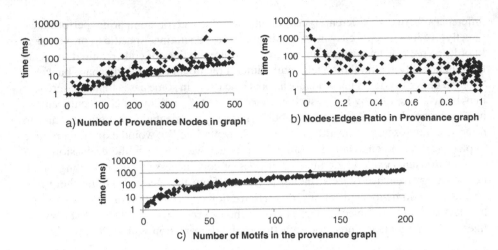

Fig. 4. (a) the time required to produce provenance test graphs, based on the number of nodes in the graph. (b) The time to create synthetic provenance graphs based on the node to edge ratio. (c) The time to create motif graphs based on the number of motifs in the final graph.

(such as Neo4j's cypher) most of the code is given over to simple housekeeping, such as query sanitization to apply safeguards to prevent the user from modifying or deleting data with a query. When using such graph databases, no new code is introduced; the user is simply given an interface to perform queries as they might with SQL, and a few utilities to visualize or report the results.

7.3   Protection

As discussed above, we need to protect sensitive data in provenance graphs, while maximizing the graphs' utility. We start with some basic graphs in classic patterns shown in Fig. 2(b), and "hide" the dashed edge within the graph. Figure 3(b) shows the difference between breaking the graph at the sensitive edge, as would occur with basic access control strategies, and surrogating. Since more of the graph is available for consumption with surrogating, the utility of the final provenance graph is higher.

7.4   Testing

The testing package included with the PLUS system has the ability to create generic provenance graphs of varying shapes and sizes. We are mostly concerned that the creation of a suite of provenance test graphs does not take undue time or resources. Figure 4 shows the time it takes to generate a set of provenance test graphs. Our test runs indicate that the cost in time is not exorbitant, allowing the system to be easily used for scalability testing.

8 Related Work

Closed World Systems: The overriding characteristic of current provenance systems is the assumption of a closed world system – a contained environment over which the provenance system has full knowledge of all the data and processes used within the contained environment. Workflow-based systems such as [5, 27, 30] contain provenance for all of the executions and data that are executed by the system. Because the workflow is executed within this closed world system, complete provenance capture of the workflow run is possible. Moreover, since the provenance is used within the system, it can use the identity and storage based within those systems. In application-based provenance, certain applications are provenance capture enabled. For instance, in ES3 [15], or MapReduce [23], the applications used by scientists for data analysis are modified to capture provenance of their use. While these applications could be run over open, heterogeneous-style systems, they specifically create assumptions to form a closed world.

Identity: The MD5 hashing function was created in 1992 [24], while SHA-0 was developed by the National Security Administration (NSA) in 1993 and approved for use by the National Institute of Standards and Technology (NIST) in 2001 [22]. The work of [29] showed that the MD5 and SHA-1 algorithms were vulnerable to attack based on hash collisions. At present, SHA-256 is considered a secure algorithm.

Storage: Past efforts (e.g., [3]) have found relational databases to be of limited use, and achieved maximal performance once a native database for the given format was chosen; provenance, as a graph, is no different. Of interest, the tutorial guide for graph databases [25] cites provenance as an inherently good use of a graph database.

Testing: The provenance community has two styles of testing: actual generated provenance [1, 8, 16, 21] and the scalable but less empirical style presented in this work. As a community, we should be heading towards a benchmarking standard that tests query workload, use cases and scalability, just like the database community [2].

9 Conclusions

We have outlined some of the engineering decisions required to support a provenance system in an open world, one in which systems are not controlled or homogenous. New engineering designs are needed to support the real U.S. government applications we have observed. These systems tend to be less concerned with fine-grained and deeply detailed provenance, and more concerned with issues of maintaining graph connectivity, providing flexible and expansive query, and enabling capture in very heterogeneous environments with as little performance impact as possible. We describe solutions to identity, base storage, protection with utility, and scalability testing; all needed to make provenance a viable open-world solution. Our open-source provenance solution, PLUS, is at https://github.com/plus-provenance/plus.

Acknowledgements. The authors thank Len Seligman, Arnie Rosenthal, Maggie Lonergan, Paula Mutchler, Jared Mowery, Erin Noe-Payne, Zack Panitzke, Brenda Davies, Jesse Freeman, Blake Coe, and Sung Kim for their contributions to the PLUS system.

References

1. Provenance Challenge (2010). http://twiki.ipaw.info/bin/view/Challenge/
2. Transaction Processing Performance Council (2013). http://www.tpc.org/
3. Al-Khalifa, S., Yu, C., Jagadish, H.V.: Querying structured text in an XML database. In: SIGMOD (2003)
4. Allen, M.D., Chapman, A., Blaustein, B., Seligman, L.: Getting it together: enabling multi-organization provenance exchange. In: TaPP (2011)
5. Anand, M.K., Bowers, S., McPhillips, T., Ludascher, B.: Efficient provenance storage over nested data collections. In: EDBT, pp. 958–969 (2009)
6. Artem Chebotko, S.L., Fei, X., Fotouhi, F.: RDFPROV: a relational RDF store for querying and managing scientific workflow provenance. Data Knowl. Eng. **69**, 836–865 (2010)
7. Belhajjame, K., Gomez-Perez, J.M., Sahoo, S.: ProvBench (2013). https://sites.google.com/site/provbench/provbench-at-bigprov-13
8. Belhajjame, K., Zhao, J., Garijo, D., Garrido, A., Soiland-Reyes, S., Alper, P., Corcho, O.: A workflow PROV-corpus based on taverna and wings. In: Khalid Belhajjame, J.M.G.-P., Sahoo, S. (ed.) ProvBench (2013)
9. Benjelloun, O., Sarma, A.D., Halevy, A., Widom, J.: ULDBs: databases with uncertainty and lineage. In: VLDB, pp. 953–964, Seoul, Korea (2006)
10. Blaustein, B., Chapman, A., Seligman, L., Allen, M.D., Rosenthal, A.: Surrogate parenthood: protected and informative graphs. In: PVLDB (2010)
11. Chapman, A., Allen, M.D., Blaustein, B.: It's about the data: provenance as a tool for assessing data fitness. In: TaPP (2012)
12. Chapman, A., Blaustein, B.T., Seligman, L., Allen, M.D.: PLUS: a provenance manager for integrated information. In: IEEE Computer Information Reuse and Integration (2011)
13. Dey, M. Agun, M. Wang, Ludäscher, B., Bowers, S., Missier, P.: A provenance repository for storing and retrieving data lineage information. Technical Report, DataONE Provenance and Workflow Working Group (2011)
14. Foster, J.N., Green, T.J., Tannen, V.: Annotated XML: queries and provenance. In: PODS, pp. 271–280 (2008)
15. Frew, J., Metzger, D., Slaughter, P.: Automatic capture and reconstruction of computational provenance. Concurr. Comput. Pract. Exper. **20**, 485–496 (2008)
16. L. M. R. G. Jr., M. Wilde, Mattoso, M., Foster, I.: Provenance traces of the swift parallel scripting system. In: Khalid Belhajjame, J.Z., Gomez-Perez, J.M., Sahoo, S. (ed.) ProvBench (2013)
17. Mason, C.: Cryptographic Binding of Metadata. National Security Agency's Review of Emerging Technologies, vol. 18 (2009)
18. Missier, P., Chen, Z.: Extracting PROV provenance traces from Wikipedia history pages. In: EDBT (2013)
19. Missier, P., Embury, S.M., Greenwood, M., Preece, A., Jin, B.: Managing information quality in e-science: the qurator workbench. In: SIGMOD, pp. 1150–1152 (2007)
20. Moreau, L., Groth, P.: Provenance An Introduction to PROV. Morgan & Claypool Publishers, San Rafael (2013)
21. Moreau, L., Ludäscher, B., et al.: Special issue: the first provenance challenge. Concurr. Comput. Pract. Experience **20**, 409–418 (2008)

22. NIST, Descriptions of SHA-256, SHA-384, and SHA-512 (2001)
23. Park, H., Ikeda, R., Widom, J.: RAMP: A system for capturing and tracing provenance in MapReduce workflows. In: VLDB (2011)
24. Rivest, R.: The MD5 message-digest algorithm. IETF Working Memo (1992). http://tools. ietf.org/html/rfc1321
25. Robinson, I., Webber, J., Eifrem, E.: Graph Databases. O'Reilly Media Inc, Sebastopol (2013)
26. Rosenthal, A., Seligman, L., Chapman, A., Blaustein, B.: Scalable access controls for lineage. In: Theory and Practice of Provenance (2008)
27. Scheidegger, C.E., Vo, H.T., Koop, D., Freire, J., Silva, C.: Querying and re-using workflows with VisTrails. In: SIGMOD (2008)
28. W3C, Provenance Data Model (2013). http://www.w3.org/TR/prov-dm/
29. Wang, X., Yu, H.: How to break MD5 and other hash functions. In: Cramer, R. (ed.) EUROCRYPT 2005. LNCS, vol. 3494, pp. 19–35. Springer, Heidelberg (2005)
30. Wolstencroft, K., Haines, R., et al.: The taverna workflow suite: designing and executing workflows of web services on the desktop, web or in the cloud. Nucleic Acids Res. **41**, w557–w561 (2013)
31. Xiey, Y., Muniswamy-Reddy, K.-K., Fengy, D., Liz, Y., Longz, D.D.E., Tany, Z., Chen, L.: A hybrid approach for efficient provenance storage. In: CIKM (2012)

Towards Supporting Provenance Gathering and Querying in Different Database Approaches

Flavio Costa[1(✉)], Vítor Silva[1], Daniel de Oliveira[2],
Kary A.C.S. Ocaña[1], and Marta Mattoso[1]

[1] COPPE, Federal University of Rio de Janeiro, Rio de Janeiro, Brazil
{flscosta, silva, kary, marta}@cos.ufrj.br
[2] Fluminense Federal University, Niteroi, Brazil
danielcmo@ic.uff.br

Abstract. The amount of provenance data gathered from Scientific Workflow Management Systems (SWfMS) and stored in databases has been growing considerably. Some difficulties are related to representation, access and query provenance databases. Despite the effort of PROV W3C group, data analyses may require different strategies of query specification because of the volume of data to be analyzed and the nature of queries. Another important point is the new approaches to store and retrieve provenance, some technologies are more appropriate than others. However, when applications are tightly coupled to specific technologies, it is difficult to take advantage of innovation. Based on these issues, we have built WfP-API, an API to store and perform queries in different provenance databases.

1 Introduction

Due to specific characteristics of Scientific Workflow Management Systems (SWfMS), experiments can generate provenance data in many different ways, in many different formats or even in many different repositories [1, 2]. To diminish the difficulties to deal with provenance coming from different repositories, W3C defined the PROV data model, which is currently a recommendation [3]. To represent typical properties on provenance from scientific workflows, we proposed PROV-Wf [4], an specialization of PROV. PROV-Wf represents provenance data gathered from scientific workflow executions to be queried during or after execution. We implemented PROV-Wf in a relational database, enabling the analysis of provenance data in a well-structured way with SQL. However, the interaction of scientists with PROV-Wf databases is typically through an interface with parameterized pre-defined relational queries. In fact, there is no consensus on the best representation to deal with provenance and database systems can vary in performance significantly even within the same data schema representation. For example, different database indexing and storage approaches may present different

The research presented in this paper was partially funded by CNPq and FAPERJ grants.

B. Ludäscher and B. Plale (Eds.): IPAW 2014, LNCS 8628, pp. 254–257, 2015.
DOI: 10.1007/978-3-319-16462-5_26

performance characteristics to execute provenance queries [5]. We can also mention that learning new database semantics for querying provenance is not an easy activity, especially for a non-specialist in computer science. In this paper, we propose WfP-API as an alternative way to SWfMS to have more flexibility when storing and querying provenance data. The API aims at storing provenance data in a variety of databases without having to concern about database system specific features. Our contribution is towards a PROV-Wf – based API, to be invoked from SWfMS, which is agnostic to the underlying database system. The API allows for querying provenance associated with workflow systems using one data model.

2 WfP-API: Storing and Querying Workflow Provenance Data

WfP-API is a provenance API that queries provenance databases based on the elements of PROV-Wf data schema [4]. WfP-API has two layers: *WfP Object Layer* and *WfP Connector Layer*. The former layer represents scientific workflows using adapted elements from PROV-Wf. In this first version, *WfP Object Layer* does not represent the agent elements (*Scientist* and *Machine*), while the software agent (*Program*) and *Execute activity* (PROV core structure of activity) are represented within the *Activation* concept. *WfP Object Layer* relies on object-oriented model to ease the integration with SWfMS to perform queries in DBMS. *WfP Connector Layer* establishes a connection between WfP-API object representation and DBMS. For each DBMS, a new instance of the connector has to be implemented. WfP-API currently supports Neo4J DBMS. Users of WfP-API need to choose the type of database to define connectors, while invocation to *WfP Object* layer is the same for every database connector.

3 Implementation and Final Remarks

WfP-API was developed according to the class diagram of Fig. 1. The dark gray classes describe each element of a scientific workflow (defined by *WfP Object Layer*) and scientists manipulate properties by calling getters and setters methods, such as *getStartTime* (that returns the activity start time) method in *Activity* class. Light gray classes represent internal controllers to define workflow structure (*Object* class) and connect WfP-API and the developed queries for a specific DBMS system (through *Connector* class). According to the specified database system, *WfP Connector* layer instantiates an object to use the DBMS, such as *Neo4J Connector* class. This class implements every abstract method from *Connector* class, with respect to the DBMS query language. Users may also need other queries than defined by WfP-API. In this case, they have to define their queries using the workflow object representation and extend connectors of the chosen DBMS.

Finally, the white classes represent DBMS connectors to the WfP-API. For example, for Neo4J DBMS we developed a *Neo4JConnector* class, which presents methods to establish a connection with this system (*start* method), to close this connection (*close* method), to determine workflow structure (*storeActicity* method), to store provenance data at runtime (*updateRunningActivations* method) or to execute custom queries developed by users (*getWorkflowExecutionTime* method).

WfP-API represents provenance based on the PROV-Wf data model, which follows W3C PROV recommendations. Furthermore, specialists only need to learn workflow semantics, since database semantics are already defined in *WfP Connector Layer*. Preliminary results showed that WfP-API was able to perform several queries that allow for steering of scientific workflow executions.

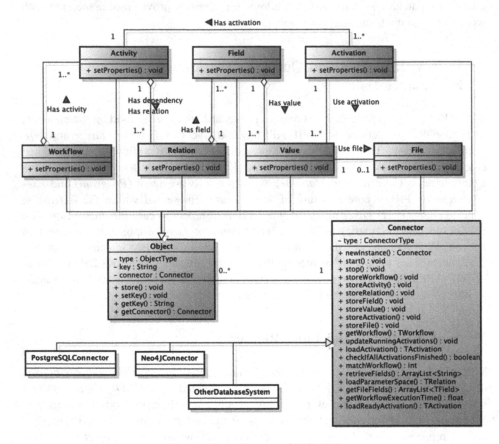

Fig. 1. Class diagram of WfP-API

References

1. Chirigati, F., Freire, J.: Towards integrating workflow and database provenance. In: Groth, P., Frew, J. (eds.) IPAW 2012. LNCS, vol. 7525, pp. 11–23. Springer, Heidelberg (2012)
2. Allen, M.D., Chapman, A., Blaustein, B., Seligman, L.: Getting it together: enabling multi-organization provenance exchange. In: TaPP (2011)
3. Missier, P., Belhajjame, K., Cheney, J.: The W3C PROV family of specifications for modelling provenance metadata. In: EDBT/ICDT 2013, pp. 773–776. ACM, New York, NY, USA (2013)

4. Costa, F., Silva, V., De Oliveira, D., Ocaña, K., Ogasawara, E., Dias, J., Mattoso, M.: Capturing and querying workflow runtime provenance with PROV: a practical approach. In: EDBT/ICDT 2013 Workshops, pp. 282–289. ACM, New York, NY, USA (2013)
5. Muniswamy-Reddy, K.-K.: Deciding how to store provenance. Technical report 03-06, Computer Science, Harvard University (2006)

Provenance for Explaining Taxonomy Alignments

Mingmin Chen[1]($\boxtimes$), Shizhuo Yu[1], Parisa Kianmajd[1], Nico Franz[2],
Shawn Bowers[3], and Bertram Ludäscher[1]

[1] Department of Computer Science, UC Davis, Davis, USA
{michen,szyu,pkianmajd,ludaesch}@ucdavis.edu
[2] School of Life Sciences, Arizona State University, Tempe, USA
nico.franz@asu.edu
[3] Department of Computer Science, Gonzaga University, Spokane, USA
bowers@gonzaga.edu

Derivations and proofs are a form of provenance in automated deduction that can assist users in understanding how reasoners derive logical consequences from premises. However, system-generated proofs are often overly complex or detailed, and making sense of them is non-trivial. Conversely, without any form of provenance, it is just as hard to know why a certain fact was derived.

We study provenance in the application of EULER/X [1], a logic-based toolkit for aligning multiple biological taxonomies. We propose a combination of approaches to explain both, logical inconsistencies in the input alignment, and the derivation of new facts in the output taxonomies.

Taxonomy Alignment. Given taxonomies T_1, T_2 and a set of *articulations* A, all modeled as monadic, first-order constraints, the *taxonomy alignment problem* is to find "merged" taxonomies that satisfy $\Phi = T_1 \cup T_2 \cup A$. An alignment can be *inconsistent* (Φ is unsatisfiable), *unique* (Φ has exactly one minimal model), or *ambiguous* (Φ has more than one minimal model). For example, let T_1 be given by *isa* (subset) constraints $b \subseteq a$, $c \subseteq a$, *coverage* constraint $a = b \cup c$, and *sibling disjointness* $b \cap c = \emptyset$. Similarly, T_2 is given by isa constraints $e \subseteq d$, $f \subseteq d$, coverage $d = e \cup f$, and sibling disjointness $e \cap f = \emptyset$.

An expert aligns T_1 and T_2 using *articulations* $a = d$, $b \subsetneq e$, $c \subsetneq f$, and $b \subsetneq d$; see Fig. 1. We would like to "apply" all of these relations between the two taxonomies, and output a merged taxonomy.

Inconsistency Explanation. Usually T_1 and T_2 are considered immutable or correct by definition, whereas A might contain modeling errors. EULER/X applied to Fig. 1 finds that the constraints are unsatisfiable, and performs a model-based diagnosis. The result lattice (Fig. 2) highlights *minimal inconsistent subsets* (MIS) and *maximal consistent subsets* (MCS). The MIS $\{A_1, A_2, A_3\}$ indicates which articulations are inconsistent with T_1, T_2. To further explore the inconsistency, the system-derived MCS can be employed: Fig. 3 shows the merged taxonomies (a.k.a. "possible worlds") obtained from the MCS. Here, each MCS corresponds to one possible world.[1]

---

[1] In general, a MCS can yield many possible worlds. Such ambiguities arise when the alignment input is underspecified.

© Springer International Publishing Switzerland 2015
B. Ludäscher and B. Plale (Eds.): IPAW 2014, LNCS 8628, pp. 258–260, 2015.
DOI: 10.1007/978-3-319-16462-5_27

Taxonomy T_1	Taxonomy T_2	Articulations
r_1: b isa a	r_5: e isa d	A_1: a = d
r_2: c isa a	r_6: f isa d	A_2: b $\subsetneq$ e
r_3: a = $b \cup c$	r_7: d = $e \cup f$	A_3: c $\subsetneq$ f
r_4: b $\cap$ c = $\emptyset$	r_8: e $\cap$ f = $\emptyset$	A_4: b $\subsetneq$ d

Fig. 1. Alignment problem: Taxonomies T_1 (given by set constraints $r_1, \ldots, r_4$) and T_2 (constraints $r_5, \ldots, r_8$) are related via articulations A (constraints $A_1, \ldots, A_4$).

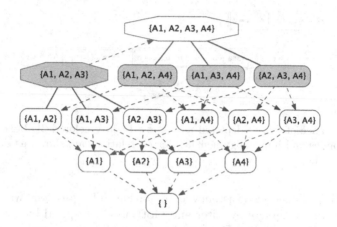

Fig. 2. Diagnosis for $A = \{A_1, \ldots, A_4\}$: solid red octagons and solid green boxes denote MIS and MCS, respectively. The (in)consistency of all other combinations are implied (Color figure online).

Using expert knowledge or further constraints[2] a preferred merge result can be selected to further analyze and then repair the inconsistency. Here, suppose the user chose the first maximal consistent subset $\{A_1, A_2, A_4\}$. It follows from A_1, A_2 and the input taxonomies T_1, T_2 that f $\subsetneq$ c. However, A_3 is c $\subsetneq$ f yielding a contradiction. Now the problem is to explain why f $\subsetneq$ c is inferred.

Derivation Explanation. To understand how f $\subsetneq$ c is inferred, we may need to inspect its logical derivation or an abstraction of it. We obtain this provenance in EULER/X by keeping track of the rules $r_1, \ldots, r_8$ and input alignments $A_1, \ldots, A_4$ used by the reasoner. Figure 4 depicts the resulting provenance overview.

Related Work. Data provenance is an actively researched area and is closely related to proofs and derivations in logical reasoning. Our inconsistency explanation is based on Reiter's model-based diagnosis [6], which has been studied extensively and applied to many areas, e.g., type error debugging, circuit diagnosis, OWL debugging, etc. We have adapted the HST algorithm in [4] to compute

---

[2] E.g., the output for MCS $\{A_2, A_3, A_4\}$ might be less desirable since it is not a tree.

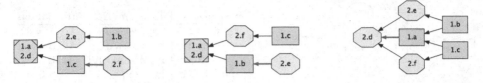

Fig. 3. Merged taxonomies (*possible worlds*) for MCS $\{A_1, A_2, A_4\}$, $\{A_1, A_3, A_4\}$, and $\{A_2, A_3, A_4\}$. Grey boxes are fused concepts; bold, red edges represent inferred relations (Color figure online).

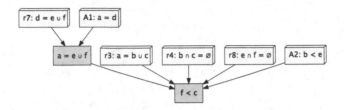

Fig. 4. Provenance of $f \subsetneq c$ (depicted as $f < c$). Lightly colored 3D-boxes are input facts (taxonomies and input alignment). Inferred relations are shown as darker boxes (Color figure online).

all MIS and MCS for inconsistency explanation. The problem was shown to be TRANS-ENUM-complete by Eiter and Gottlob [2]. Inspired by the ideas of a provenance semirings [3] and Datalog debugging [5], our approach explains the derivation of the inferred relations.

Acknowledgments. Supported in part by NSF IIS-1118088 and DBI-1147273.

References

1. Chen, M., Yu, S., Franz, N., Bowers, S., Ludäscher, B.: Euler/X: A toolkit for logic-based taxonomy integration. In: 22nd International Workshop on Functional and (Constraint) LogicProgramming (WFLP), Kiel, Germany (2013)
2. Eiter, T., Gottlob, G.: Hypergraph transversal computation and related problems in logic and AI. In: Flesca, S., Greco, S., Leone, N., Ianni, G. (eds.) JELIA 2002. LNCS (LNAI), vol. 2424, pp. 549–564. Springer, Heidelberg (2002)
3. Green, T., Karvounarakis, G., Tannen, V.: Provenance semirings. In: ACM Symposium on Principles of Database Systems (PODS), pp. 31–40 (2007)
4. Horridge, M., Parsia, B., Sattler, U.: Explaining inconsistencies in OWL ontologies. In: Godo, L., Pugliese, A. (eds.) SUM 2009. LNCS, vol. 5785, pp. 124–137. Springer, Heidelberg (2009)
5. Köhler, S., Ludäscher, B., Smaragdakis, Y.: Declarative datalog debugging for mere mortals. In: Barceló, P., Pichler, R. (eds.) Datalog 2.0 2012. LNCS, vol. 7494, pp. 111–122. Springer, Heidelberg (2012)
6. Reiter, R.: A theory of diagnosis from first principles. Artif. Intell. **32**(1), 57–95 (1987)

Challenges for Provenance Analytics
Over Geospatial Data

Daniel Garijo[1]([✉]), Yolanda Gil[2], and Andreas Harth[3]

[1] Ontology Engineering Group,
Universidad Politécnica de Madrid, Madrid, Spain
dgarijo@fi.upm.es
[2] Information Sciences Institute,
University of Southern California, Los Angeles, USA
gil@isi.edu
[3] Institute AIFB, Karlsruhe Institute of Technology,
Karlsruhe, Germany
harth@kit.edu

Abstract. The growing availability of geospatial data online, the increased use of crowdsourced maps and the advent of geospatial mashups have led to systems that deliver data to users after integration from many sources. In such systems, understanding the provenance of geospatial data is crucial for assessing the quality of the data and deciding on whether to rely on the data for decision making. To be able to use and analyze provenance in geospatial integration systems in a principled manner, we identify different levels of provenance in the geospatial domain, provide a set of provenance questions from the point of view of end users, and relate our geospatial provenance model to the W3C PROV recommendation.

1 Introduction

The Open Geospatial Consortium and the World Wide Web Consortium are working jointly towards standards for linking and integrating geospatial data [1]. As geospatial data is often used in decision making (e.g., navigation), the accuracy of integrated data is important. While we specifically cover provenance for geospatial information, some of these challenges are present in many other domains as well. The area of geospatial data integration is a prime scenario for provenance management, as the involved data and systems are complex and exhibit many challenging characteristics:

- External sources: when integrating two geospatial datasets, an algorithm might consult other sources.
- Human-in-the-loop processes: in some cases, the integration might involve manual intervention, to check particular values by seeking additional confirmation or even perhaps with eyes on target.
- Crowdsourcing: datasets may have been collected from many small contributions, which should attacj provenance too.

© Springer International Publishing Switzerland 2015
B. Ludäscher and B. Plale (Eds.): IPAW 2014, LNCS 8628, pp. 261–263, 2015.
DOI: 10.1007/978-3-319-16462-5_28

- Granularity: geospatial information may be represented at different levels of granularity in space; a geographical feature can be a point in space (e.g., a road intersection), a one-dimensional segment (e.g., a bridge that connects two points) or a two-dimensional region (e.g., a parking lot).
- Computation: spatial reasoning may be needed to compute relationships between features; the integration system may have to integrate computed relations from different sources.
- Versioning: maps are updated as the original data sources are updated. The objects in a map themselves can have multiple revisions.

We present an initial study on the requirements and challenges of tracking geospatial provenance, based on discussions with researchers and practitioners at several meetings and workshops on geospatial data.

2   Geospatial Provenance Model

Before we explain how to apply the W3C PROV standard model [2] to the geospatial domain, we present a classification of provenance levels on geospatial data:

- Dataset-level provenance: provenance assertions about a map as a single entity. The map contains objects, and these objects contain properties and values, but provenance is associated with the map as a whole.
- Object-level provenance: how different objects were created in the map.
- Property-level provenance: enables us to answer questions about attributes and attribute values of objects shown in the map.

Modeling detailed provenance across all levels presents a challenge of scale. Maps can have millions of objects, and if we represented each of the integration processes for each object, the amount of information could become larger than the map itself, especially if we assume updates at regular intervals. Property-level provenance aggravates the scale issues of object-level provenance.

In Fig. 1, we list user questions concerning geospatial provenance, grouped according to our provenance model for geospatial data.

Applying PROV to the geospatial domain is straightforward for dataset-level and object-level provenance, as we can use dataset and object identifiers as handle for attaching provenance records to. Property-level provenance requires a more involved approach, as properties are typically accessed through the object and cannot be referenced as a separate entity. Therefore, we would either need to create new identifiers for each property assertion, or to repeat the property assertion itself to be able to attach the provenance record to. Tracking appearing and disappearing objects or values across versions would require to store the entire history of all datasets, including provenance records.

PROVENANCE OF DATASETS:	PROVENANCE OF SETS OF DATASETS:
Q1: Where does the information in this map come from?	Q7: What maps were generated after a given date?
Q2: Who created the map?	Q8: Which maps were generated by a given organization/person?
Q3: How was the map created?	Q9: Which maps were generated with a given version of a source dataset?
Q4: What is the most recent version of this map?	
Q5: Why was the map updated?	Q10: Which maps were generated with a given version of the integration algorithm?
Q6: How was the map updated?	
PROVENANCE OF OBJECTS:	**PROVENANCE OF SETS OF OBJECTS:**
Q11: What original data source did this object come from?	Q16: What other objects in the map (or selected region) come from the same data source as a given selected object?
Q12: Who created the object?	Q17: What objects were taken from data from a given organization?
Q13: How was this object created?	Q18: What objects were taken from a specific original data source?
Q14: When was this object created?	Q19: What objects were taken from a type of data source (e.g., a crowdsourced data source)?
Q15: How was this object included in the original data source?	
	Q20: What objects were generated with an older version of the algorithm?
PROVENANCE OF PROPERTIES:	**PROVENANCE OF SETS OF PROPERTIES:**
Q21: What original data source did this property come from?	Q26: What properties of the selected objects come from the same data source as the selected property of that object?
Q22: Who created the property?	Q27: What properties of the selected objects
Q23: How was this property created?	Q28: What properties of a selected objects were taken from a specific original data source?
Q24: When was this property created?	
Q25: How was this property included in the original data source?	Q29: What properties of a selected objects were taken from a type of data source (e.g., a crowdsourced data source)?
	Q30: What properties were generated with an older version of the algorithm?
	Q31: What properties from other objects come from the same data source as a given selected property of an object?

OTHER PROVENANCE QUESTIONS:
Q32: How did the selected information come about in each of the input data sources?
Q33: How did a given set of manual corrections help improve later versions of the map?
Q34: What is new in this new version of the map?
Q35: What objects were integrated with confidence > 0.8?
Q36: Why is the object I am looking for not appearing?
Q37: Which datasets were used for generating a selected area?
Q38: Can I see some highlights of important things about this map, e.g., where is the information more uncertain, where is the information really recent, where has the information changed the most, etc?

Fig. 1. User questions concerning geospatial provenance.

References

1. Archer, P.: Joint W3C/OGC Workshop on Linking Geospatial Data, March 2014. http://www.w3.org/2014/03/lgd/
2. Moreau, L., Missier, P.: PROV-DM: The PROV Data Model (2012). http://www.w3.org/TR/prov-dm/

Adaptive RDF Query Processing
Based on Provenance

Marcin Wylot[1], Philippe Cudré-Mauroux[1], and Paul Groth[2]($\boxtimes$)

[1] University of Fribourg, Fribourg, Switzerland
{marcin,phil}@exascale.info
[2] VU University Amsterdam, Amsterdam, The Netherlands
p.t.groth@vu.nl

Given the increasing amounts of RDF data available from multiple heterogeneous sources, as evidenced by the Linked Open Data Cloud, there is a need to track provenance within RDF data management systems [1]. In [8], we presented TripleProv, a database system supporting the transparent and automatic capture of detailed provenance information for arbitrary queries. A key focus of TripleProv is the efficient implementation of provenance-enabled queries over large scale RDF datasets. TripleProv is based on a native RDF store, which we have extended with two different physical models to store provenance data on disk in a compact fashion. In addition, TripleProv supports several new query execution strategies to derive provenance information at two different levels of aggregation. At one level, the exact sources for a query results can be identified. The second, more detailed level, provides the full lineage of the query results including the various constraints, projections and joins involved in answering the query. In addition to these levels of aggregation at the data source level, we support tracking the provenance at the quadruple level. That is, every quad (i.e. tuple) is annotated and those annotations are tracked through the query processing pipeline. This tracking is done by leveraging the concept provenance polynomials [3]. That is capturing the provenance representation as a formula over tuples. Our work follows on from previous work on annotating or coloring RDF triples [2,9] by focusing on both scale and query adaptivity.

At the logical level, we use two basic operators to express the provenance polynomials. The first one ($\oplus$) to represent unions of sources, and the second ($\otimes$) to represent joins between sources.

Unions are used in two cases when generating the polynomials. First, they are used when a constraint or a projection can be satisfied with triples coming from multiple sources (meaning that there are more than one instance of a particular triple which is used for a particular operation). The following polynomial:

$$l1 \oplus l2 \oplus l3$$

for instance, encodes the fact that a given result can originate from three different sources ($l1$, $l2$, or $l3$). Second, unions are also used when multiple entities satisfy a set of constraints or projections.

As for the join operator, it can also be used in two ways: to express the fact that sources were joined to handle a constraint or a projection, or to handle

B. Ludäscher and B. Plale (Eds.): IPAW 2014, LNCS 8628, pp. 264–266, 2015.
DOI: 10.1007/978-3-319-16462-5_29

object-subject or object-object joins between a few sets of constraints. The following polynomial:

$$(l1 \oplus l2) \otimes (l3 \oplus l4)$$

for example, encodes the fact that sources $l1$ or $l2$ were joined with sources $l3$ or $l4$ to produce results.

Provenance polynomials can be used to compute a trust or information quality score based on the sources used in the result.

TripleProv works on large scale real world data. We have tested the system on two datasets consisting of over 110 million triples each. Each dataset is roughly 25 GB in size. The datasets are drawn, respectively, from two crawls of the Web: the Billion Triple Challenge[1] and the Web Data Commons[2] [7].

Based on this foundation, this work presents preliminary results on *adaptively modifying query execution* based on provenance. Specifically, we have extended TripleProv to allow a specific list of sources (e.g. trusted sources) to be provided which are to be used when answering a query. Additionally, one can also specify a list of sources to avoid during query execution (e.g. a list of untrusted sources). The specified lists are checked at every stage of query execution process. This means that even at the level of intermediate results, which are not necessarily presented as an output, we ensure that these data sources are not touched. We note that this trigger based approach allows for potentially dynamic changes in the source list at query execution.

Such adaptive query processing is useful for a number of use cases. For instance, one could restrict the results of a query to certain subsets of sources or use provenance for access control such that only certain sources will appear in a query result. Identifying results (i.e., particular triples) with overlapping provenance is also another prospective use case. Additionally, one could detect whether a particular result would still be valid when removing a source dataset. We could also extend our approach to with Hartig's tSPARQL [4] to be able to query trust annotations in combination with provenance sources.

In [8], we found that provenance tracking within the database caused between a 60–70% overhead. While this is acceptable for many use cases, it would be beneficial if the performance would be faster. We believe that by taking advantage of knowing data provenance one could potentially optimize the performance of the database. We note that our approach focused on adjusting the pipeline of query processing verses querying provenance after the fact as in other systems [5,6]. An interesting area of work would be to study the trade off between runtime query adaptation based on provenance and post hoc provenance queries.

This work is a first step towards showing how provenance can be used to make it easier to work with heterogenous RDF data.

Acknowledgements. This work was funded in part by the Swiss National Science Foundation under grant number PP00P2_128459 and by the Data2Semantics project in the Dutch national program COMMIT.

---

[1] http://km.aifb.kit.edu/projects/btc-2009/.
[2] http://webdatacommons.org/.

References

1. Ding, L., Peng, Y., da Silva, P.P., McGuinness, D.L.: Tracking RDF graph provenance using RDF molecules. In: International Semantic Web Conference (2005)
2. Flouris, G., Fundulaki, I., Pediaditis, P., Theoharis, Y., Christophides, V.: Coloring RDF triples to capture provenance. In: Bernstein, A., Karger, D.R., Heath, T., Feigenbaum, L., Maynard, D., Motta, E., Thirunarayan, K. (eds.) ISWC 2009. LNCS, vol. 5823, pp. 196–212. Springer, Heidelberg (2009)
3. Green, T.J., Karvounarakis, G., Tannen, V.: Provenance semirings. In: Proceedings of the Twenty-Sixth ACM SIGMOD-SIGACT-SIGART Symposium on Principles of Database Systems, pp. 31–40. ACM (2007)
4. Hartig, O.: Querying trust in RDF data with tSPARQL. In: Aroyo, L., et al. (eds.) ESWC 2009. LNCS, vol. 5554, pp. 5–20. Springer, Heidelberg (2009)
5. Karvounarakis, G., Ives, Z.G., Tannen, V.: Querying data provenance. In: Proceedings of the 2010 ACM SIGMOD International Conference on Management of data, pp. 951–962. ACM (2010)
6. Miles, S.: Electronically querying for the provenance of entities. In: Moreau, L., Foster, I. (eds.) IPAW 2006. LNCS, vol. 4145, pp. 184–192. Springer, Heidelberg (2006)
7. Mühleisen, H., Bizer, C.: Web data commons - extracting structured data from two large web corpora. In: Bizer, C., Heath, T., Berners-Lee, T., Hausenblas, M. (eds.), LDOW. CEUR Workshop Proceedings, vol. 937. CEUR-WS.org (2012)
8. Wylot, M., Cudré-Mauroux, P., Groth, P.: Tripleprov: efficient processing of lineage queries over a native rdf store. In: Proceedings of the 23rd Intenational World Wide Web Conference (WWW'2014) (2014)
9. Zimmermann, A., Lopes, N., Polleres, A., Straccia, U.: A general framework for representing, reasoning and querying with annotated semantic web data. Web Semant. 11, 72–95 (2012)

Using Well-Founded Provenance Ontologies to Query Meteorological Data

Thiago Silva Barbosa[1], Ednaldo O. Santos[1], Gustavo B. Lyra[1],
and Sérgio Manuel Serra da Cruz[1,2,3(✉)]

[1] UFRRJ – Universidade Federal Rural do Rio de Janeiro, Seropédica, RJ, Brazil
{thiago, ednaldo, gblyra, serra}@ufrrj.br
[2] PPGMMC/UFRRJ – Programa de Pós Graduação Modelagem
Matemática e Computacional, Seropédica, RJ, Brazil
[3] PET-SI/UFRRJ – Programa de Educação Tutorial - Sistemas de Informação,
Seropédica, RJ, Brazil

Abstract. The analysis of increasing flow of data about Tropical rainfall is a big challenge faced by meteorologists. This work presents an approach to pre-process, organize and query high quality meteorological data. Thus, we present a semantic approach that uses well-founded ontologies that help meteorologists to develop SPARQL queries that navigate over high quality data and provenance metadata collected during the execution meteorological in silico experiments.

Keywords: Provenance · Foundational ontology · Meteorology

1 Introduction

There is great interest in determining the periods and the probability of occurrence of extreme hydrometeorological events so as to mitigate possible associated risks to citizens and agribusiness. Briefly, meteorological data flows from lots of sensors through heterogeneous apparatus to scientists' databases where they perform statistics, analytics to tune mathematical models to study the occurrences extreme events. Therefore, in this work, we present an approach that uses well-founded ontologies [1, 3, 8] and provenance management techniques to aid researchers to investigate the cause of erroneous values detected at any point of the pre-processing chain and to query high quality meteorological.

2 Materials and Methods

Meteorological Data and Pre-processors - Daily raw rainfall data were obtained from 75 weather stations geographically scattered in the southeast region of Rio de Janeiro State, Brazil, one of the regions subject to the occurrence of extreme rainfall events. The datasets are part of long meteorological series (bigger than 20 years since 1960). The series were extracted over the Web from FAO and HidroWeb systems [4] by a Web framework named "Meteoro", previously developed by our research group [2], which uses several Vistrails workflows as chains of pre-processors to generate higher

© Springer International Publishing Switzerland 2015
B. Ludäscher and B. Plale (Eds.): IPAW 2014, LNCS 8628, pp. 267–270, 2015.
DOI: 10.1007/978-3-319-16462-5_30

quality curated meteorological data. The pre-processors checks: high–low extreme daily values, internal consistency, temporal and spatial outliers, missing and erroneous data. The framework allows meteorologists to rectify gap data and annotate datasets with provenance to reduce error propagation on long-term meteorological investigations. Besides, the framework also generates a structured relational repository of high quality meteorological data. The quality of data in the repository generated was evaluated by Precinoto et al. (2013) [5]. However, despite the computations, data are still faulty and presents some semantic inconsistencies. Thus, in order to reduce the semantic gaps, we developed well founded provenance ontology to annotate meteorological data of the repository.

Well-Founded Ontologies - In this work, we have used the ontologically well-founded UML modeling profile named OntoUML presented by Guizzardi and Halpin [3] to develop well-founded ontologies. This profile comprises a number of stereotyped classes and relations implanting a metamodel that reflect the structure and axiomatization of a foundational and domain independent ontology named Unified Foundation Ontology (UFO). We also used the Open proVenance Ontology (OvO) [1] which is based in three other theories: the lifecycle of scientific experiments, presented by Mattoso et al. [6], PROV-O and PROV-DM specifications and UFO itself. OvO's concepts are modeled as UML profile because of the widespread understanding of classes and relations and their suitability. OvO was developed as a set of three sub-ontologies: (i) in silico scientific experiment sub-ontology, (ii) experiment composition sub-ontology, (iii) experiment execution sub-ontology. The sub-ontologies complement each other; they are connected by relations between their concepts as well as by formal axioms.

3   Meteoro Ontology and WebOntology Query Tool

Meteoro is an application ontology that maps the concepts of (i) the pre-processing steps of raw meteorological data into curated data; (ii) provenance metadata about data transformations executed by the pre-processors and; (iii) the characteristics about the in silico experiments performed by the meteorologists. It makes these concepts explicit, extends the OvO to that domain, besides reuses the concepts of provenance in large scale scientific experiments described by Cruz et al. [1, 8]. *Meteoro*, like OVO, was designed using OLED (OntoUML Lightweight Editor) [3], it is an editor for OntoUML, aimed to provide a simple, lightweight and integrated set of features such as model editing, syntax verification, instances simulation via Alloy, anti-pattern management and transformations to OWL. In other words, *Meteoro* is first modeled in an ontologically well-founded language that explicitly commits to fundamental ontological distinctions in their metamodels comprising type such as: Rigid (*Kinds* and *subKinds*), Anti-Rigid (*Phases* and *Roles*) and Semi-Rigid (*Mixins*). After that, it can be converted to another language that supports inferences and reasonings.

Meteoro **Ontology** - To be computed, the ontology has to be codified into another language that supports automated inferences. Besides, it must consider legacy applications and other relevant requirements such as reasonable computational efficiency and compatibility with Semantic Web standards. Thus, we transformed *Meteoro* from OLED to OWL taking advantage of the Protégé editor. The codification of well-founded ontologies to OWL is complex. The mappings between two radically different languages need for customizations to represent each domain element. During the execution of this work OLED was still under development; thus we used two rounds of mapping. As the first round, we used the mapping rules defined by Zamborlini et al. [7]. As the second round of mapping, we used rules to match the concepts of the ontology to the relations of the meteorological repository. This approach allows relational databases to offer their contents as virtual RDF graphs without the replication of the RDB in RDF triples. Besides, it permits meteorologists to develop SPARQL queries and navigate over meteorological data and provenance metadata thought the concepts of the ontology.

WebOntology Tool - We have noticed that it was not trivial for meteorologists to create SPARQL queries that involve meteorological data, provenance metadata and also ontology classes. Thus, we developed a simple web-based graphical query tool named WebOntology that uses the *Meteoro* ontology to assist meteorologists with respect to the process of query formulation over the meteorological repositories. There are two main functionalities that we considered important to be mentioned: (i) *Manage Queries*: It aims to reduce the researcher's (re)work. It allows them to create, execute, delete and update SPARQL queries over the data repository; (ii) *SPARQL EasyBuilder*: It lets meteorologists create simple queries even without knowing the syntax of the language. Therefore, it allows users to navigate through the concepts and properties and graphically develop simple queries by selecting features like ontology class, object, properties and values to be searched.

4   Conclusion

This work presented an approach to help meteorologist to manage curated data about Tropical rainfall. Our proposal incorporates well-founded ontologies, provenance and Semantic Web standards to recover high quality meteorological data annotated with provenance metadata generated during early stages of data transformation.

Acknowledgements. We are grateful by the financial support provided by FAPERJ (E-26/112.588/2012 and E-26/110.928/2013) and FNDE-MEC-SeSU.

References

1. Cruz, S.M.S, Campos, M.L.M., Mattoso, M.: A foundational ontology to support scientific experiments (2012). ceur-ws.org/Vol-728/paper6.pdf
2. Lemos Filho, G.R., et al.: Assimilação, Controle de Qualidade e Análise de Dados de Meteorológicos Apoiados por Proveniência. In: VII Brazilian E-science Workshop (2013)
3. Guizzardi, G., Halpin, T.: Ontological foundations for conceptual modeling. Appl. Ontol. **3**, 91–110 (2008)

4. HidroWeb: Sistemas de Informação Hidrológicas (2014). http://hidroweb.ana.gov.br/
5. Precinoto, R.S., et al.: Aplicação de Regressão Linear Múltipla para Preenchimento de Falhas de Dados Pluviométricos no Estado do Rio de Janeiro. In: Anais XVII SBMET (2012)
6. Mattoso, M., et al.: Towards supporting the life cycle of large scale scientific experiment. Int. J. Bus. Process Integr. Manage. 5(1), 79–92 (2010)
7. Zamborlini, V., Gonçalves, B., Guizzardi, G.: Codification and application of a well-founded heart-ECG ontology (2011). http://www.inf.ufes.br/~gguizzardi/camera-ready_paper48363.pdf
8. Cruz, S.M.S.: Uma Estratégia de Apoio à Gerência de Dados De Proveniência em Experimentos Científicos. Ph.D. Thesis, Federal University of Rio de Janeiro - COPPE, Brazil (2011)

Applying W3C PROV to Express Geospatial Provenance at Feature and Attribute Level

Joan Masó[1]([✉]), Guillem Closa[1], and Yolanda Gil[2]

[1] Center for Ecological Research and Forestry Applications,
08193 Cerdanyola del Vallès, Spain
joan.maso@uab.cat, g.closa@creaf.uab.cat
[2] Information Sciences Institute, University of Southern California,
4676 Admiralty Way, Marina del Rey, CA 90292, USA
gil@isi.edu

Abstract. This paper presents the application of PROV to geospatial data. In particular, it is applied to the vector model, where geospatial phenomena are represented as a collection of individual objects (called features) that are described with a lot of geographical (point, lines, polygons, etc.) and non-geographical (names, measures, etc.) properties (sometimes called attributes). We present an approach to describe in W3C PROV the distributed data sources and the processes involved in the generation/revision of a geospatial dataset.

Keywords: W3C · Geospatial provenance · RDF · Distributed environments

1 Geospatial Provenance in W3C PROV

This paper presents an application of PROV to describe geospatial provenance generated on a distributed environment and encoded in RDF. To apply PROV in the geospatial domain it is important to identify the different elements that PROV provides and map them to geospatial concepts. The PROV Data Model relies on the definition of entities, activities, and agents and the relations among them [1]. In the geospatial world information is stored in features. A feature is described as a set of geographical and non-geographical properties (sometimes called attributes). Features can be tangible, such as rivers; or an abstract concept, such as political boundaries [2]. Geographical properties are the position and shape of a feature that can be expressed as a point a line or a polygon (as a sequence of coordinates). Non-geographical property can be for example the name of a river.

Each geospatial feature can be considered a PROV *entity,* and we refer to the provenance associated with it as *feature-level provenance.* Geospatial features are grouped in collections of features. A feature collection (called *datasets*) can also be considered an *entity* in PROV (in fact, an *entity collection*), the *dataset-level provenance.* In many occasions, feature properties are processed with different techniques and can come from different origins. In that case, their attributes (also considered *entities),* have their own provenance, the *attribute-level.* Therefore, we capture

B. Ludäscher and B. Plale (Eds.): IPAW 2014, LNCS 8628, pp. 271–274, 2015.
DOI: 10.1007/978-3-319-16462-5_31

geospatial provenance information at three different levels of granularity. In a Geospatial Information System (GIS) context, *activities* are executions that create and manipulate datasets, features and attributes (such as buffer generation or conflation execution). Activities can be executed in a GIS platform or a web processing service. Each of the individual activities can be associated with a general process that can be represented as a PROV *Plan*. The GIS platform or the web processing service can be considered a *plan collection*. Another important aspect to consider is identifying the PROV *agents,* that can be either responsible of an individual process execution (*activity*) or be the developer of a general process (*plan*).

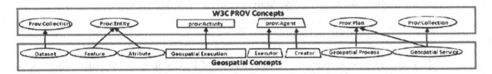

Fig. 1. The correspondence between W3C PROV and Geospatial concepts

We use the RDF subclass mechanism to map geospatial elements to PROV classes, as shown in Fig. 1. In addition, we use the Turtle notation here to show examples, with geospatial concepts shown with the "ows" namespace. For example:

```
ows:Feature rdfs:subClassOf prov:Entity .
```

2 W3C PROV Relations Applied to Geospatial Provenance

In our application, we can derive a new dataset by combining two data sources through an *activity* requested by an *agent*. A new features *wasGeneratedBy* the combination process and *wasDerivedFrom* the two initial features. In RDF:

```
combinationProcessExec1 prov:used feature1 ;
                        prov:used feature2 ;
newFeature1 prov:wasGeneratedBy combinationProcessExec1 .
```

At the same time, the geospatial process *wasAssociatedWith* an *agent,* which can be considered the author *(wasAttributedTo)* of the new *features*:

```
newFeature1 prov:wasAttributedTo processExecutor .
combinationProcessExec1 prov:wasAssociatedWith
processExecutor .
```

We can associate the individual execution with the generic GIS tools used (*plan*) and with the developer of the tools:

```
combinationProcessExec1 prov:used combinationProcess .
gisApplication prov:wasMember combinationProcess .
combinationProcess prov:wasAttributedTo processDeveloper .
```

These examples describe feature-level provenance, but the same relations can be used at dataset or attribute level. This is an excerpt of the provenance for 2 attributes of newFeature1:

```
newPosition1 prov:wasDerivedFrom position1 .
```

3 W3C PROV and RDF to Express Geospatial Provenance

The Open Geospatial Consortium has defined a standard for geospatial processing on the web called Web Processing Service (WPS) [3]. As a use case, we have defined how to implement a distributed process for the conflation of two datasets as a WPS process. In the geospatial field, a conflation process is defined as the process of combining geographic information from overlapping sources so as to retain accurate data, minimize redundancy, and reconcile data conflicts [4]. In our case, a U.S. Geological Survey (USGS) dataset was enhanced with Open Street Map (OSM) dataset by adding new features or updating the geometry or other attributes. The conflation process uses a matching and enrichment algorithm controlled by a distance parameter (that acts as a threshold for the conflation step where features in the OSM beyond that distance will not be conflated with a given USGS feature). Dataset-level provenance information captures the purpose of each parameter, the name of the authors of the data and the processes involved, the date and time of both the process development and the execution. During conflation, some completely new features are added, and for them feature-level provenance is provided. Other features are conflated by modifying only the geometrical property (location) or the non-geometrical properties, and a more detailed and granular attribute-level provenance is used.

4 Conclusions

PROV can be used to express, store and query geospatial information. The model presented defines geospatial entities and captures provenance at 3 levels of granularity. The RDF encoding of PROV can express well the provenance of the geospatial objects, roles and relations with a uniform approach. PROV was found more flexible, easier to understand, and more compact than ISO19115 XML encoding that is traditionally used in the geospatial community.

Acknowledgments.   This work is a continuation of the GeoViQua FP7 project, and organized and funded by the Open Geospatial Consortium as part of the OWS10 Interoperability Experiment. It was also supported in part by the US Air Force Office of Scientific Research with grant FA9550-11-1-0104.

References

1. Moreau, L., Missier, P. (eds.): PROV-DM: The PROV Data Model. World Wide Web Consortium (2013)
2. Lake, R., et al.: Geography Mark-Up Language. Wiley, Chichester (2004). ISBN 978-0470871546
3. Schut, P.: OpenGIS Web Processing Service Version 1.0.0. OGC 05-007r7 (2007)
4. Chen, C.-C., et al.: Automatically and accurately conflating raster maps with orthoimagery. Geoinformatica **12**(3), 377–410 (2008). doi:10.1007/s10707-007-0033-0

ProvStore: A Public Provenance Repository

Trung Dong Huynh[✉] and Luc Moreau

Electronics and Computer Science, University of Southampton,
Southampton SO17 1BJ, UK
{tdh,l.moreau}@ecs.soton.ac.uk

Abstract. ProvStore is the first online public provenance repository supporting the new PROV standards by W3C. It allows users and applications to store and (optionally) publish the provenance of their data on the Web. Provenance documents can be transformed, visualized, and shared in various serializations, with all the functionality also available to third-party applications via a RESTful API (OAuth supported).

1 Provenance Repository

ProvStore (https://provenance.ecs.soton.ac.uk/store/) is the first public repository of provenance documents supporting the PROV standards for provenance on the Web by the World Wide Web Consortium [MM13]. Users can register for a free account, allowing them to upload and share provenance documents either privately or publicly in various representations (see Fig. 1 for an example[1]). Specifically, it supports the Provenance Notation (PROV-N), RDF encoded using the PROV Ontology (PROV-O) in Turtle or TriG formats, PROV-XML, and PROV-JSON [HJK+13].

By default, documents submitted to ProvStore are private and can only be accessed by their owners. Document owners, however, can choose to share their documents with others in two ways: making a document *public*, i.e. available to any visitor to ProvStore, or sharing it with specific ProvStore's users. The former is useful for users who want to expose the provenance of their resources (e.g. papers, reports, data sets) to the public; the link to a document on ProvStore can be attached as the provenance URI along with the corresponding resource.[2] In the latter, different access roles can be set to authorized users for fine-grain access control: administrator, editor, contributor, or reader. Except reader, all other roles and the owner can append new provenance bundles to a document after it has been created. It is suitable for sharing provenance between a team of collaborating humans and/or applications (see Sect. 3 for more information about the application programming interface provided by ProvStore).

ProvStore was funded by the UK Engineering and Physical Sciences Research Council (EPSRC) as part of project Orchid, grant EP/I011587/1.

[1] Online address: https://provenance.ecs.soton.ac.uk/store/documents/1979/.
[2] See www.w3.org/TR/prov-aq for more information on provenance access and query. Document links on ProvStore support HTTP content negotiation. For example, if the HTTP request specify a header `Accept: application/json`, the PROV-JSON representation of the provenance document will be returned.

B. Ludäscher and B. Plale (Eds.): IPAW 2014, LNCS 8628, pp. 275–277, 2015.
DOI: 10.1007/978-3-319-16462-5_32

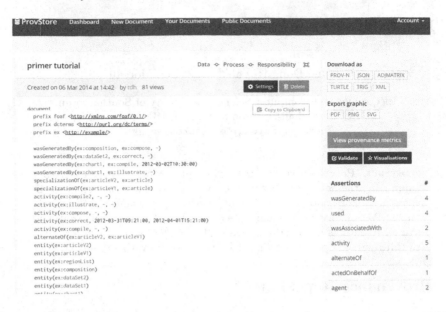

Fig. 1. The screen-shot of a ProvStore document.

On each document (Fig. 1), users can see its provenance descriptions in PROV-N, along with some statistics about the numbers of assertions. ProvStore also provides a number of provenance network metrics [EHM+12] calculated on the graph representation of the document. As mentioned above, access links to various provenance representations are included, in addition to a numbers of provenance transformations and visualizations (see Sect. 2). The provenance of the document can be checked directly from inside the document page (provided by the external ProvValidator service[3]).

2   Provenance Transformation and Visualization

A provenance document can contain bundles, which are a PROV construct to support bundling a set of provenance descriptions (so allowing provenance of provenance to be expressed) [MM13]. To support relating provenance statements within a document across its bundles, ProvStore can produce a *flattened* representation of the document in which all of its provenance statements are merged into a flat document. In this representation, the provenance of entities distributed in multiple bundles can be "connected" for further examination.

In addition to the flattened representation, ProvStore provides a number of provenance views: Data Flow (concerned with the flow of information or the transformations of things), Process Flow (concerned with the processes that took place), and Responsibility (assigning responsibility for what happened) [MG13, Chap. 3].

---

[3] provenance.ecs.soton.ac.uk/validator.

These views are simplified versions of the original document produced by selecting only the relevant provenance descriptions from it. They can facilitate the examination of provenance information by allowing users to focus on a single aspect of it rather than the full descriptions. Each of the views can be applied either on the original document or its flattened version.

All versions (original or flattened, optionally simplified in a provenance view) of a ProvStore document can be visualized in a (static) graphical representation (in the SVG, PNG, or PDF formats). In addition, ProvStore provides interactive visualization tools for users to explore a provenance graph through a Hive plot (highlighting input, output, and intermediary nodes), a Wheel plot (showing the density of connections to/from nodes), a Gantt chart (presenting entities, activities, and agents on a time line), and a Sankey diagram (showing flows of 'influence' between provenance elements). All the interactive visualizations, except the Gantt chart, also allow filtering on provenance assertion types to simplify the visualizations.

3   RESTful Application Programming Interface (API)

All of the functionality described in the previous sections (with the exception of interactive features like validation and visualizations) can be accessed programmatically via a RESTful API[4] over the Hypertext Transfer Protocol. ProvStore, hence, can serve as a provenance storage-and-publish service on the cloud, providing applications a means to make the provenance of their data available online as soon as it is generated/recorded. Authorized applications must authenticate with ProvStore's API either by using their (revocable) secret API keys or by following the OAuth (version 1) protocol. With the latter, ProvStore enables users of any third-party applications or web sites (that registered with it) to store or access their provenance data directly from inside such applications in a seamless fashion.

References

[EHM+12] Ebden, M., Huynh, T.D., Moreau, L., Ramchurn, S., Roberts, S.: Network analysis on provenance graphs from a crowdsourcing application. In: Groth, P., Frew, J. (eds.) IPAW 2012. LNCS, vol. 7525, pp. 168–182. Springer, Heidelberg (2012)

[HJK+13] Huynh, T.D., Jewell, M.O., Sezavar Keshavarz, A., Michaelides, D.T., Yang, H., Moreau, L.: The PROV-JSON serialization. Technical report, World Wide Web Consortium, April 2013

[MG13] Moreau, L., Groth, P.: Provenance: An Introduction to PROV. Morgan & Claypool, San Rafael (2013)

[MM13] Moreau, L., Missier, P.: PROV-DM: The PROV Data Model. Technical report, World Wide Web Consortium, W3C Recommendation (2013)

---

[4] See provenance.ecs.soton.ac.uk/store/help/api for the full specification of the API and example codes.

Sentence Templating for Explaining Provenance

Heather S. Packer$^{(\boxtimes)}$ and Luc Moreau

Web And Internet Science Group, University of Southampton, Southampton, UK
{hp3,L.Moreau}@ecs.soton.ac.uk

Abstract. Disseminating provenance data to users can be challenging because of its technical content, and its potential scale and complexity. Textual narrative and supporting images can be used to improve a user's understanding of provenance data. This early work aims to support the exploration of provenance data by allowing users to query provenance data with a *provenance subject* (either an entity, activity or agent) recorded in it.

1 Introduction

Provenance data can be hard for both expert and non-expert users to understand because of its technical content, and its potential scale and complexity. In order to address these obstacles, we propose allowing users to explore provenance data via an explanation service. This service requires provenance data and a single subject (either an entity, activity or agent) described in the data, as parameters. It returns a description of the subject, which includes text and a provenance graph.

Section 2 describes the sentence templates used to generate a textual narrative of a *provenance subject*. Following that, Sect. 3 describes the provenance graphs generated to support the textual narrative. We then provide conclusions and discuss future work in Sect. 4.

2 Sentence Templating

The explanation service uses sentence templates to explain the provenance types defined in the PROV [1] W3C's standard for provenance (see Table 1 for examples). The sentence templates are strung together to form a paragraph describing the entities, agents and activities which relate to the *subject*. For example, the following paragraph has been generated about the *provenance subject* **rs:/ rideRequest/1** from the provenance in Fig. 1.

The rs:/rideRequest/1 is a UserInput entity. It was generated by the activity rs:post_ride_request_103. It was attributed to the agent rs:/users/agent2. It was used by the activity rs:store_ride_request81935.

B. Ludäscher and B. Plale (Eds.): IPAW 2014, LNCS 8628, pp. 278–280, 2015.
DOI: 10.1007/978-3-319-16462-5_33

```
entity(rs:/rideRequest/1, [prov:type='prsm:UserInput'])
activity(rs:post_ride_request_103, -, -, [prov:type='prsm:Provide_Info'])
activity(rs:store_ride_request81935, -, -, [prov:type='prsm:StoreData'])
agent(rs:ride_server, [prov:type='prsm:webserver'])
agent(rs:/users/agent2, [prov:type='prsm:loggedInUser'])
wasGeneratedBy(rs:/rideRequest/1, rs:post_ride_request_103, -)
used(rs:store_ride_request81935, rs:/rideRequest/1, -)
wasInformedBy(rs:store_ride_request81935, rs:post_ride_request_103)
wasAttributedTo(rs:/rideRequest/1, rs:/users/agent2)
wasAssociatedWith(rs:post_ride_request_103, rs:/users/agent2, -)
wasAssociatedWith(rs:store_ride_request81935, rs:ride_server, -)
```

Fig. 1. Provenance extract used for the ride share example.

3   Provenance Graphs

As well as providing sentences which describe a subject, we also generate provenance graphs highlighting the agents, activities, entities and relationships which are in the textual narrative. The graphs represent the provenance data described in the narrative using the standard colours used in PROV and greys out data that was not used. In our example from the previous section, Fig. 2 shows which items were used in the narrative.

Table 1. Template Sentence examples, where items in {} are variables which can be either a single item or a list.

Prov Types	Sentence template
Entity	The {subject} is a {type} entity
Agent	The {subject} is a {type} agent
Activity	The {subject} is a {type}activity
Alternate	It was an alternate of {alternate/s}
Association	It was associated with agent/s {agent/s}
Attribution	It was attributed to agent/s {agent/s}
Collections	It was a member of the {collection/s} collection/s
Communication	It was informed by {agent/s}
Delegation	It acted on behalf of {agent/s}
Derivation	The {subject} was derived from the entity/ies {entity/ies}
Specialization and Revision	The {subject} was a specialisation of the entity {entity}, and is a revision of {entity/ies}
Generation	It was generated by the activity {activity/ies}
Usage	It was used by the activity/ies {activity/ies}

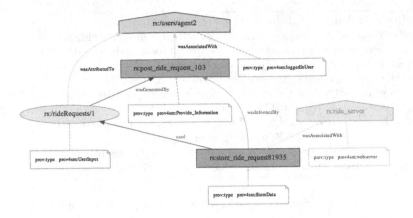

Fig. 2. A graph generated using the ride share example.

4   Conclusion

The explanation service provides users with a description of a *provenance subject* using text and images. For future work, we plan to expand and develop two categories of sentence templates: inspection, which are used to describe facts; and comparison, which are to rank a subject against others. We will also consider policies to support privacy and security in the templates. Finally, we will explore how to foster trust using templates by adopting different authorial tones in the narrative and granularities of explanations about policies, such as privacy and how provenance data is used.

Acknowledgments. The research leading to these results has received partially funding from the European Community's Seventh Framework Program (FP7/2007-2013) under grant agreement n. 600854 Smart Society: hybrid and diversity-aware collective adaptive systems: where people meet machines to build smarter societies http://www.smart-society-project.eu/.

Reference

1. Moreau, L., Missier, P. (eds.) Belhajjame, K., B'Far, R., Cheney, J., Coppens, S., Cresswell, S., Gil, Y., Groth, P., Klyne, G., Lebo, T., McCusker, J., Miles, S., Myers, J., Sahoo, S., Tilmes, C.: PROV-DM: The PROV Data Model. W3C Recommendation REC-prov-dm-20130430, World Wide Web Consortium, Oct 2013. http://www.w3.org/TR/2013/REC-prov-dm-20130430/

Extending PROV Data Model
for Provenance-Aware Sensor Web

Peng Yue[⊠], Xia Guo, Mingda Zhang, and Liangcun Jiang

State Key Laboratory of Information Engineering in Surveying,
Mapping and Remote Sensing, Wuhan University,
129 Luoyu Road, Wuhan 430079, China
geopyue@gmail.com

Abstract. Provenance has become a fundamental issue in Sensor Web, since it allows applications to answer "what", "why", "where", "when", and "how" queries related to the consumption process, which finally helps to determine the usability and reliability of data products. This paper proposes how the W3C PROV Data Model (PROV-DM) [1] can be used for creating a lineage model for Sensor Web to support interoperability.

In the sensor domain, the observation values, phenomenon measurement, observation location, time of observation, and observation procedure are important parts to answer sensor discovery queries. They are categorized as "what", "why", "where", "when", and "how" queries in this paper. These five perspectives, together, construct the lineage for an observation. In this paper, OCG standards and W3C SSN ontology [2] are leveraged to provide comprehensive domain vocabularies for Sensor Web, which are later mapped into concepts in PROV-DM for modeling observation lineage. It is possible to adopt SSN solely as the vocabularies and map them to W3C PROV. However, we argue that the solution of adopting O&M basic observation model [3] as a core with its complements by SSN ontology could facilitate the extraction of PROV data from the large amount of existing observation data following the OGC Sensor Web standards.

The domain vocabularies adopt the base Observation model in the O&M, enriched by classes and properties in the SSN ontology (Fig. 1). Within the O&M standard, an observation (OM_Observation) is defined as "an act of observing a property or phenomenon, with the goal of producing an estimate of the value of the property", and a feature (GFI_Feature) is "an abstraction of real world phenomenon". Result (Result-Data) records the value of an observation. featureOfInterest and observedProperty together sketch the phenomenon to be measured. The "what" and "why" questions can then be answered using these entities. Furthermore, responsible party information is added using the class CI_ResponsibleParty from ISO19115:2003 to record the person or party responsible for the observation. An observation often involves a procedure, which can be a sensor, a human observer, or a series of process steps. Thus, a procedure (OM_Process) has two subconcepts: Sensor and Process. Observers (Observer) and sensing devices (SensingDevice) are modeled as subconcepts of Sensor. The Process can be understood as a processing method with Input and Output to describe how observations were made. These definitions together, answer the "how" question in

© Springer International Publishing Switzerland 2015
B. Ludäscher and B. Plale (Eds.): IPAW 2014, LNCS 8628, pp. 281–284, 2015.
DOI: 10.1007/978-3-319-16462-5_34

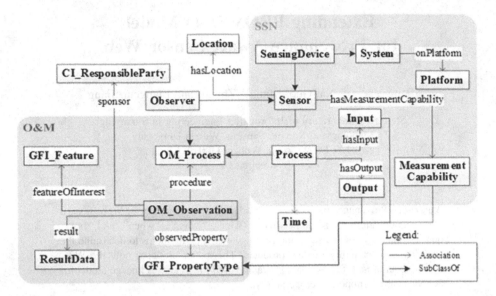

Fig. 1. Domain vocabularies for Sensor Web

provenance queries. Besides, the System and Platform are also added according to relationships among the sensor, system, and platform defined from the system perspective of the SSN ontology. Location and time, which are not described in the SSN ontology, answer "Where" and "When" questions, using associations with Sensor and Process respectively.

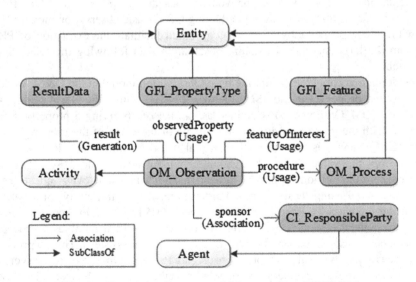

Fig. 2. Observation lineage model by extending PROV-DM

Mapping domain vocabularies from the Sensor Web to PROV-DM can facilitate interoperable provenance modeling. Figure 2 shows domain-specific extensions of W3C PROV by creating mapping from the domain vocabularies in Fig. 1 to PROV-DM.

GFI_PropertyType and GFI_Feature are entities that together can be used to describe the phenomenon observed by an observation. An observation (OM_Observation) is then a kind of Activity. The relationships observedProperty and featureOfInterest are categorized as the relation concept Usage. The procedure associates OM_Observation and OM_Process, and thus can be also seen as a kind of Usage. The relation result follows the relation concept Generation as the results are generated by observation activities. CI_ResponsibleParty is responsible for the observation, and then the relation sponsor is categorized as the relation concept Association. The subconcepts of OM_Process, such as Process, Sensor, and SensingDevices are all entities.

In the paper, an ontology is used to represent the observation lineage model which are extended to PROV-O, using rdfs:subClassOf and rdfs:subPropertyOf relationships. The observation lineage model is then enriched according to the specific sensors and database schema when dealing with the PM cases. A relational database is used to store datasets including observation values and corresponding metadata. The datasets content is then mapped into RDF, which is published as linked data and thereby allows to be browsed and searched.

Three typical query examples, including temporal and spatial provenance filtering, are conducted and showed through a prototype system. One of the query examples following the SPARQL syntax is showed in Table 1. Specially, to demonstrate the potential of interoperability, a query example is also conducted with combining generic concepts in PROV-O and domain-specific concepts in observation lineage ontology. Using OWL reasoners, concepts and relations that are mapped to PROV can be discovered by applying PROV-related queries.

Table 1. The query example

```
SELECT ?sensor ?geonames ?latitude ?longitude
WHERE {
    ?Observation prov-pmsw:procedure ?sensor.
    ?sensor prov-pmsw:type "sensingdevice".
    ?Observation prov-pmsw:resultTime ?instanceTime.
    ?instanceTime prov-pmsw:xsdDateTime ?xsdDateTime.
    FILTER(?xsdDateTime >= "2013-06-16T08:00:00+08" && ?xsdDateTime <= "2013-
06-16T08:00:00+08").
    ?sensor prov-pmsw:hasLocation ?location.
    ?location prov-pmsw:geonames ?geonames.
    ?location prov-pmsw:wgs84_lat ?latitude.
    ?location prov-pmsw:wgs84_long ?longitude.
    FILTER(?geonames="Nanjing").
}
```

Acknowledgements. We are grateful to the anonymous reviewers for their constructive comments. The work is supported jointly by National Basic Research Program of China (2011CB707105), National Natural Science Foundation of China (41271397), and Program for New Century Excellent Talents in University (NCET-13-0435).

References

1. Moreau, L., Missier, P.: ROV-DM: The PROV Data Model. WWW document (2013). http://www.w3.org/TR/prov-dm/
2. W3C 2005 Semantic Sensor Network Ontology. WWW document. http://www.w3.org/2005/Incubator/ssn/ssnx/ssn
3. Cox S 2007 Observation and Measurements Implementation Specification, Version 1.0. Open Geospatial Consortium document No. OGC 07-022r1

SC-PROV: A Provenance Vocabulary for Social Computation

Milan Markovic[✉], Peter Edwards, and David Corsar

Computing Science and dot.rural Digital Economy Hub,
University of Aberdeen, Aberdeen AB24 5UA, UK
{m.markovic,p.edwards,dcorsar}@abdn.ac.uk

Abstract. In this paper we present SC-PROV - an extension to PROV-O and P-PLAN that is designed to capture the provenance of social computations.

1 Introduction

The Web has enabled the rapid growth of various forms of social computation [RG13] - hybrid workflows that consist of tasks executed by both computational agents and humans. Such workflows are typically used to solve problems that are difficult for machines (e.g. image classification). We have previously argued [MEC13] that existing social computation systems suffer from a lack of transparency, that makes decisions about the reliability of participants and the quality of generated solutions difficult. We believe that such transparency issues could be addressed by recording the provenance of social computation executions. While PROV-O[1] can be used to document retrospective provenance (such as execution traces of workflows) this would not include details of why or how a workflow was expected to execute [MDB+13, GG12]. For this purpose, P-PLAN[2] extends PROV-O with the ability to document workflow plans in terms of steps and variables. However, in order to improve the transparency of social computations and support enhanced reasoning about human participants (and their contributions), we believe that plans should also include additional elements describing important characteristics of the social computation [MEC13]. These include pre and post conditions associated with social computation tasks, e.g. a participant must be an English speaker and the outcome has to be validated by two additional participants. Also needed is a means to describe incentives that are associated with successful completion of a task (e.g. receive 10 points). We have developed SC-PROV as an extension of PROV-O and P-PLAN to enable descriptions of such conditions and incentives as part of the social computation plan. In addition, SC-PROV enables such concepts to be mapped to a provenance record describing the execution trace (Fig. 1).

The research described here is supported by the award made by the RCUK Digital Economy programme to the dot.rural Digital Economy Hub; award reference: EP/G066051/1.

[1] http://www.w3.org/TR/prov-o/.
[2] http://vocab.linkeddata.es/p-plan/.

B. Ludäscher and B. Plale (Eds.): IPAW 2014, LNCS 8628, pp. 285–287, 2015.
DOI: 10.1007/978-3-319-16462-5_35

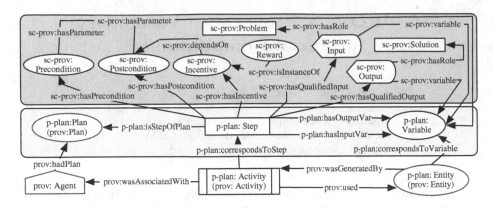

Fig. 1. PROV-O and corresponding extensions including P-PLAN and SC-PROV.

2   Model Description

SC-PROV reuses the concepts defined by P-PLAN to enable the basic structure
of a social computation workflow to be captured. P-PLAN describes plans in
terms of *p-plan:Step* and *p-plan:Variable*. Steps represent activities that should
be executed as part of the workflow. A variable can be related to a particular
step as either an input or output variable. The *p-plan:correspondsToVariable*
property maps a variable to a *p-plan:Entity* that was used or generated by a
p-plan:Activity during execution. Similarly, steps can be mapped to a *p-plan:
Activity* via the *p-plan:correspondsToStep* property. To augment such descriptions of tasks in the context of social computations, SC-PROV defines *sc-prov:
Precondition, sc-prov:Postcondition, sc-prov:Incentive* and *sc-prov:Reward*. A
precondition defines a subclass of *prov:Entity* representing constraints that should
be satisfied before a plan step can be fulfilled (e.g. the required location of a
human worker). A precondition is associated with a step via the *sc-prov:has
Precondition* property and can be linked to parameters of type *p-plan:Variable*
(e.g. GPS coordinates) using the *sc-prov:hasParameter* property. As every precondition is a subclass of *prov:Entity*, it can be linked to the retrospective provenance described by PROV-O. For example, a provenance record might include a
prov:Activity that evaluated whether the precondition was satisfied and therefore
used the entity representing the precondition as well as entities corresponding
to its parameters. A postcondition defines a subclass of *prov:Entity* representing
constraints that should be satisfied after the completion of a particular step for
it to be considered successful. For example, a postcondition of a human task
might require an agent to produce a solution that should be validated at least
by another two agents. The properties *sc-prov:hasPostcondition* and *sc-prov:
hasParameter* are analogous to those described for *sc-prov:Precondition*. The
sc-prov:Incentive class is a subclass of *prov:Entity* representing an incentive associated with the successful completion of a task. This concept can be understood
as a thing (e.g. £10, increased knowledge, etc.) that would be realised by a

worker following successful completion of a task. An incentive is associated with a step via the *sc-prov:hasIncentive* property. A property *sc-prov:dependsOn* is defined to link the concept of the incentive and a postcondition, where the postcondition is used to describe circumstances under which a worker should receive the reward described by the incentive. The concept of *sc-prov:Reward* defines a subclass of *prov:Entity* representing a realisation of the promised incentive (e.g. a voucher worth £10). The *sc-prov:isInstanceOf* property can be used to map a promised task incentive with such a reward. In a social computation context, there are two important types of variables, namely problems and solutions, which describe the purpose and outcomes of the computation. Using P-PLAN concepts, a problem would be described by a set of variables that represent a problem statement and serve as an input to a step (e.g. human task). Similarly, a solution would be described by a set of variables that specify the answer to the problem. SC-PROV defines two *sc-prov:Role*'s (*sc-prov:Problem* and *sc-prov:Solution*) to describe the expected function of a variable in a step. The qualified relation[3] pattern is used to model properties *p-plan:hasInputVar* and *p-plan:hasOutputVar* as resources. For this *sc-prov:Input* describes a variable that will be taken as an input for a step and *sc-prov:Output* describes a variable that will be produced as an output of a step in the planned execution. Properties *sc-prov:hasRole* and *sc-prov:variable* can then be used to associate the role with a variable.

3   Future Work

In our future work we aim to develop a framework utilising the SC-PROV ontology to record the provenance of a number of social computations. The aim is to demonstrate the utility of provenance records documented using SC-PROV by evaluating the potential of such data to support reasoning about participants' trustworthiness and thus aid workforce selection.

References

[GG12]   Garijo, D., Gil, Y.: Augmenting prov with plans in p-plan: scientific processes as linked data. In: Proceedings of the Second International Workshop on Linked Science 2012 - Tackling Big Data, CEUR (2012)

[MDB+13] Missier, P., Dey, S., Belhajjame, K., Cuevas-Vicenttin, V., Ludaescher, B.: D-prov: extending the prov provenance model with workflow structure. Technical report, Newcastle University (2013)

[MEC13]   Markovic, M., Edwards, P., Corsar, D.: Utilising provenance to enhance social computation. In: Alani, H., et al. (eds.) ISWC 2013, Part II. LNCS, vol. 8219, pp. 440–447. Springer, Heidelberg (2013)

[RG13]   Robertson, D., Giunchiglia, F.: Programming the social computer. Philos. Trans. R. Soc. A: Math. Phys. Eng. Sci. **371**(1987), 20120379 (2013)

---

[3] http://patterns.dataincubator.org/book/qualified-relation.html.

RDataTracker and DDG Explorer

Capture, Visualization and Querying of Provenance from R Scripts

Barbara S. Lerner[1](✉) and Emery R. Boose[2]

[1] Mount Holyoke College, South Hadley, MA 01075, USA
blerner@mtholyoke.edu
[2] Harvard Forest, Harvard University, Petersham, MA 01366, USA

Scientific data provenance is gaining interest among both scientists and computer scientists. The current state of the art of provenance capture requires scientists to adopt new technologies, most commonly workflow systems such as Kepler [BML+06], Vistrails [SKS+08] or Taverna [MBZ+08], among others. While there are likely additional benefits to adopting these systems, they present a hurdle to scientists who are more interested in focusing on science than in learning new technologies. The work described in this poster is aimed at exploring the extent to which we can support scientists while expecting a minimal investment in terms of additional effort on their part.

This work has been developed in collaboration with ecologists at Harvard Forest, a 3500 acre facility operated by Harvard University and serving as a Long-Term Ecological Research (LTER) site funded by the National Science Foundation. Many of these ecologists perform data analysis using R, a widely used scripting language that includes extensive statistical analysis and plotting functionality. These scientists are committed to understanding their data, making sure that their data analyses are done in an appropriate manner, and sharing their data and results with others. For these reasons, they appreciate the value that collecting data provenance may have, but they are not enthusiastic about learning new tools. In this poster, we present two tools aimed at this audience: RDataTracker and DDG Explorer. RDataTracker [LB14] is used to collect data provenance during the execution of an R script. DDG Explorer is the tool that is used to examine and query the resulting data provenance.

1 Capturing Data Provenance with RDataTracker

RDataTracker is an R library that contains functions to build a provenance graph based on the execution of an R script and/or user activity in the R console. At a minimum, the scientist needs to load the library, initialize the provenance graph at the start of execution, and save the provenance graph at the end. As a script executes or the user enters commands at the console, a provenance graph is constructed that records the operations that are executed, the data that are used, and where variables are assigned.

© Springer International Publishing Switzerland 2015
B. Ludäscher and B. Plale (Eds.): IPAW 2014, LNCS 8628, pp. 288–290, 2015.
DOI: 10.1007/978-3-319-16462-5_36

The user can increase the amount of information collected during execution by including more instrumentation. In particular, by doing this the user can:

– Save copies of input and output files as well as copies of plots created.
– Include details of provenance that occurs within the execution of functions.
– Introduce levels of abstraction that allow the provenance graph to be viewed with a varying amount of detail.
– Checkpoint the entire R state and restore it later, capturing the checkpoint and restore operations in the provenance graph so that the data derivation links correctly show the effects of the checkpoint and restore operations and files are restored to the contents they had at the time of the checkpoint.
– Capture error messages generated by the R interpreter or RDataTracker and include them in the provenance graph as an aid to debugging.

This work differs from CXXR [SR10, RS12], an implementation of the R interpreter that includes automated provenance collection. In CXXR, the data provenance is made available to the programmer via functions within the R session, but there is no provenance recorded within functions and the data provenance is not stored persistently.

2   Viewing and Querying Provenance with DDG Explorer

DDG Explorer is a tool that supports the querying and visualization of the provenance graphs created by RDataTracker. DDG Explorer has been carefully designed to be language agnostic and also supports the display and querying of provenance graphs created from the execution of Little-JIL processes [OCE+10, LBO+11]. This poster focuses on provenance collected in R.

With DDG Explorer, the user can load a provenance graph written by RData-Tracker. In addition to the usual navigation and querying facilities provided by provenance browsers, DDG Explorer takes advantage of the abstraction and checkpoint/restore features of RDataTracker to provide additional navigation capabilities. The levels of abstraction captured in RDataTracker allow for sections of the full provenance graph to be collapsed to an individual node. This allows for navigation at a high level of abstraction. By clicking on a collapsed node, the node is expanded to expose more detail.

DDG Explorer also uses checkpoint/restore information to hide detail and selectively expose it. In particular, the provenance that occurs between a checkpoint and when that checkpoint is restored is collapsed to a single node. By clicking on the collapsed node, the user can see the details of the activity that occurred between the checkpoint and restore.

The normal mode of operation that we expect is for users to write and execute their scripts, examine the resulting provenance graphs and use the information to refine the scripts, iterating until the script behaves as expected and the provenance graph contains the desired amount of detail. At that point, the user can save the provenance graph and associated files to a database.

3   Conclusion

RDataTracker and DDG Explorer support the collection of data provenance from the execution of R scripts and R console commands. Our goal is to provide tools that are easy for scientists to learn and that offer an immediate payback for a small effort and increasing value as the scientist becomes familiar with the tools and invests more effort in their use. Initial results have been encouraging and we will continue to improve upon the types of information that we capture and to reduce the effort required by scientists.

Acknowledgments. The authors acknowledge intellectual contributions from collaborators Leon Osterweil and Aaron Ellison and Harvard Forest REU students Sophia Taskova, Antonia Oprescu, and Shaylyn Adams. The work was supported by NSF grants DEB-0620443, DEB-1237491, and DBI-1003938, the Charles Bullard Fellowship at Harvard University, and a faculty fellowship from Mount Holyoke College and is a contribution from the Harvard Forest Long-Term Ecological Research (LTER) program.

References

[BML+06] Bowers, S., McPhillips, T., Ludäscher, B., Cohen, S., Davidson, S.B.: A model for user-oriented data provenance in pipelined scientific workflows. In: Moreau, L., Foster, I. (eds.) IPAW 2006. LNCS, vol. 4145, pp. 133–147. Springer, Heidelberg (2006)

[LB14] Lerner, B.S., Boose, E.R.: RDataTracker: collecting provenance in an interactive scripting environment. In: TAPP 2014, Cologne, Germany, June 2014

[LBO+11] Lerner, B., Boose, E., Osterweil, L.J., Ellison, A.M., Clarke, L.A.: Provenance and quality control in sensor networks. In: Proceedings of the Environmental Information Management (EIM) 2011 Conference, Santa Barbara, California, September 2011

[MBZ+08] Missier, P., Belhajjame, K., Zhao, J., Roos, M., Goble, C.: Data lineage model for Taverna workflows with lightweight annotation requirements. In: Freire, J., Koop, D., Moreau, L. (eds.) IPAW 2008. LNCS, vol. 5272, pp. 17–30. Springer, Heidelberg (2008)

[OCE+10] Osterweil, L.J., Clarke, L.A., Ellison, A.M., Boose, E.R., Podorozhny, R., Wise, A.: Clear and precise specification of ecological data management processes and dataset provenance. IEEE Trans. Autom. Sci. Eng. **7**(1), 189–195 (2010)

[RS12] Runnalls, A., Silles, C.: Provenance tracking in R. In: Groth, P., Frew, J. (eds.) IPAW 2012. LNCS, vol. 7525, pp. 237–239. Springer, Heidelberg (2012)

[SKS+08] Scheidegger, C., Koop, D., Santos, E., Vo, H., Callahan, S., Freire, J., Silva, C.: Tackling the provenance challenge one layer at a time. Concurr. Comput. Pract. Exp. **20**(5), 473–483 (2008)

[SR10] Silles, C.A., Runnalls, A.R.: Provenance-awareness in R. In: McGuinness, D.L., Michaelis, J.R., Moreau, L. (eds.) IPAW 2010. LNCS, vol. 6378, pp. 64–72. Springer, Heidelberg (2010)

Provenance Support for Medical Research

Richard McClatchey(✉), Jetendr Shamdasani,
Andrew Branson, and Kamran Munir

Centre for Complex Cooperative Systems, FET, UWE Bristol,
Coldharbour Lane, Bristol, UK
{richard.mcclatchey,jetendr.shamdasani,
andrew.branson,kamran.munir}@cern.ch

Abstract. This poster paper introduces a system known as CRISTAL [1] and the experience using it for medical research, primarily in the neuGRID [2] and neuGridforUsers (N4U) projects. These projects aim to provide detailed traceability for research analysis processes in the study of biomarkers for Alzheimer's disease. They have faced major challenges in managing data volumes and algorithm complexity leading to problems associated with information tracking, analysis reproducibility and scientific data verification. We present a working system that supports provenance data management for medical researchers.

Medical informatics has increasingly required systems that facilitate historical data capture and management in order to support researchers' analyses through workflow based algorithms. To facilitate the requirement of tracking large scale analyses, we have adopted CRISTAL [1], a workflow and 'provenance data' tracking solution. Its use has provided a rich environment for neuroscientists to track and manage the evolution of both data and workflows in neuGRID and N4U. In the N4U project in particular we have developed a so called Virtual Laboratory (VL). One major goal of the VL is to ensure the reproducibility of results and to allow sharing of analysis information between researchers. All of the workflows in N4U after design are automated, their complete history from design to orchestration being captured and stored. Another feature of the VL is its collaborative environment, allowing for 'provenance' information to be shared and used by various researchers. The N4U VL is based on services layered on top of the neuGRID infrastructure, described in detail in [2].

The VL was developed for neuroscientists involved in Alzheimer's studies but has been designed to be reusable across other medical research communities. It has been designed to provide access to infrastructure resident data and to enable the analyses required by the medical research community. This has been achieved by basing the N4U virtual laboratory on an integrated Analysis Base [3], which has been developed following the detail requirements from both neuGRID and N4U projects. This Analysis Base provides an integrated medical data analysis environment to exploit neuroscience workflows, large image datasets and algorithms for scientific analyses. Once researchers conduct their analyses information from the Analysis Base, the analysis definitions and resulting data along with the user profiles are also made available in the Base for tracking and reusability purposes in a so-called Analysis Service via a Science Gateway, Analysis Workarea and Information Services. (see Fig. 1).

The N4U Analysis Service provides access to tracked information (images, pipelines and analysis outcomes) for querying/browsing, visualization, pipeline authoring

B. Ludäscher and B. Plale (Eds.): IPAW 2014, LNCS 8628, pp. 291–293, 2015.
DOI: 10.1007/978-3-319-16462-5_37

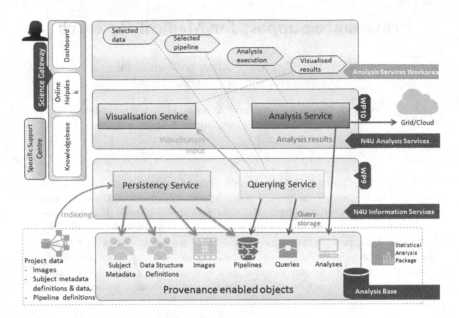

Fig. 1. The N4U Virtual Laboratory

and execution. Its Work Area is a facility for users to define new pipelines or configure existing pipelines to be run against selected datasets and dispatch to conduct analysis. The N4U Science Gateway provides facilities that include a Dashboard, Online Help and Service interfaces for users to interact with the underlying set of N4U services. The N4U Analysis Base: (a) indexes all external clinical datasets (b) registers neuroscience pipeline definitions and/or associated algorithms (c) stores provenance and user-derived data resulting from pipeline executions on the Grid (d) provides access to all datasets stored on the infrastructure and (e) stores users' analysis definitions and linking them with the existing pipelines and datasets definitions.

CRISTAL is a data and workflow tracking system which was used to trace the construction of the CMS experiment at the CERN LHC [4]. Using the facilities for description and dynamic modification in CRISTAL in a generic and reusable manner, CRISTAL is able to provide dynamically modifiable and reconfigurable workflows. It uses the "description-driven" nature of CRISTAL models to act dynamically on process instances already running, and can intervene in the actual process instances during execution (for further detail refer to [1]). These processes can be dynamically (re)-configured based on the context of execution without compiling or stopping the process and the user can make modifications directly upon any process parameter whilst preserving all historical versions so they can run alongside the new version. In neuGRID/N4U, we have used CRISTAL to provide the provenance needed to support neuroscience analysis and to track individualized analysis definitions and usage patterns, thereby creating a practical knowledge base for neuroscience researchers.

CRISTAL captures provenance data that emerges in the specification and execution of the stages in analysis workflows. The provenance management service also keeps track of the origins of the data products generated in an analysis and their evolution between different stages of research analysis. CRISTAL is a system that records every change made to its objects, which are referred to as CRISTAL Items. Whenever a modification is made to any piece of data, the definition of that piece of data or application logic, the change and the metadata associated with that change (e.g. who made the change, when and for what purpose) are stored alongside that data. This makes CRISTAL applications fully traceable, and this data may be used to assemble detailed provenance information.

In N4U, CRISTAL manages data from the Analysis Service as Items, containing the full history of computing task execution; it can also provide this level of traceability for any piece of data in the system, such as the datasets, pipeline definitions and queries. Provenance querying facilities are provided by the Querying Service in neuGRID/N4U. The ability of description-driven systems to both cope with change and to provide traceability of such changes (i.e. the 'provenance' of the change) we see as one of the main contributions of the CRISTAL approach to building flexible and maintainable systems and we believe this makes a significant contribution to how enterprise systems can be implemented.

In the future we will develop a so-called User Analysis module which will enable applications to learn from their past executions and improve and optimize new studies and processes based on the previous experiences and results. Using machine learning approaches, models will be formulated that can derive the best possible optimisation strategies using the past execution of experiments and processes. These models will evolve over time and will facilitate decision support in designing, building and running the future processes and workflows in a domain. A provenance analysis mechanism will be built on top of the data that has been captured in CRISTAL. It will employ approaches to learn from the data that has been produced, find common patterns and models, classify and reason from the information accumulated and present it to the system in an intuitive way. Work is also ongoing to make CRISTAL compliant with emerging provenance standards such as the Open Provenance Model, OPM [5].

References

1. Branson, A., et al.: CRISTAL : A practical study in designing systems to cope with change. Inf. Syst. J. **42**, 139–152 (2014). Elsevier Publishers
2. Anjum, A. et al.: Provenance management for neuroimaging workflows in neuGRID. In: International Conference on P2P, Parallel, Grid, Cloud and Internet Computing. Barcelona, Spain (2011)
3. Munir, K., et al.: An integrated e-science analysis base for computational neuroscience experiments and analysis. Procedia – Soc. Behav. Sci. **73**, 85–92 (2013)
4. Chatrchyan, S. et al.: The compact muon solenoid experiment at the CERN LHC. The Compact Muon Solenoid Collaboration. J. Instr. **3**, Article No: S08004, pp. 1–361 (2008). Institute of Physics Publishers
5. Shamdasani, J. et al.: Towards semantic provenance in CRISTAL. In: Proceedings of the 3rd International Workshop on the Role of Semantic Web in Provenance Management (SWPM12), pp. 29–36. IEEE Press, Heraklion May (2012). ISBN: 978-1-4673-1328-5

Experiencing PROV-Wf for Provenance Interoperability in SWfMSs

Wellington Oliveira[1,2(✉)], Daniel de Oliveira[1],
and Vanessa Braganholo[1]

[1] Instituto de Computação, Universidade Federal Fluminense (UFF),
Niterói, Brazil
{wellmor,danielcmo,vanessa}@ic.uff.br
[2] Departamento Acadêmico de Ciência da Computação,
Instituto Federal de Educação, Ciência e Tecnologia do Sudeste de Minas Gerais,
Rio Pomba Campus, Juiz de Fora, Brazil

Abstract. Analyzing disperse and heterogeneous provenance data usually requires using higher-level tools which scientists need to learn. In our view, scientists should be able to analyze provenance in the SWfMS of their choice. In this paper, we propose Géfyra, an architecture based on the PROV-Wf model, which provides a way to capture heterogeneous provenance data from different SWfMSs into a single format. Géfyra exports and imports provenance data to/ from different SWfMSs, allowing scientists to use the system of their choice.

1 Introduction

Depending on the size and complexity of the scientific experiment, it can be divided/ modelled into two or more workflows (*i.e.* fragments) [1]. This division can ease the management of the experiment, reducing the total execution time, and enables a cooperative work where each research team works on parts of the experiment in an "independent" way [2]. From there, data provenance management becomes a challenge when the workflow (and their fragments) needs to be executed in more than one SWfMS, and each SWfMS has its own associated provenance model.

For scientists to analyze, share, and combine provenance data generated by different systems, it is necessary to ensure the interoperability between these SWfMSs. Some authors propose an additional layer in a higher level of abstraction [3] to perform the mediation between the provenance data items collected in the various SWfMSs. In our view, the provenance data should be "imported" to one of the SWfMSs used (preferably that the scientist is used to) so that the analysis is performed in a single system, taking advantage of the existing analysis infrastructure of these SWfMSs. Thus, in this paper we propose Géfyra, an approach for provenance data interoperability between existing SWfMSs. Géfyra is based on a recently proposed provenance model called PROV-Wf [4].

B. Ludäscher and B. Plale (Eds.): IPAW 2014, LNCS 8628, pp. 294–296, 2015.
DOI: 10.1007/978-3-319-16462-5_38

2   Géfyra: Making Provenance Interoperable

Our main goal in this paper is to provide a bridge between different SWfMSs so that it allows scientists to analyze provenance data generated by other SWfMS. Thus, we named our approach as Géfyra, which means "bridge" in Greek. We designed a representation schema in XML Schema (which we call *Prov-Wf Schema*) to create and/or validate provenance data from heterogeneous data sources. While designing it, we used some elements of PROV-XML [5] and included all entities and relationships of the PROV-Wf conceptual model. The resulting schema is available at www.ic.uff.br/~vanessa/papers/PROV-Wf.xsd.

The Géfyra architecture is shown in Fig. 1. To convert provenance data from SWfMS *A* to SWfMS *B*, the *Géfyra Broker* triggers the cartridge of SWfMS *A*, which converts the data stored in SWfMS *A*'s provenance repository to an XML file that follows the *PROV-Wf Schema*. This XML file is then sent to the *Géfyra Broker*, which stores it in the *PROV-Wf Repository* and sends it to the cartridge within SWfMS *B* for conversion. The cartridge of SWfMS *B* then converts the XML file to SWfMS *B*'s provenance repository format, and stores the provenance information in the repository of that SWfMS. Note that each *Cartridge* knows how to convert from a specific SWfMS format to the PROV-Wf XML format, and vice versa.

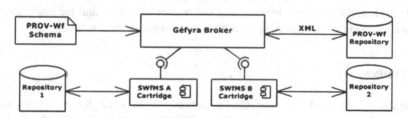

Fig. 1. The Géfyra conceptual architecture.

3   Experimental Evaluation and Final Remarks

To evaluate Géfyra, we use the SciPhy [6] workflow that is executed in two SWfMSs that can collect and store provenance data in a relational database: SciCumulus and VisTrails. This way, we develop two cartridges (*PROV-Wf_Sci* and *PROV-Wf_Vis*) to map the provenance data from SciCumulus and VisTrails to XML (according the PROV-Wf Schema) and in the opposite direction, from XML to the SWfMS itself. In order to assess the quality of our mapping, we developed a series of queries to evaluate the amount of tuples and fields, types and values of attributes and the compatibility between the databases of the two SWfMSs. We also were inspired by the queries of the *First and Second Provenance Challenges* [7]. Our main goal was to evaluate information loss that might occur in the import process (since there are some attributes that do not exist in both models), and capture mistakes in our mapping.

To evaluate our results we use the concepts of *precision* and *recall*. Thus, we execute the queries in two provenance databases (SciCumulus and VisTrails) to assess

Table 1. Results for SciCumulus

Query	Precision		Recall	
	Tuples	Fields	Tuples	Fields
1	100%	100%	100%	100%
2	100%	100%	100%	86%
3	100%	100%	100%	100%
4	100%	100%	100%	100%
5	100%	100%	100%	50%

Table 2. Results for VisTrails

Query	Precision		Recall	
	Tuples	Fields	Tuples	Fields
1	100%	100%	100%	100%
2	100%	100%	100%	100%
3	100%	100%	100%	100%
4	100%	100%	100%	100%
5	100%	100%	100%	75%

the amount of records and check whether the fields were aligned to the attributes of the respective elements in the PROV-Wf Schema. Tables 1 and 2 show the results.

The Géfyra architecture is flexible and extensible: new cartridges of different SWfMSs can be connected to it at any time (as shown in Fig. 1). Géfyra maps heterogeneous provenance data sources, allowing the data from a SWfMS to be converted to XML and the latter to another SWfMS. This way, it is not necessary to convert provenance data from each SWfMS to all other provenance systems one wants to use, as Géfyra converts the data to a single XML format that can be shared by all SWfMSs. As a limitation, since one data model may contain data that cannot be mapped to Prov-Wf, some data may be lost in the conversion process. This is the tradeoff of being able to use a single system for analysis.

As future work, we intend to implement cartridges to other SWfMS, we intend to further explore the semantic dimension of the provenance data, and the implications of such a dimension in the mapping of different provenance data sources.

References

1. Marinho, A., Murta, L., Werner, C., Braganholo, V., da Cruz, S.M.S., Ogasawara, E., Mattoso, M.: ProvManager: a provenance management system for scientific workflows. Concurr. Comput. Pract. Exp. **24**, 1513–1530 (2012)
2. Altintas, I., Anand, M.K., Crawl, D., Bowers, S., Belloum, A., Missier, P., Ludäscher, B., Goble, C.A., Sloot, P.M.: Understanding collaborative studies through interoperable workflow provenance. In: McGuinness, D.L., Michaelis, J.R., Moreau, L. (eds.) IPAW 2010. LNCS, vol. 6378, pp. 42–58. Springer, Heidelberg (2010)
3. Ellqvist, T., Koop, D., Freire, J., Silva, C., Stromback, L.: Using mediation to achieve provenance interoperability. In: 2009 World Conference on Services – I, pp. 291–298 (2009)
4. Costa, F., Silva, V., de Oliveira, D., Ocaña, K., Ogasawara, E., Dias, J., Mattoso, M.: Capturing and querying workflow runtime provenance with PROV: a practical approach. In: Joint EDBT/ICDT 2013 Workshops, pp. 282–289. ACM, New York (2013)
5. Moreau, L.: PROV-XML: The PROV XML Schema. http://www.w3.org/TR/prov-xml/
6. Ocaña, K.A., de Oliveira, D., Ogasawara, E., Dávila, A.M., Lima, A.A., Mattoso, M.: SciPhy: A cloud-based workflow for phylogenetic analysis of drug targets in protozoan genomes. In: Norberto de Souza, O., Telles, G.P., Palakal, M. (eds.) BSB 2011. LNCS, vol. 6832, pp. 66–70. Springer, Heidelberg (2011)
7. Moreau, L., Ludäscher, B. et al.: Special issue: The first provenance challenge. Concurr. Comput. Pract. Exp. **20**, 409–418 (2008)

Author Index

Printed in the United States
By Bookmasters